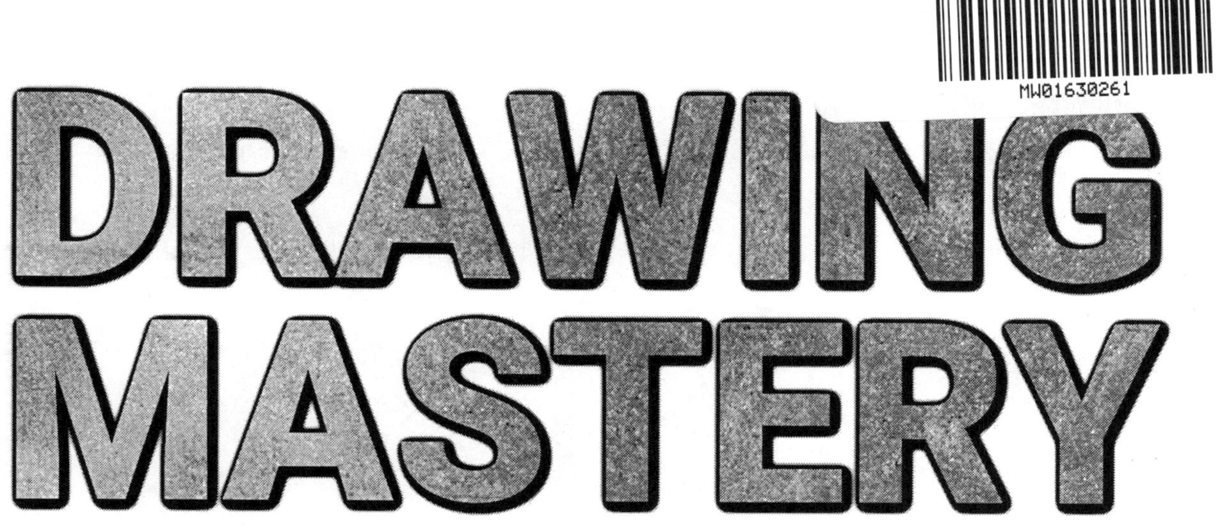

DRAWING MASTERY

HEAD & FIGURE GEOMETRY and STEREOGRAPHY

Book One

KIAR MESKO

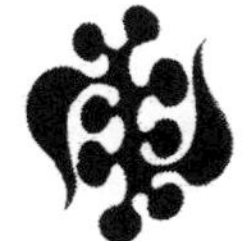

An ART MASTERY ™ Book

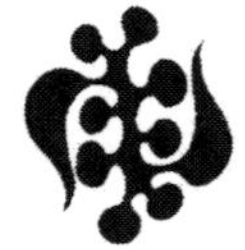

Published by
ArnicaPress.com

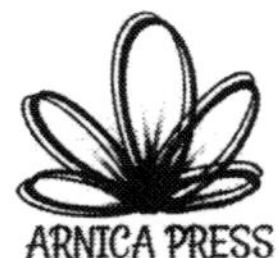

Copyright © 2022 Kiar Mesko, Sabrina Mesko
Written by Kiar Mesko
Translated by S. Mesko
Printed in the United States of America

January 2022

Manufactured in the United States of America

ISBN: 978-1-955354 -14 -1

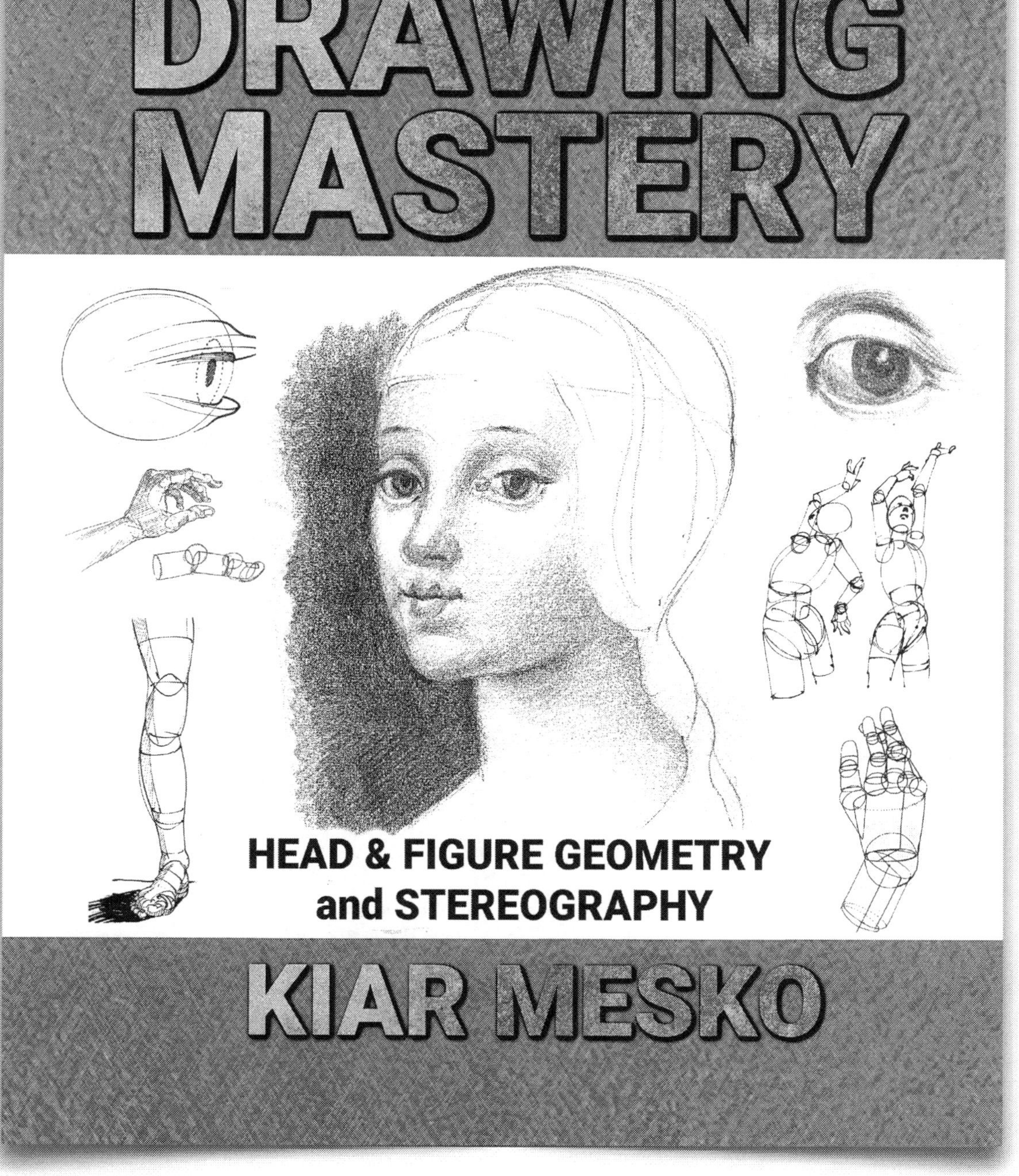

Book One

DRAWING MASTERY

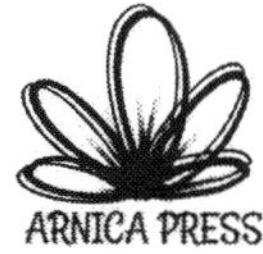

HEAD & FIGURE GEOMETRY and STEREOGRAPHY

KIAR MESKO

ARNICA PRESS

OTHER BOOKS BY KIAR MESKO

1973 Treatise on Drawing

2000 Pictorial Esthetics

2000 Slovenian Poets and Writers

2015 Pictorial Intelligence ~ Part 1.

2018 My Art in My Words

2021 Pictorial Intelligence ~ Part 2.

The DRAWING MASTERY SERIES
entails Three book volumes:

Book One
DRAWING MASTERY
Head & Figure Geometry and Stereography

Book Two
DRAWING MASTERY
Figural Composition

Book Three
DRAWING MASTERY
Dancers and Horses

For my Daughter Sabrina

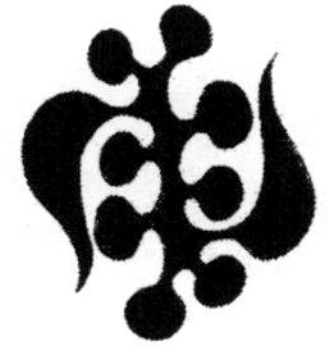

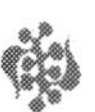

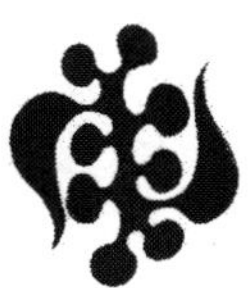

Table of Contents

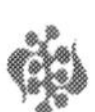

Introduction

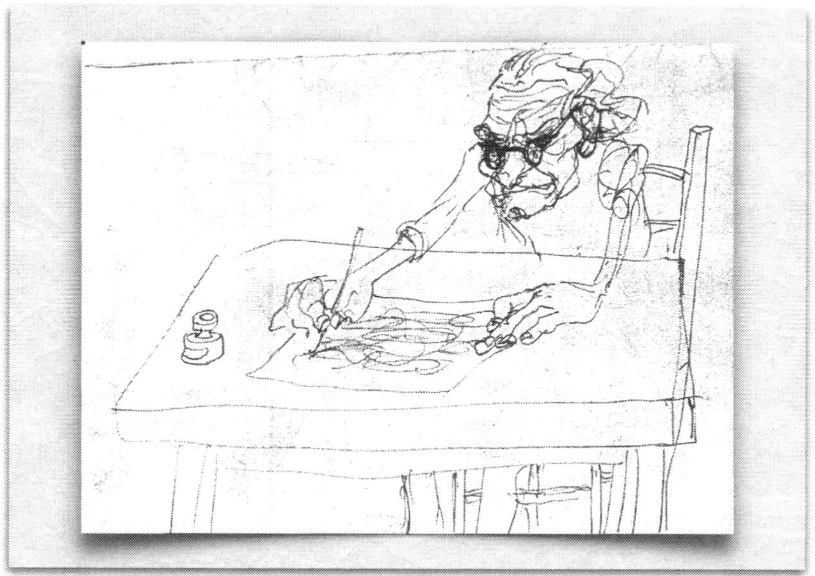

THIS BOOK IS INTENDED FOR ANYONE THAT IS INTERESTED IN THE ARTS; an admirer that simply loves observing art, a beginner with a desire to learn professional techniques and finally, a more or less educated artist that is curious and interested in the technique and working approach of an older colleague. It is also appropriate for all art enthusiasts, collectors and art lovers, as well as those that work in professions such as sculptors, architects, etching artists, and yes, also art historians or art critics.

Drawing is a very enjoyable activity. Does it require special gifts and abilities, or is it possible to learn and acquire this knowledge? The basic condition is having a genuine interest. Then, the first step is learning about the process of drawing.

There is an old rule that the basis of good painting is the artist's ability to draw. Therefore it is also a most reliable measure of painter's quality.

How many drawings are known from the great artist Velazquez?
Two. One depicts a portrait sketch of a cardinal, and the second a head of a stag deer. They look as if they were created by a moderately gifted art student.

How many drawings are known from the Master artists Tizian? Actually none! They are definitely not worth mentioning as examples of a good drawing.

Are all drawings from Leonardo Da Vinci worthy of attention or praise? Yes almost all, but not because of some special drawing quality.

Was Michelangelo flawless? Definitely not, for he had plenty of flaws, but they can only be noticed by a person who understands and knows the art of drawing.

All the artists mentioned above are great examples of good drawing masters.

Do not underestimate failures of successful people and overestimate their successes. Know that a drawing represents a decision of geometry values, symmetry, calligraphy and tectonics. These are simple values known by all. Eventually, you will master them.

To master the art of drawing, means to be able to manipulate the cylinders and balls of various sizes and shapes. This can't be easily accomplished by just anyone, but with a good level of understanding, you can learn these basics without a special ability or gift for creative drawing.

This book can teach you how to understand what is a good drawing. But most importantly, it can also help you master drawing at an enviously high level. On theses pages, you will find a rich selection of fun exercises that should not be taken too seriously, but as an incentive for reflection. Keep in mind, there is never just one good solution.

Take these drawing technique suggestions from my personal treasure chest of knowledge as a master artist painter, trained in strict classical style, that has been long forgotten these days. I am quite bored by dogmas of pseudo-realism and surprised by the nonsense that is happening nowadays in the world of art, paining and sculpture. It almost seems as if the humanity is slowly sliding into an era of darkness, perhaps ruled by the esthetic measures of insects? Well, such events seem to have happened already a few times in the history of human civilization.

Drawing mastery requires a way of thinking, never landing at the same conclusion, but always finding something different while staying creative. The best way to gradually learn to draw is with practice of drawing various lines and shaping simple objects or surfaces. This is an entertaining and increasingly demanding game, that I often repeat myself. It is also very useful as a test of your ability to concentrate and control your hand muscular-motor skills and coordination.

As you draw your way through the drawing exercises, you will find increasingly more demanding tasks. I included them into this book as my own free hand explorations of geometric patterns.

Drawing Mastery will surely take you into the world of understanding the art of drawing. It will allow you to think in the way of a drawing. Thinking is a human reality, attribute and quality. Do not denounce it.

Above all, follow your own progress with enthusiastic curiously and always evaluate your work from a cheerful and fun point of view.

Kiar

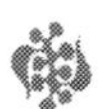

About Drawing

F**REEHAND DRAWING IS WELL FOUNDED IN STEREOMETRY.**

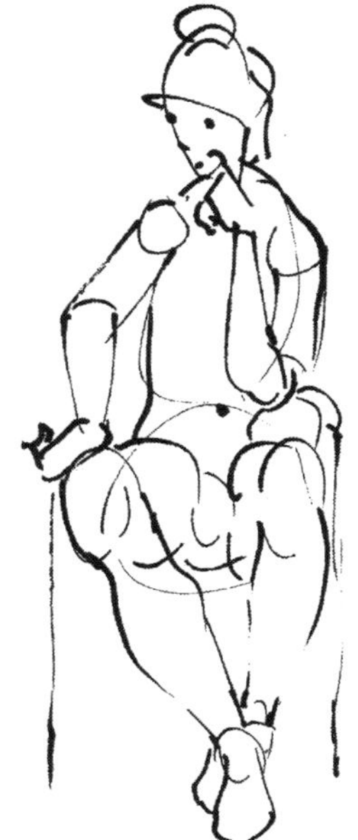

The DRAWING is the boundary:
- between the surfaces,
- between the forms,
- between the valeurs of tones, valeurs of colors,
- between textures,
- between the object and the space.

The DRAWING is the imaginary line between the points:
- it is the point in space,
- it is the mesh in the form, on and along the shape,
- it is two or three dimensional calligraphy,
- it is the division of a shape,
- it is the measurement of dimensions,
- it is the raster.

The drawing is a presentation of geometrical, perspective and proportional value. In drawings of the human figure, the fundamental value - beside stereometry - is space orientation, statics, silhouette and symmetric values, as well as the dynamic of levitation.

The pictorial space depends of geometrical bearing and perspective. The geometrical perspective regulates the diminishing of shapes with the distance. The space perspective diminishes the sharpness between the shapes and cuts down the color scale.

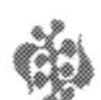

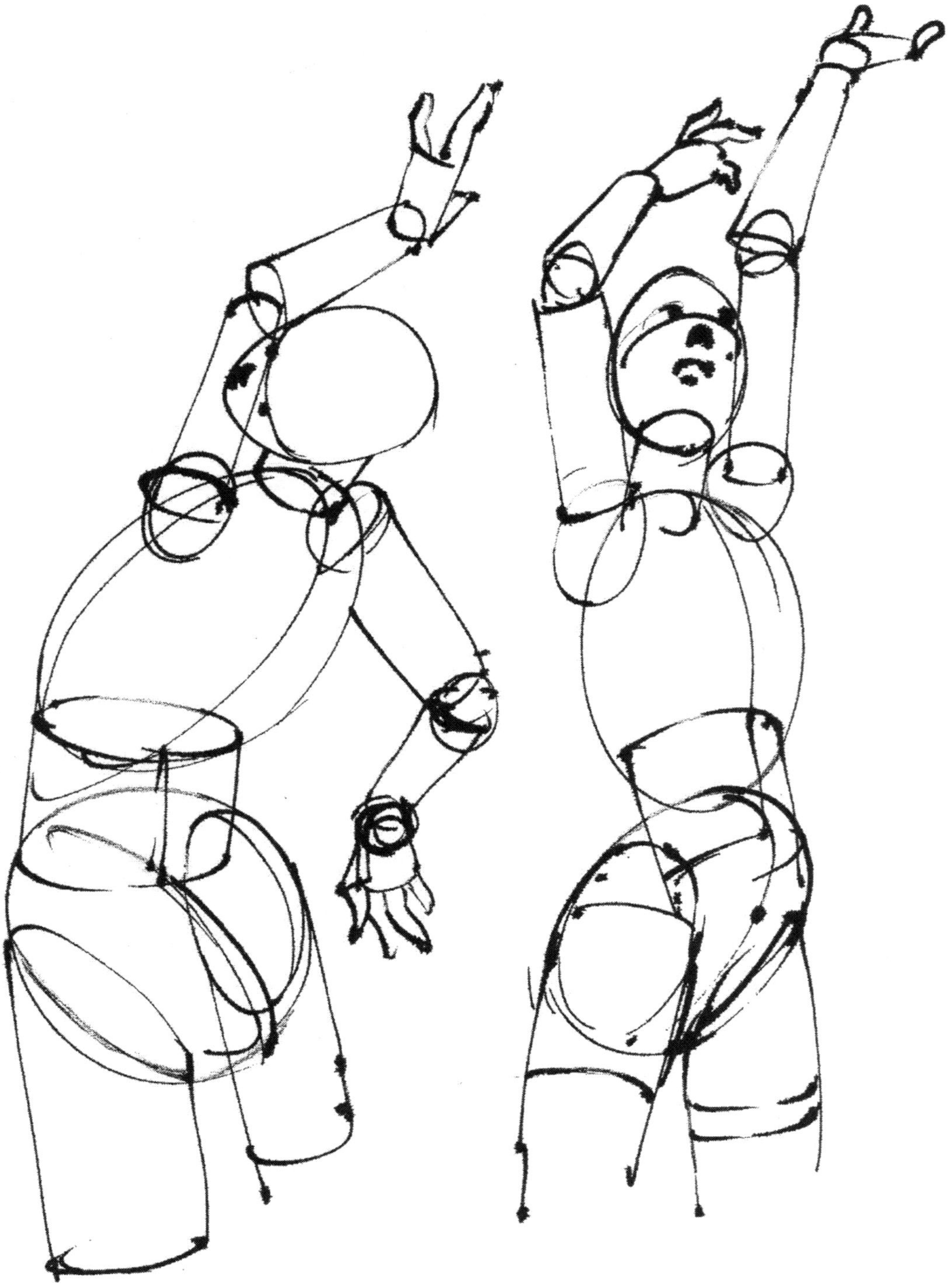

Geometry & Stereography

THIS BOOK PRESENT THE BASIS OF THE PAINTING PROFESSION - drawing from the perspective of the antique mentality. In comparison with the other civilizations, the art of the Antique Greek-Roman classics is more accomplished than the great cultures of India, China and Japan. The beautiful example of Antique Greek range of thought is the heliocentric explanation of the cosmic system by Philolaus and Hicetas 500 BC, and Aristarchus of Samos 270 BC. The Antique Greek knowledge of drawing is the groundwork for painting and sculpting. In that context the complexes of forms are representations of potential energy.

In the year 1973, as a docent on the Academy of Art, I published the book "Treatise About the Drawing," where I presented the principle of stereography in the drawing of the human body in the nude. The improved manuscript was formed in 1995; the current edition is a part of previously published book.

The understanding of anatomical and stereographic interior smaller shapes facilitates a very specific drawing approach. This approach surpasses the usual only simple observations of exterior values. The difference is in the appearance of the reflection and transparency. The reflection is presented with descriptive geometry, while the transparency is presented with the perception of depth. An illustration can be compared to an X-ray picture. This picture is presenting smaller shapes inside a larger shape.

The human body presents everything that is included in formative structure of painting and sculpturing activity. The distinctive examples of Classical Greek-Roman and Renaissance era present the formative and spacious realizations of complicated anatomical organisms. These realizations are founded on the comprehension of reduction and deduction, connected with demanding intellectual decisions. Well-known is Leonardo's quote about painting; "Painting is a matter of intelligence."

The heart of Classic Greek-Roman culture is in the manner of thinking: uniqueness, primeval depth of thought and individuality. Nobility of the mind is unreachable for the ignorant man. Strive for the manner of thinking, which exceeded the simple, hairsplitting observations. This Classic Greek-Roman approach to thinking, gradually become European. The ancient European generations recognized the uniqueness of this artistic inheritance and preserved it in harmonious concordant.

Similar principles should prevail in the American art world. The so called Western art world is connected with the power of thought and intelligence.

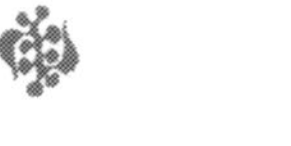

Your Preparation

YOUR **PREPARATIONS FOR THE STUDY AND WORK WITH THIS BOOK ARE QUITE SIMPLE.** I suggest you use regular white paper, for example multipurpose paper, cut into format 5,5 x 8.5 or larger, whatever gives you a feeling of a relaxed drawing practice.

Use regular pencils of various grading, anywhere from 4H to 6B and keep testing what suits you better for various drawing efforts. Same principle applies when using various kinds of charcoal and chalk.

As an old rule, the pen is the queen of drawing. Try it out see if it applies in all cases. Explore all sorts of pens, from very thin ones, all the way to the wide ones. Same principle applies when using a reed - fountain pen.

Remember, the tools are not the most important aspect, so simply chose whatever you prefer for accomplishing a specific goal.

The time required to complete a drawing, can greatly vary. And ideal drawing must give the impression of being created in "a breath". But of course, that is a deception. The essence lies in concentration, in your knowing what you want.

It is good to have the awareness, that erasing something does not translate into insecurity or failure. Quite the opposite, it can also demonstrate your courage to change an idea. The erased parts can enrich the quality of the drawing, for they represent an act of thinking.

When you are drawing the suggested drawings remember "all ticks" that could help you to accomplish the desired effect. The technique of drawing should be playful. All masters played with the technique, wether they admit it or not. The ones that didn't, were clumsy procrastinators.

You will fin each chapter more or less divided into geometry and general part. Many drawings represent a study of old masters drawings form the likes of Leonardo, Michelangelo, Rubens, Velazques and Rembrandt.

When practicing your drawing, remain relaxed and at ease. You may chose to simplify or be as picky as you wish. Most importantly, have fun. And remember, the drawing that may seem challenging at first, may be mastered by you later.

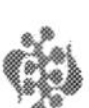

Your Drawing Tools

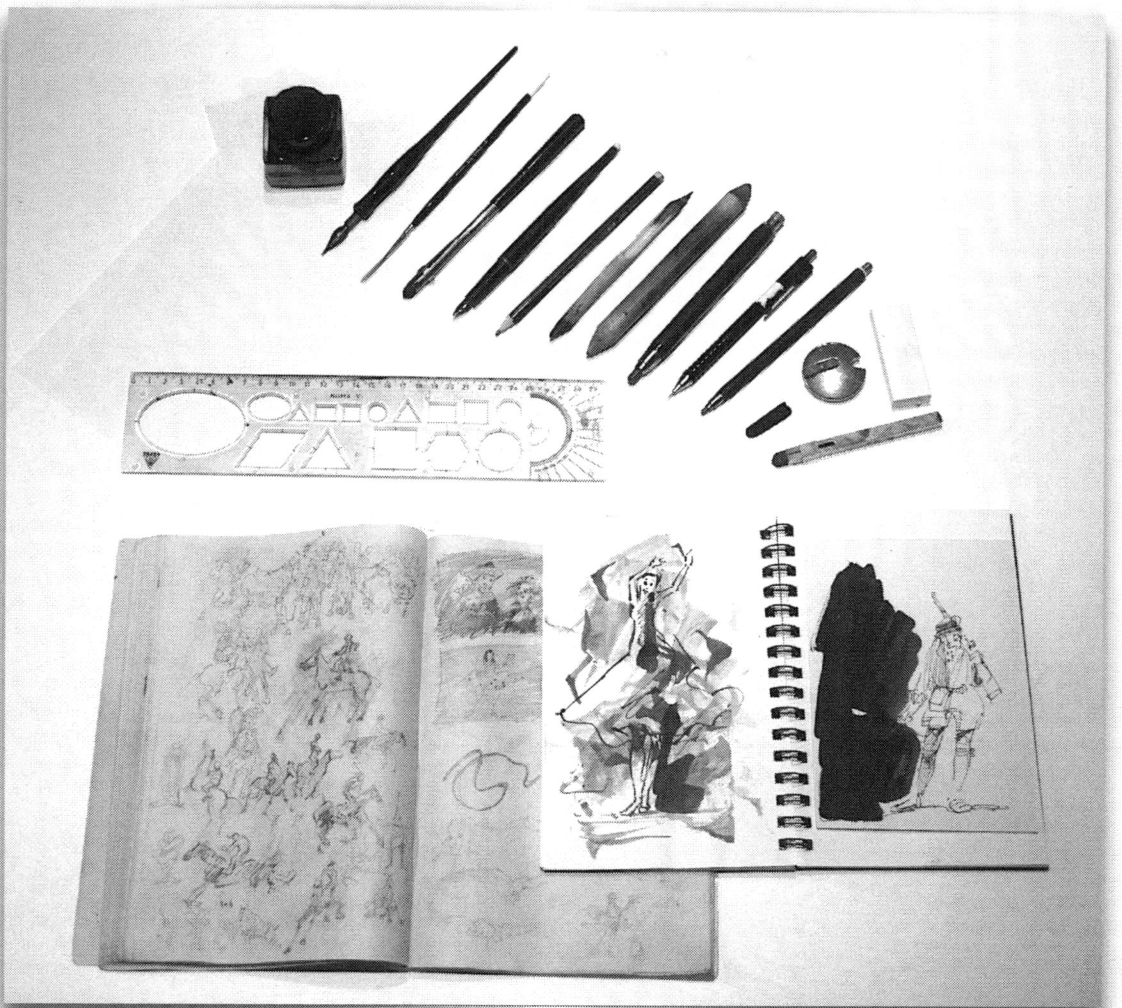

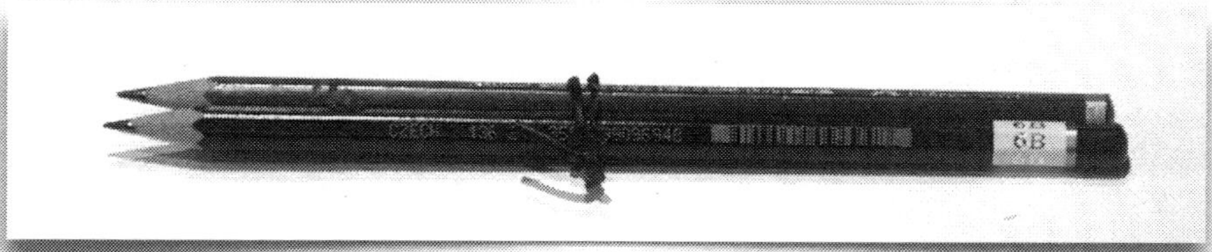

A SELECTION OF MY DRAWING TOOLS

**IN SPECIAL CASES YOU CAN USE TWO PENCILS,
TIED TOGETHER TO CREATE A DOUBLE DRAWING LINE.
SEE EXAMPLES ON PAGE 26, 27**

Masterclass in Drawing

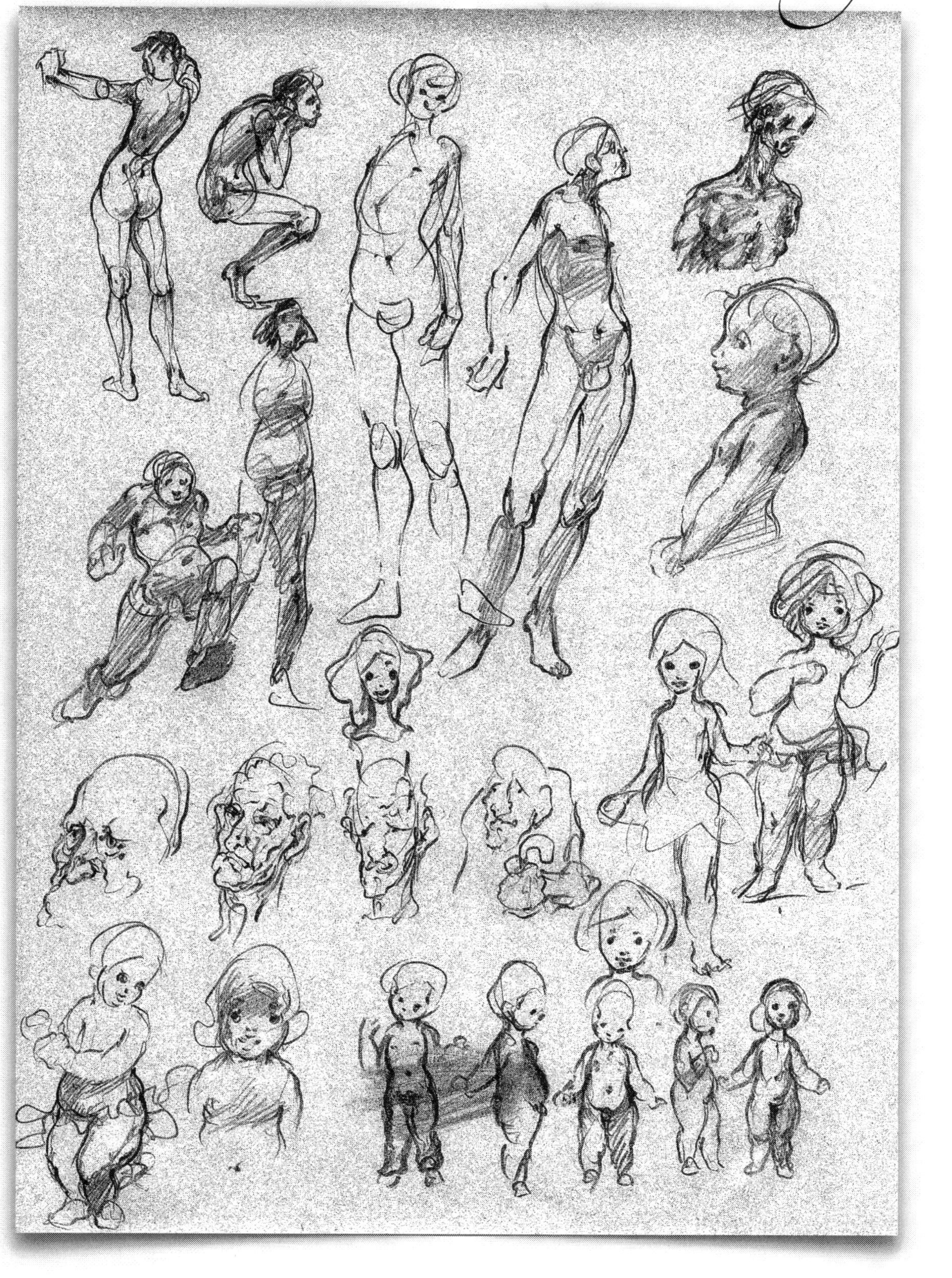

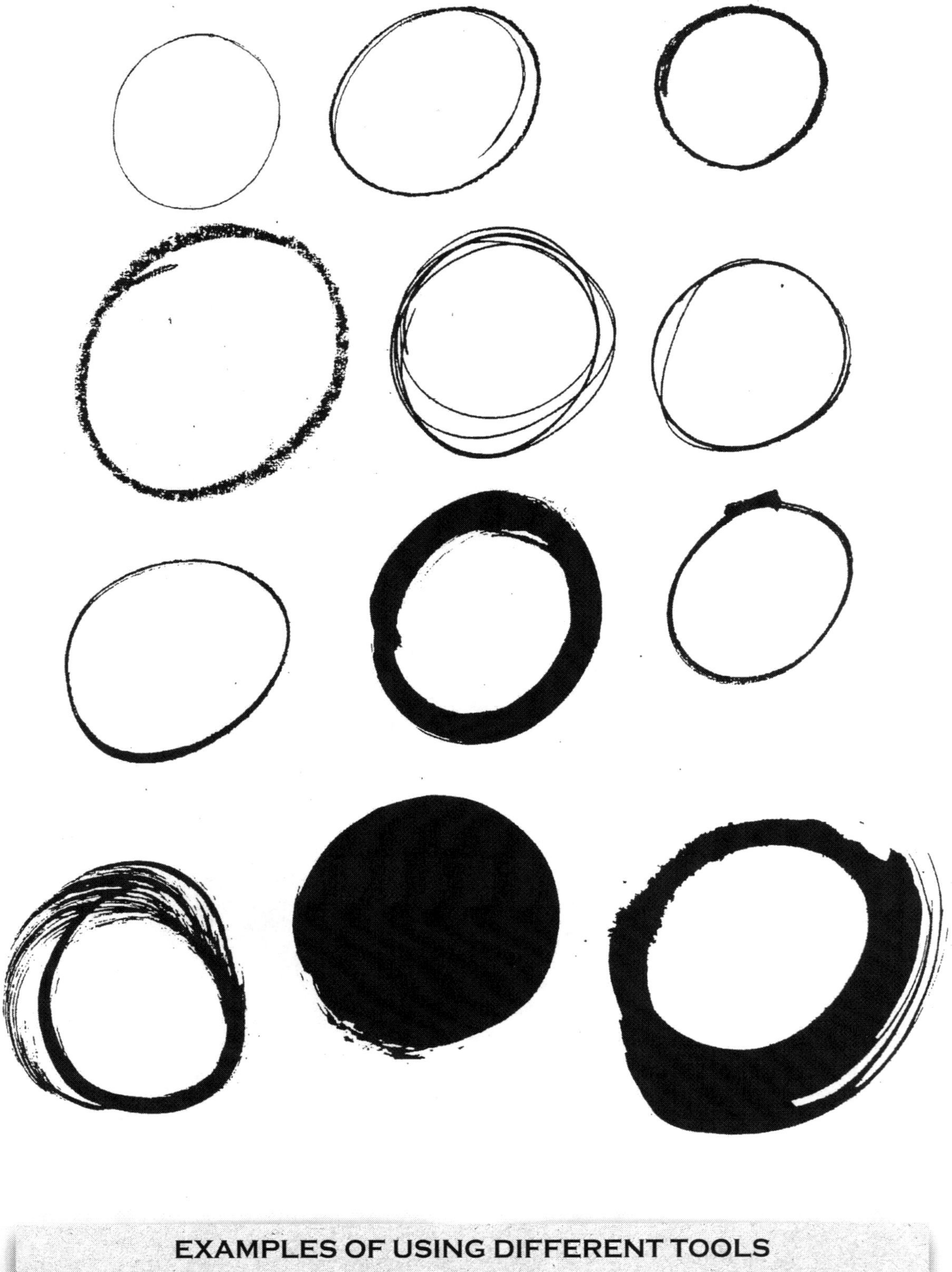

EXAMPLES OF USING DIFFERENT TOOLS
THE MATERIALS AND TOOLS WE USE AFFECT THE
CHARACTER OF THE DRAWING

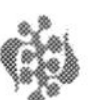

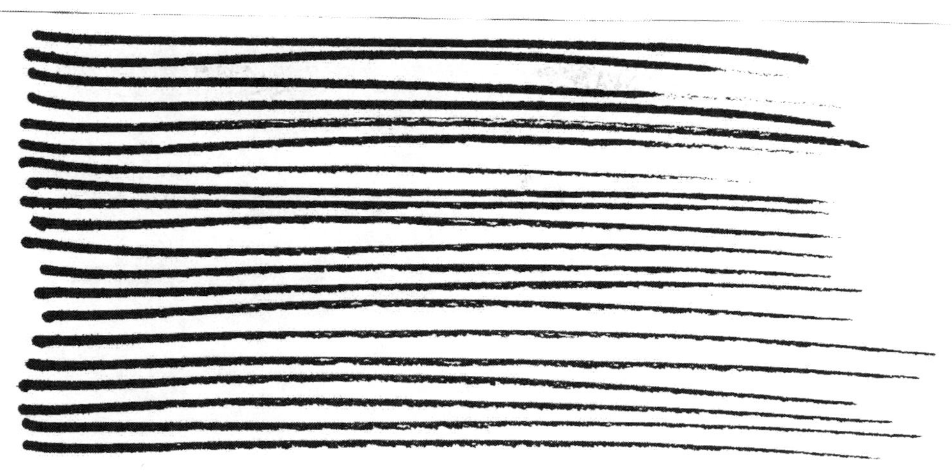

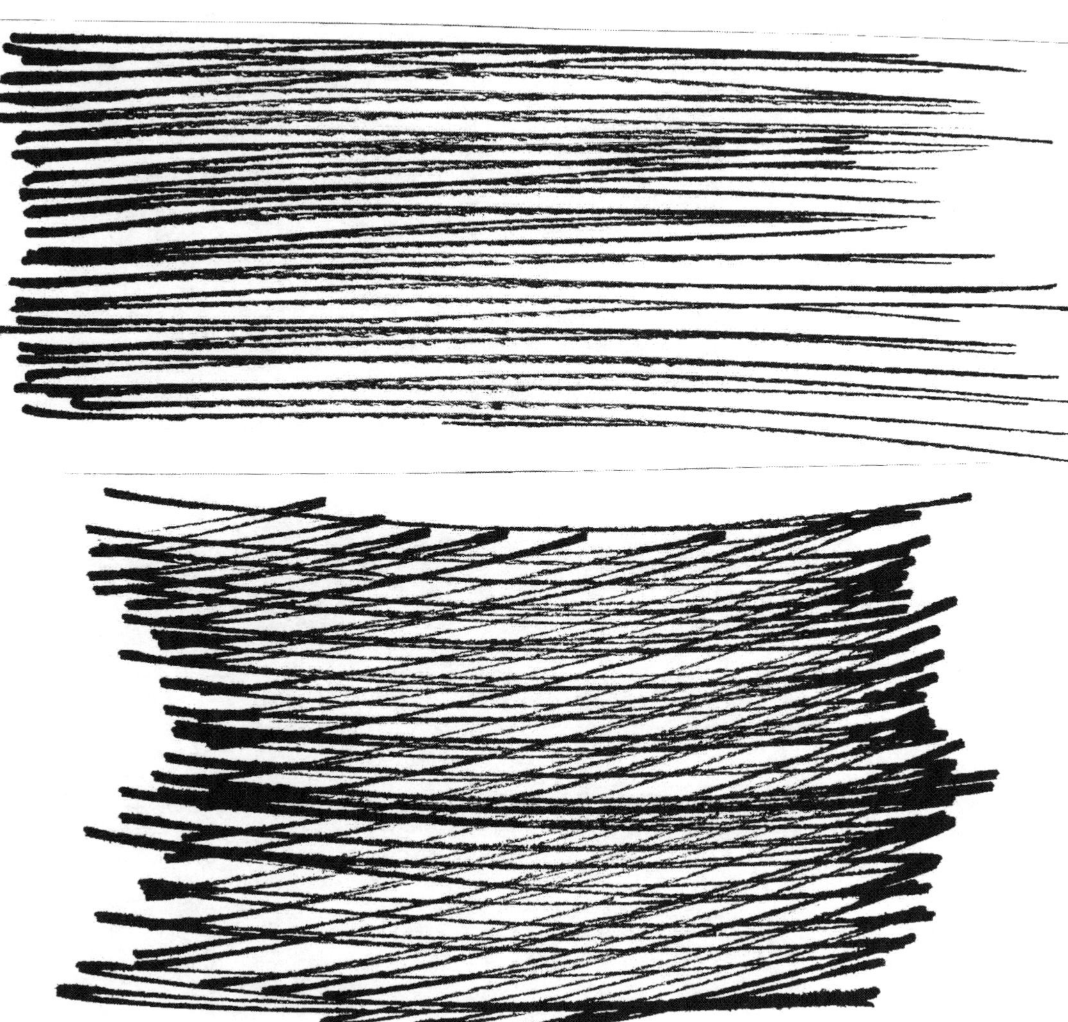

SLOW PRECISE DRAWING OF LINES

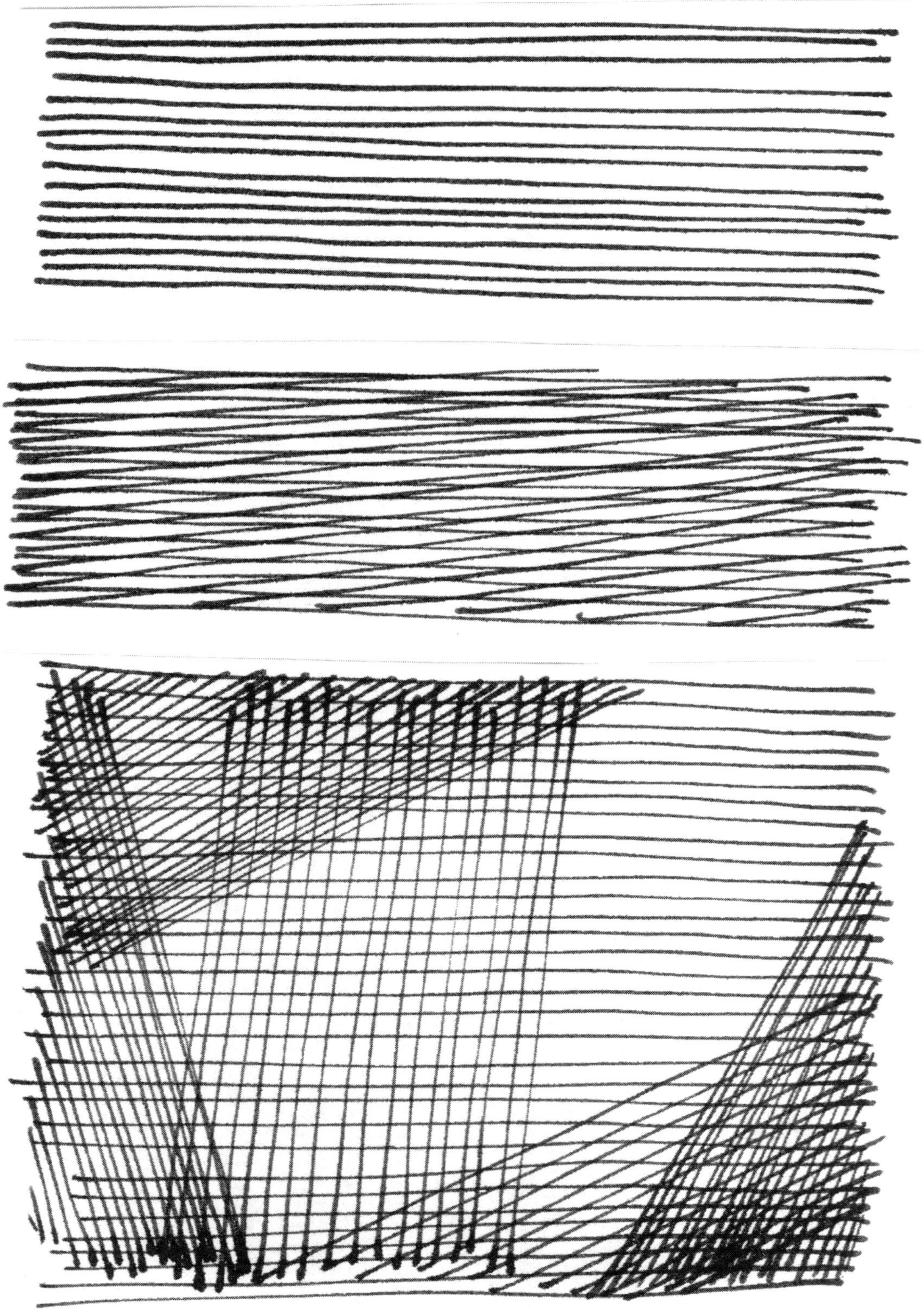

EXAMPLES OF LINES IN VARIOUS PATTERNS

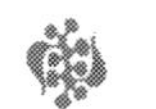

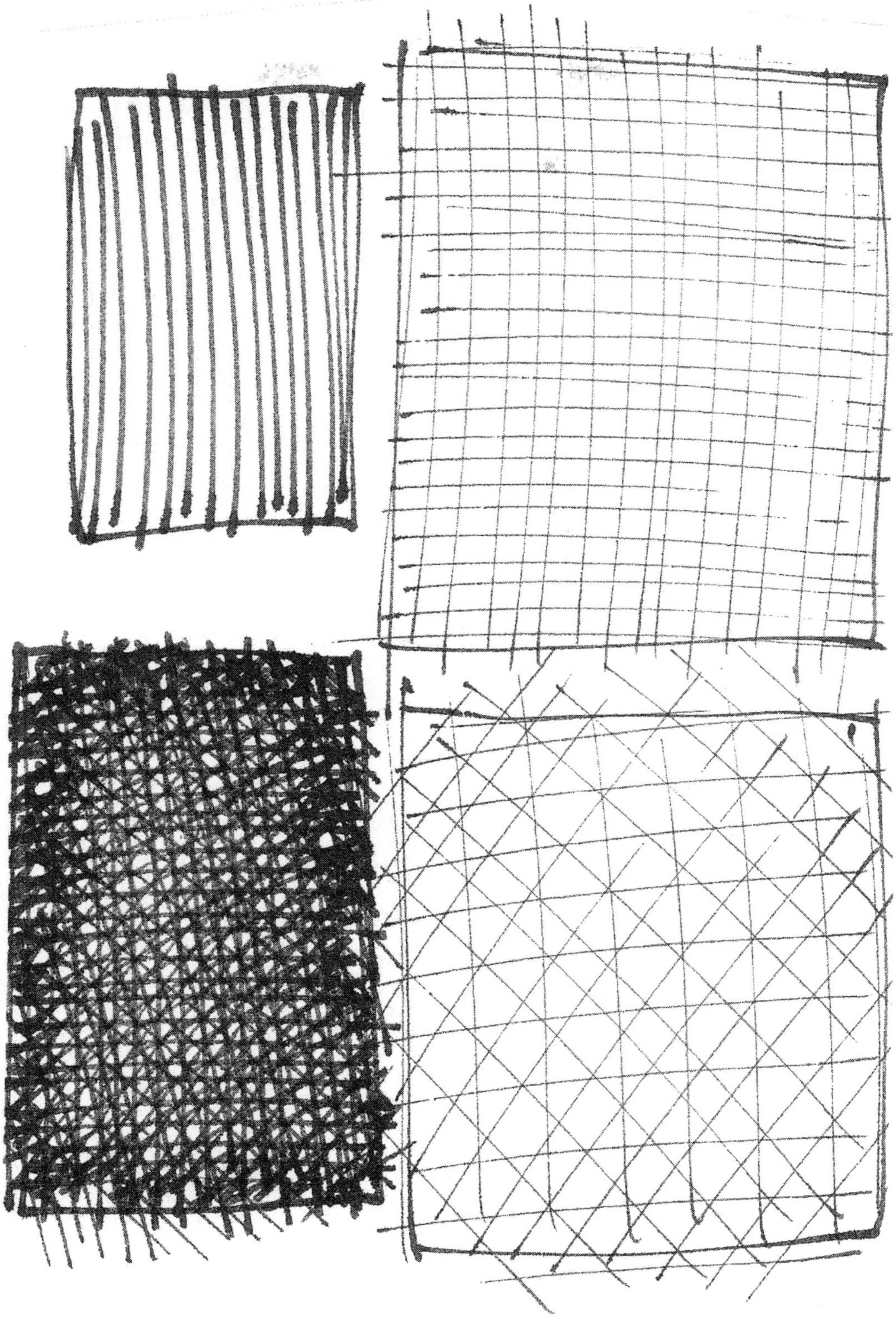

EXAMPLES OF DRAWING NETS

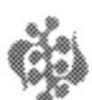

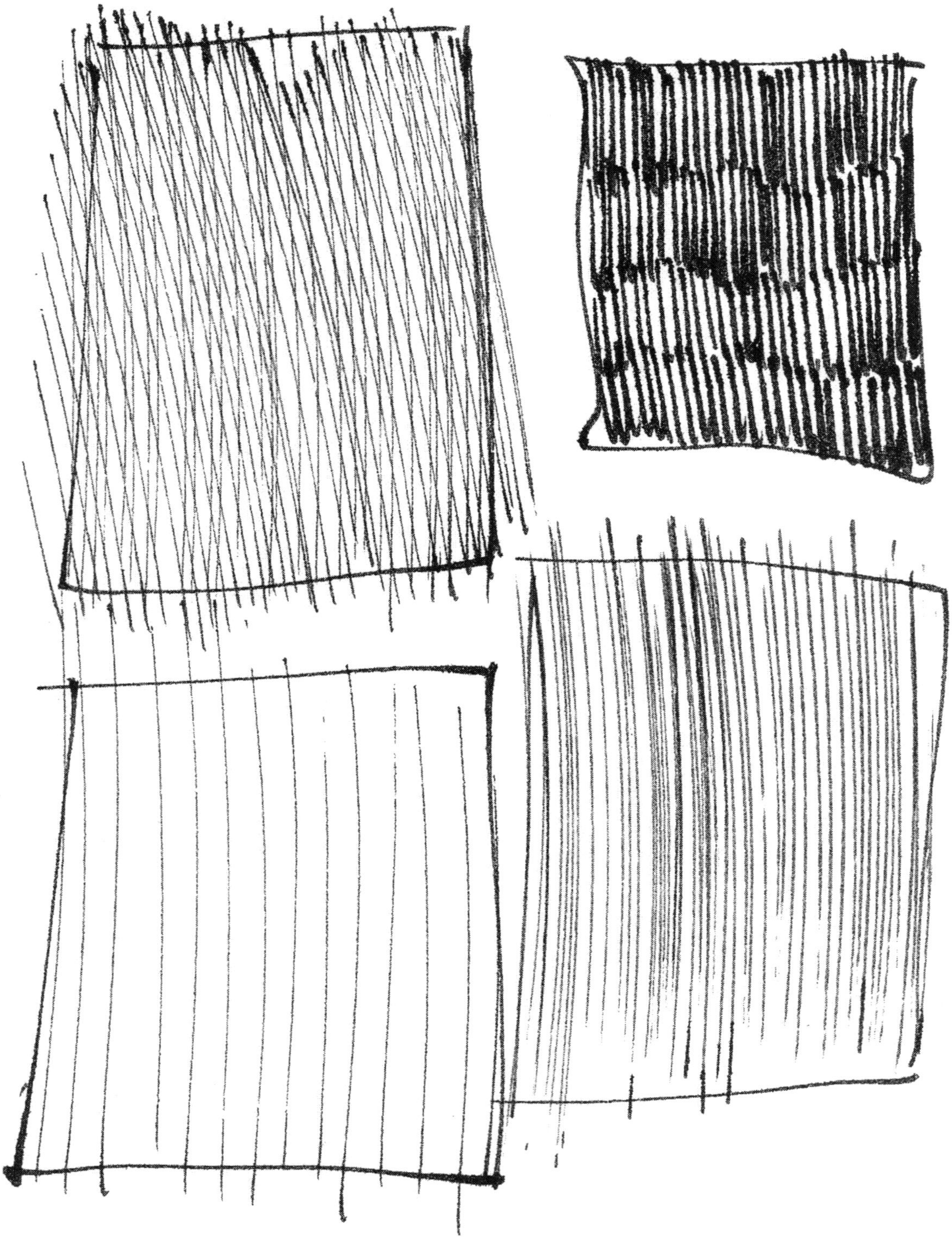

EXAMPLES OF VARIOUS DENSITY MEASURES IN LINES

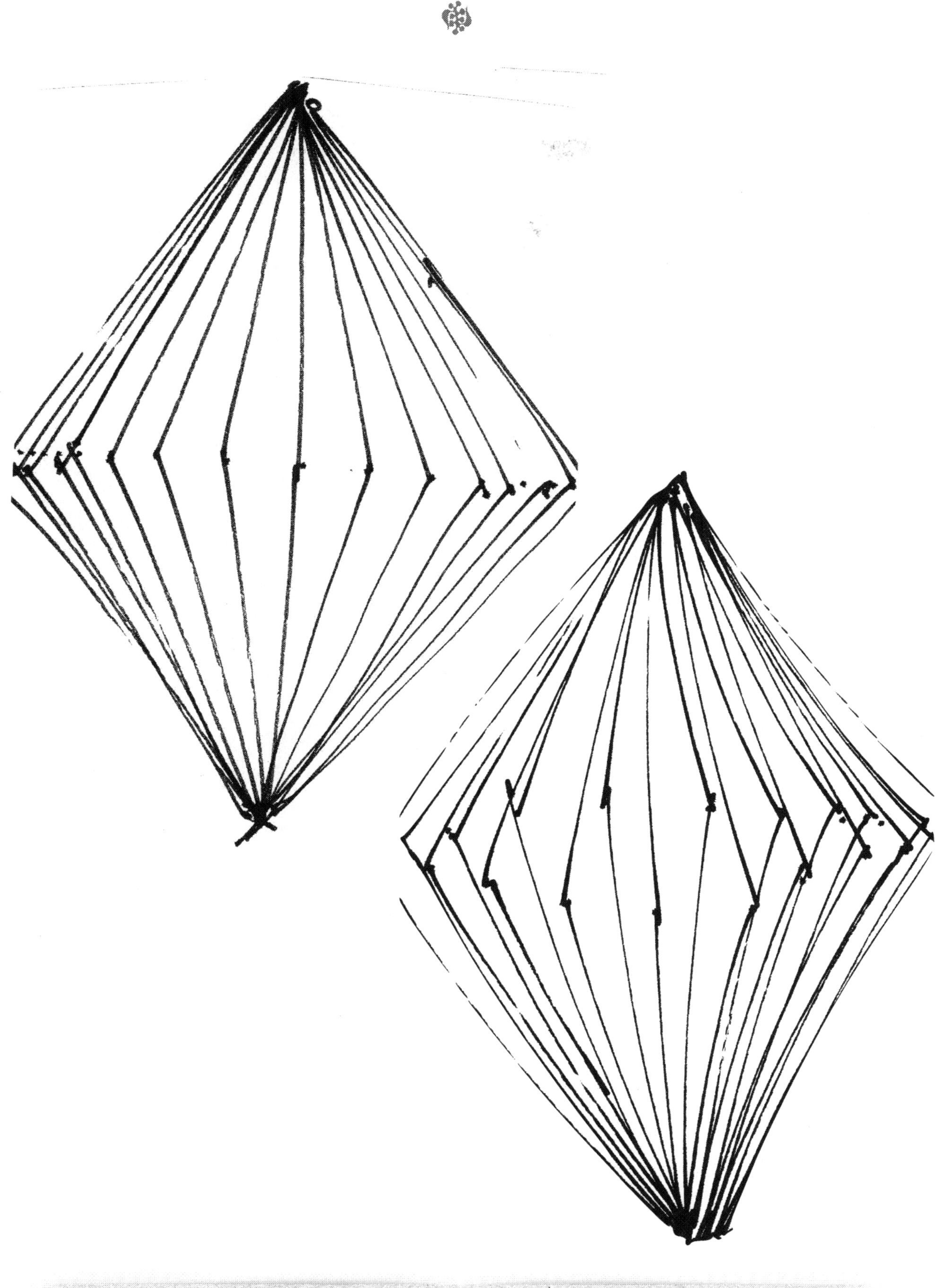

EXERCISE IN ASSESSING CONTACT POINTS OF LINES

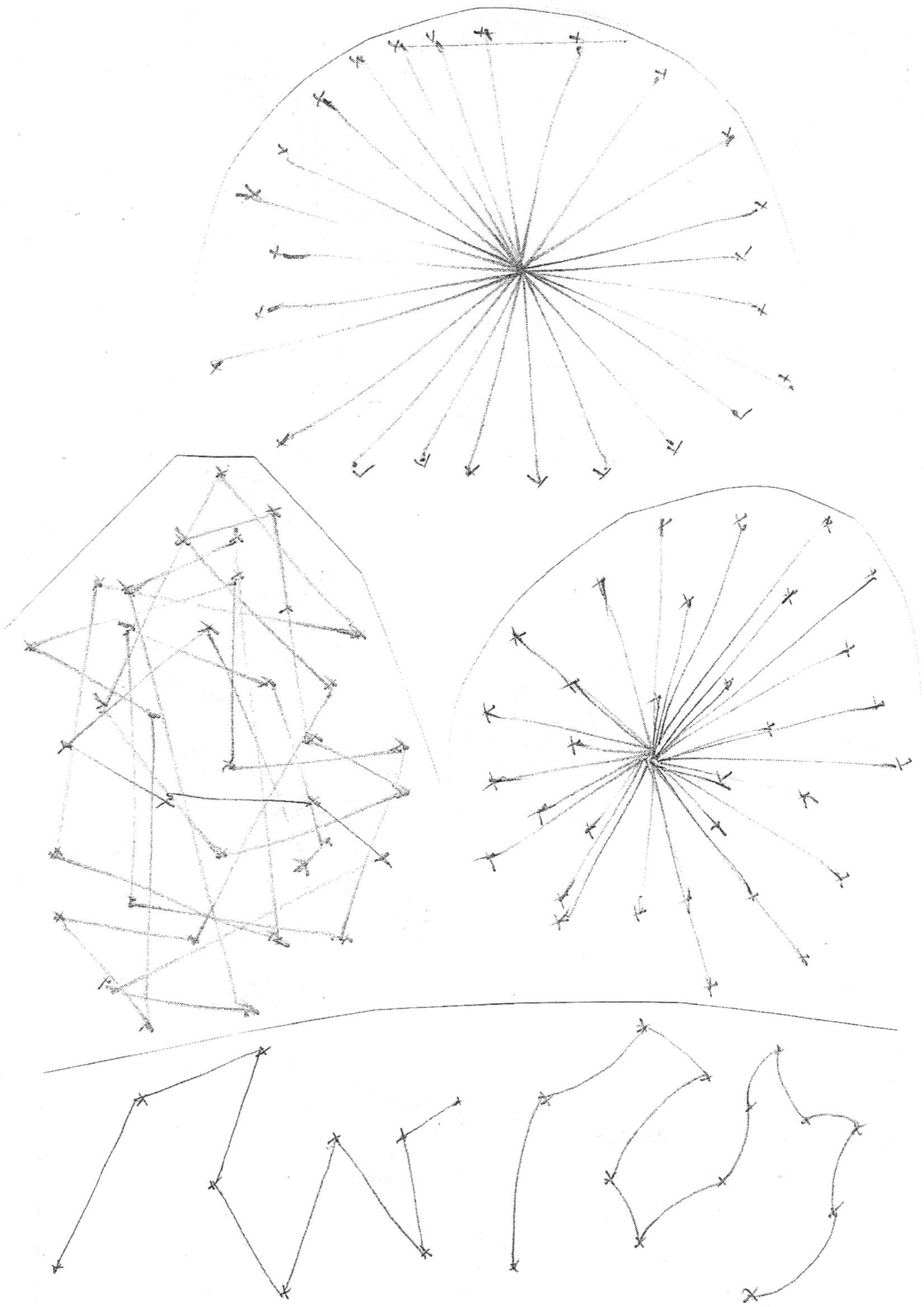

EXAMPLES OF DRAWING DOTS AND
THEN CONNECTING THEM WITH SLOW DRAWN LINES

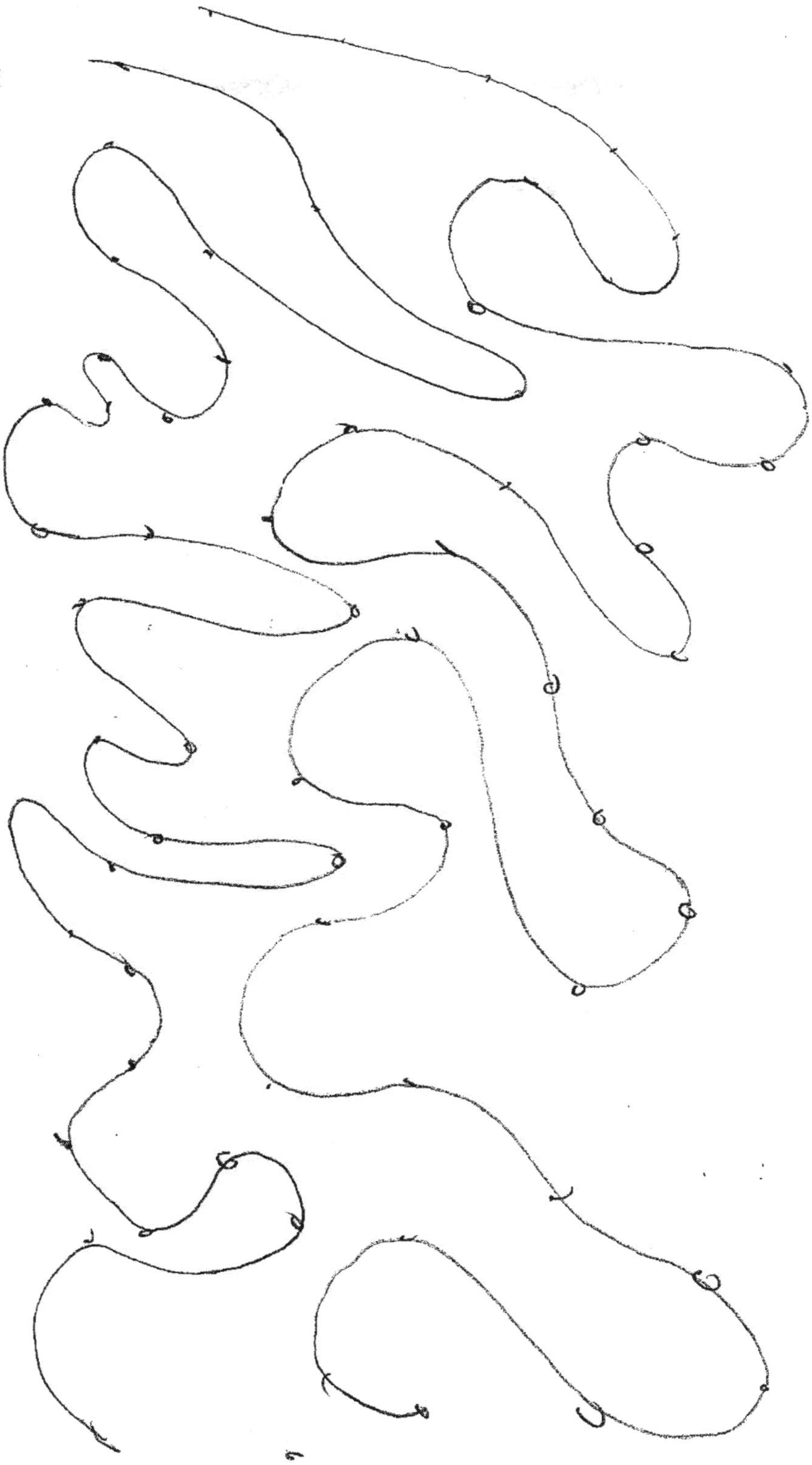

**EXAMPLES OF DRAWING DOTS AND THE CONNECTING THEM
WITH CURVED, UNINTERRUPTED, SLOW DRAWN LINES**

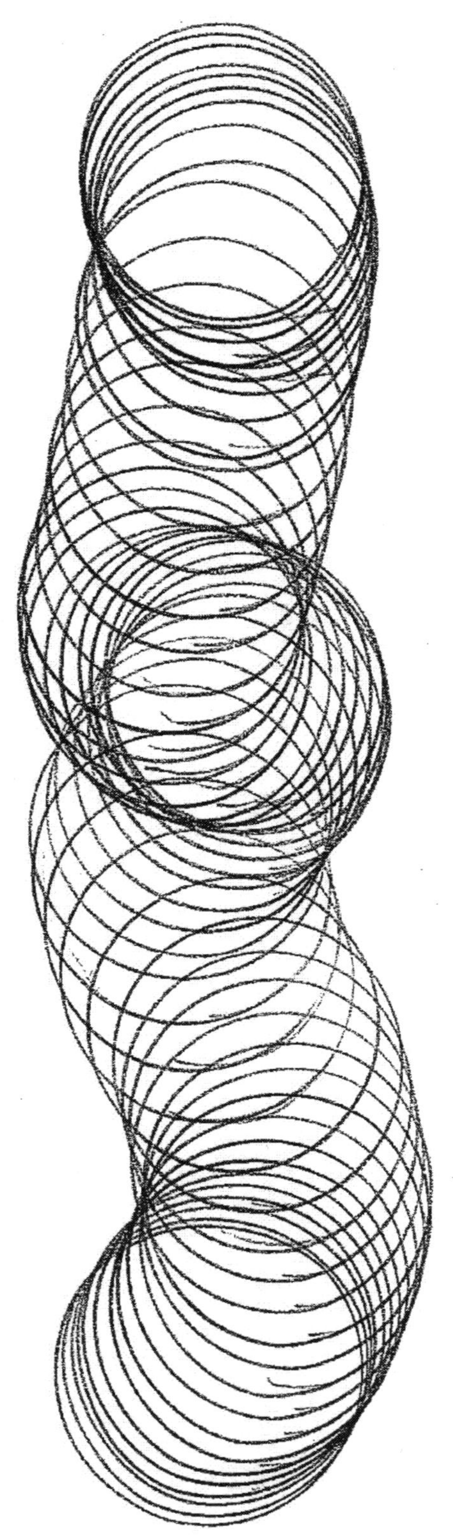

EXERCISE OF DRAWING WITH A ROUND HOLLOW TEMPLATE

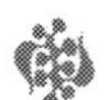

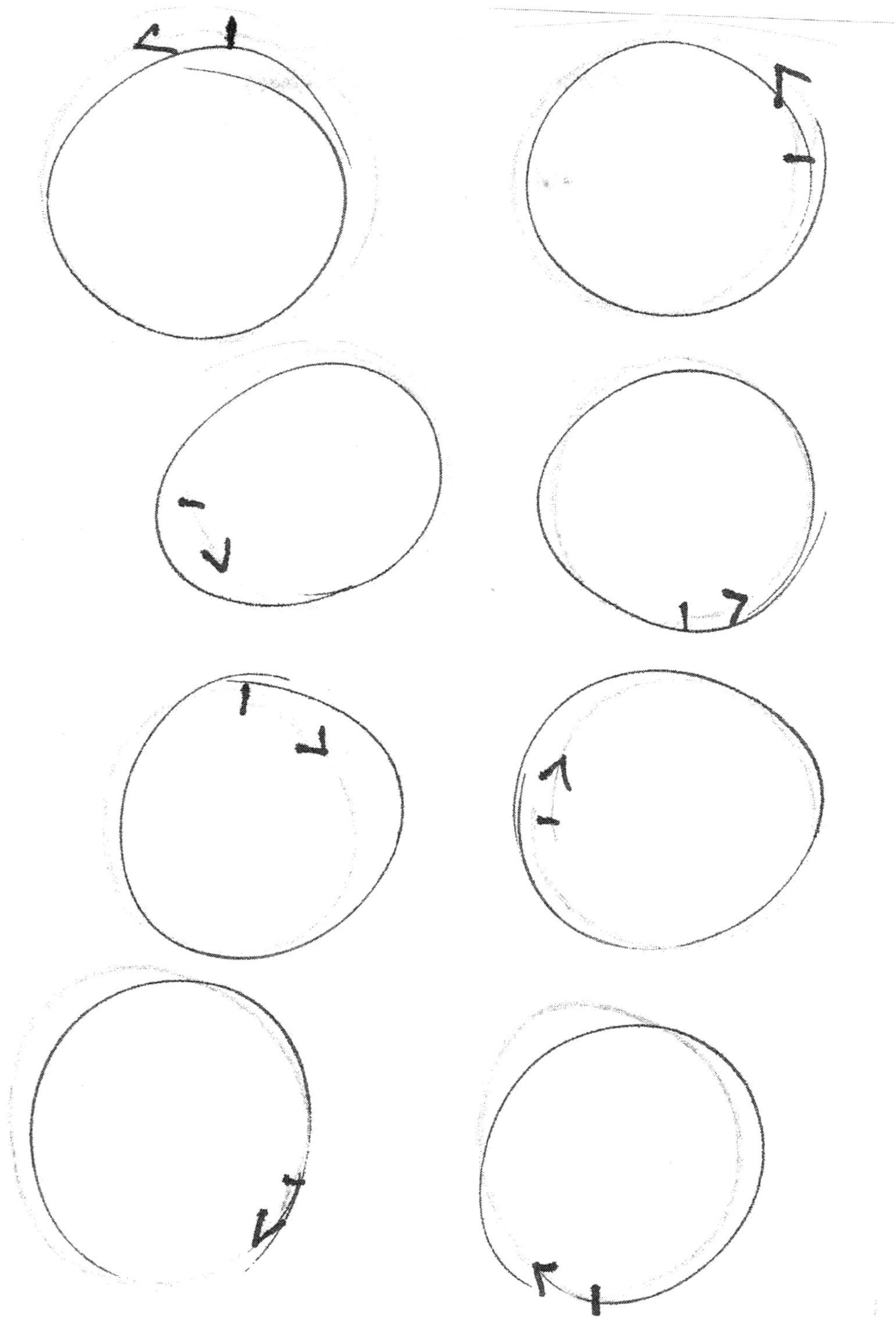

EXERCISE WITH A STARTING POINT AND DIRECTION WHEN DRAWING A FREE HAND CIRCLE

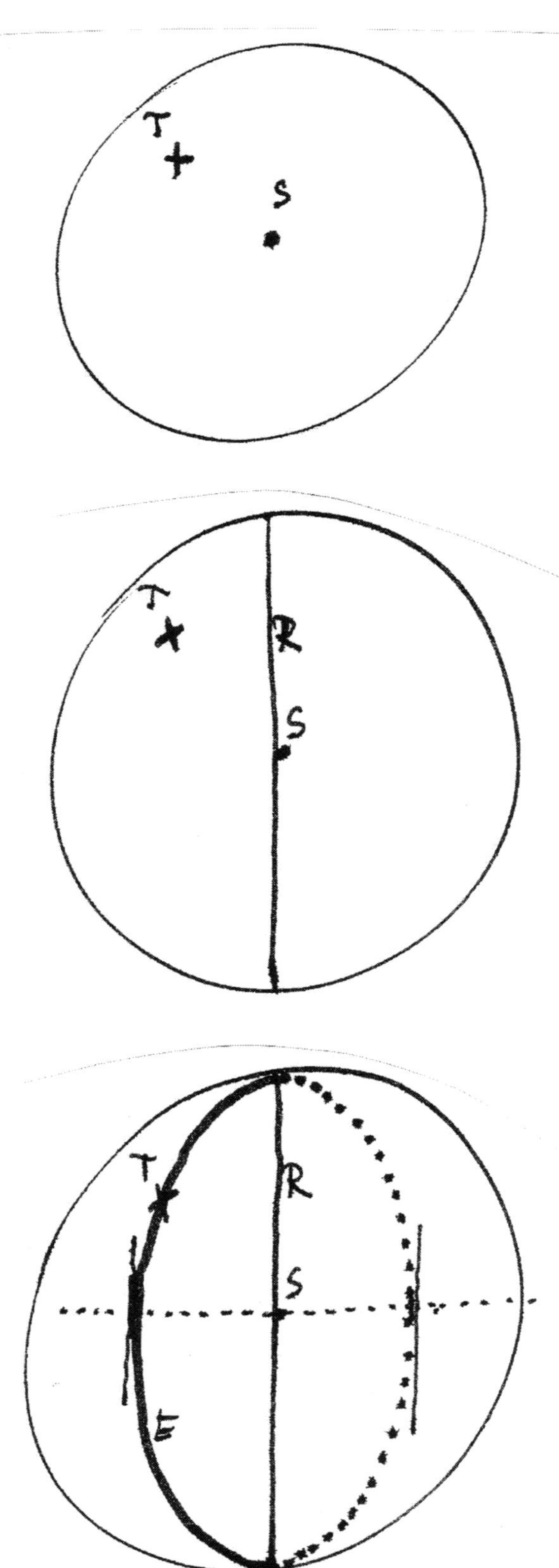

EXERCISE IN DRAWING FROM CIRCLE TO A BALL

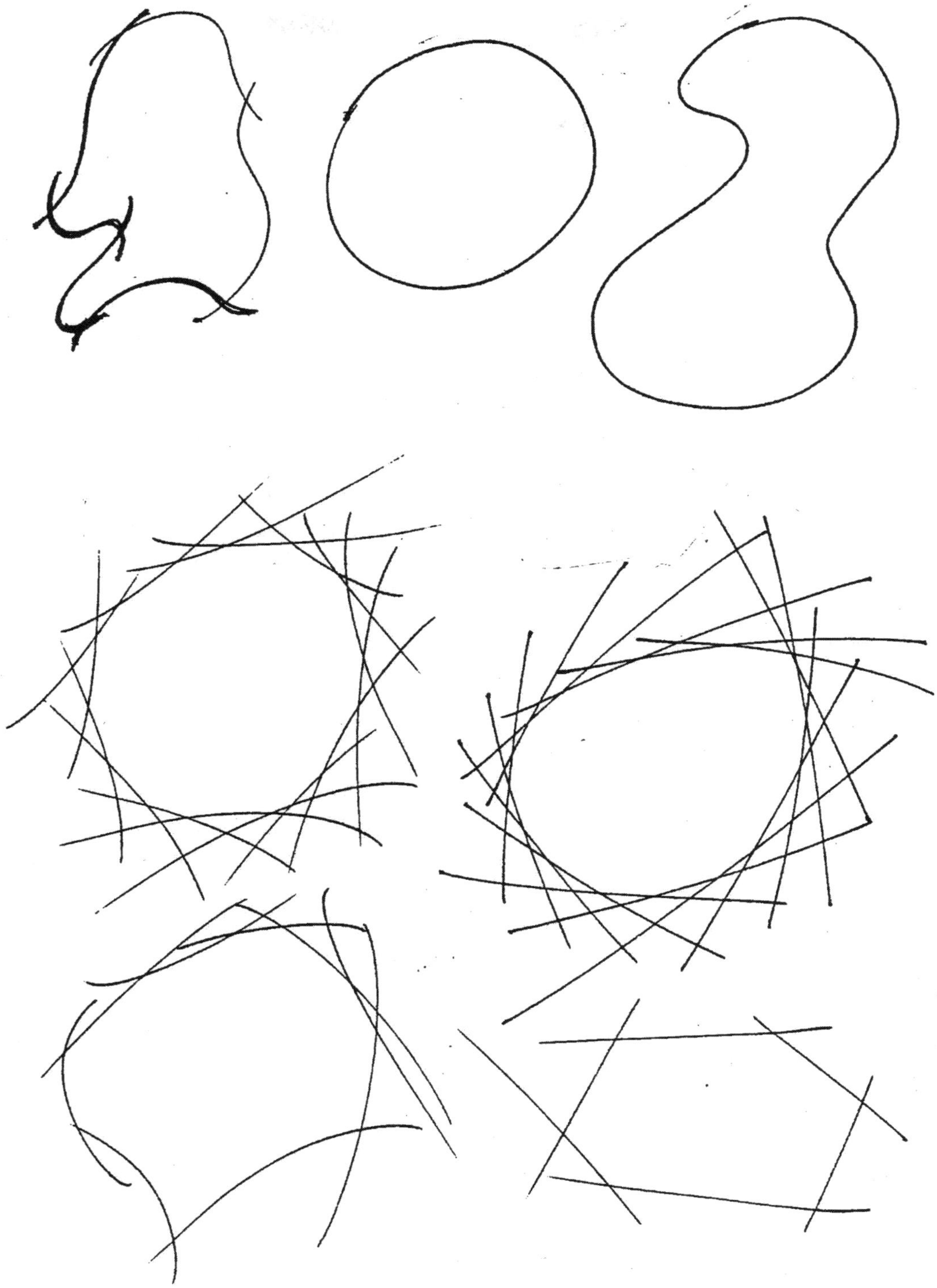

DEFINING THE SHAPES WITH STRAIGHT OR CURVED LINES

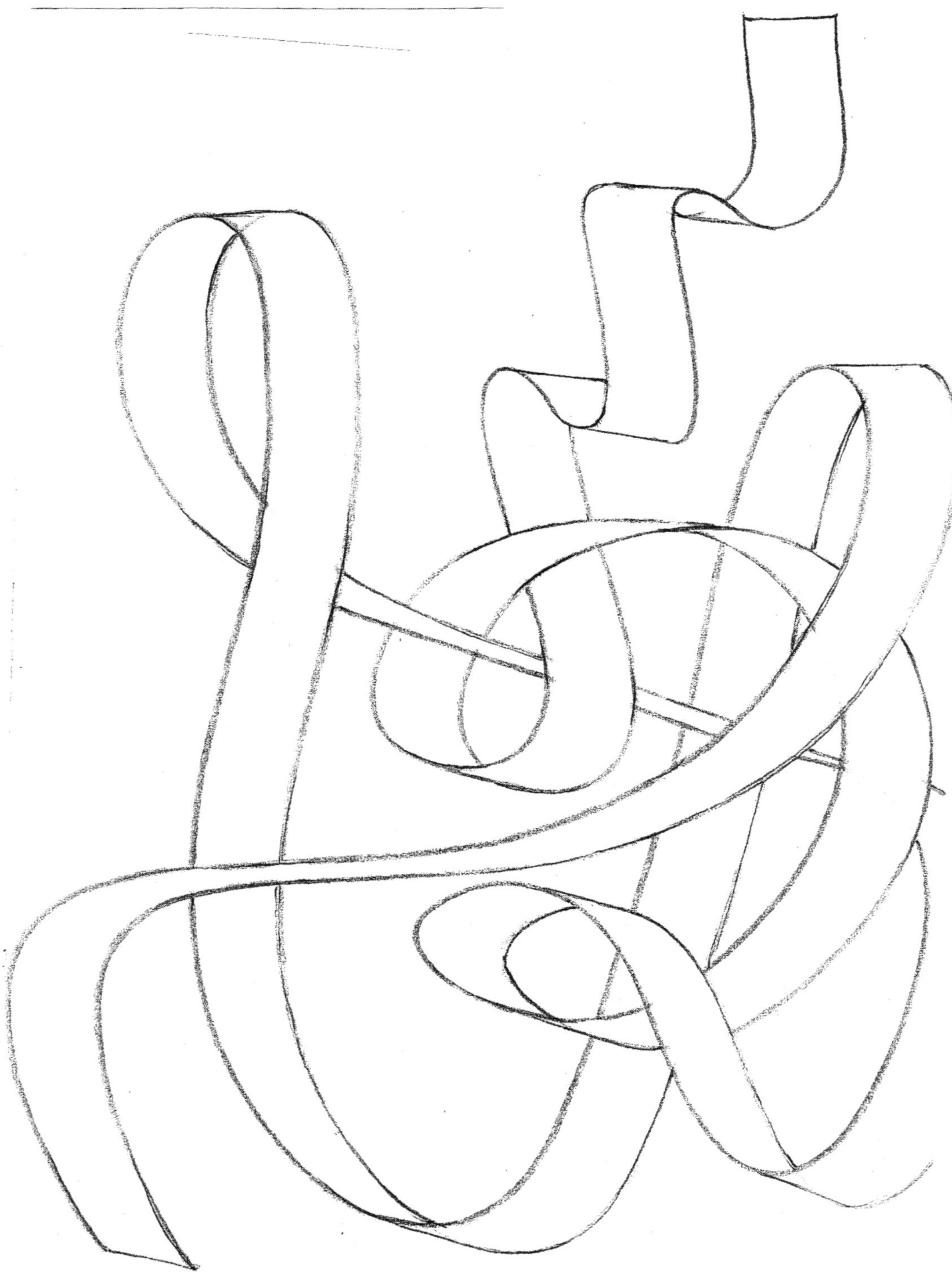

**THE CALLIGRAPHY OF A RIBBON ~
USING TWO PENCILS SIMULTANEOUSLY**

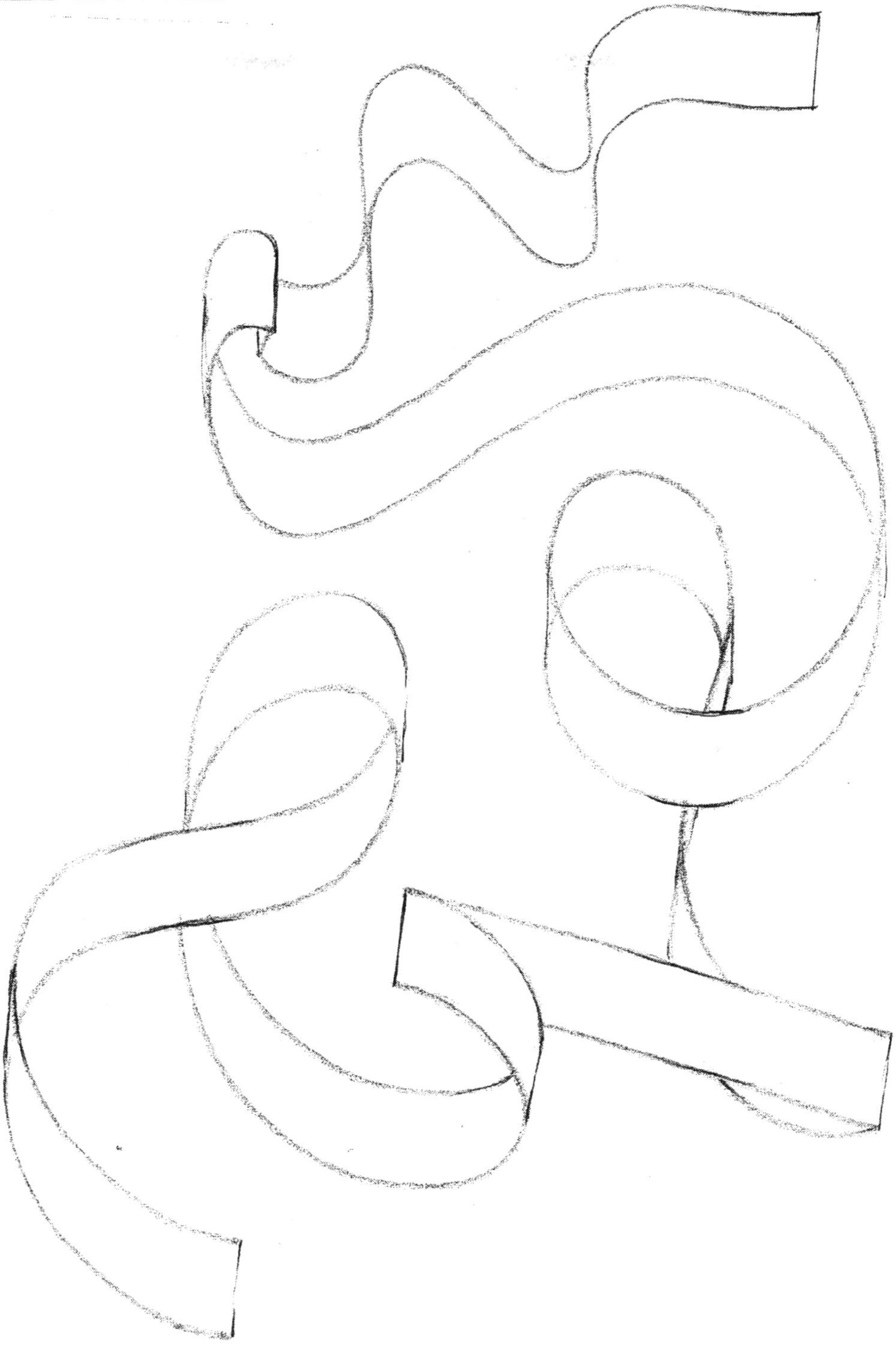

THE CALLIGRAPHY OF A RIBBON ~
USING TWO PENCILS SIMULTANEOUSLY

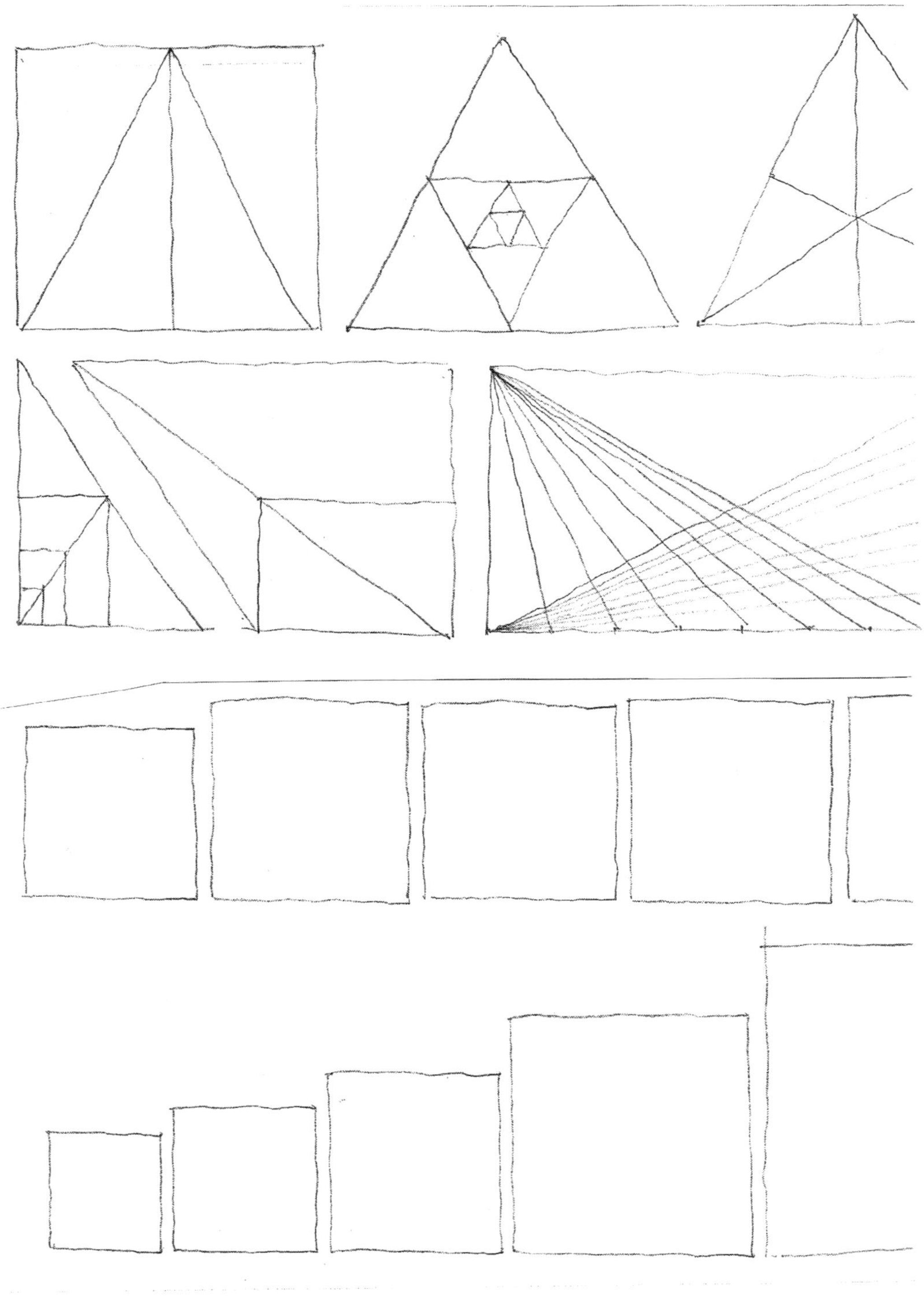

FREE HAND DRAWING PRACTICE OF VARIOUS SURFACES

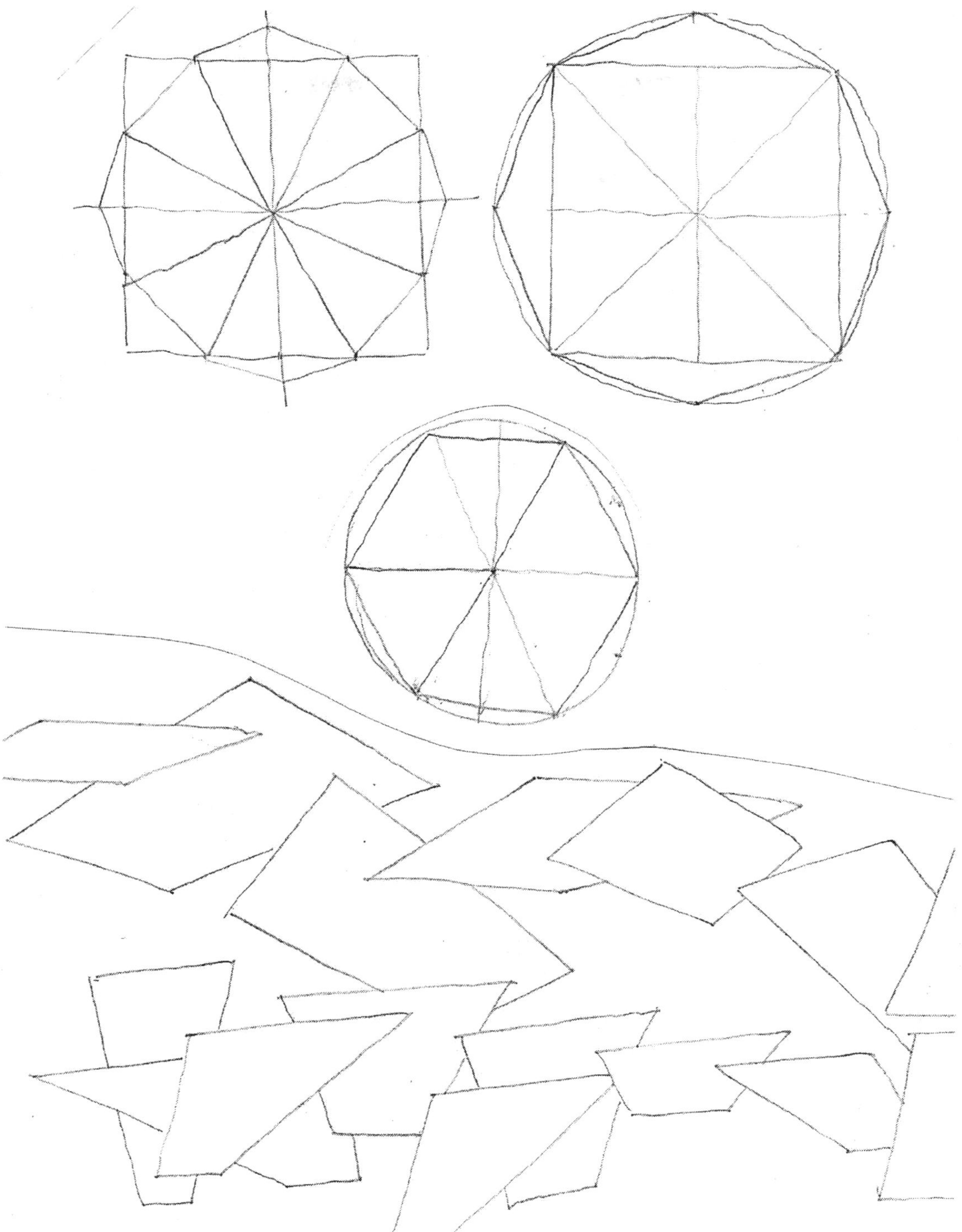

**FREE HAND DRAWING PRACTICE OF
VARIOUS SURFACES IN SPACE AND PERSPECTIVE**

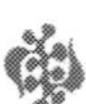

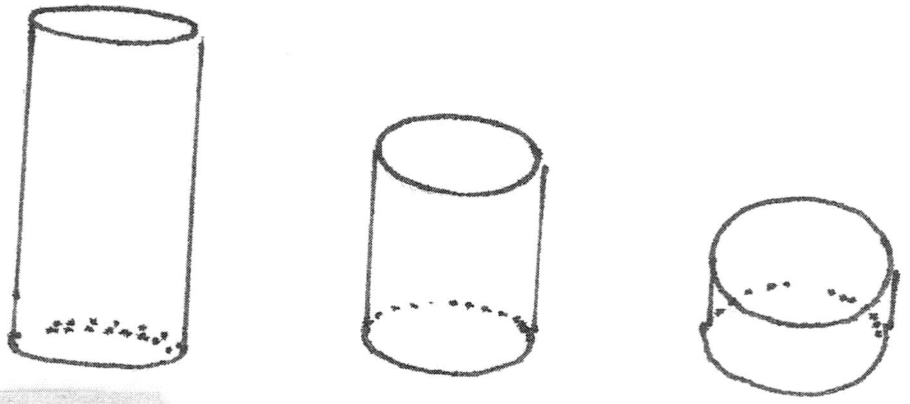

5 INCH HEIGHT

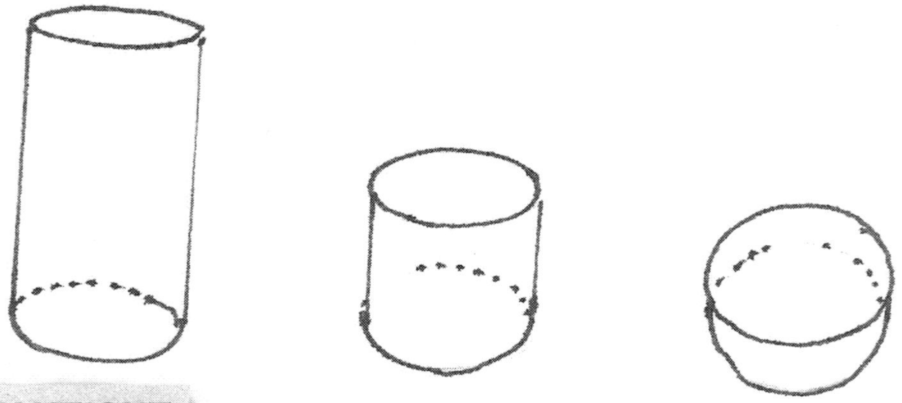

50 INCH HEIGHT

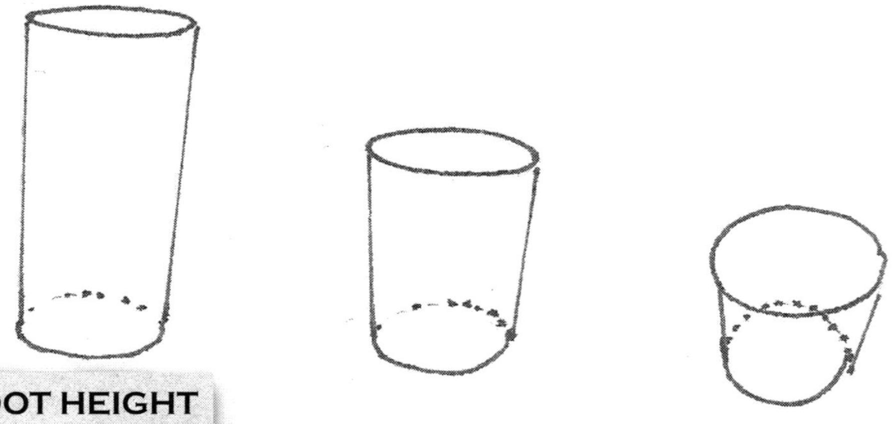

50 FOOT HEIGHT

THE ASPECTS OF CYLINDER SIZE

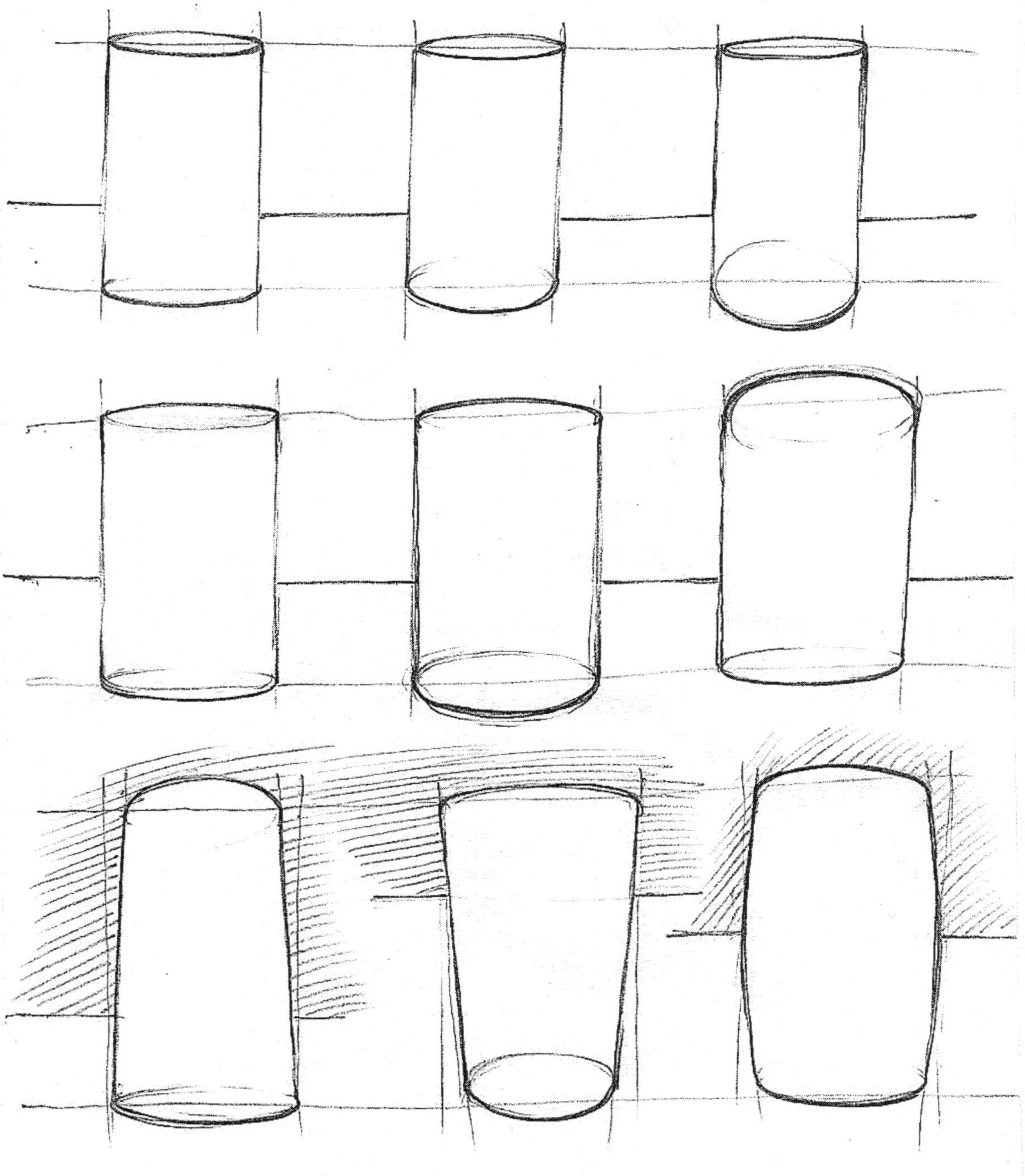

**EXERCISE FOR A FREE HAND ELIPSE CONCLUSIONS
OF A CYLINDER, DEPENDING ON SIZE**

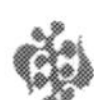

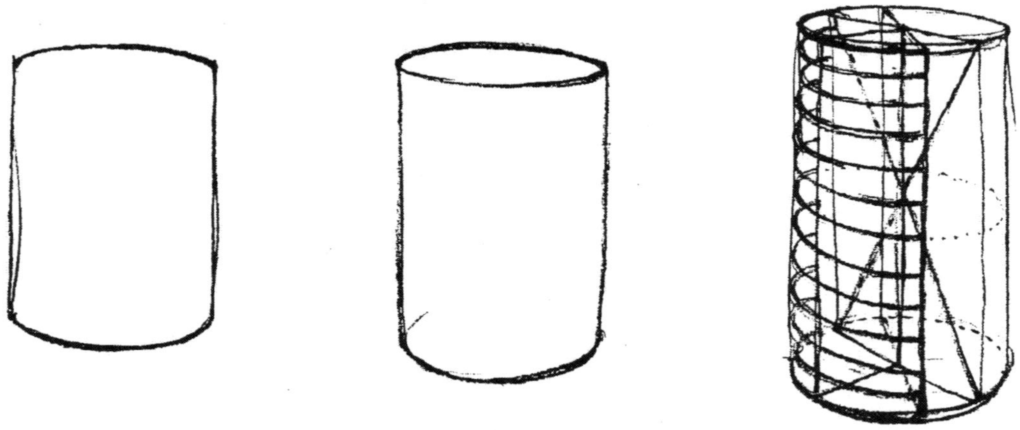

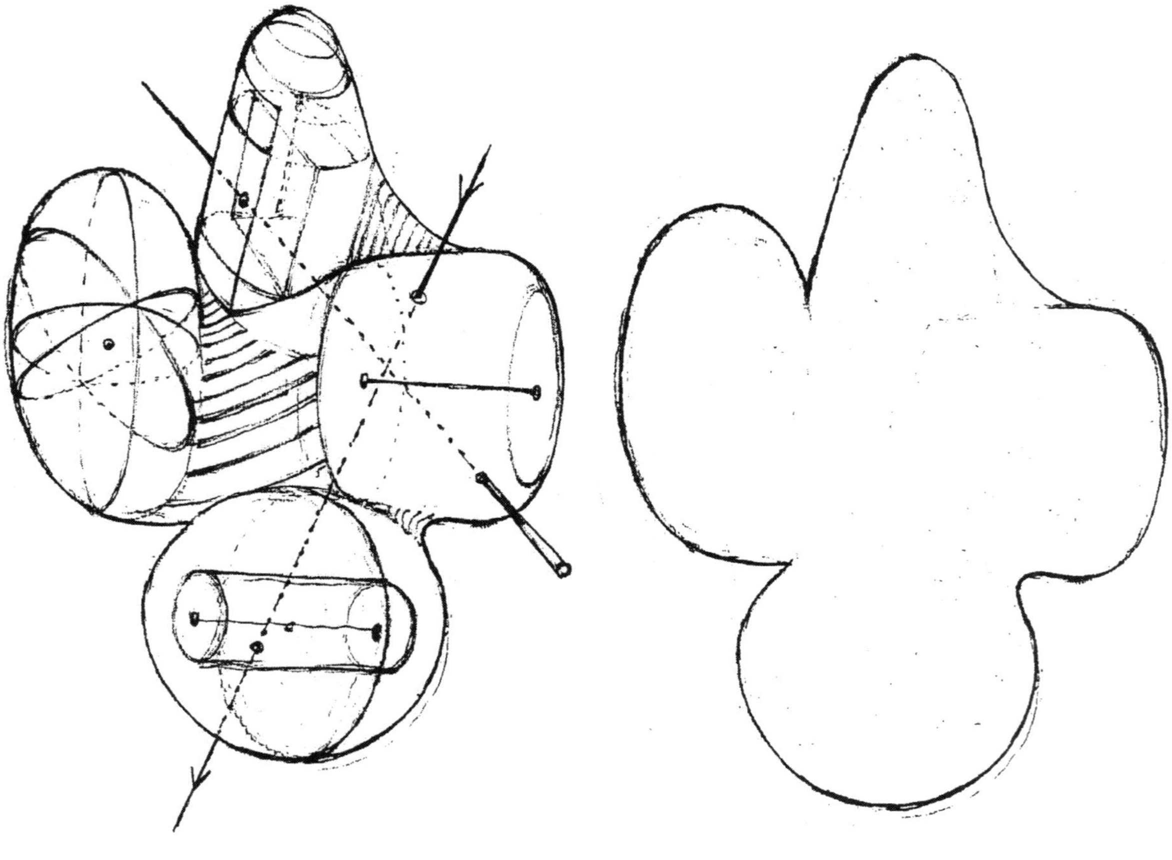

THE ANALYSIS OF A SHAPE

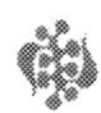

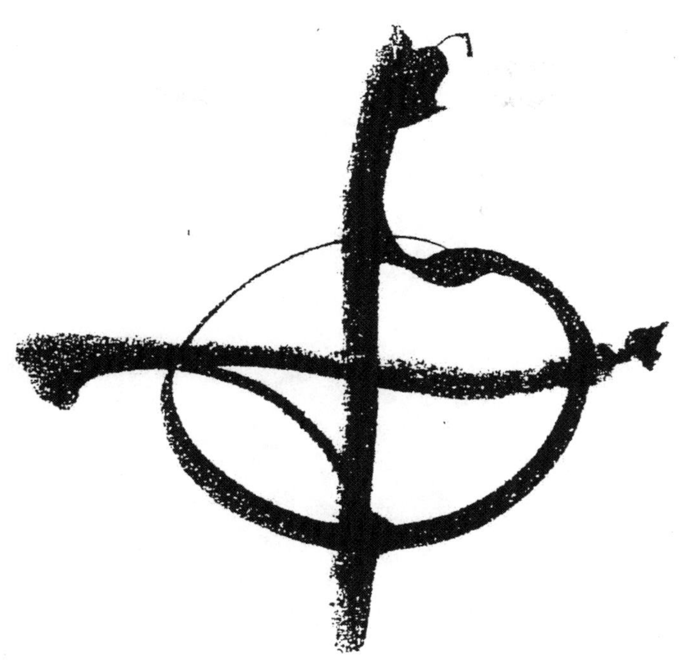

A EXAMPLE OF CALLIGRAPHY

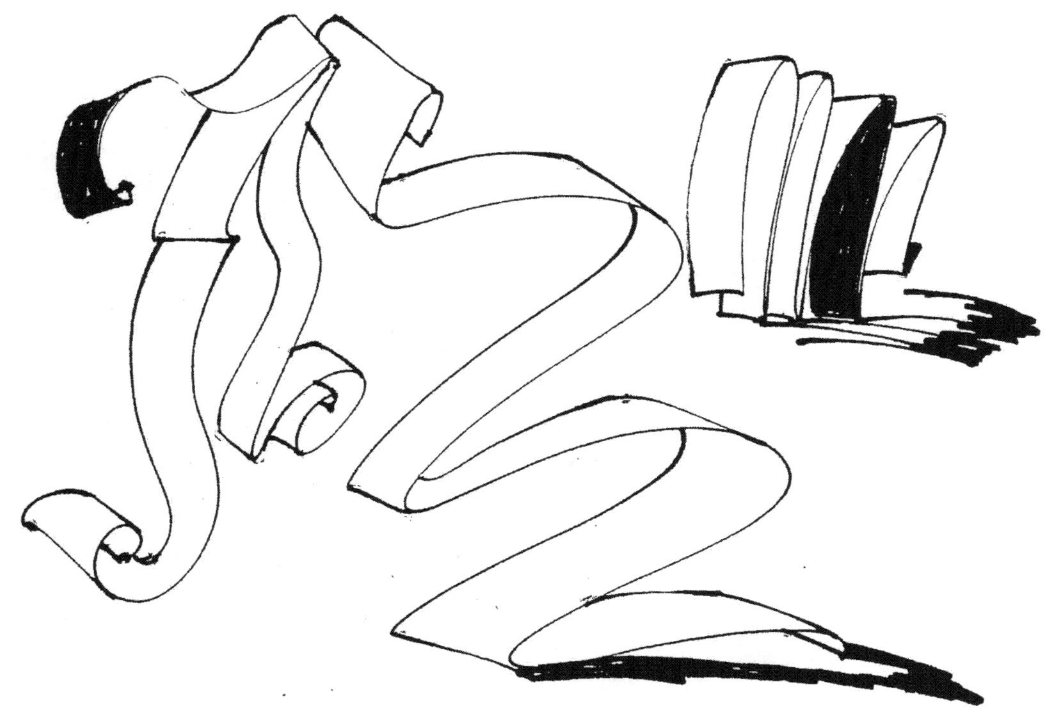

THE CALLIGRAPHY OF A RIBBON

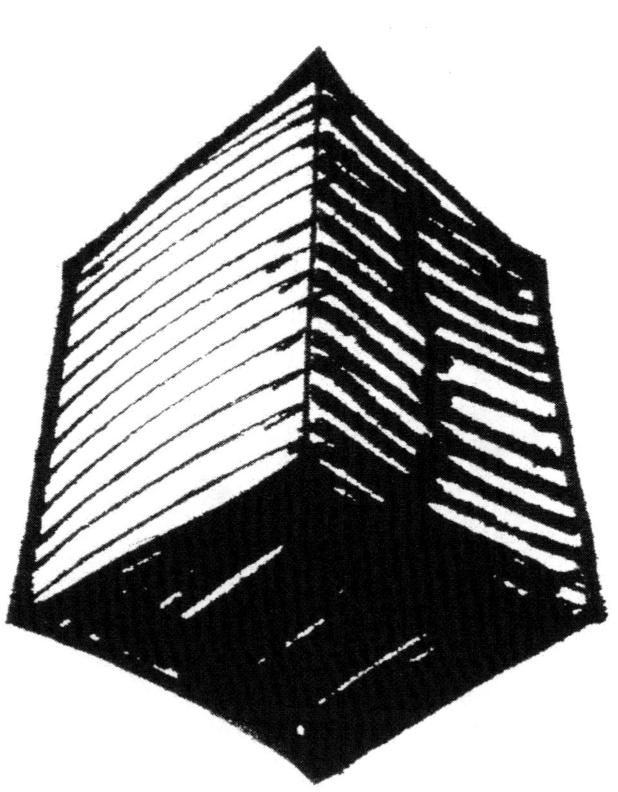

SUQARE AS AN EXAMPLE FROM ALL SIDES IN A LIMITED SPACE

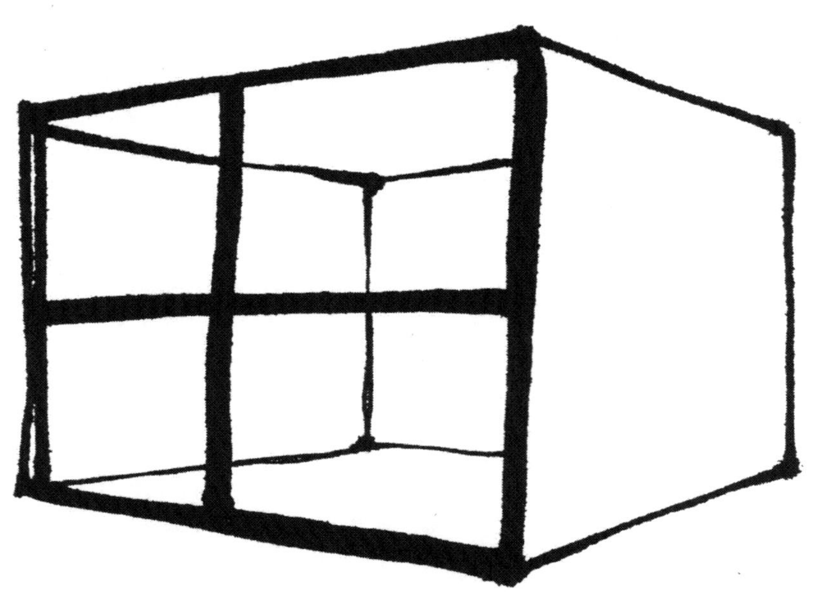

A ROOM WITH A LARGE CLOSED WINDOW IS AN OBJECT,
BUT WITH AN OPEN WINDOW IT IS AMBIENT

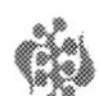

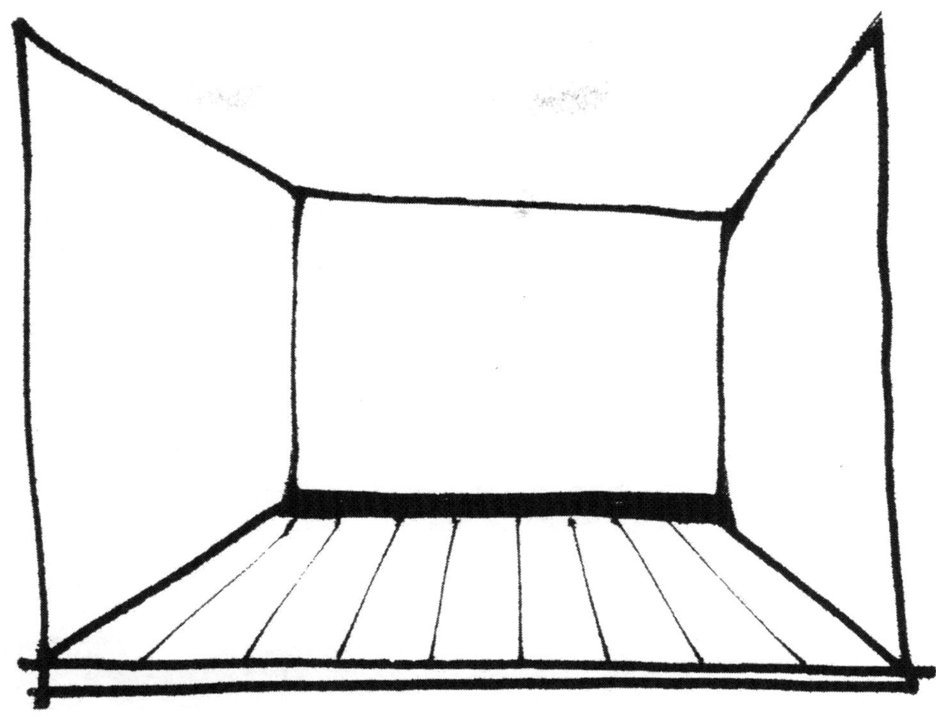

A STAGE, PARTIALLY OPEN AND LIMITED REPRESENTS AN AMBIENT

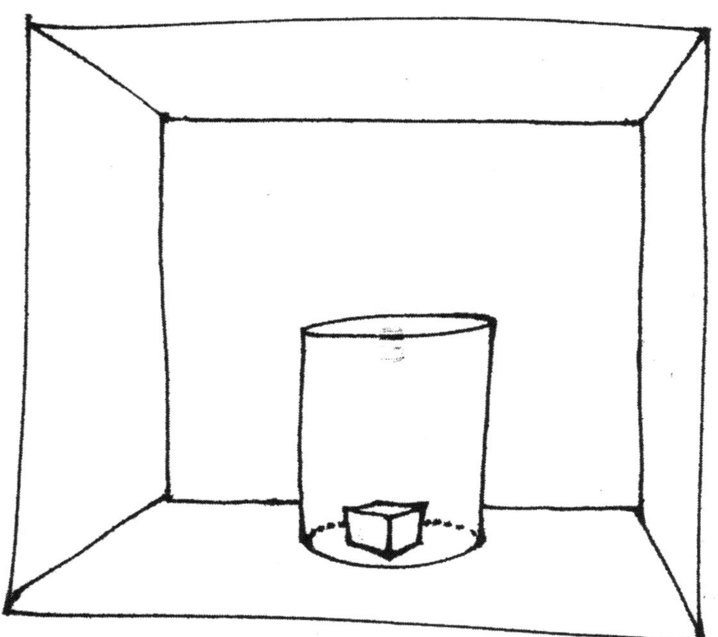

WITH A FEW EXCEPTIONS, THE CONCEPT OF POSITIVE
AND NEGATIVE SHAPE INTERTWINES

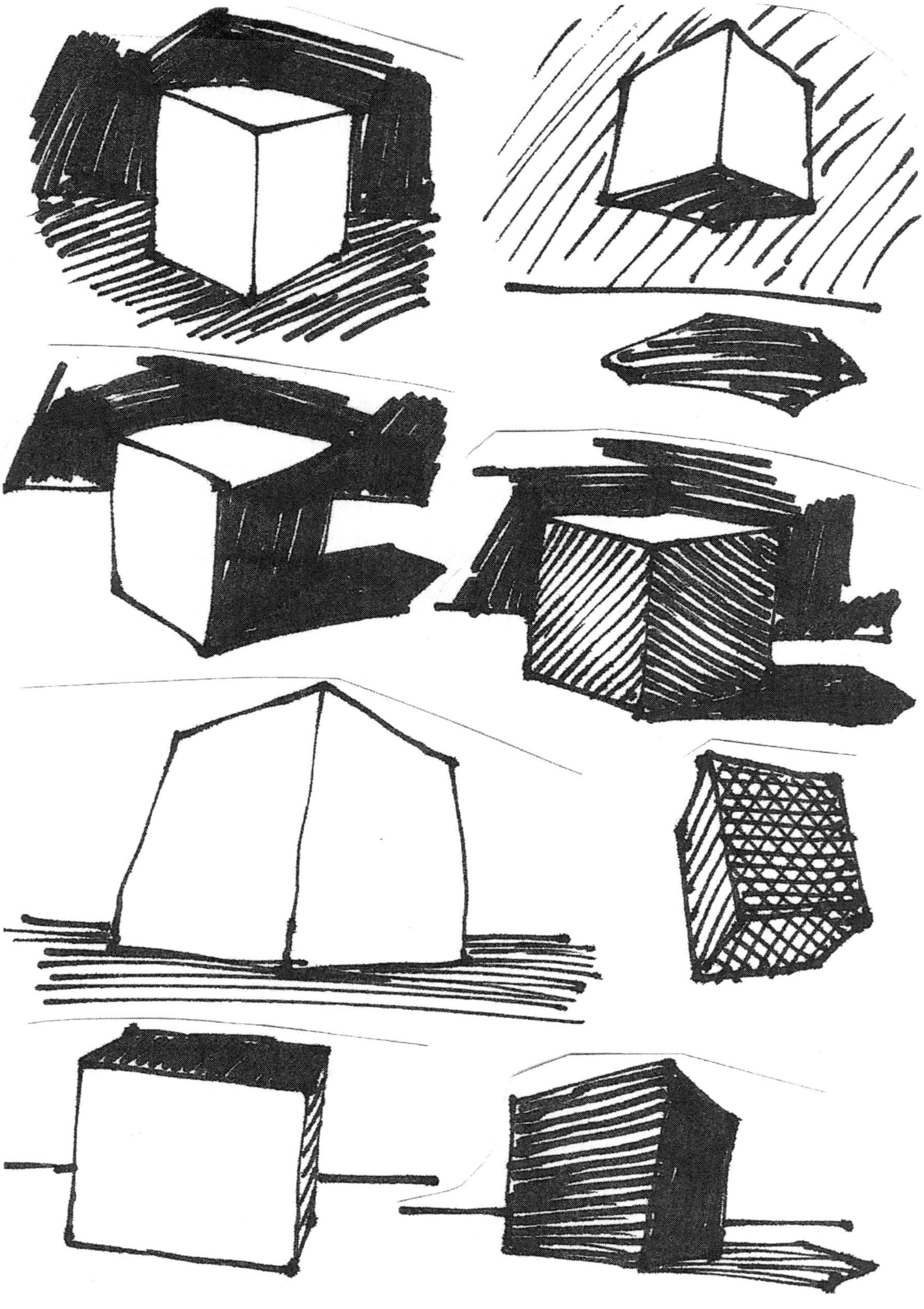

EXAMPLES OF SHADOWS AND LIGHT

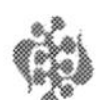

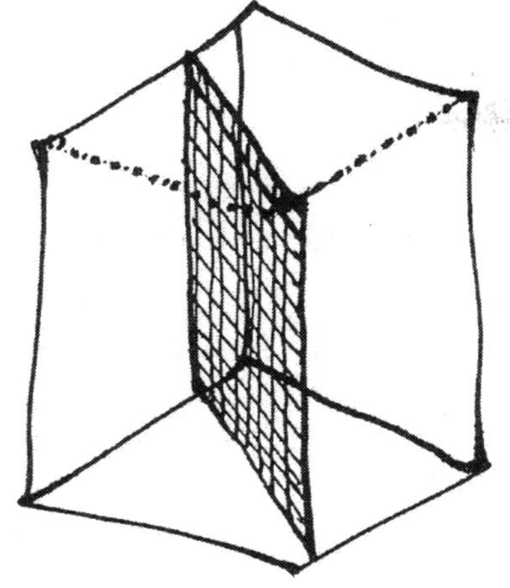

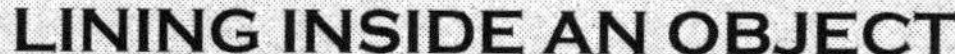
LINING INSIDE AN OBJECT

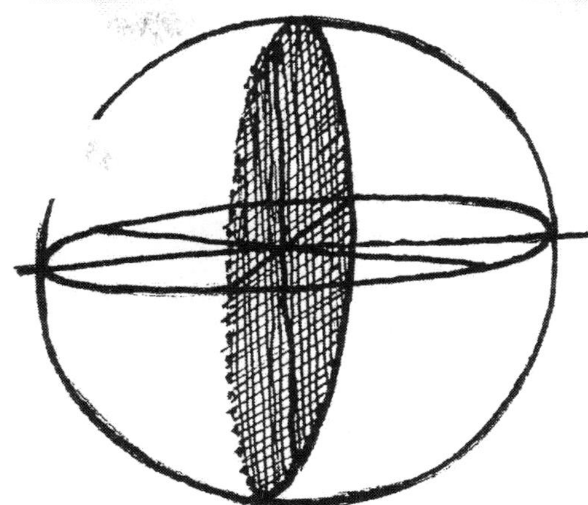

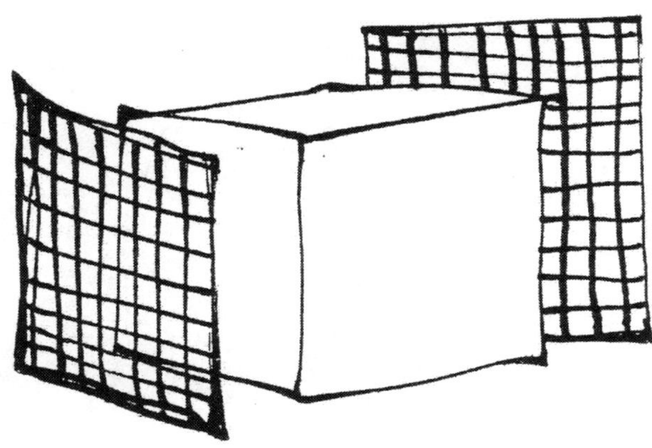

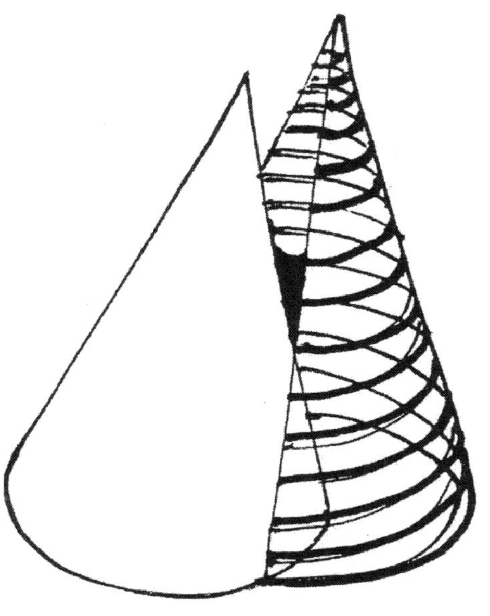

LINING AROUND AN OBJECT

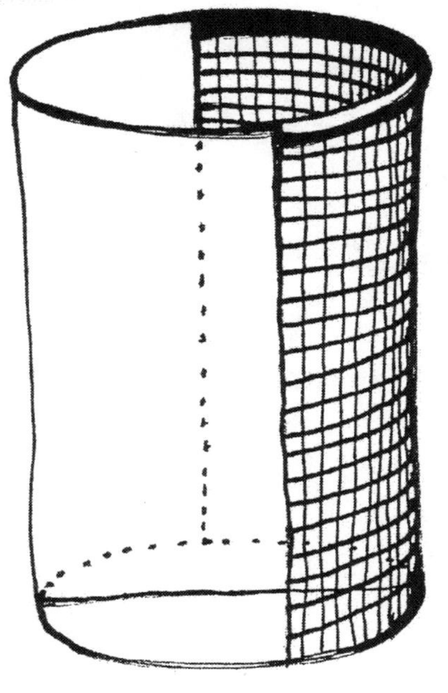

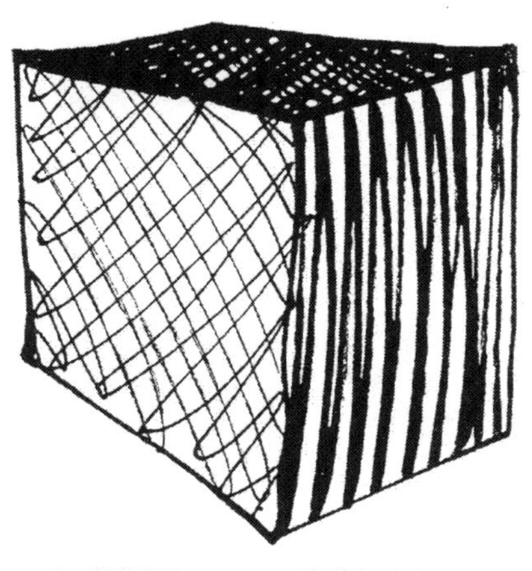
LINING ON THE OBJECT

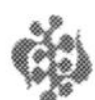

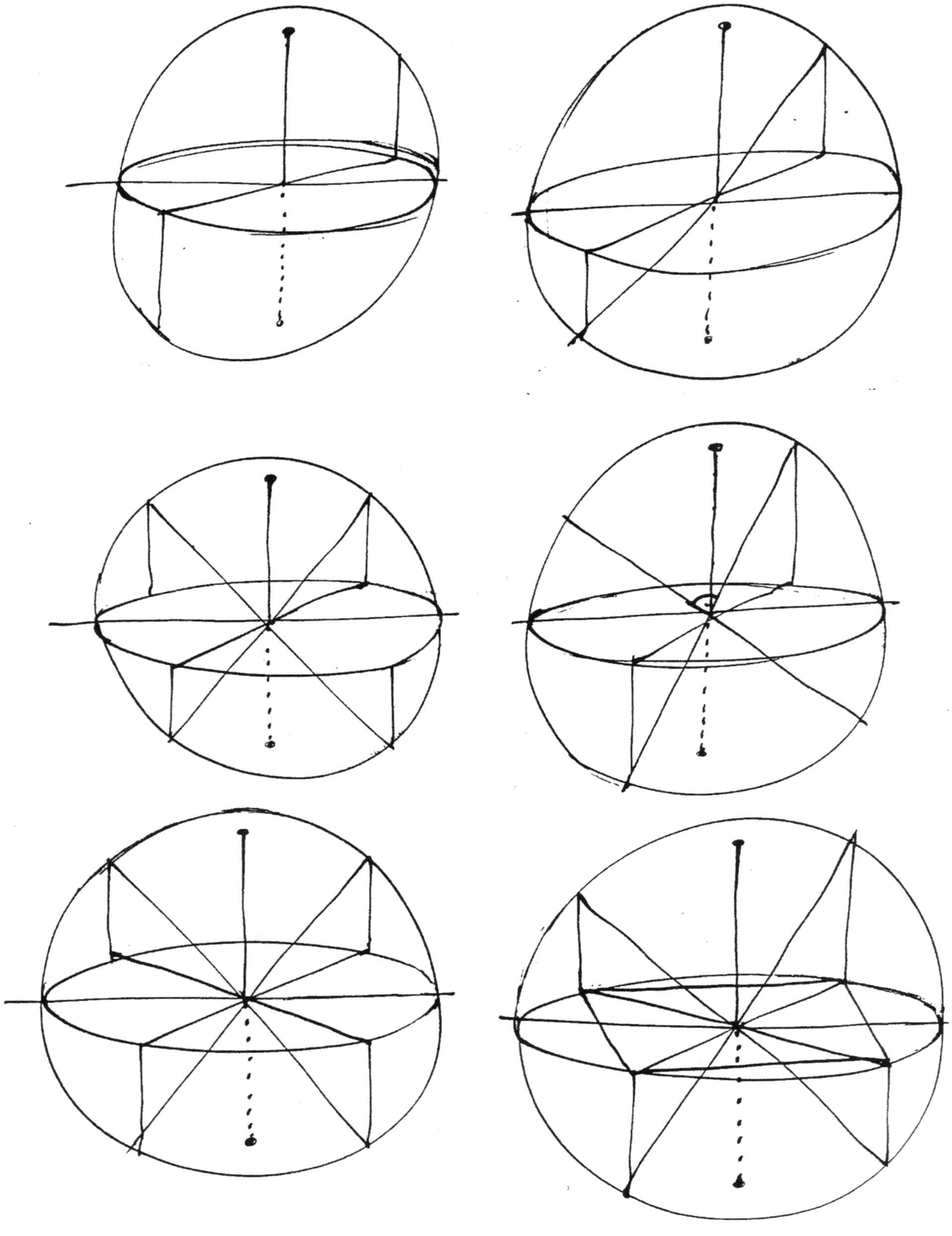

STEP BY STEP PROGRESSION OF A THOUGHT

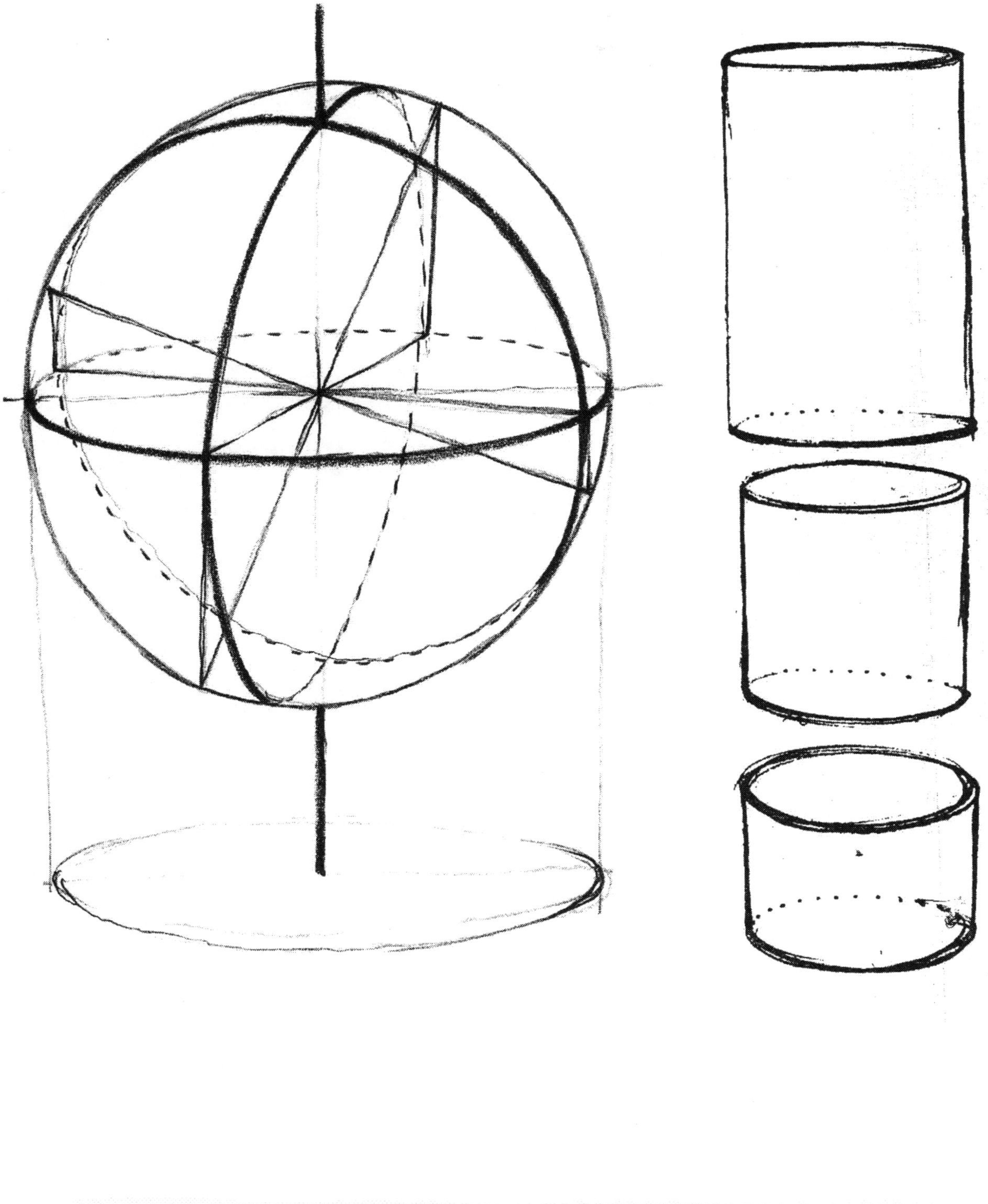

EXERCISE FOR FREE HAND GEOMETRIC ANALYSIS

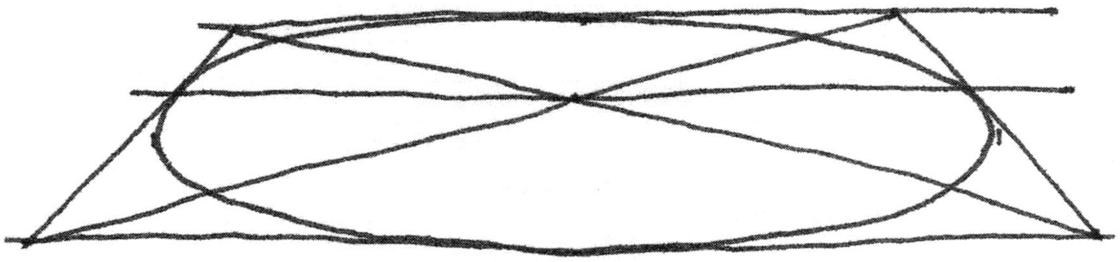

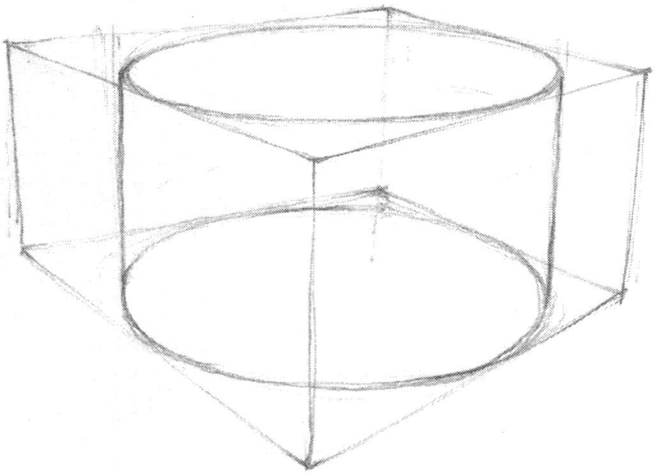

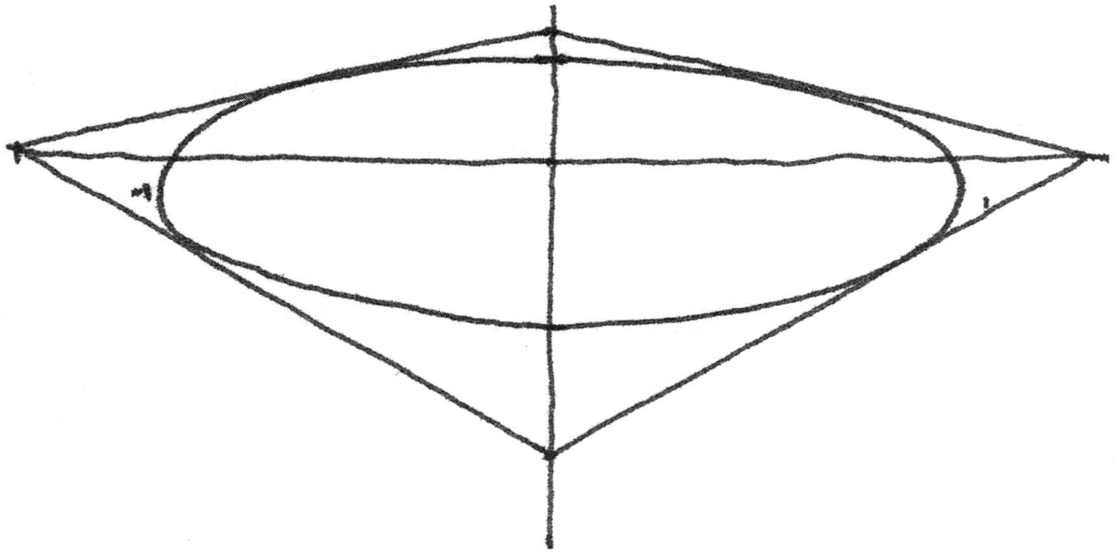

THE ENIGMA OF AN ELLIPSE IN PERSPECTIVE

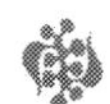

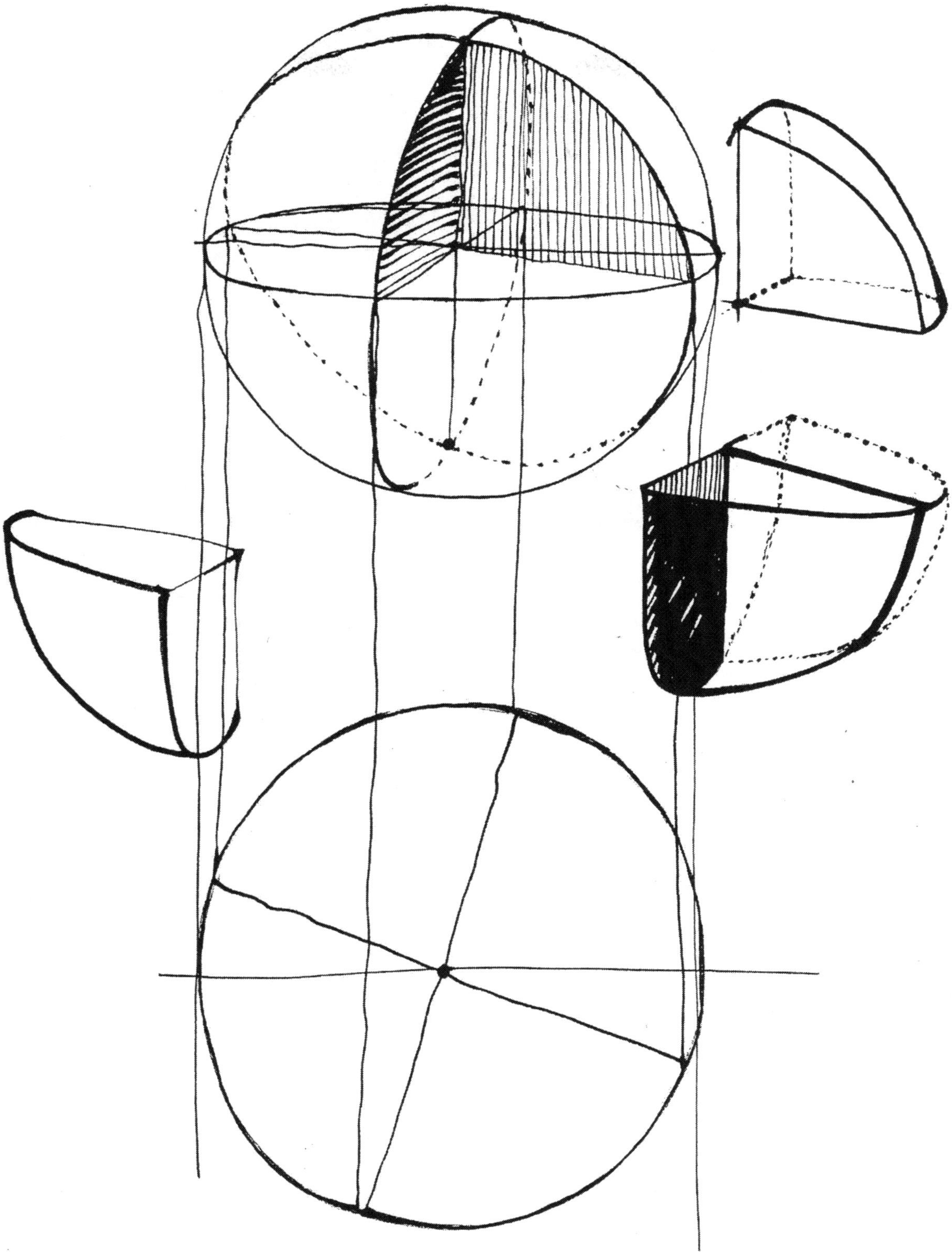

FREE HAND GEOMETRIC ANALYSIS OF A BALL

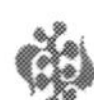

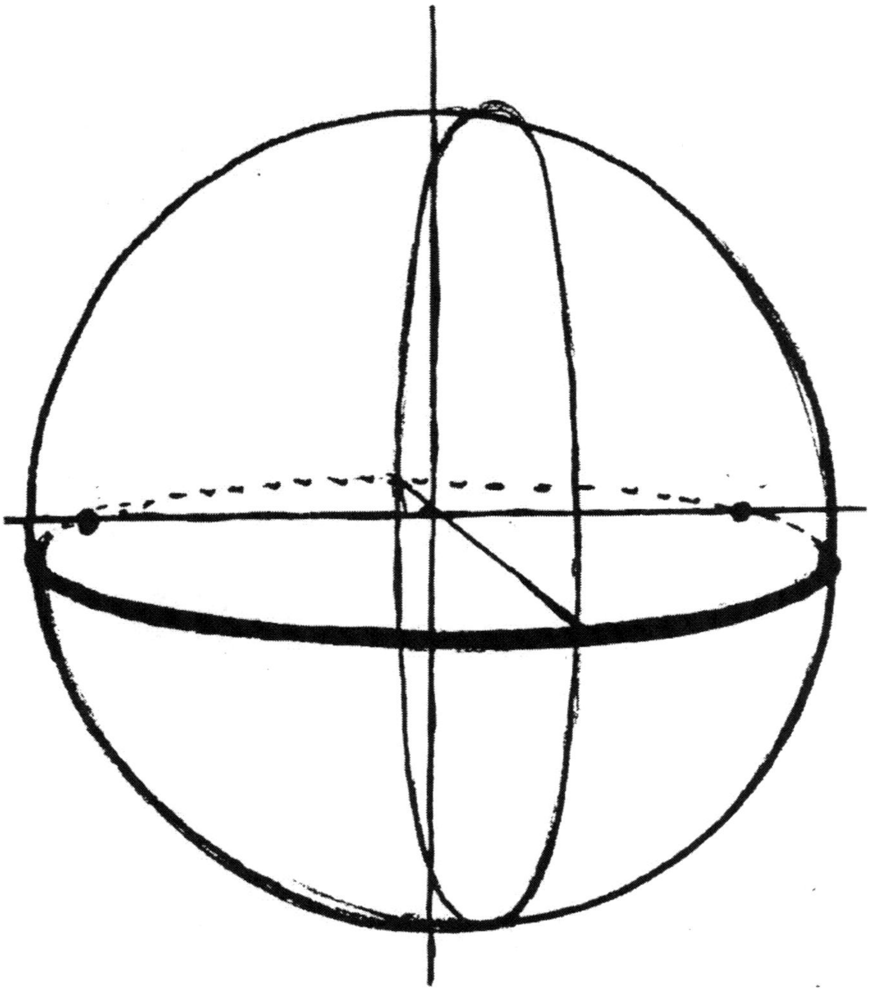

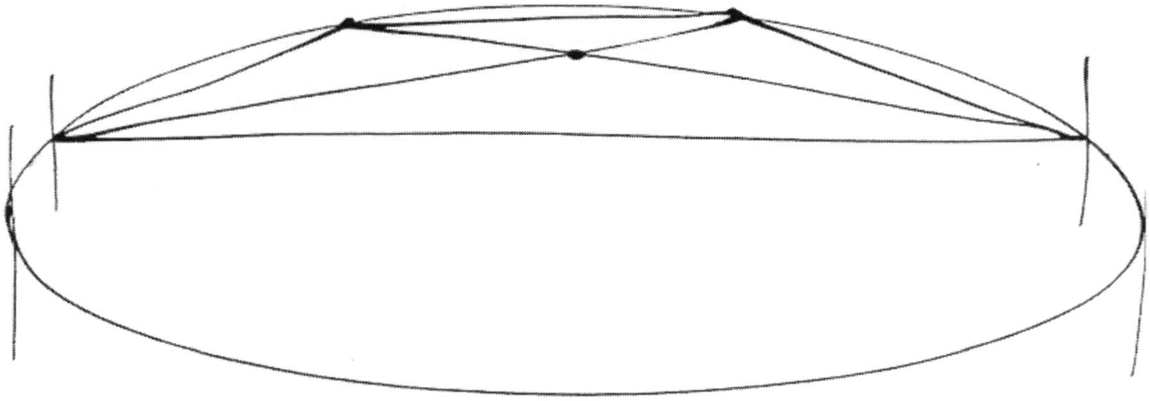

GEOMETRICAL AND PERSPECTIVE ANALYSIS
OF AN ELLIPSE IN FREE HAND

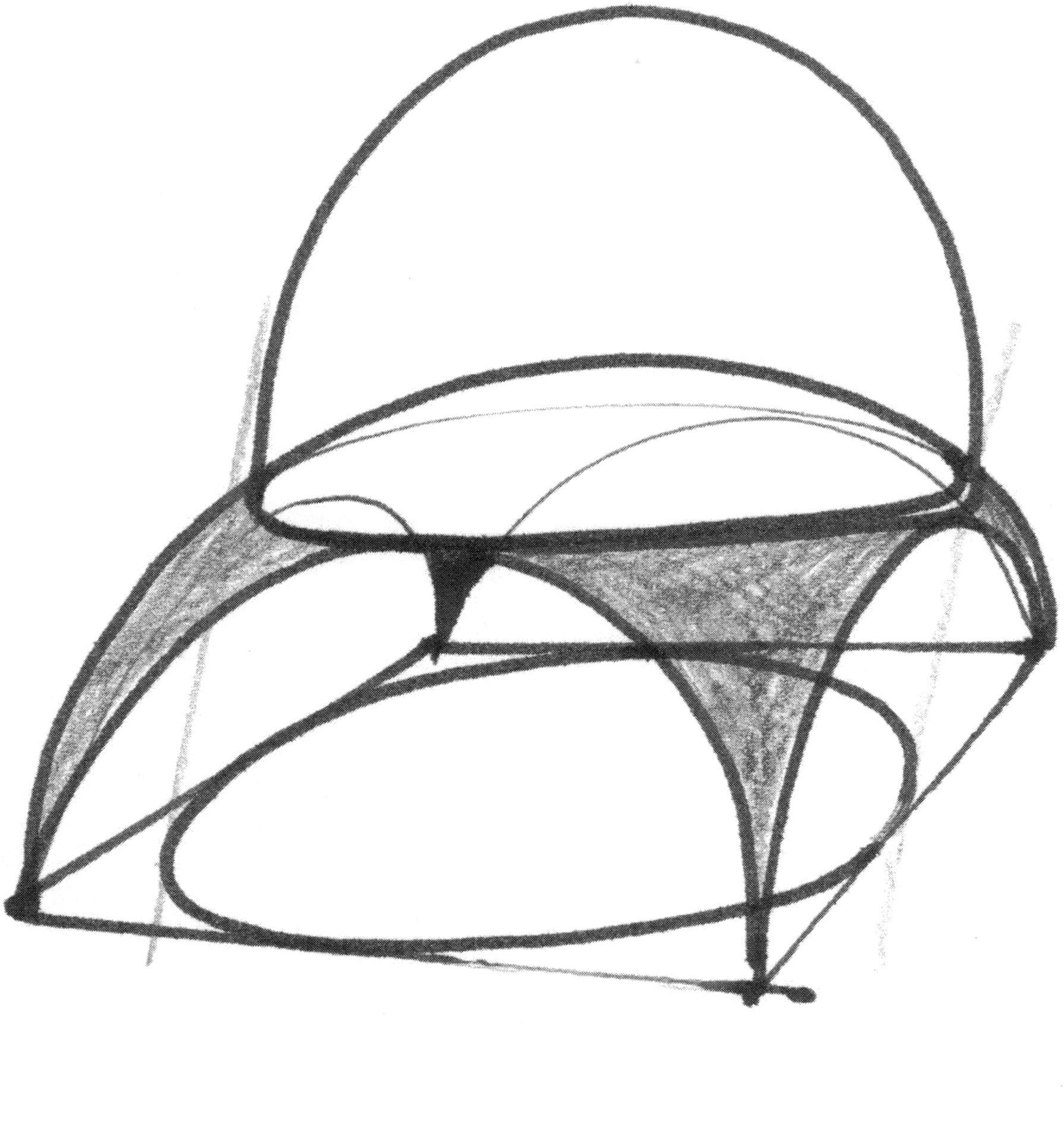

THE ARCHITECTURAL COMPLEXITY OD A DOME ON A PEDESTAL, DRAWN IN FREE HAND

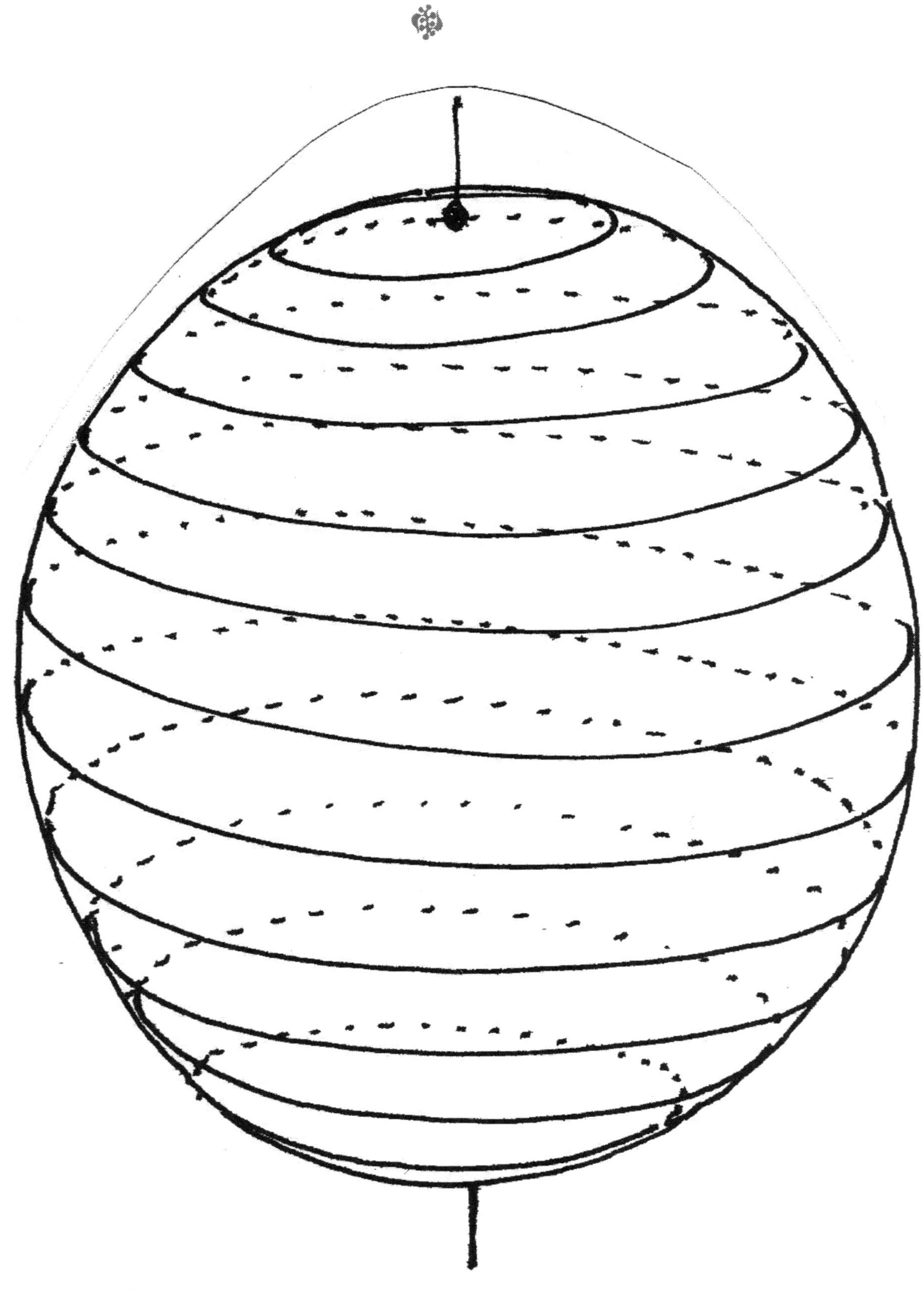

FREE HAND ANALYSIS OF A BALL AND ITS THE DEPTH

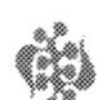

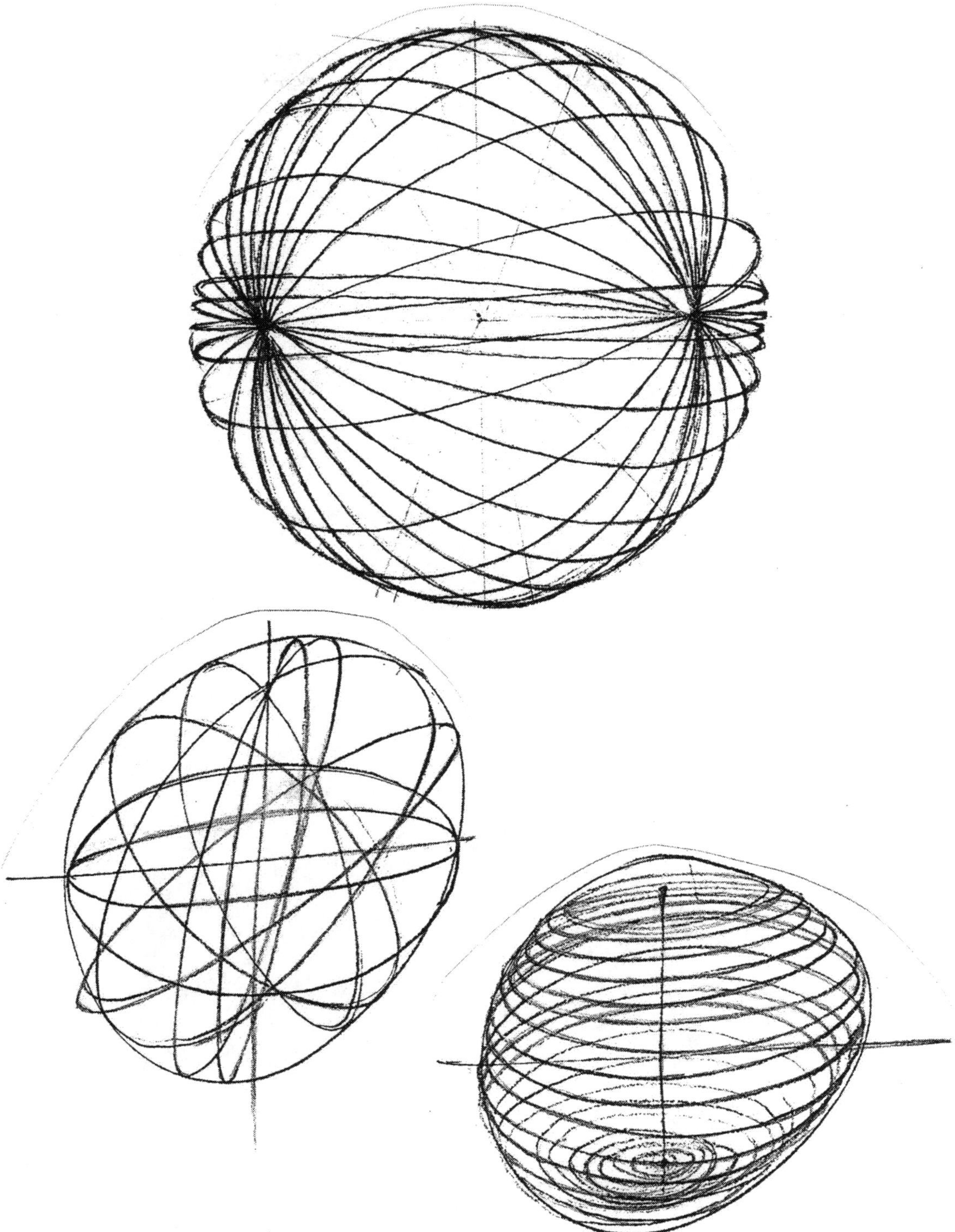

FREE HAND VARIATIONS OF A BALL

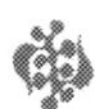

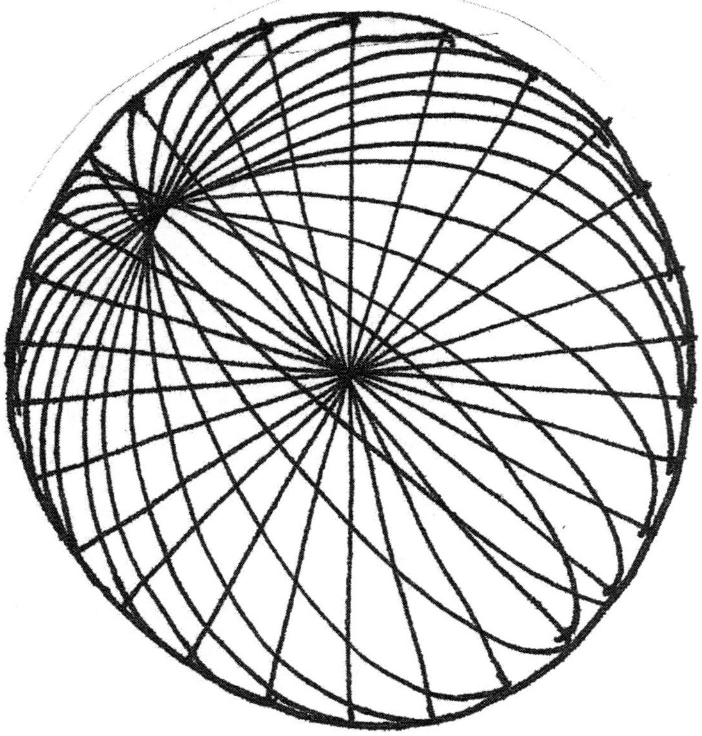

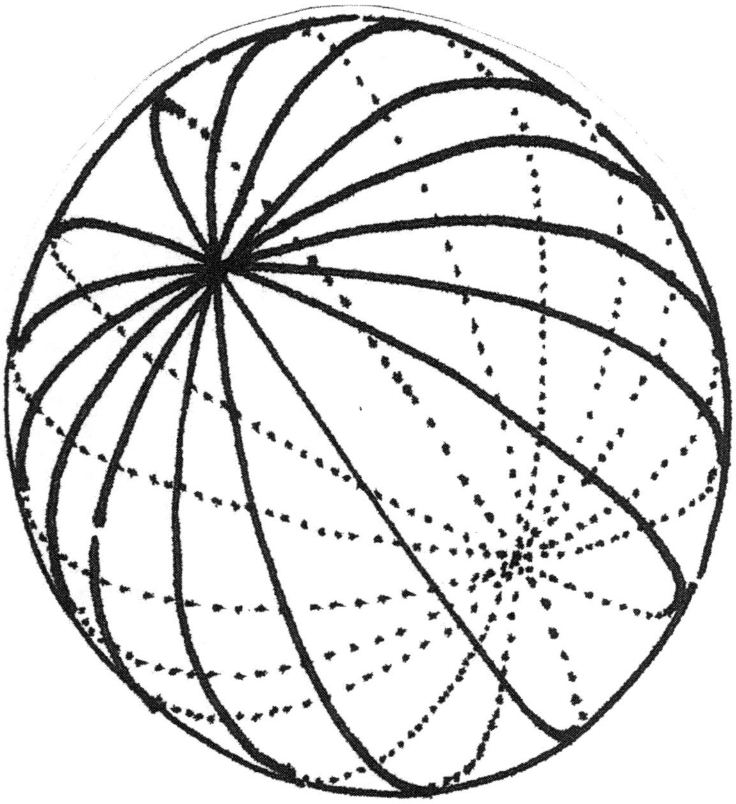

FREE HAND ELLIPSES

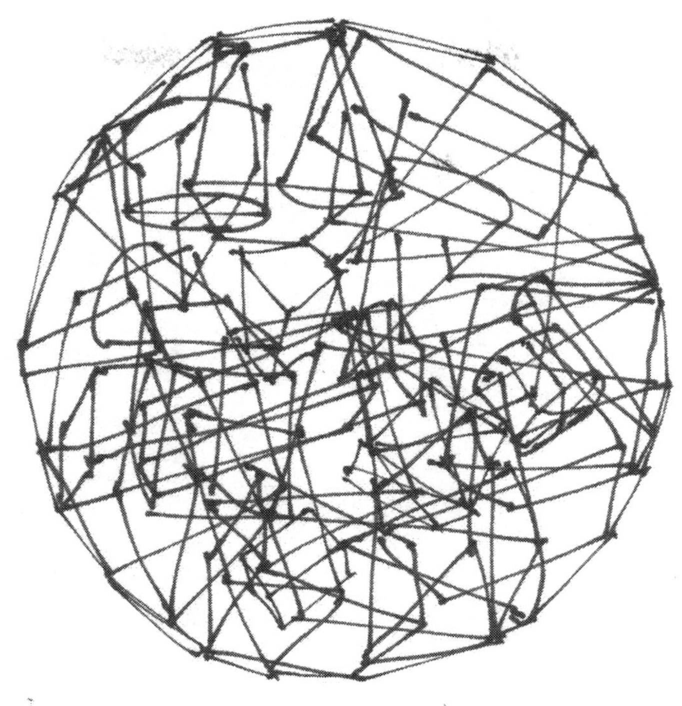

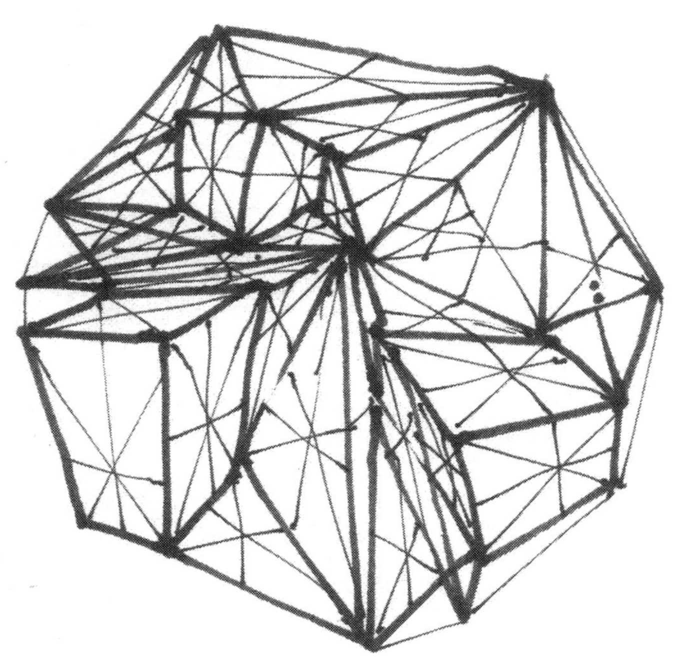

GEOMETRIC SHAPES IN A CIRCULAR SHAPE

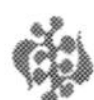

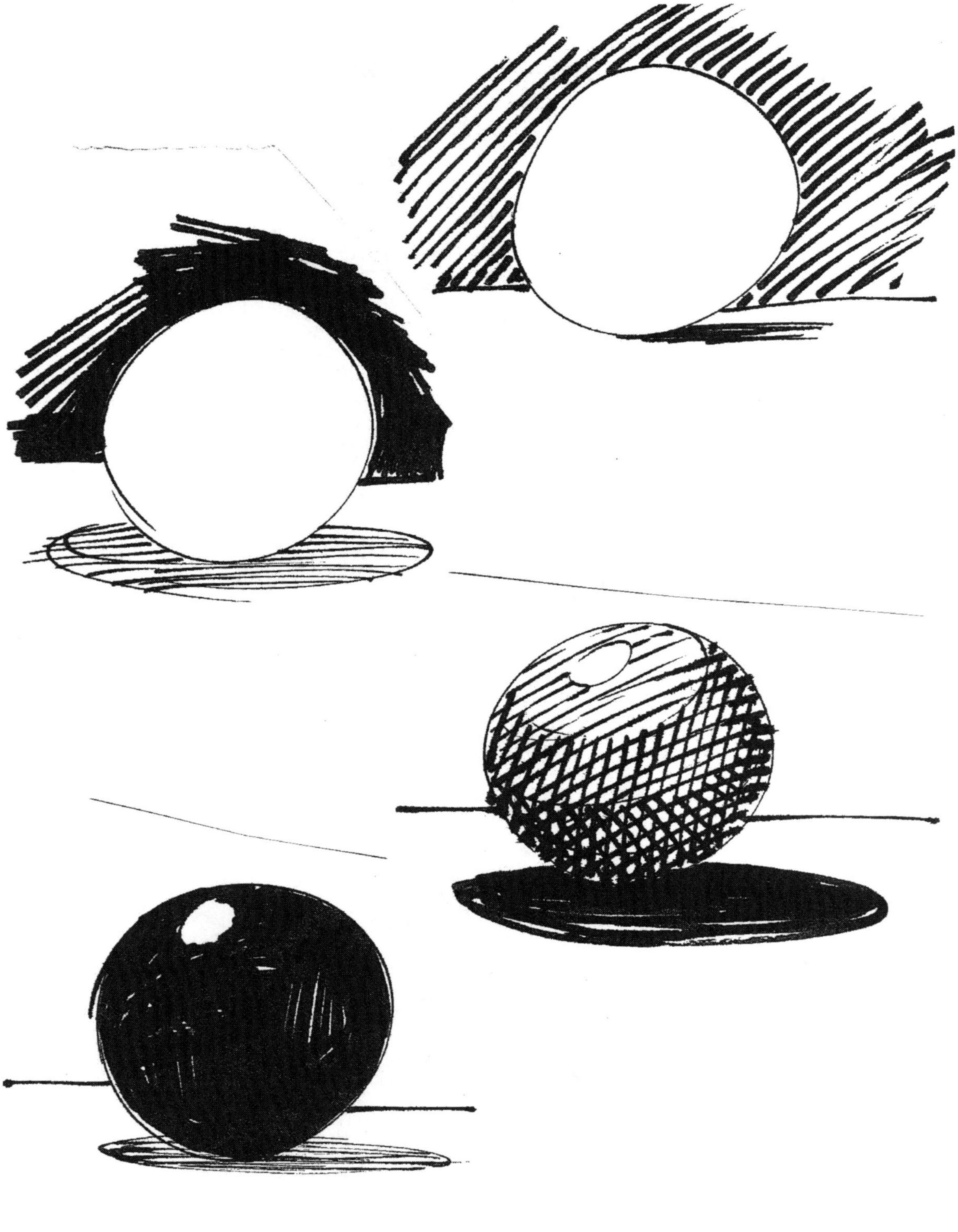

EXPERIMENTING WITH A DARK AND LIGHT BALL

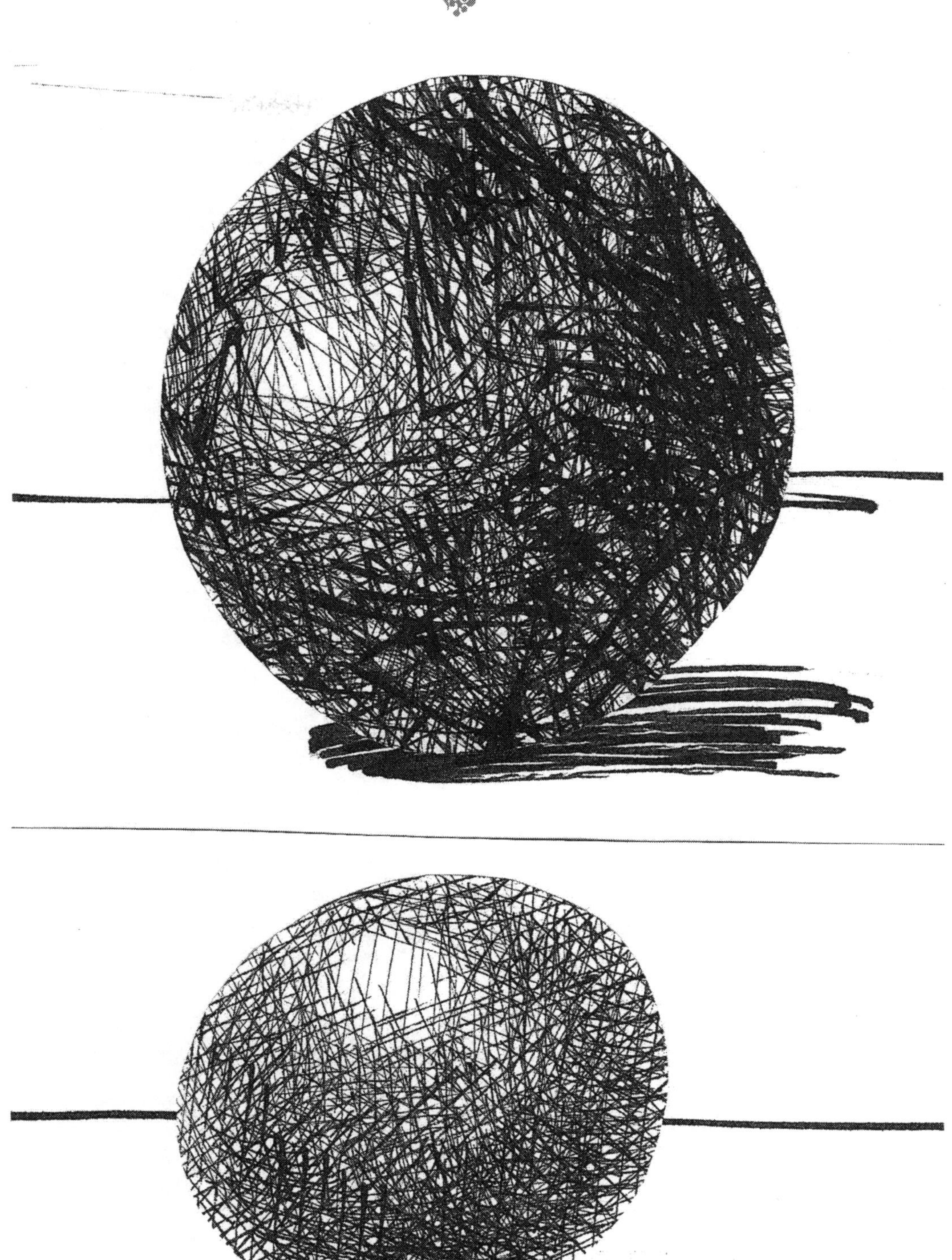

**DRAWING OF A PATTERN, CUTOUT OF DRAWING IN ROUND SHAPES
AND PLACED ON AN A EMPTY PAGE.
CREATING NEW SPACE AND PERSPECTIVE WITH CUTOUTS**

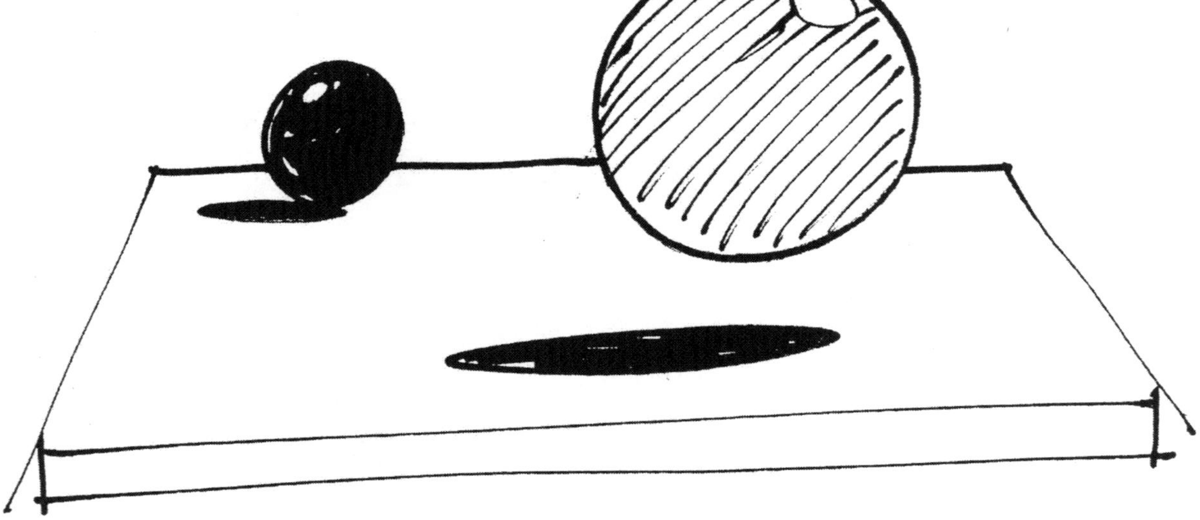

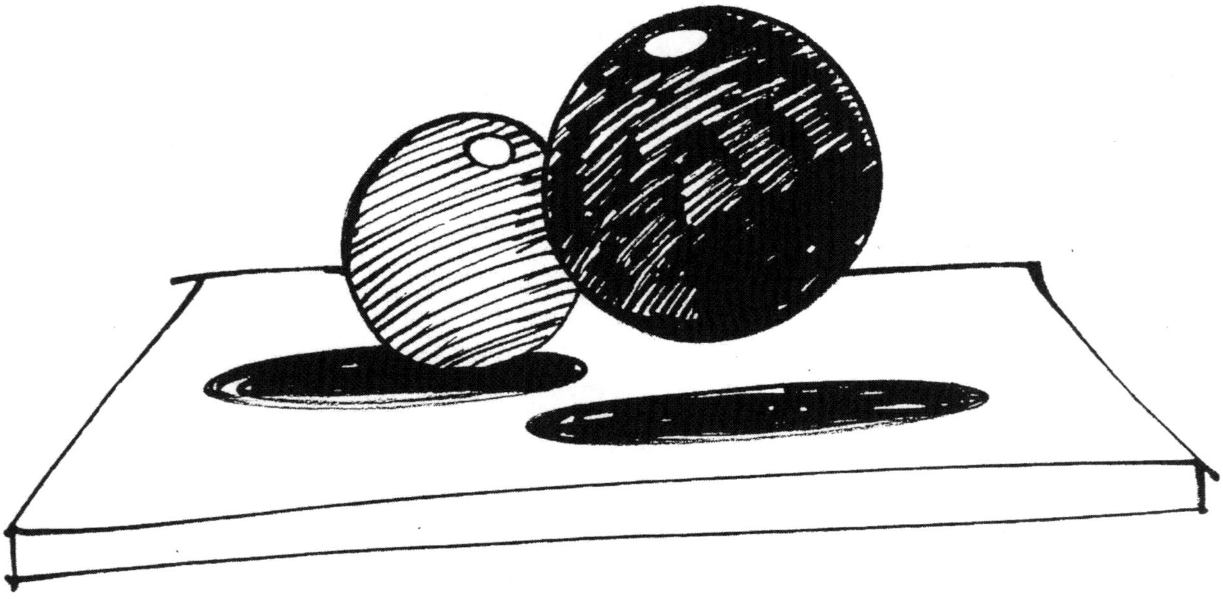

RELATIONSHIPS BETWEEN SHAPES, PLACEMENT AND SHADOWS

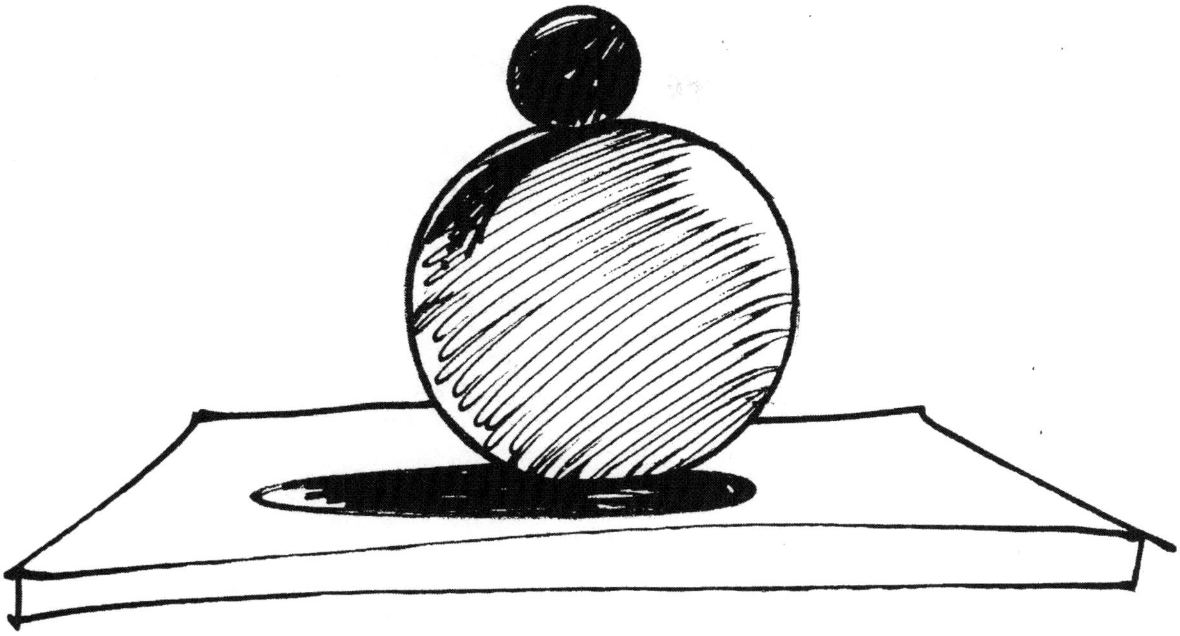

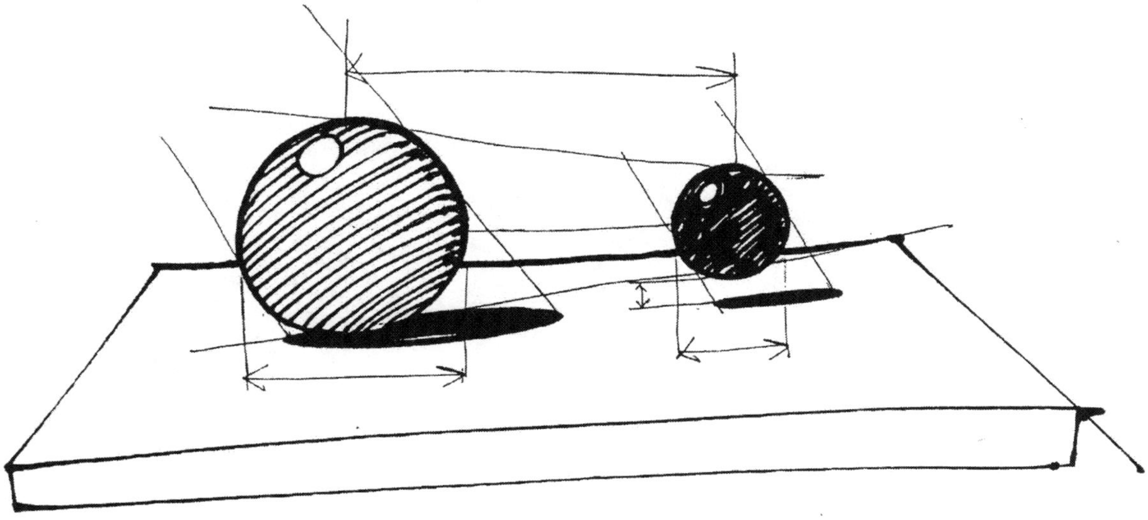

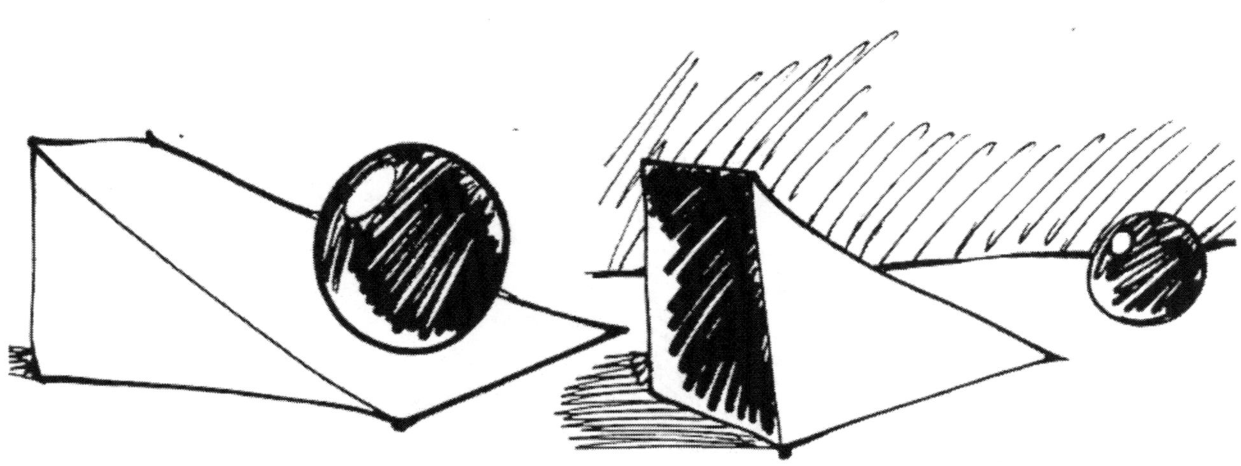

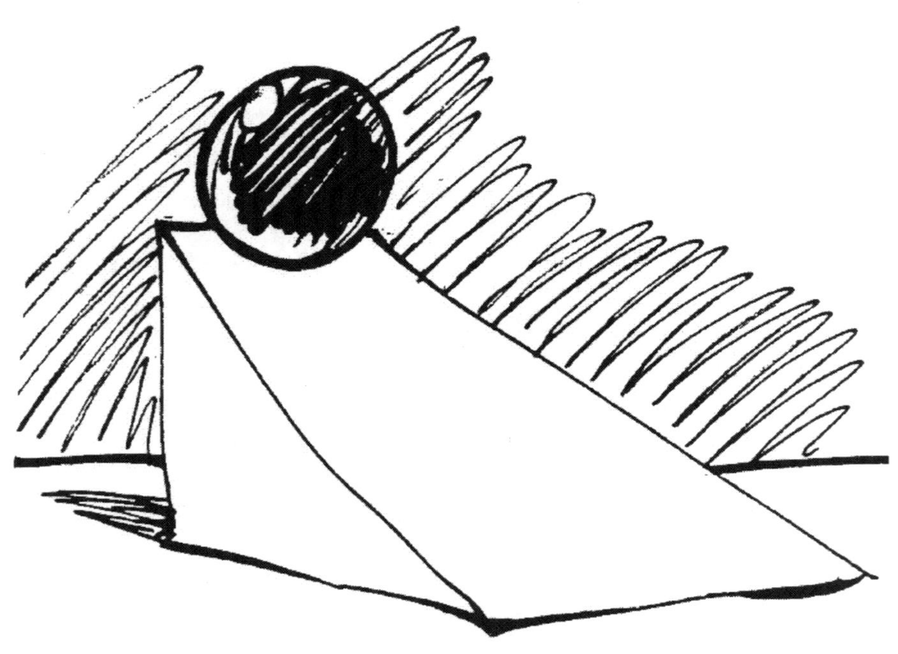

THE MOVEMENT OF A BALL IN VARIOUS CIRCUMSTANCES

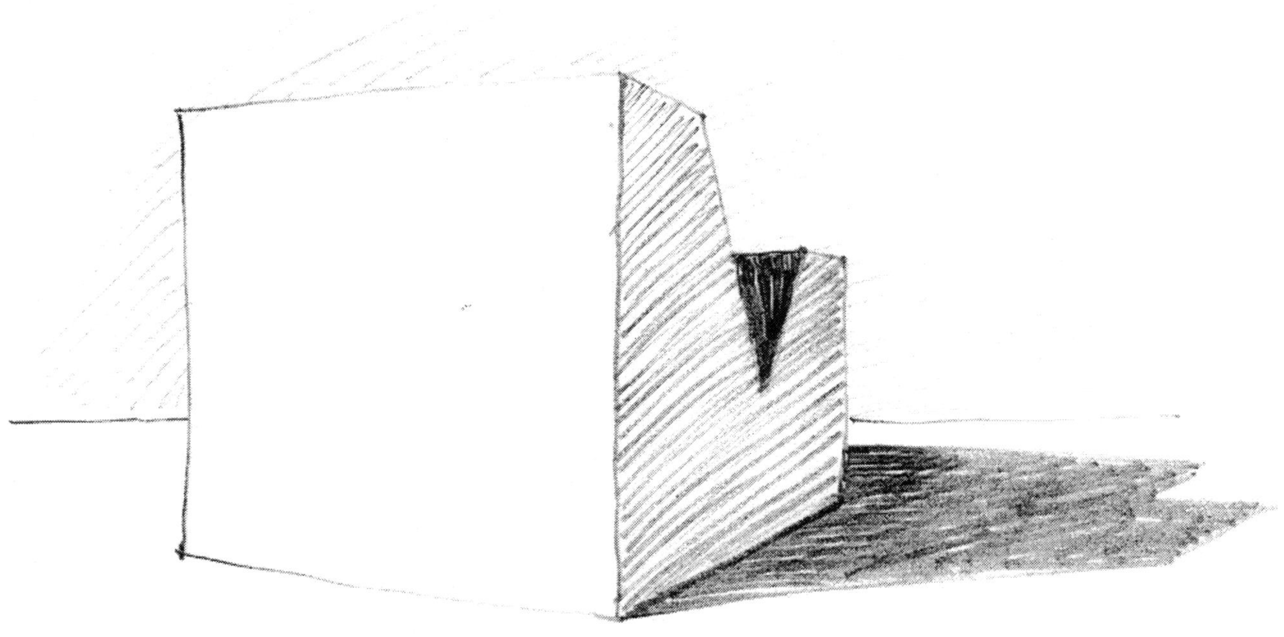

THE GRADUAL PROGRESSION OF SHADING

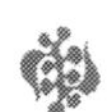

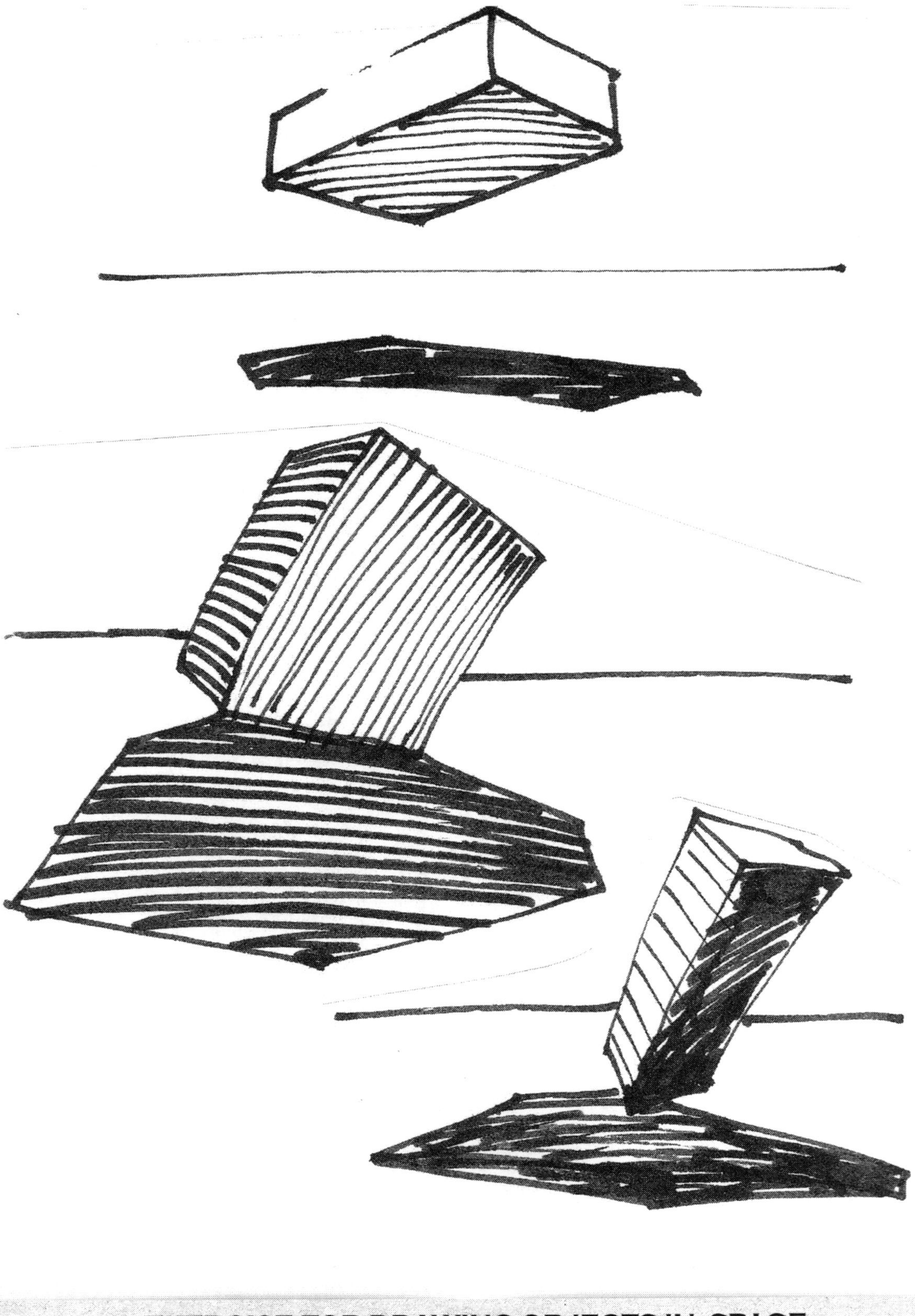

EXERCISE FOR DRAWING OBJECTS IN SPACE

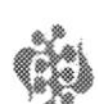

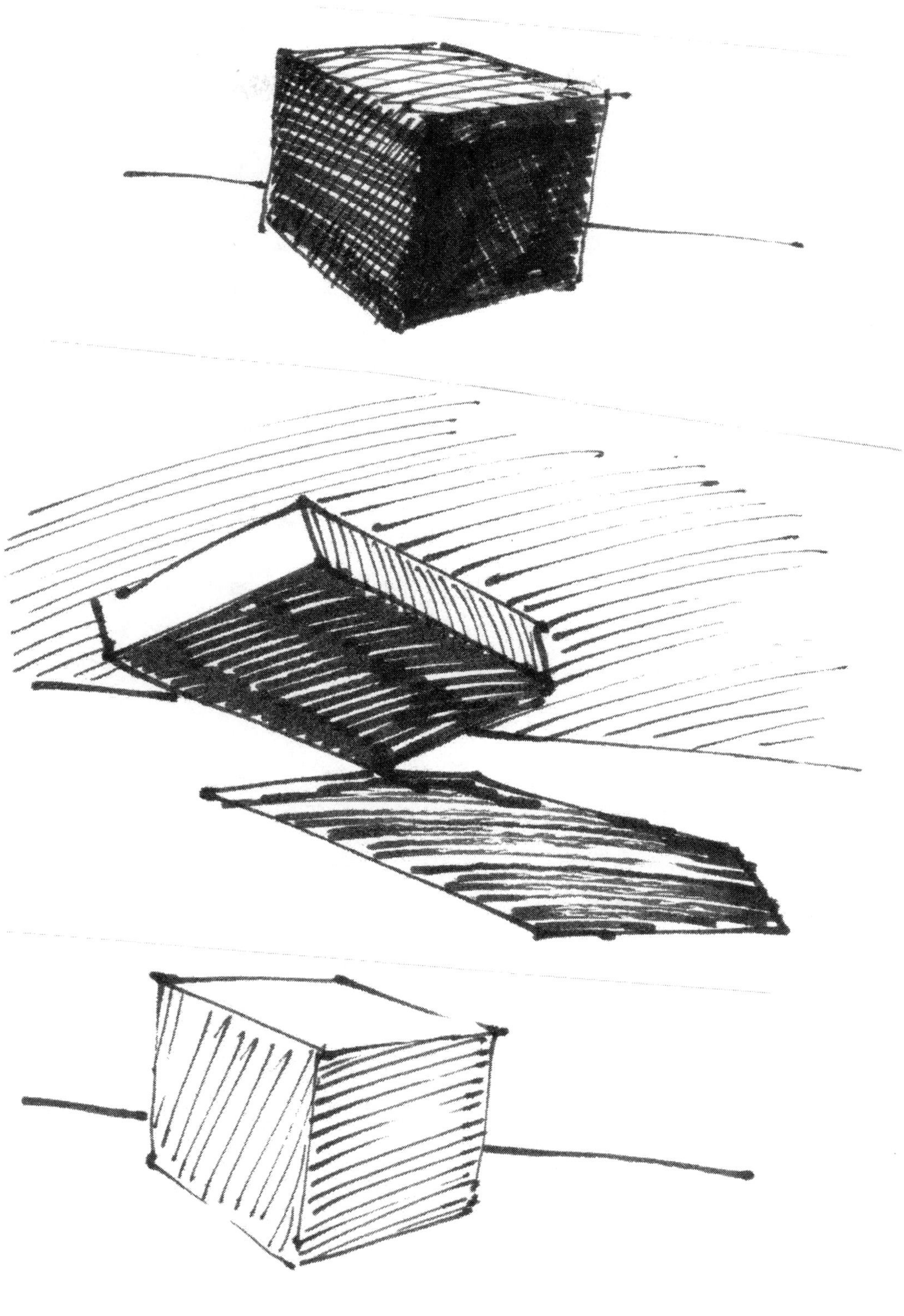

EXERCISE FOR DRAWING OBJECTS IN SPACE

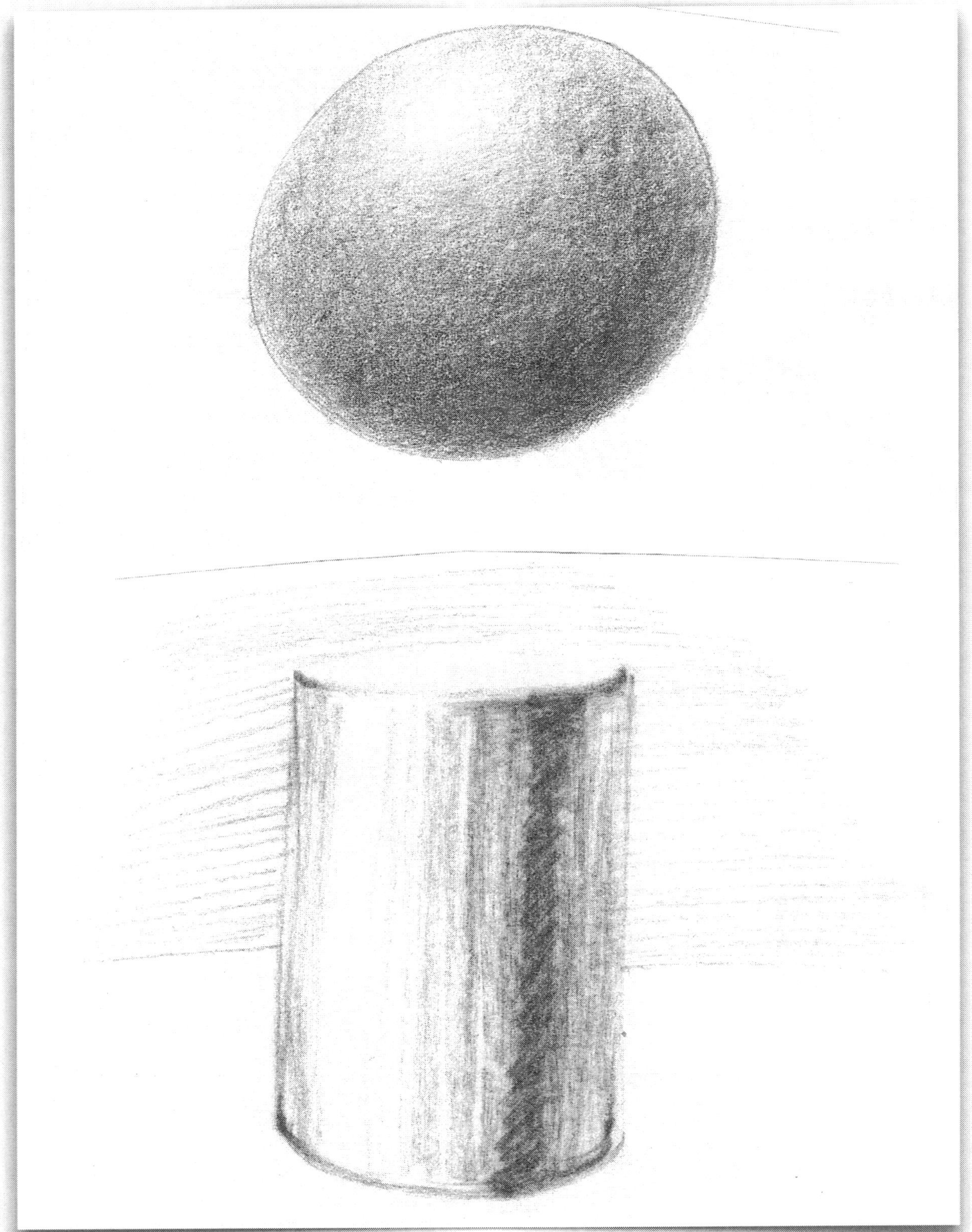

APPLICATION OF A GRADUAL SOFT SHADING

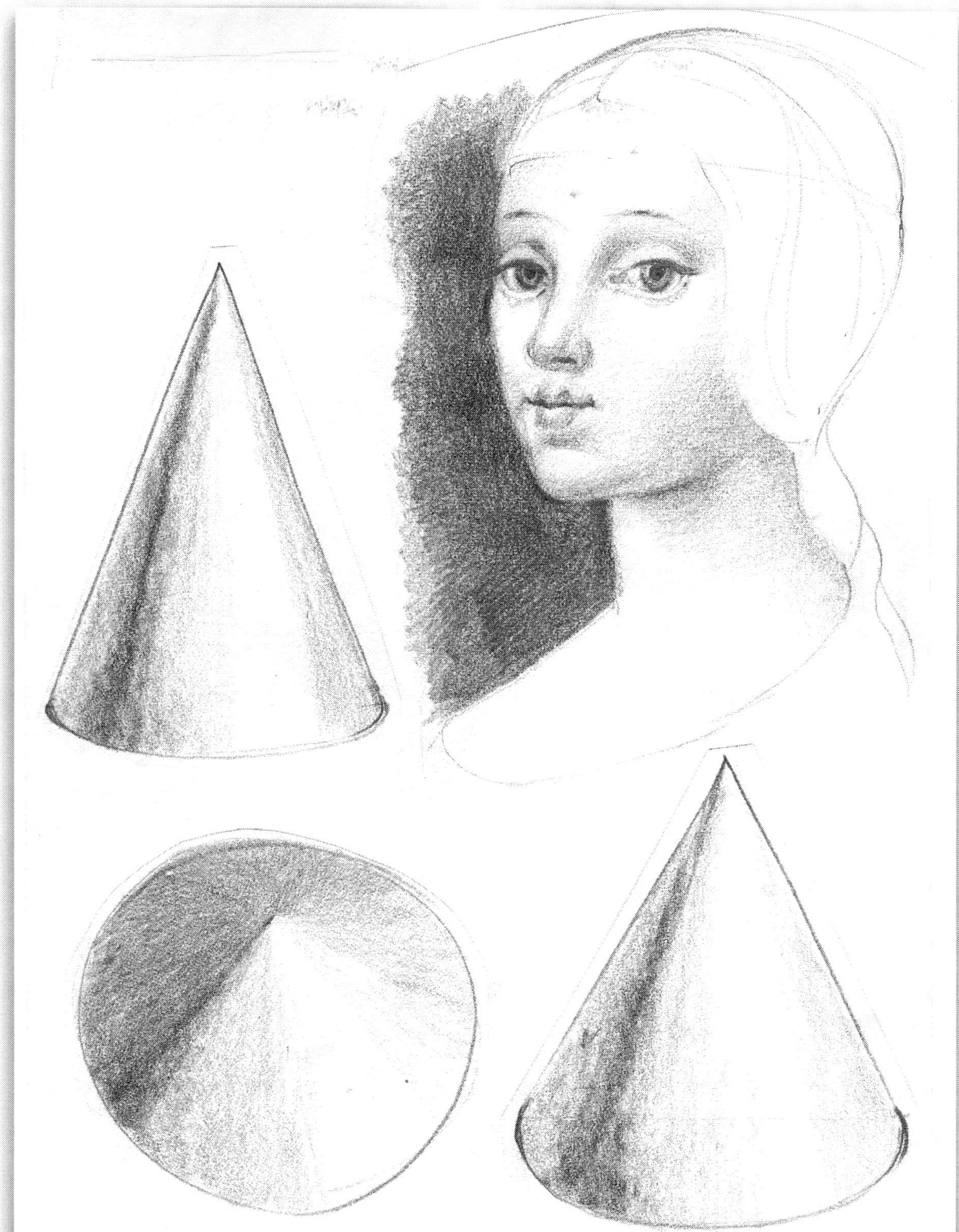

APPLICATION OF A GRADUAL SOFT SHADING

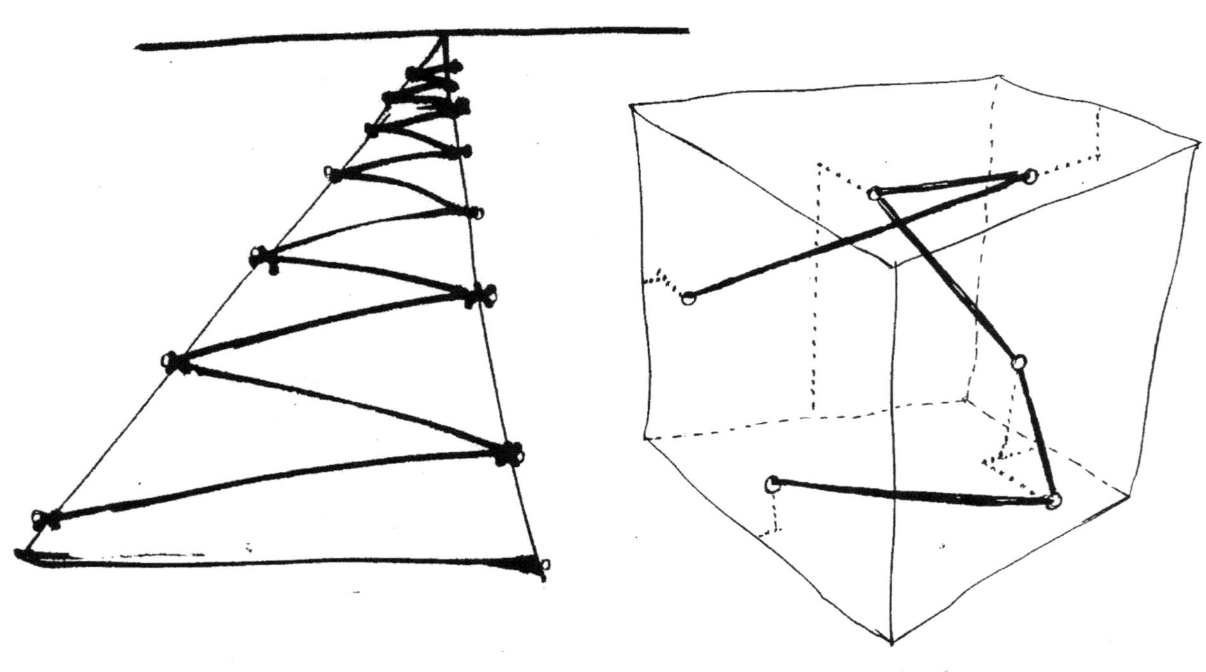

THE DRAWING OF THE LINE BETWEEN DOTS CREATES SPACE

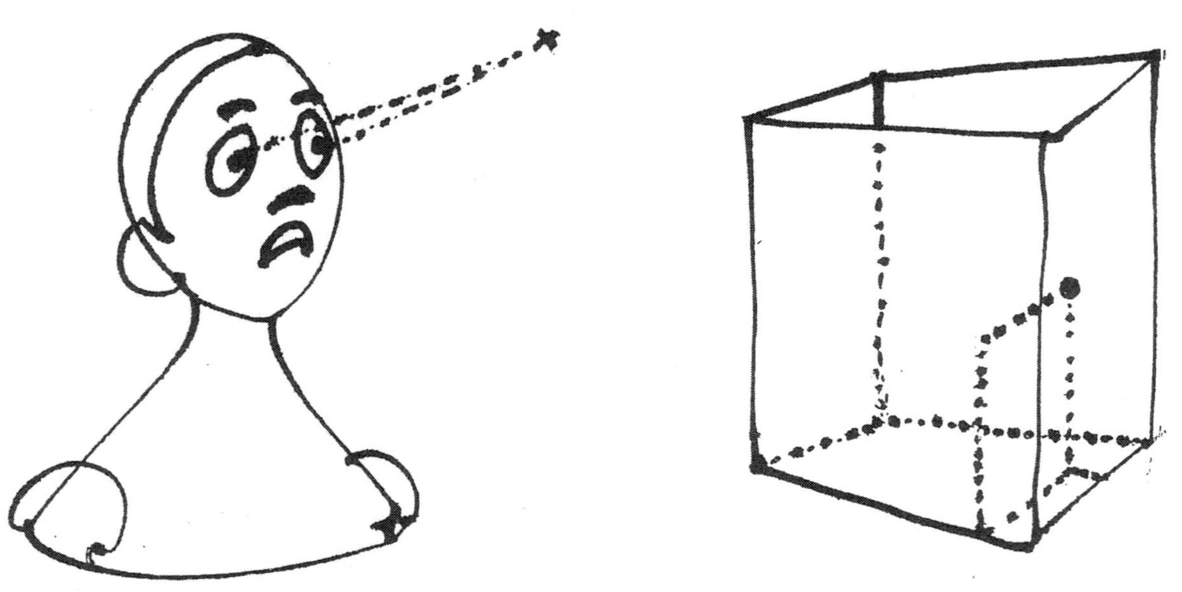

A DRAWING OF THE FOCAL POINT IN SPACE

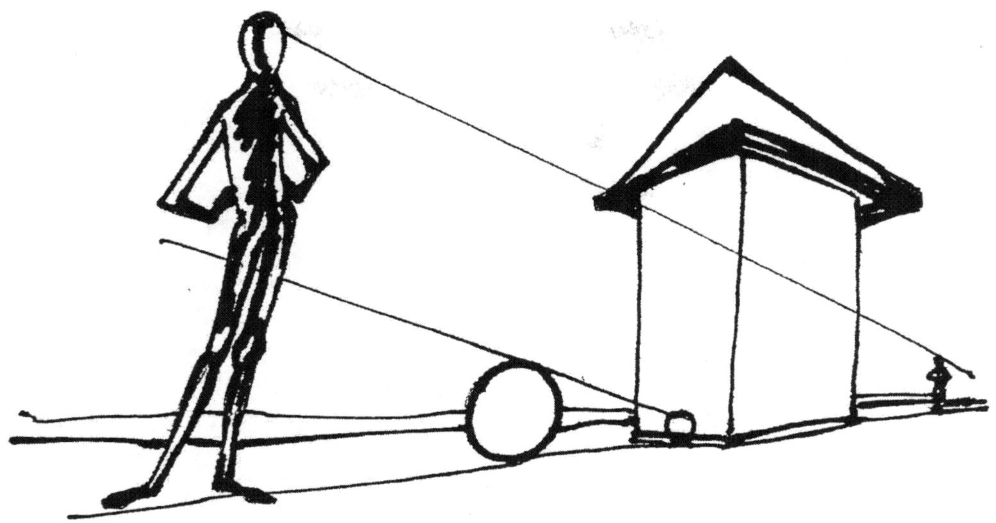

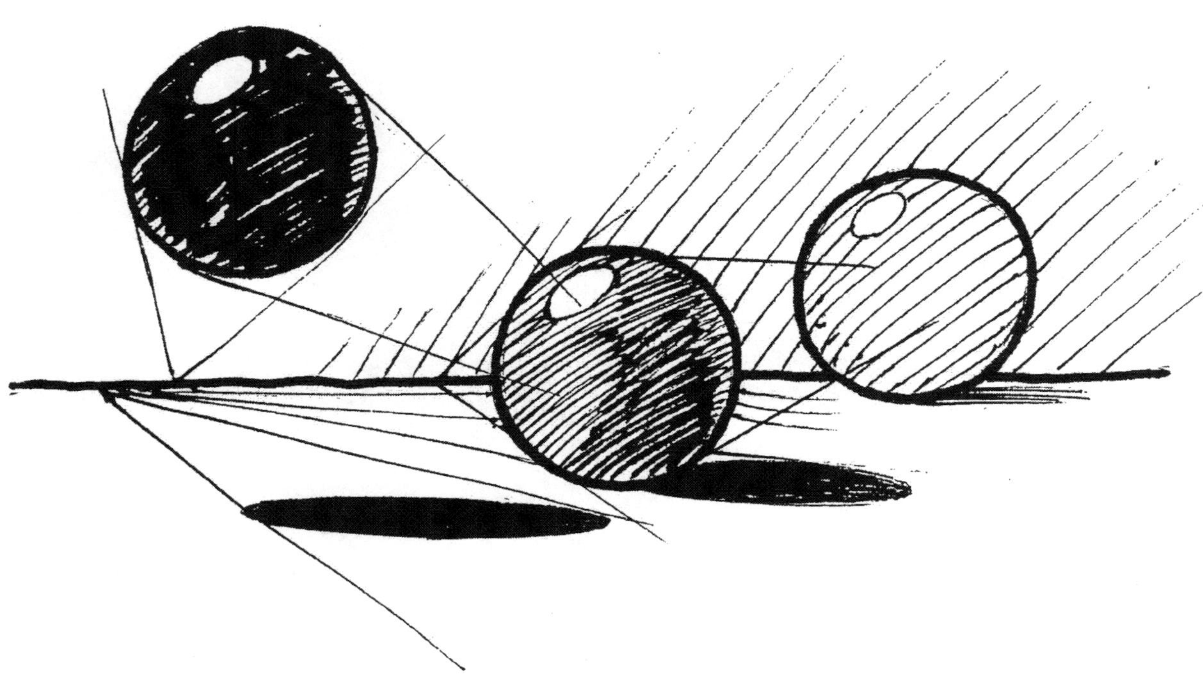

EXERCISE FOR DRAWING AND MEASURING THE DISTANCE

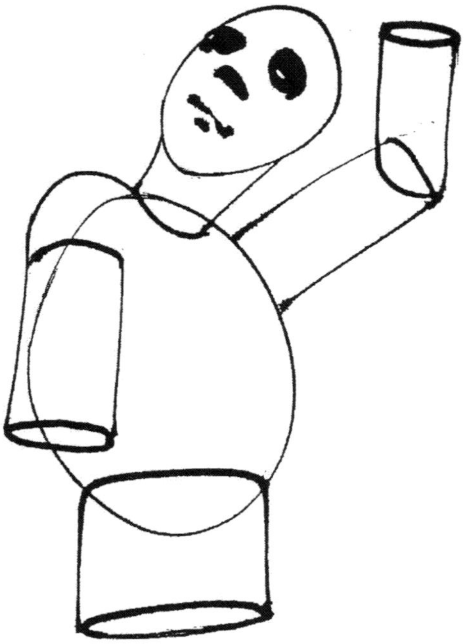

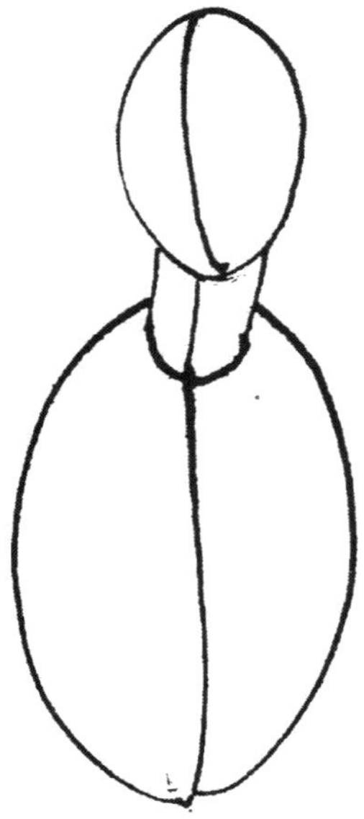

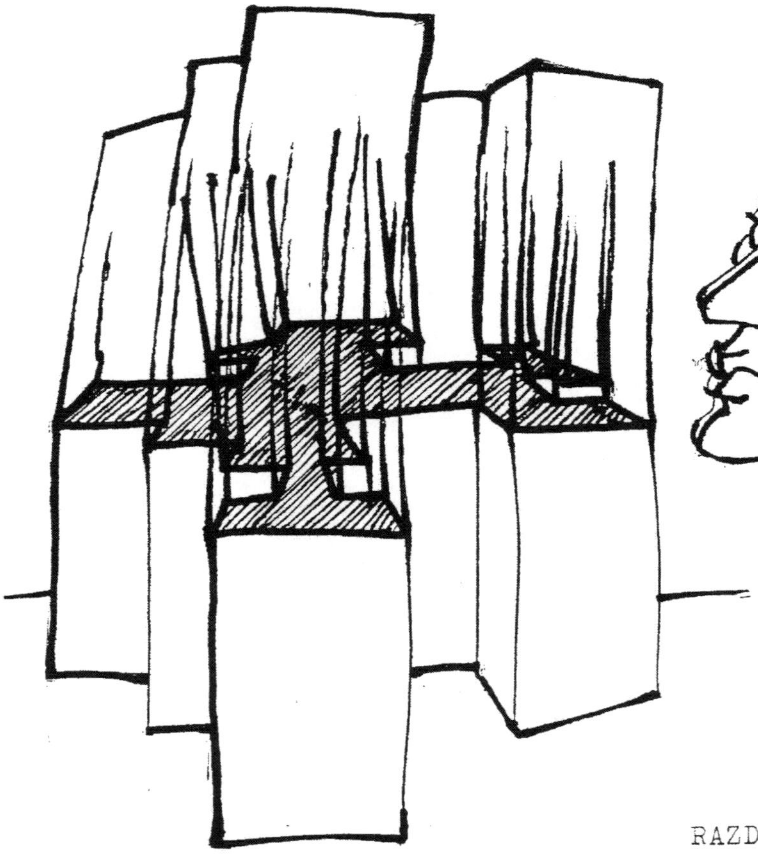

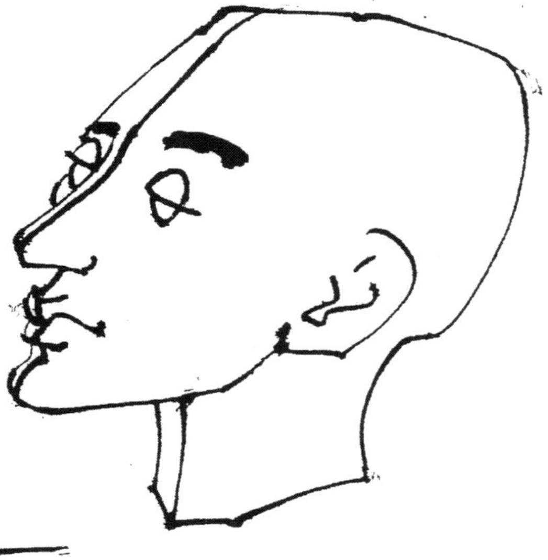

RAZDELITEV OBLIKE

**EXERCISE FOR DRAWING DIVISION OF THE FORM
INTO THE PROFILE**

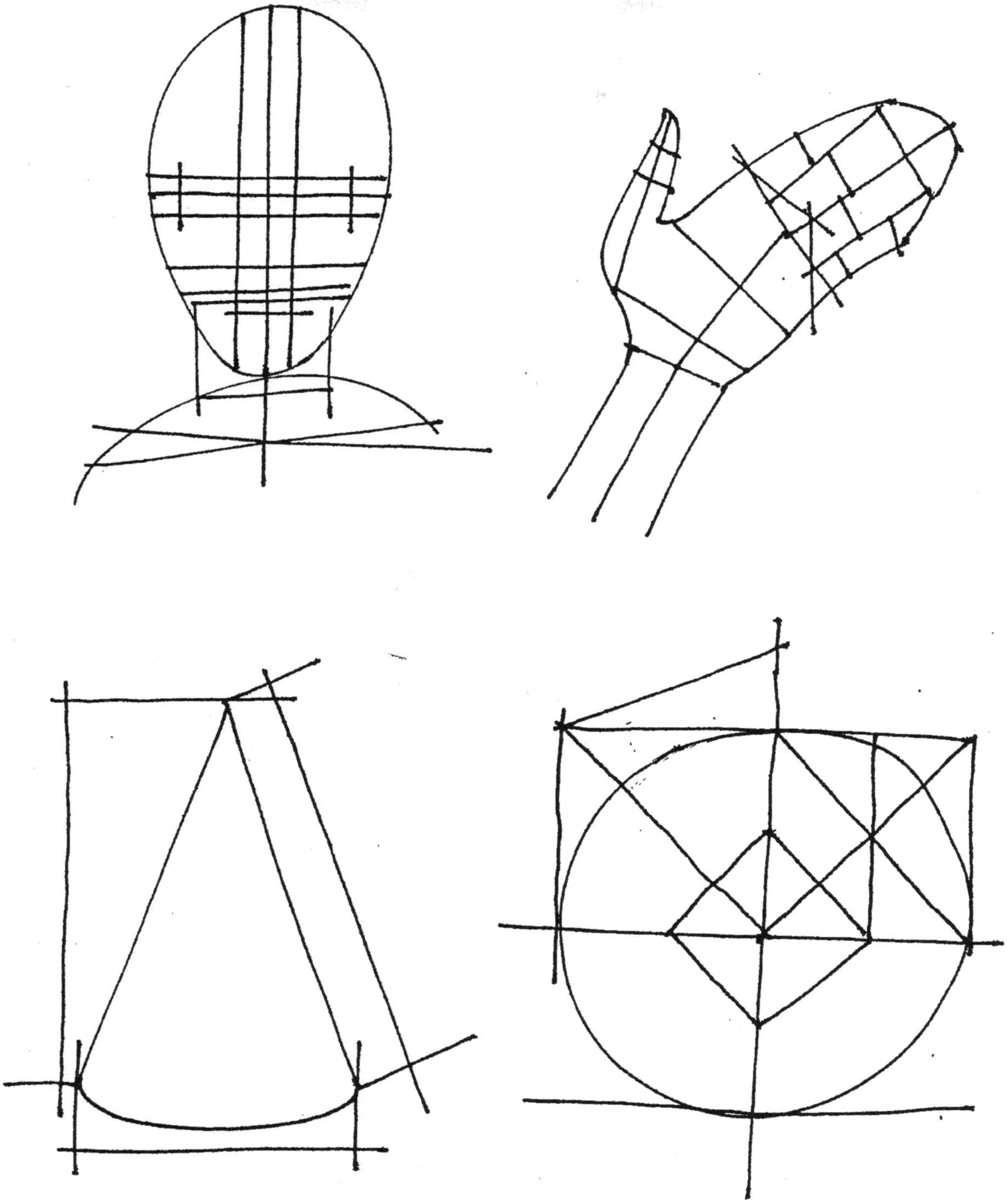

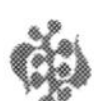

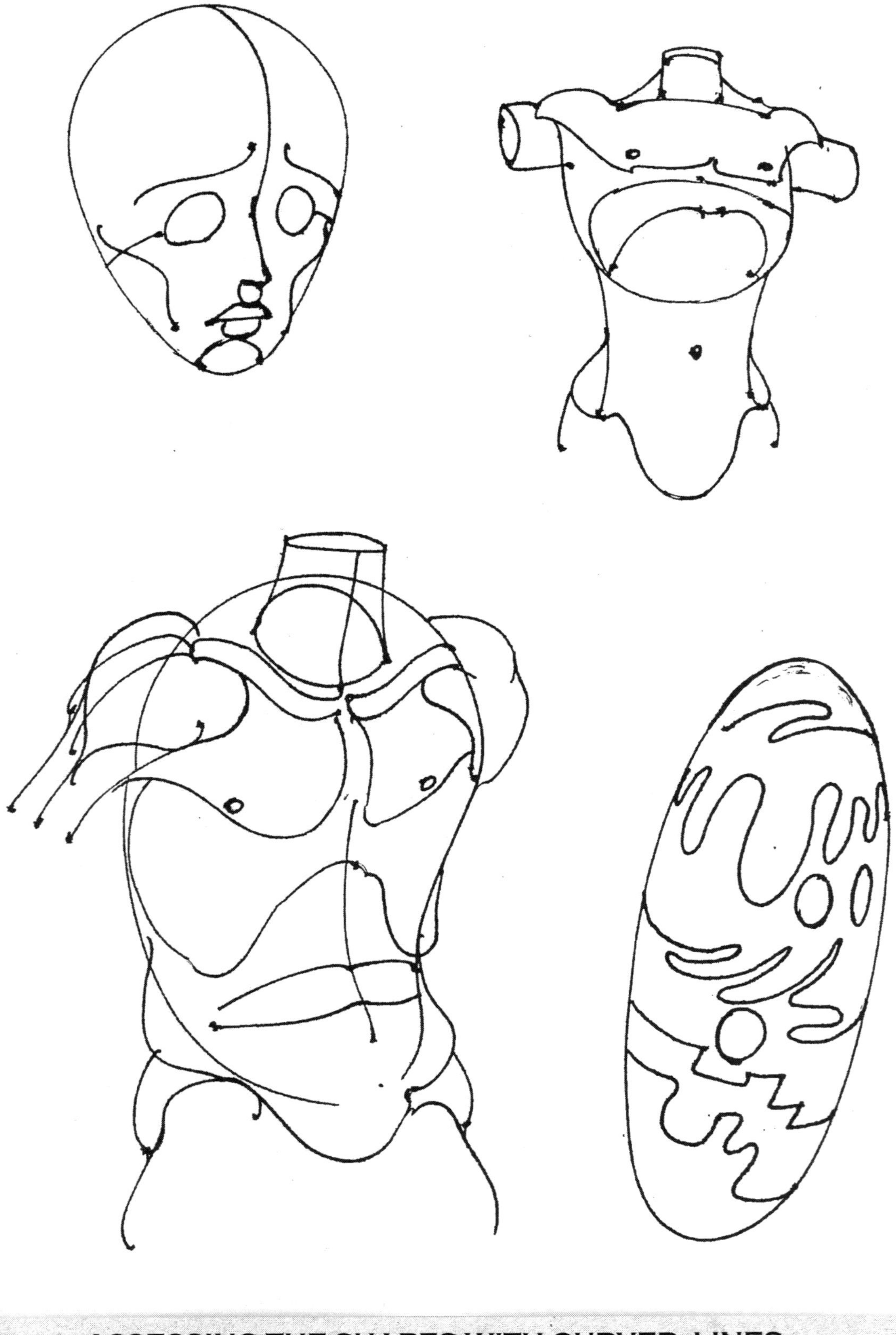

ASSESSING THE SHAPES WITH CURVED LINES
THAT CORRESPOND TO THE CHARACTER OF THE SHAPE

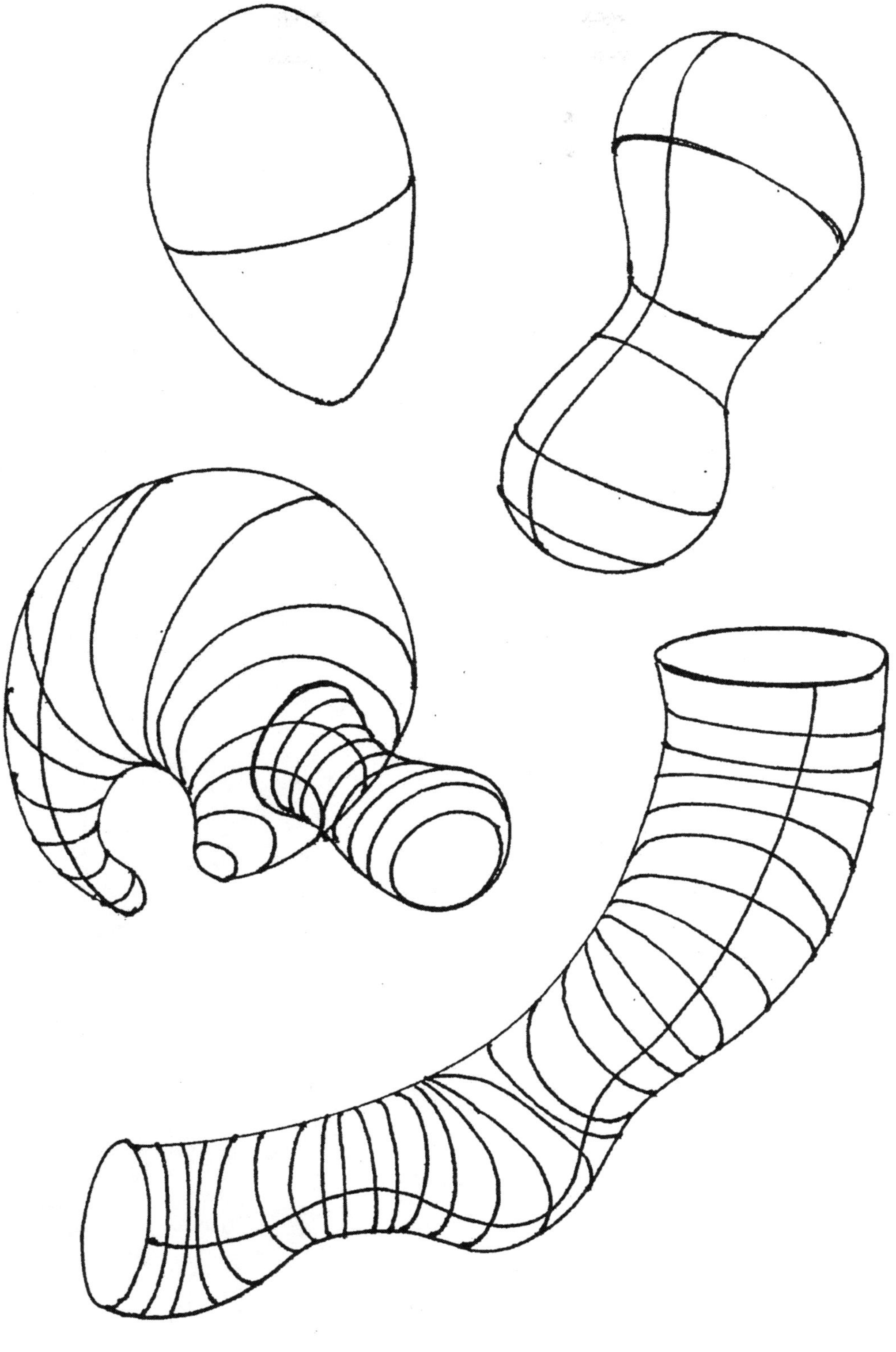

ASSESSING THE CHARACTER OF SHAPES
WITH CURVED LINES

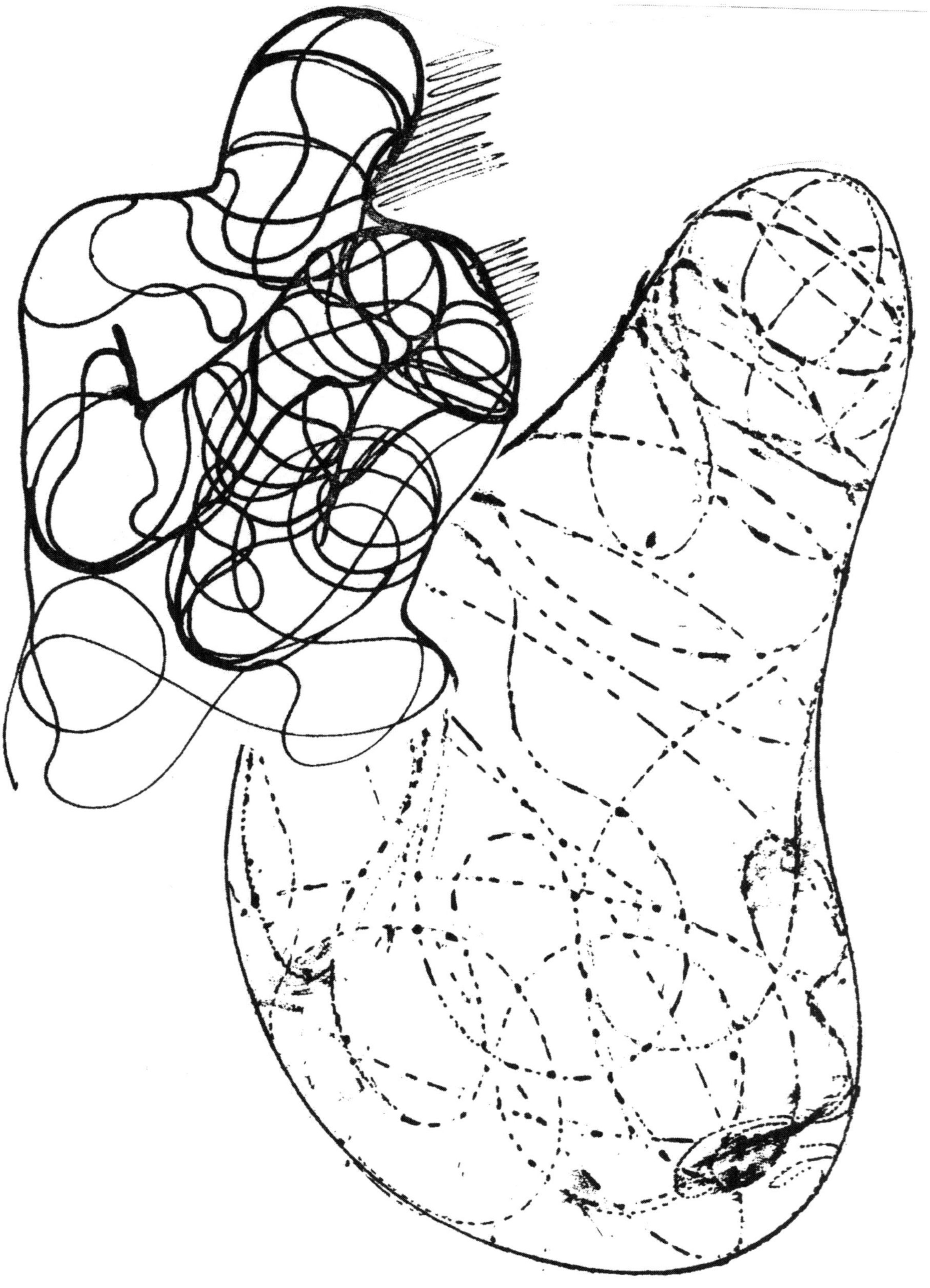

EXERCISE FOR DRAWING CURVES AND SHAPES

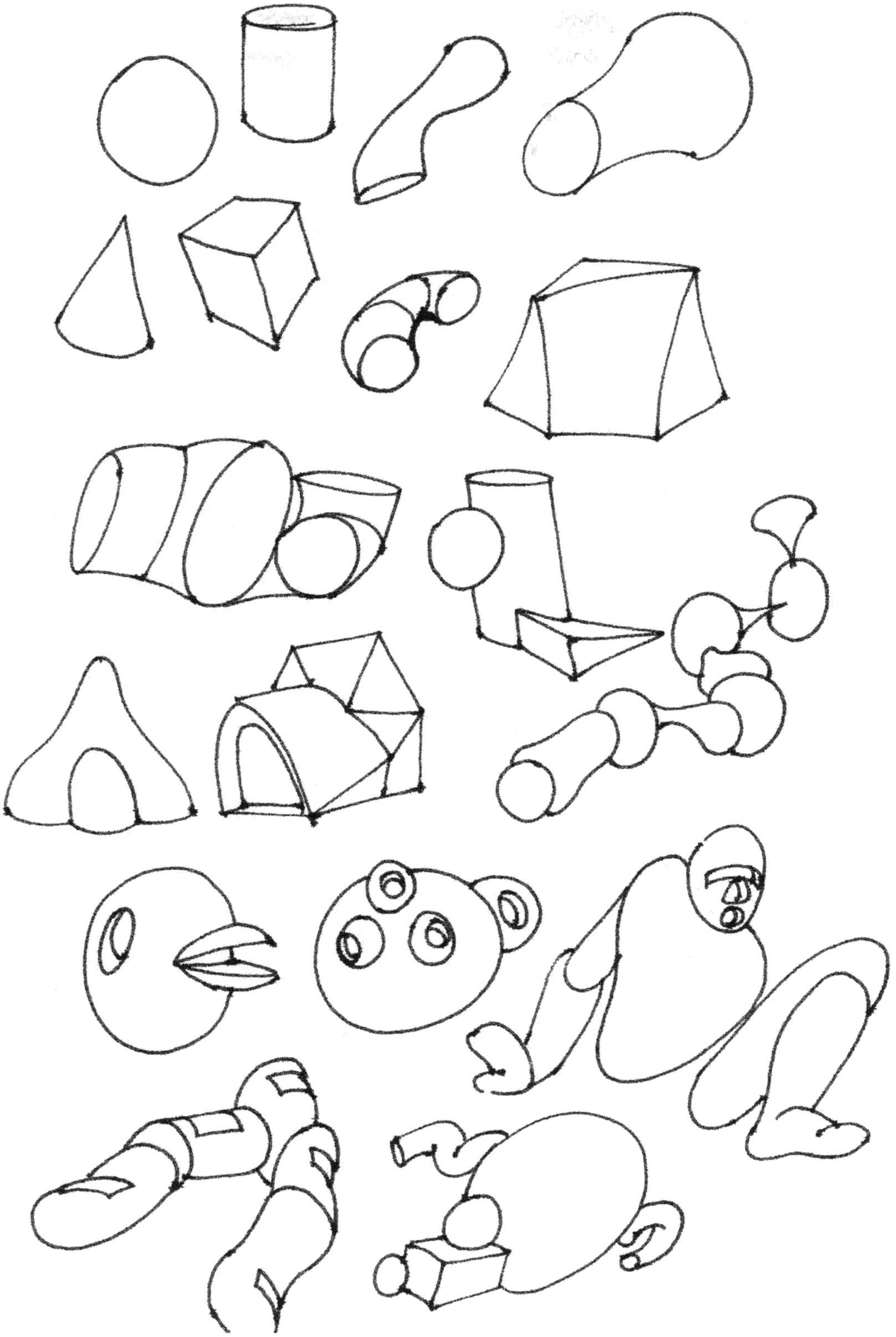

SIMPLE SHAPES ARE CLEAR GEOMETRIC BODIES.
THEIR INTERACTION CREATES MORE COMPLEX SHAPES.

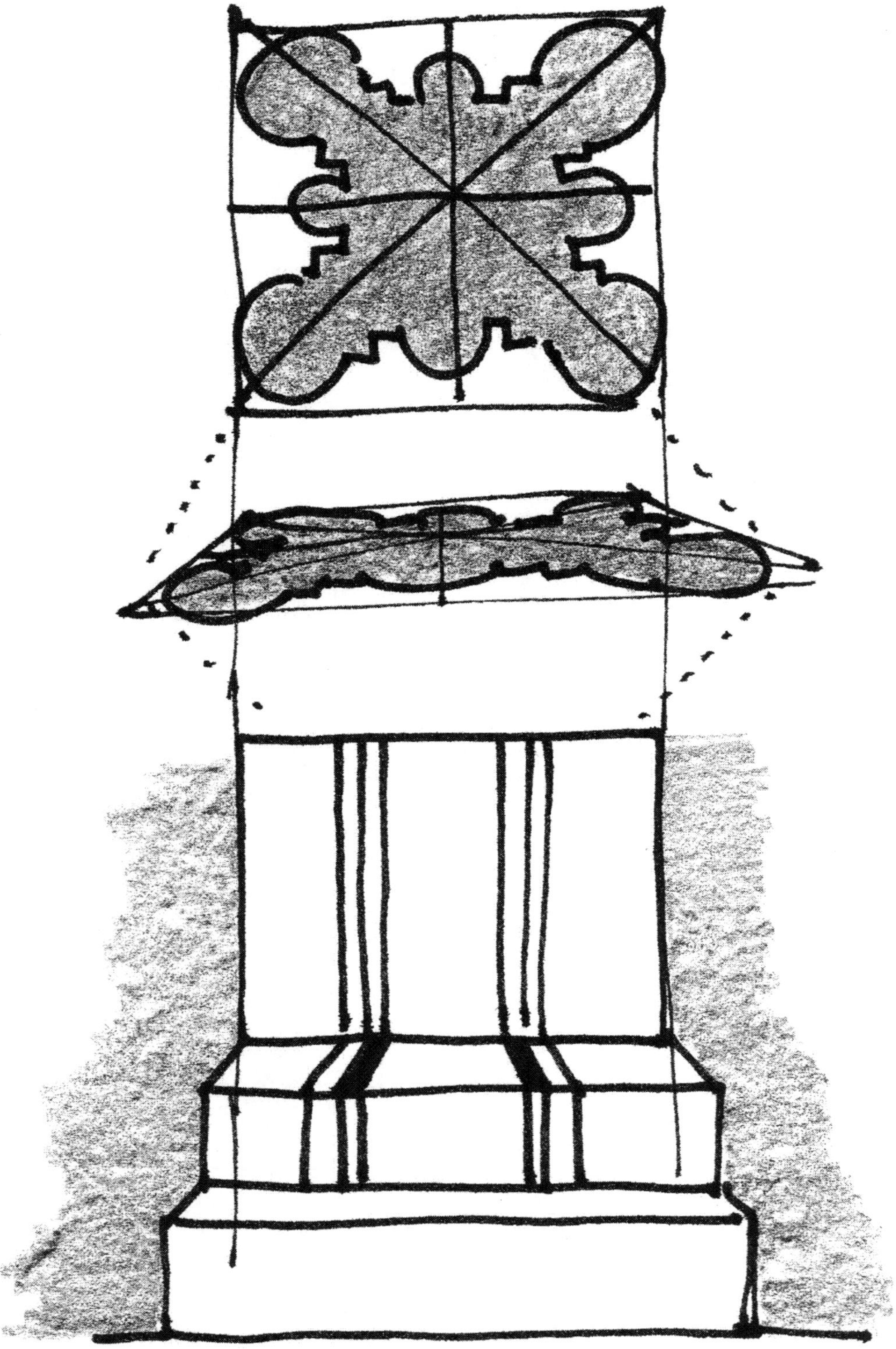

A PROFILE OF A PILLAR

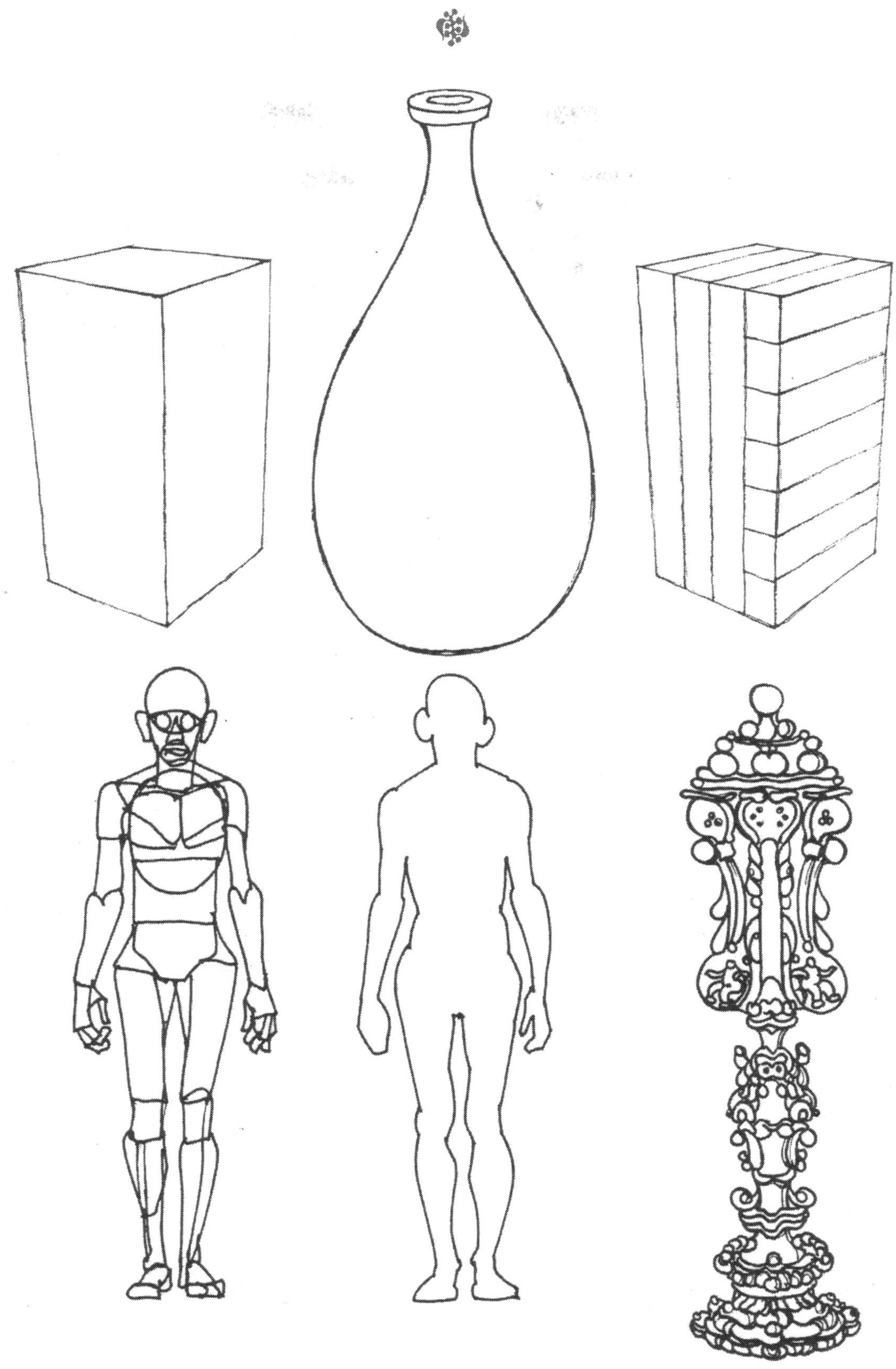

A DOMINANT SHAPE IS COMPOSED OF SMALLER SHAPES

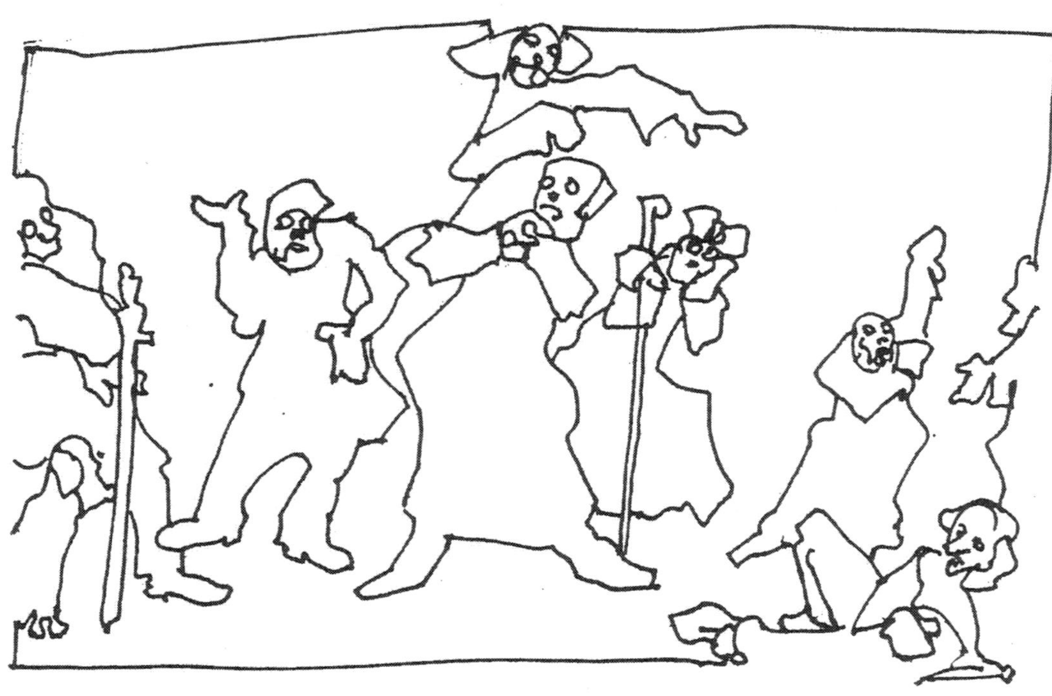

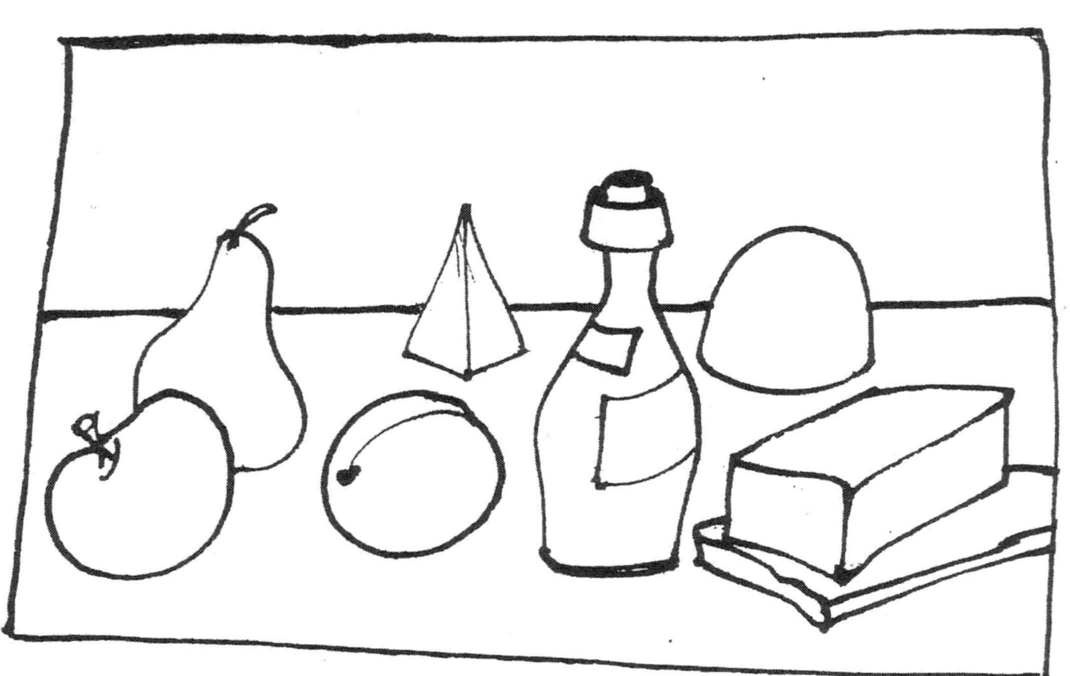

**UNDERSTANDING THE POSITIVE SHAPE ENABLES US
TO SEE THE NEGATIVE SHAPE - THE SHELL.**

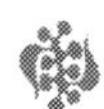

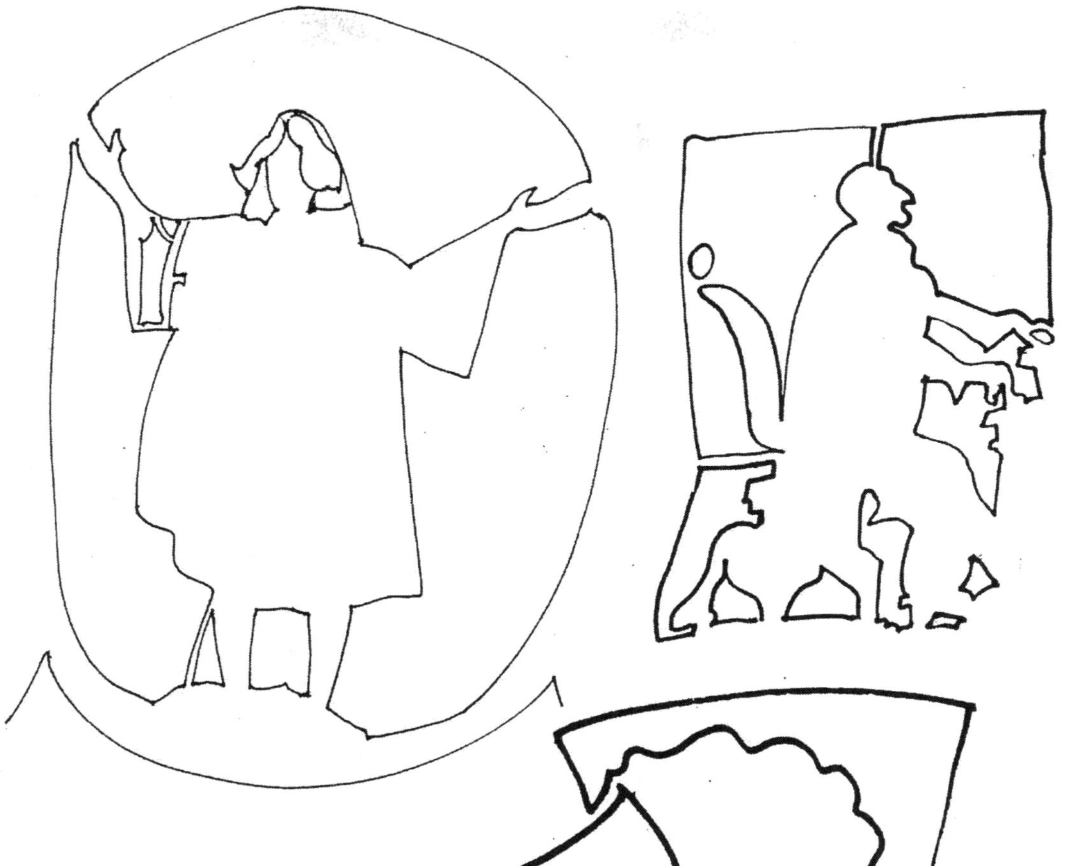

A CERTAIN NEGATIVE SPACE DEFINES ALSO POSITIVE SHAPES.

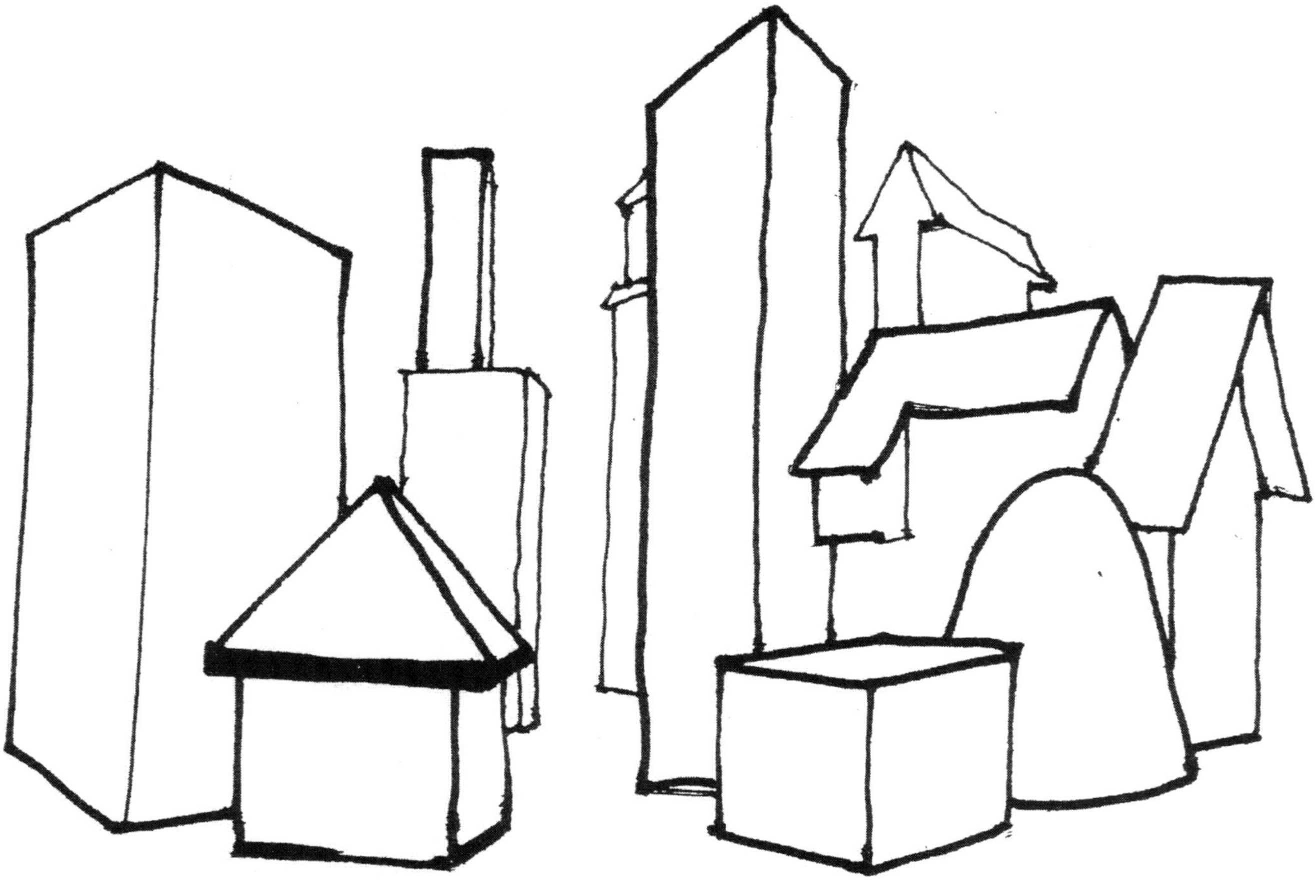

NEGATIVE SHAPE IS A SPACIAL ENVIRONMENT OF POSITIVE SHAPES

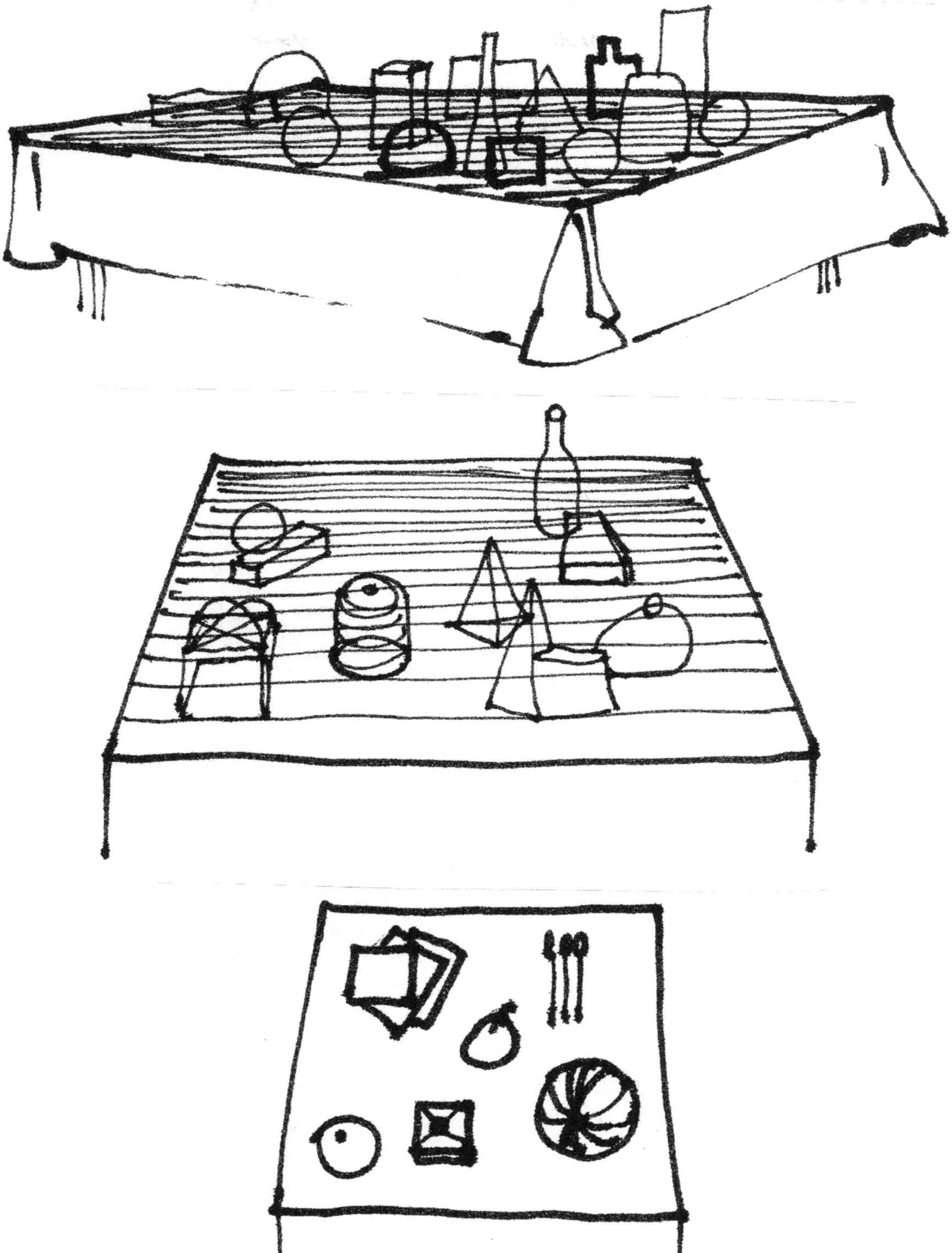

**EXERCISE FOR DRAWING TRANSPARENCY AND DEFINITION OF SPACE.
EXAMPLE IN STILLIFE**

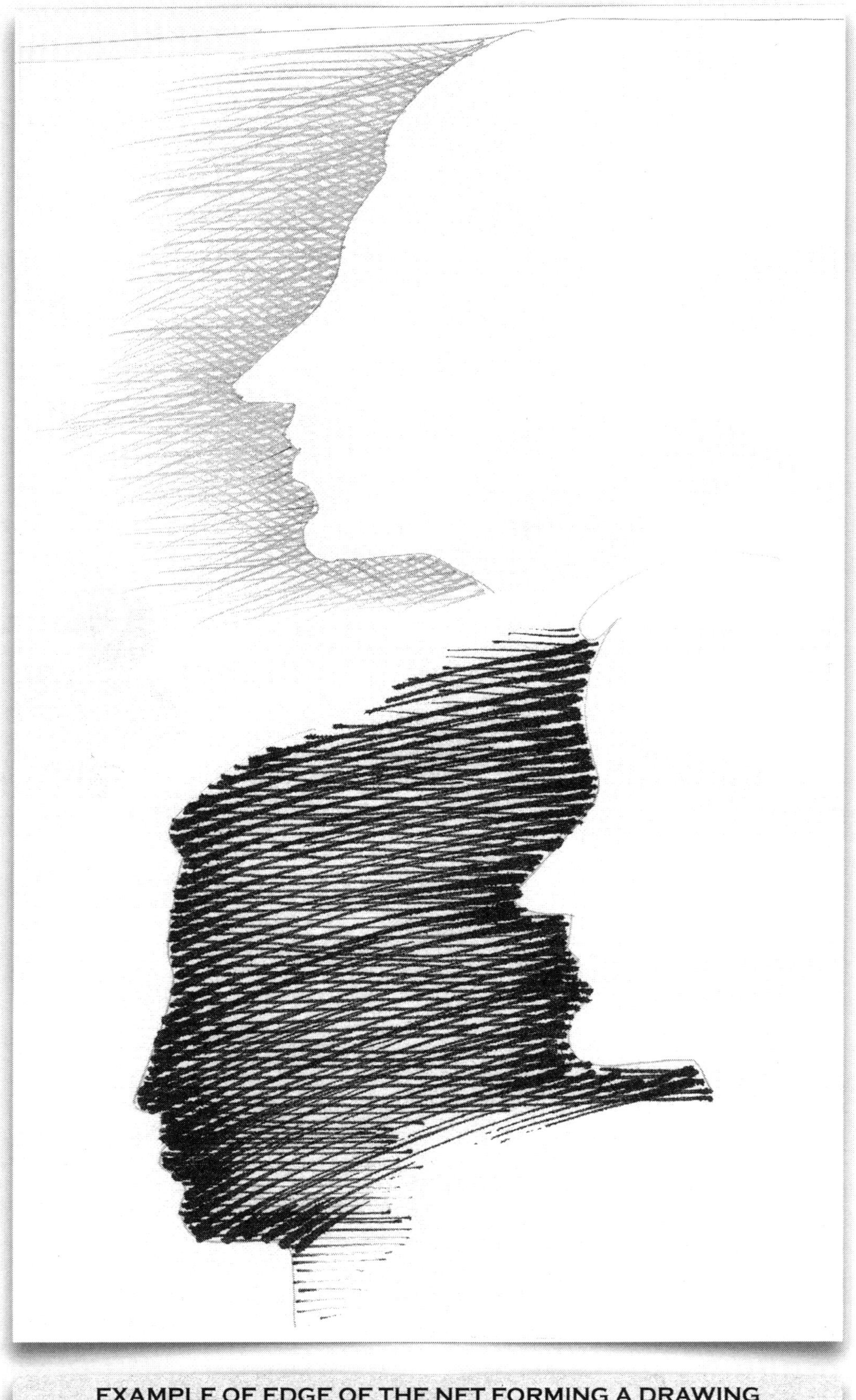

EXAMPLE OF EDGE OF THE NET FORMING A DRAWING

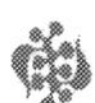

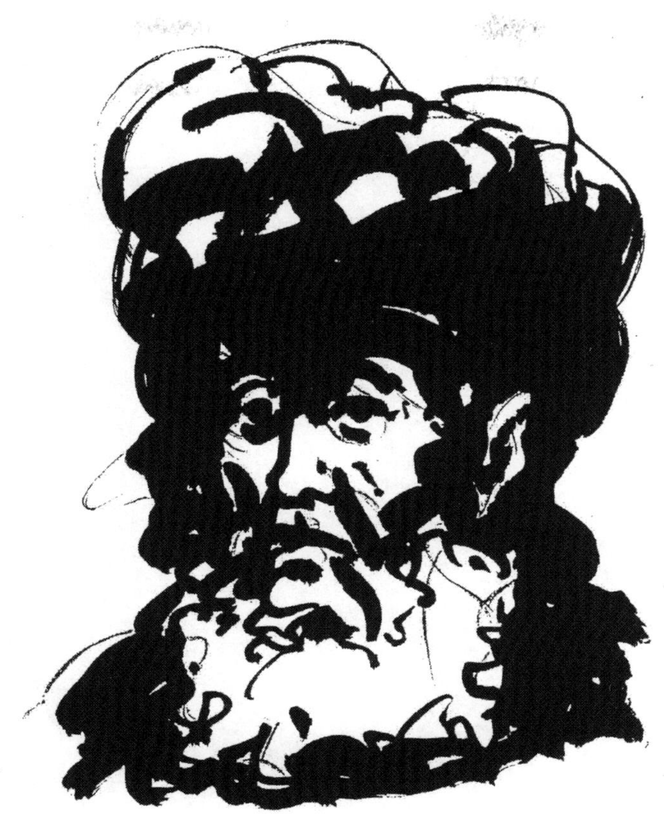

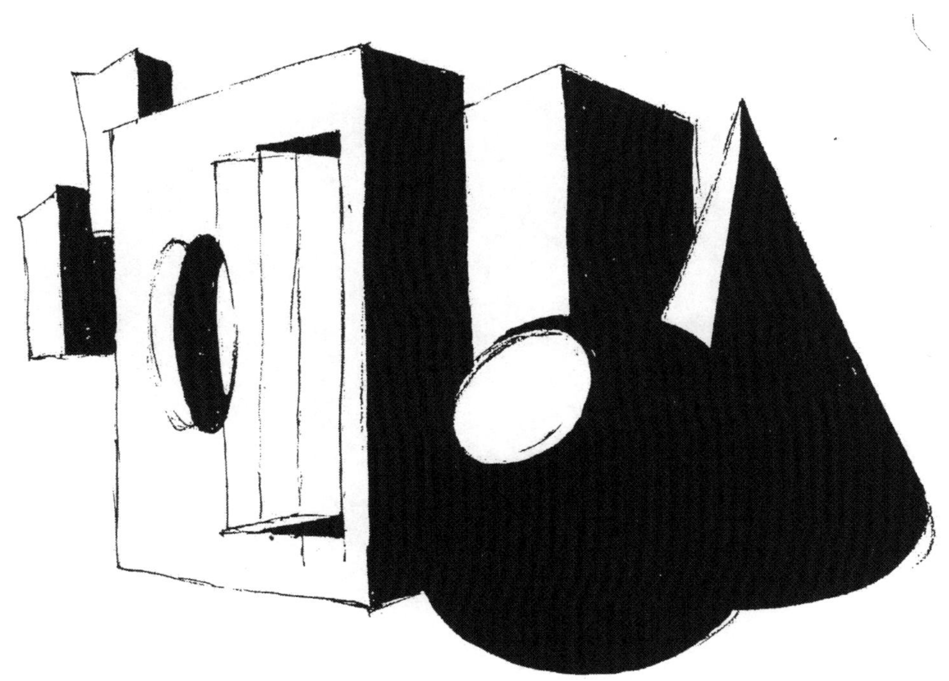

EXAMPLES OF THE EDGE BETWEEN SHADOW AND LIGH FORMING A SHAPE

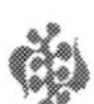

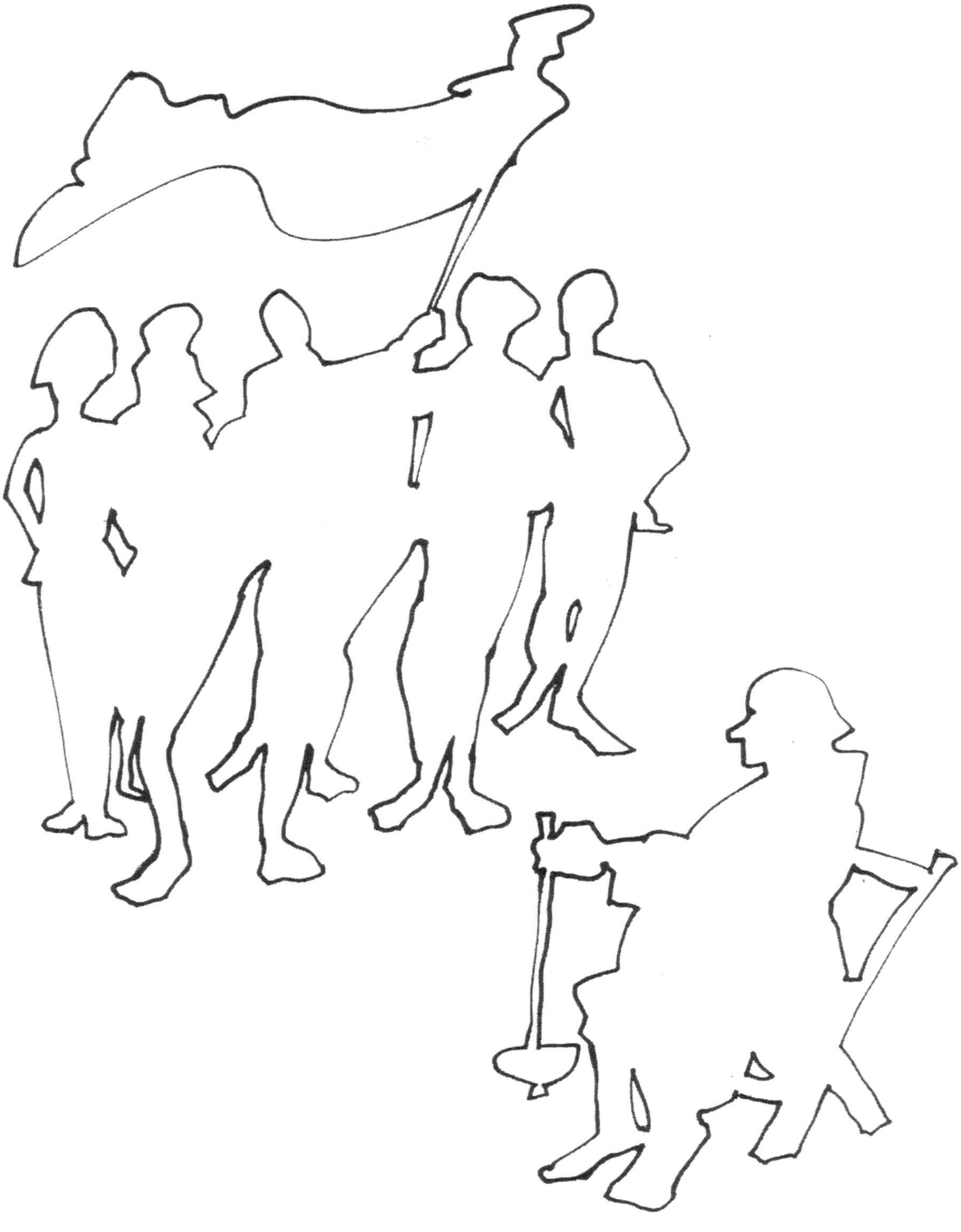

THE BOUNDARIES BETWEEN OBJECTS AND AMBIENT

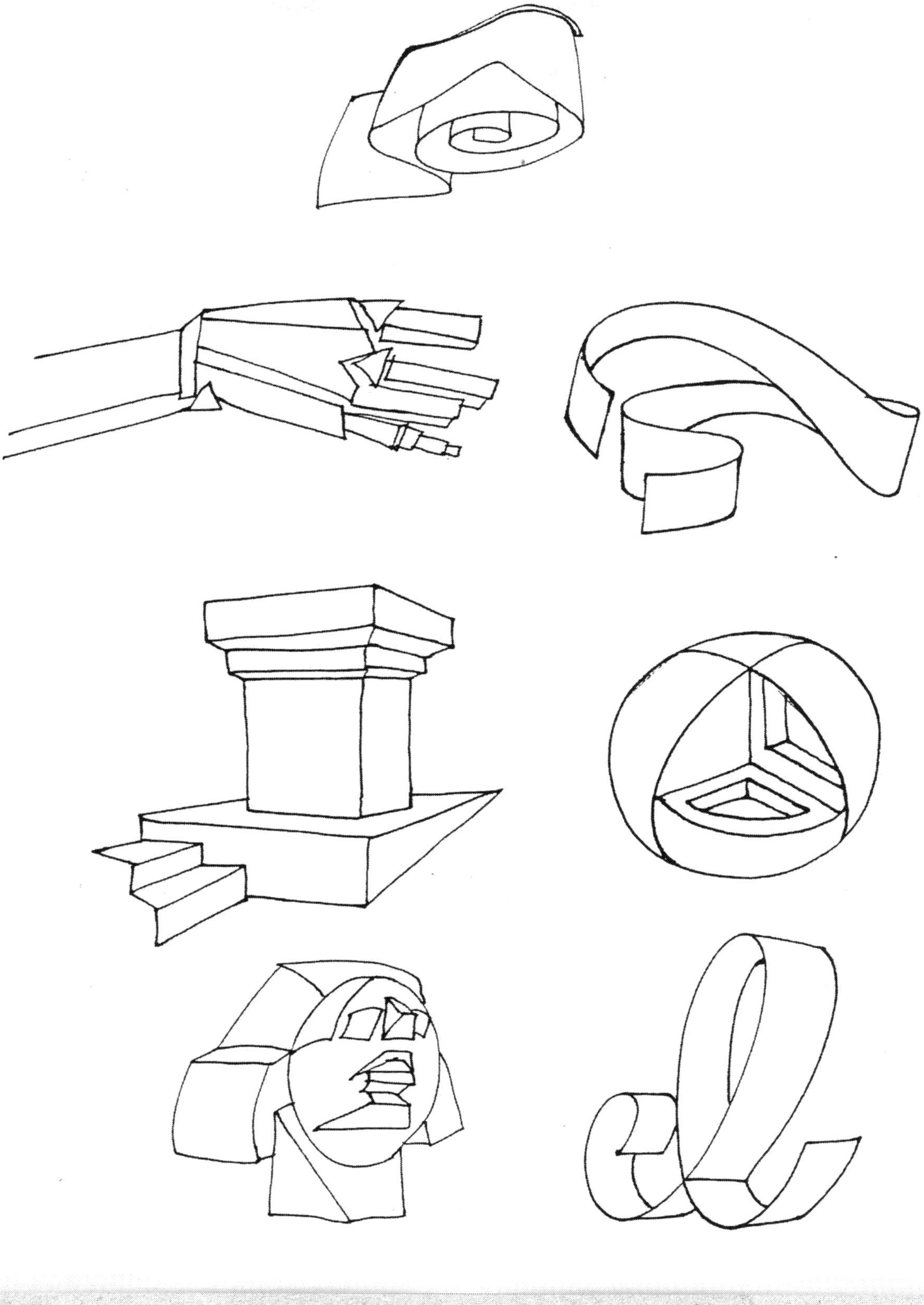

THE BOUNDARIES OF SURFACE FIELDS

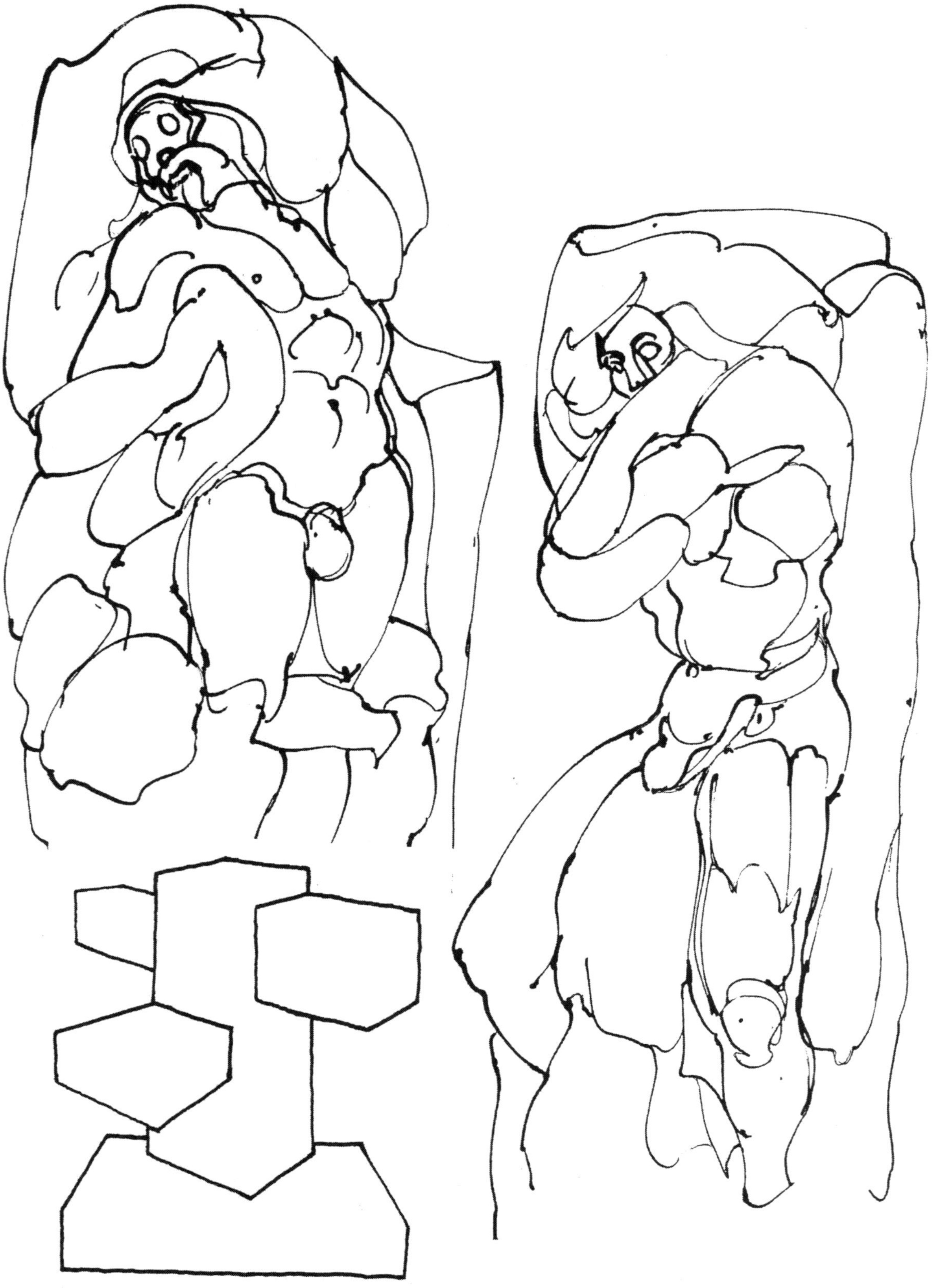

THE BOUNDARIES OF CUBIC SPACE

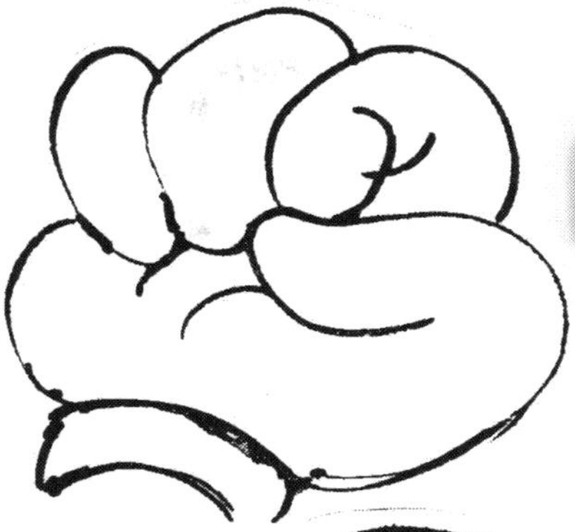

CARTOON
JAPANESE WOODCUT 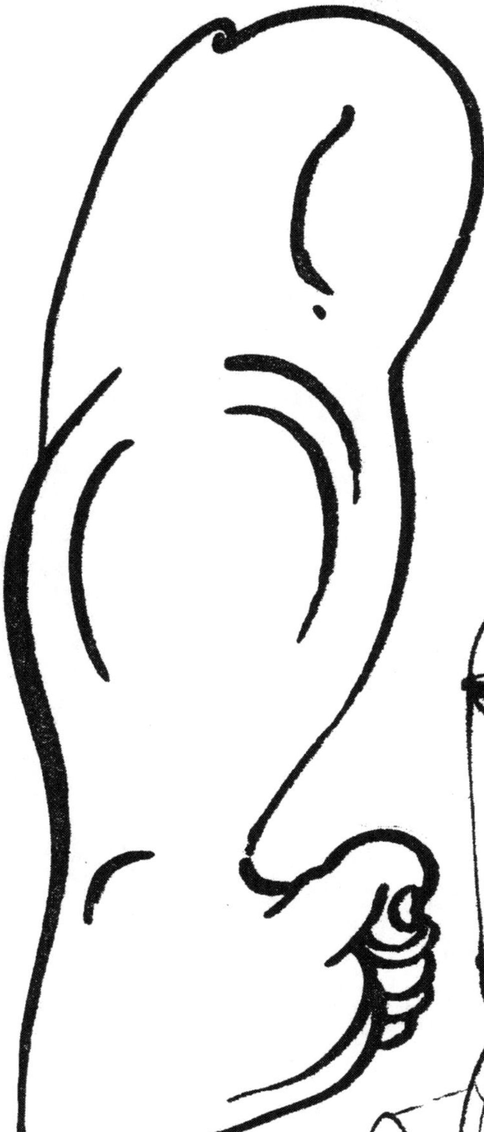
GEOMETRY IN DRAWING 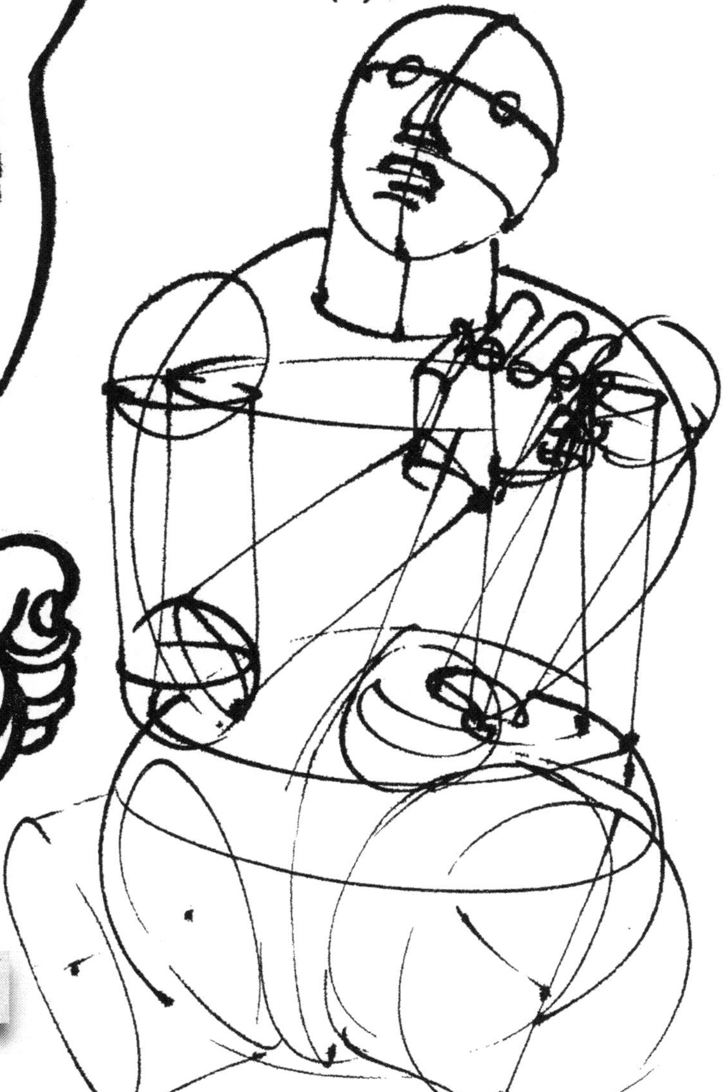
EXAMPLES OF VARIOUS DRAWING CONCEPTS

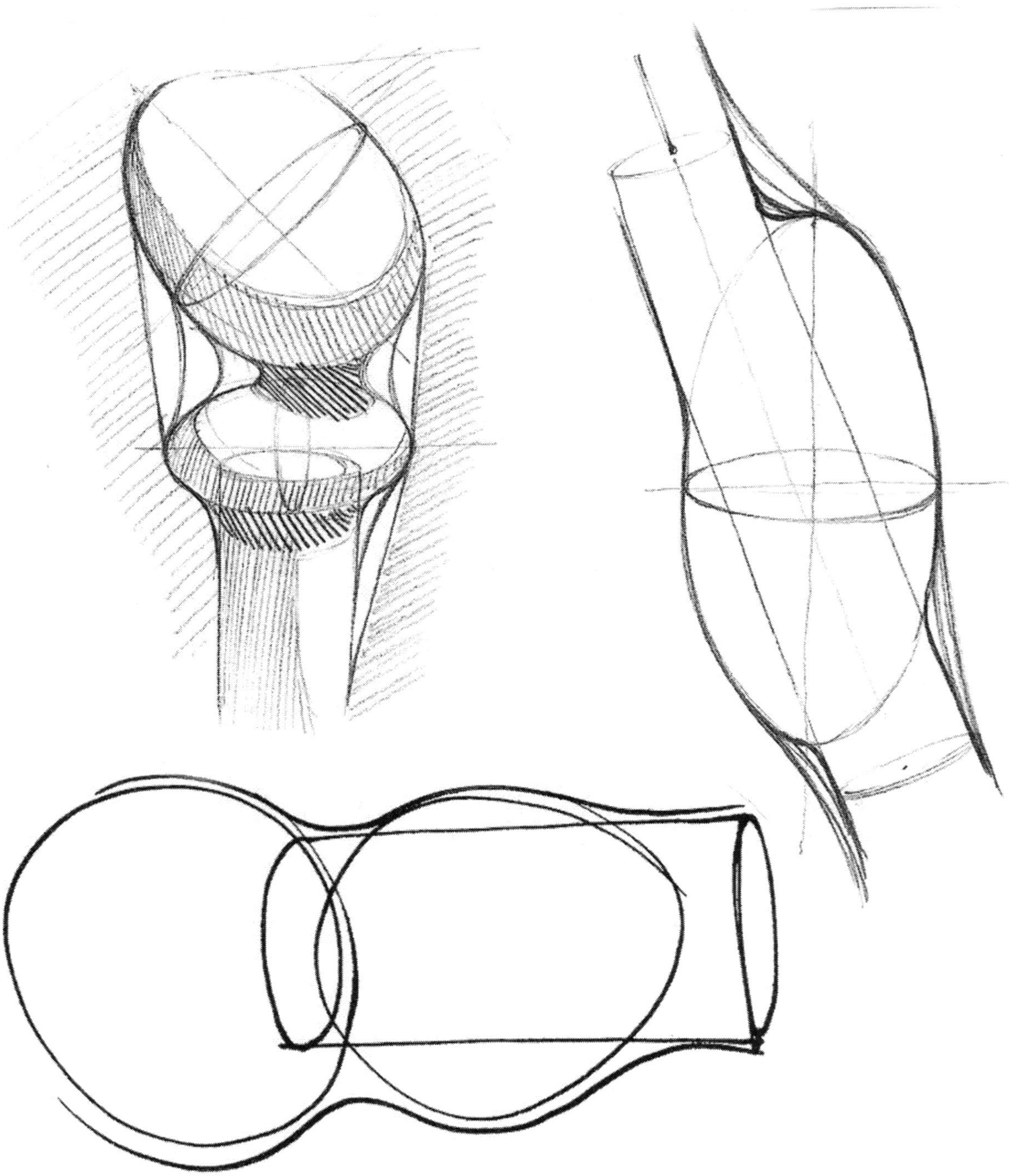

**TWO GEOMETRIC SHAPES CONNECTED WITH CURVED A LINE,
ANOTHER CONCEPT OF STEREOMETRY**

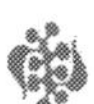

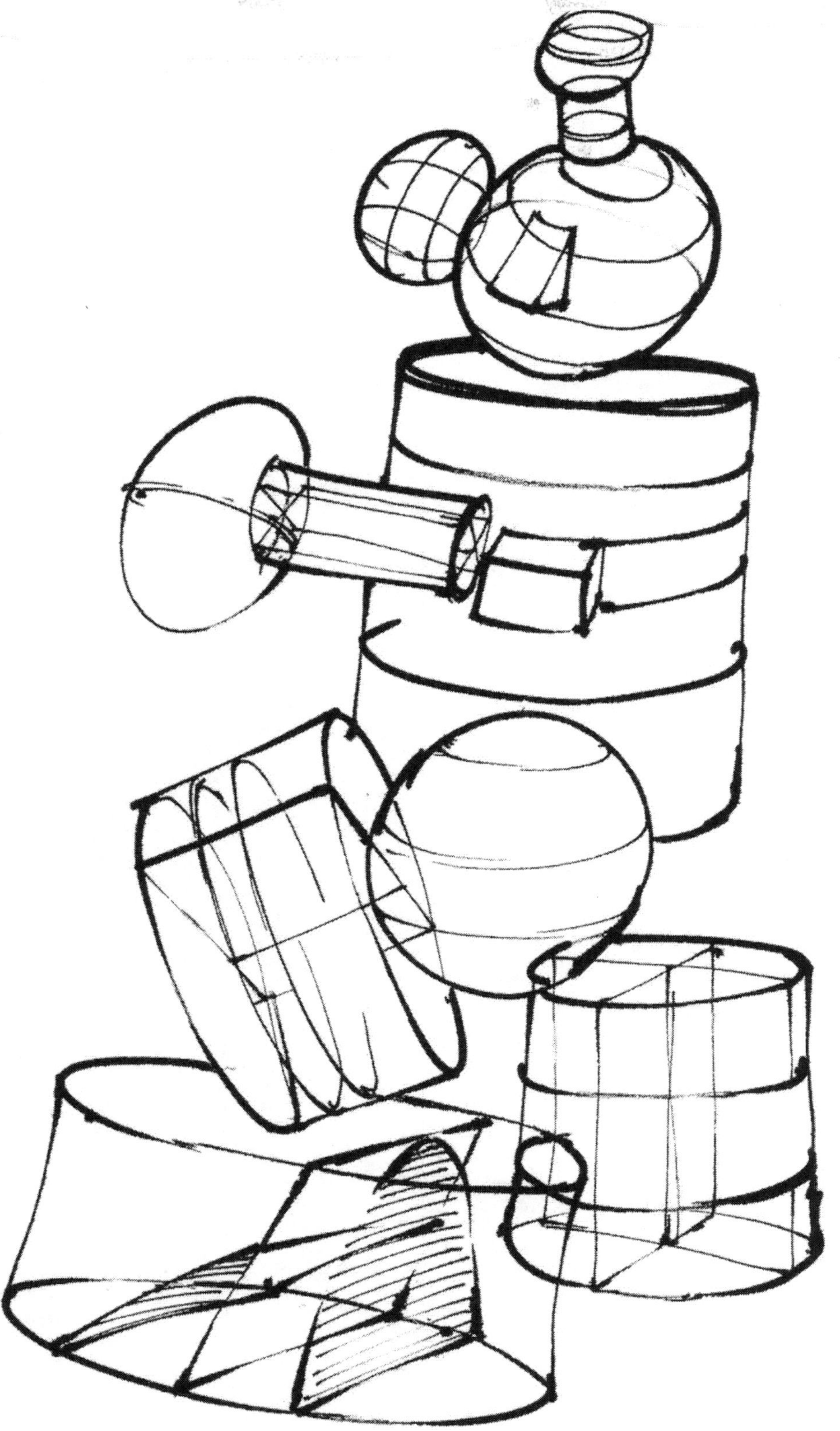

GEOMETRIC SIGNIFICANCE OF HUMAN FIGURE

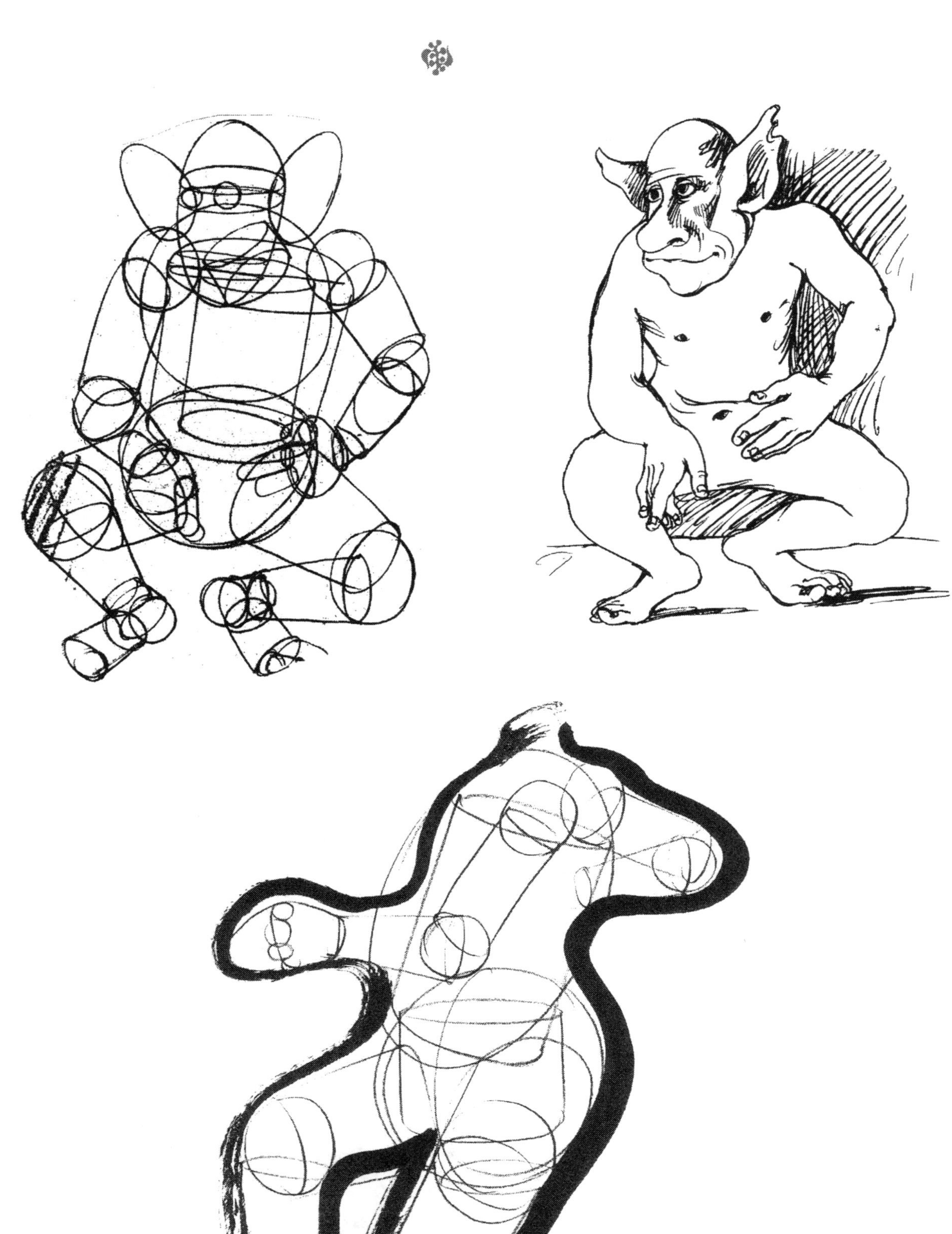

GEOMETRIC AND ORGANIC CONTENTS OF A SILHOUETTE

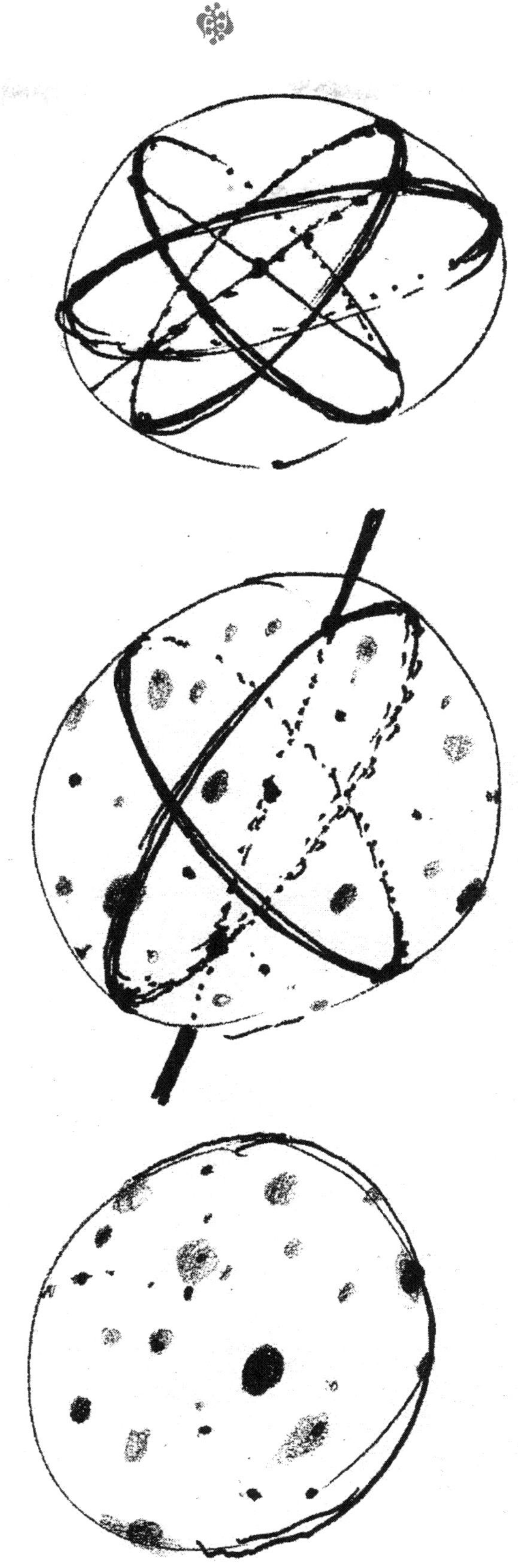

**EXAMPLES OF STEREOGRAPHY OF A BALL,
THE DOTS ARE INSIDE AND ON THE SURFACE OF THE BALL**

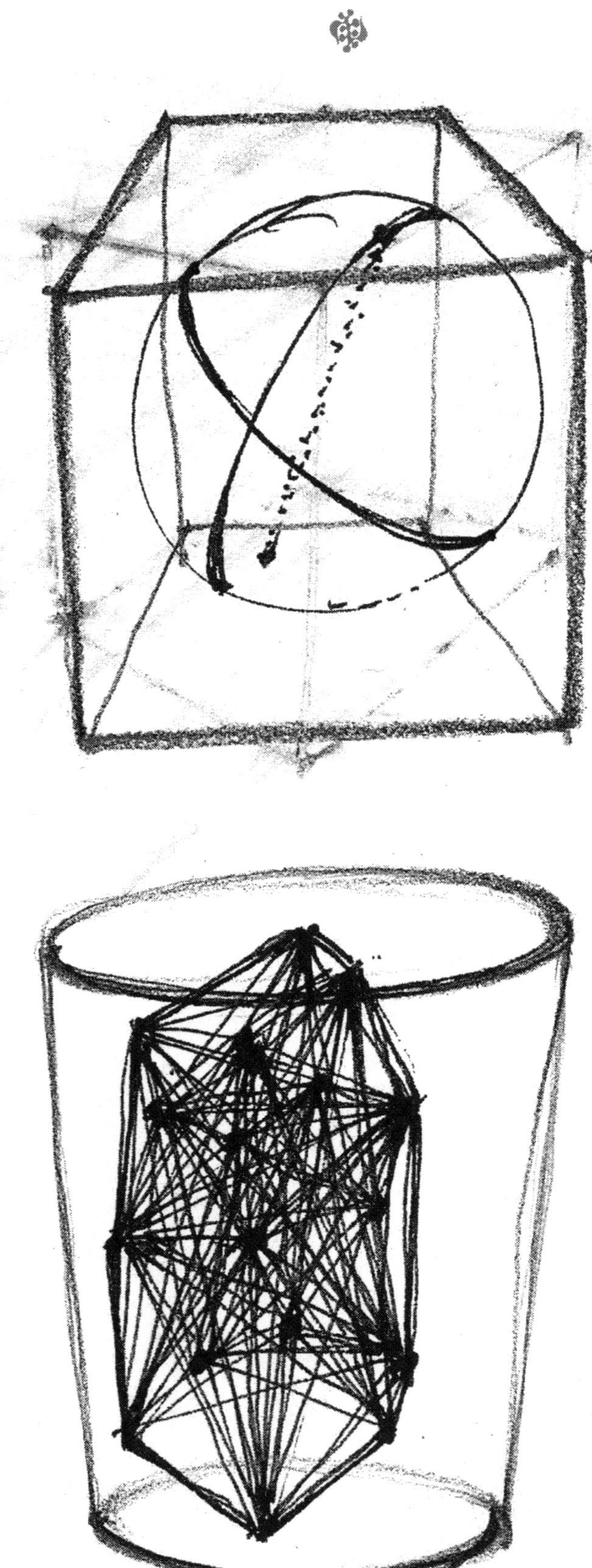

EXAMPLES OF STEREOGRAPHY: WITH THE BALL IS INSIDE A CUBE WE OBSERVE STEREOGRAPHIC PLASTICITY.
SECOND EXAMPLE: CRYSTAL SHAPE INSIDE A CYLINDER

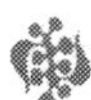

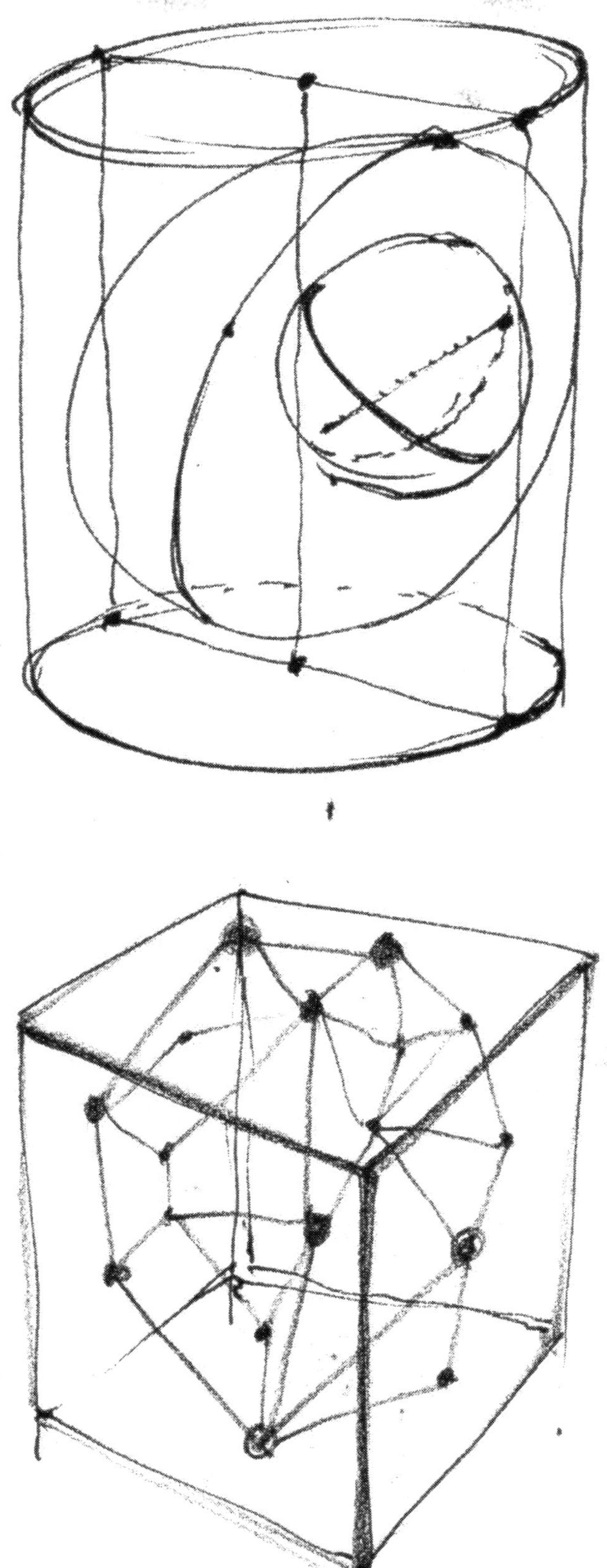

EXAMPLES OF STEREOGRAPHY

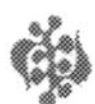

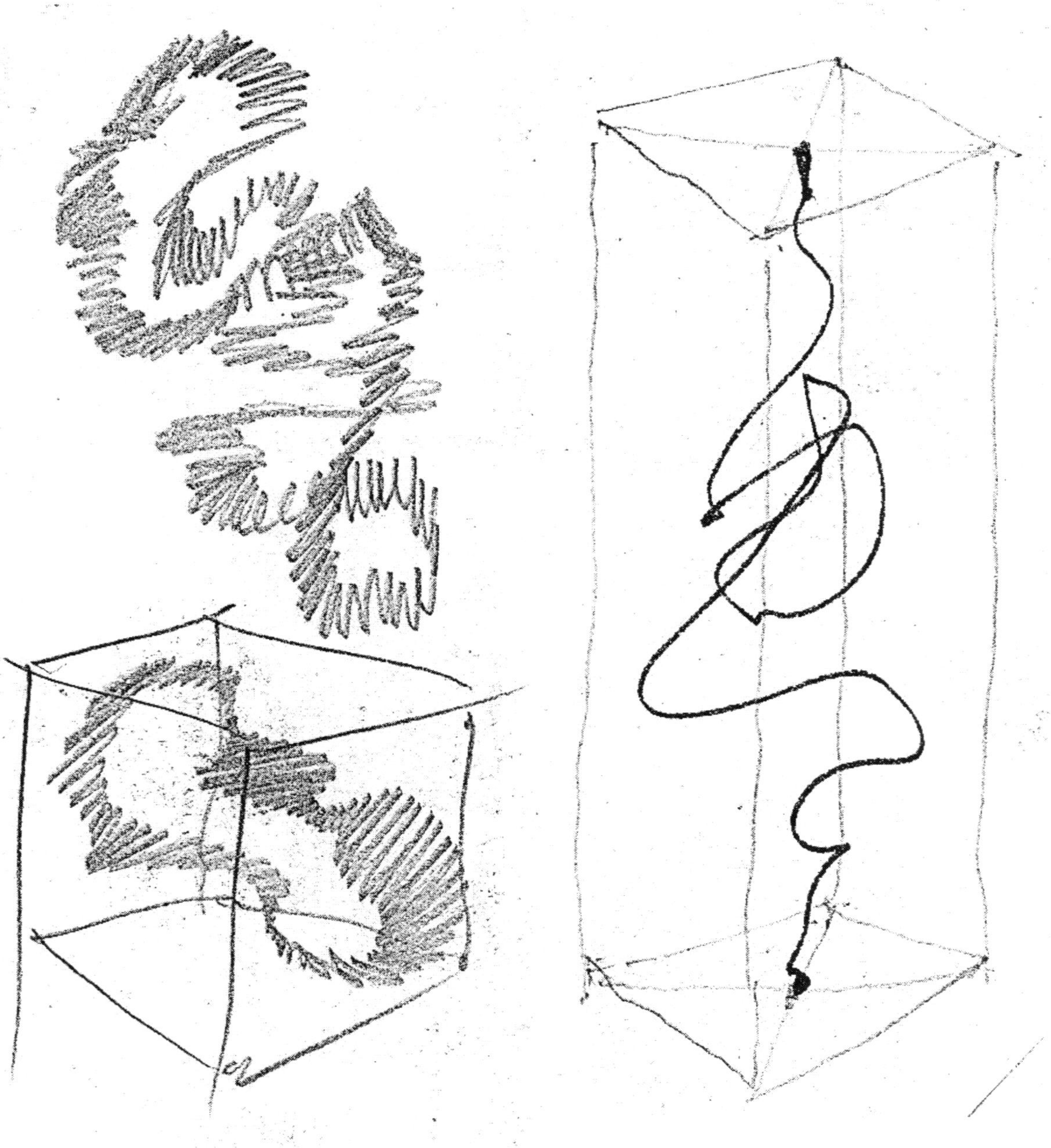

EXAMPLES OF STEREOGRAPHY EFFECTS
A LINE INSIDE OF A SQUARE

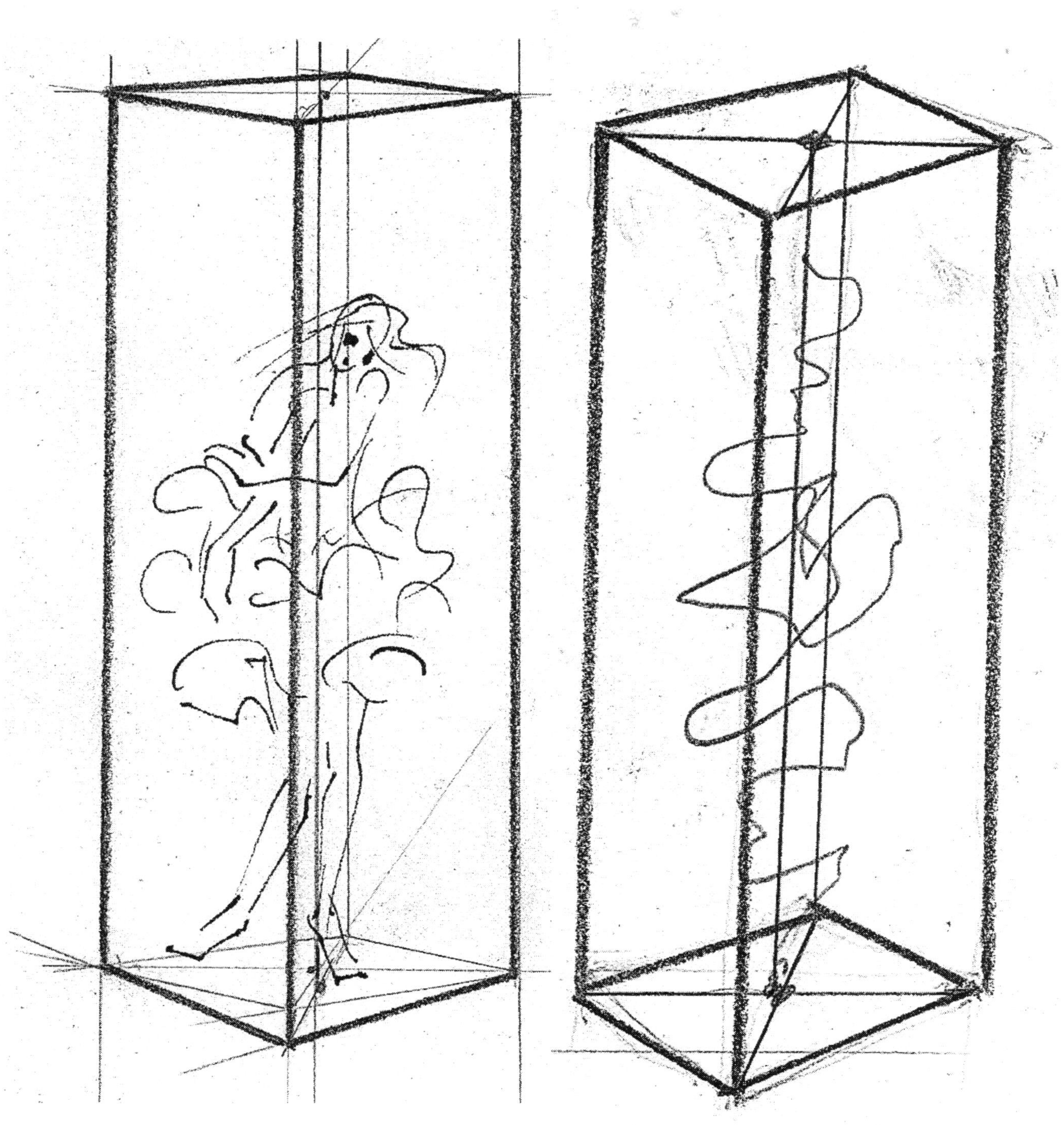

**EXAMPLES OF STEREOGRAPHY EFFECTS
A FIGURE INSIDE OF A SQUARE**

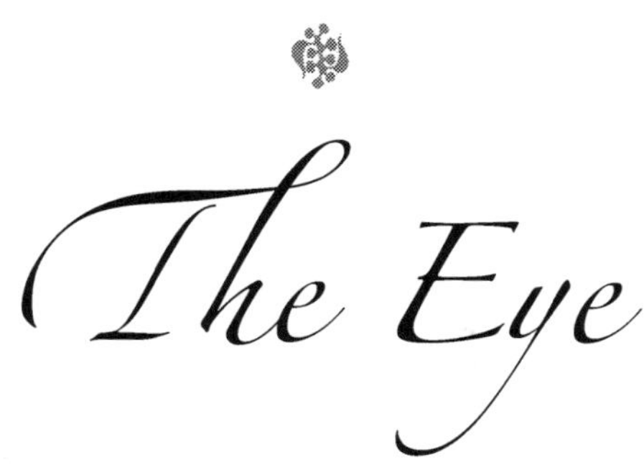

The Eye

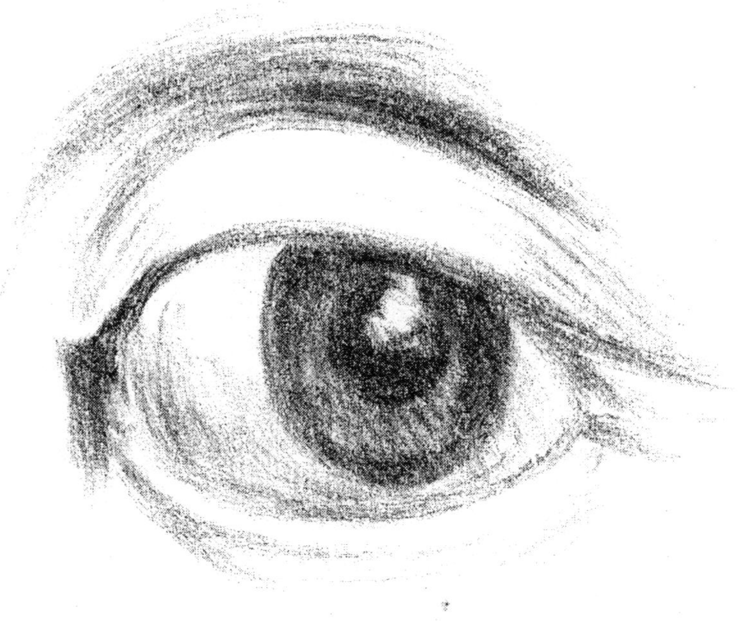

WHEN DRAWING THE EYE it is necessary to take into consideration the character of its geometrical shapes:

- ~ the eye is a ball with certain values and details
- ~ the location and positioning of the eye in the head is geometrically important

There is only a section of the ball that comes into play when drawing an eye. This visible part is partially or completely covered by the eyelids that have a certain thickness and hold a row of eyelashes. The iris and the pupil are also very geometrical in character. The harmony of both irises is important, for they define the direction of the gaze. When looking up or down the eyelids change character as well.

It is clear that geometrical values are very important when drawing an eye. In fact, geometry is more important than perfectly executed eye as a singular detail. This is why sometimes you may be surprised when observing masterful paintings you'll notice how the eyes are not finished in detail.

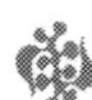

TECHNICAL ADVICE AND SUGGESTIONS

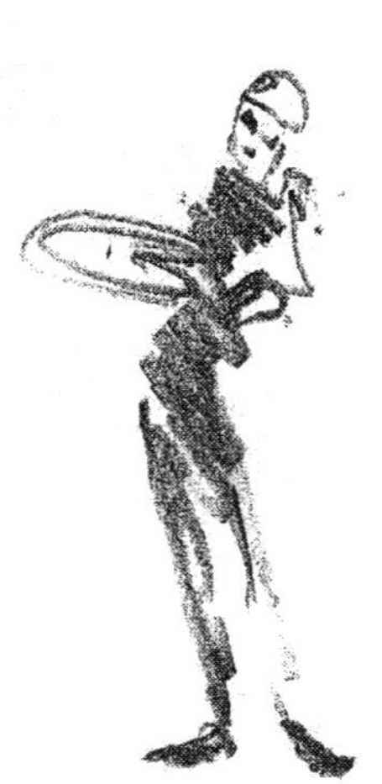

S OME DRAWINGS REQUIRE A SOFT PENCIL OR CHARCOAL. To achieve a calligraphy effect with a fluid line, you may try repeating the lines. You can also complete them with gentle touches while adding dots.

For larger drawings of the eye, I suggest you use a harder pencil. First lightly mark the fundamental pattern, then continue by accentuating the darkness. You may also turn the paper while drawing, for easier and even application.

In certain cases you may try using a thicker pen, softer pencil or charcoal.

Pay attention to the inner corner of the eye, and take into consideration the small, pink, globular nodule at the inner corner.

Also pay attention to the elliptical quality of the iris and location of the pupil.

The eyelashes are presented by accentuating the darkness.

Experiment with various size drawings, including very small ones and emphasize the geometrical qualities. Enforce the lines with light strokes.

Special instructions for geometrical drawings:

Begin by lightly marking the size of objects. Use the help of a ruler or compass - drawing tool.

Pay attention to each line and keep repeating, improving and perfecting them.

Use a combination of harder, softer, sharper or dull-pointed pencils.

Experiment and observe the difference between controlled fast lines and thoughtful slow moves.

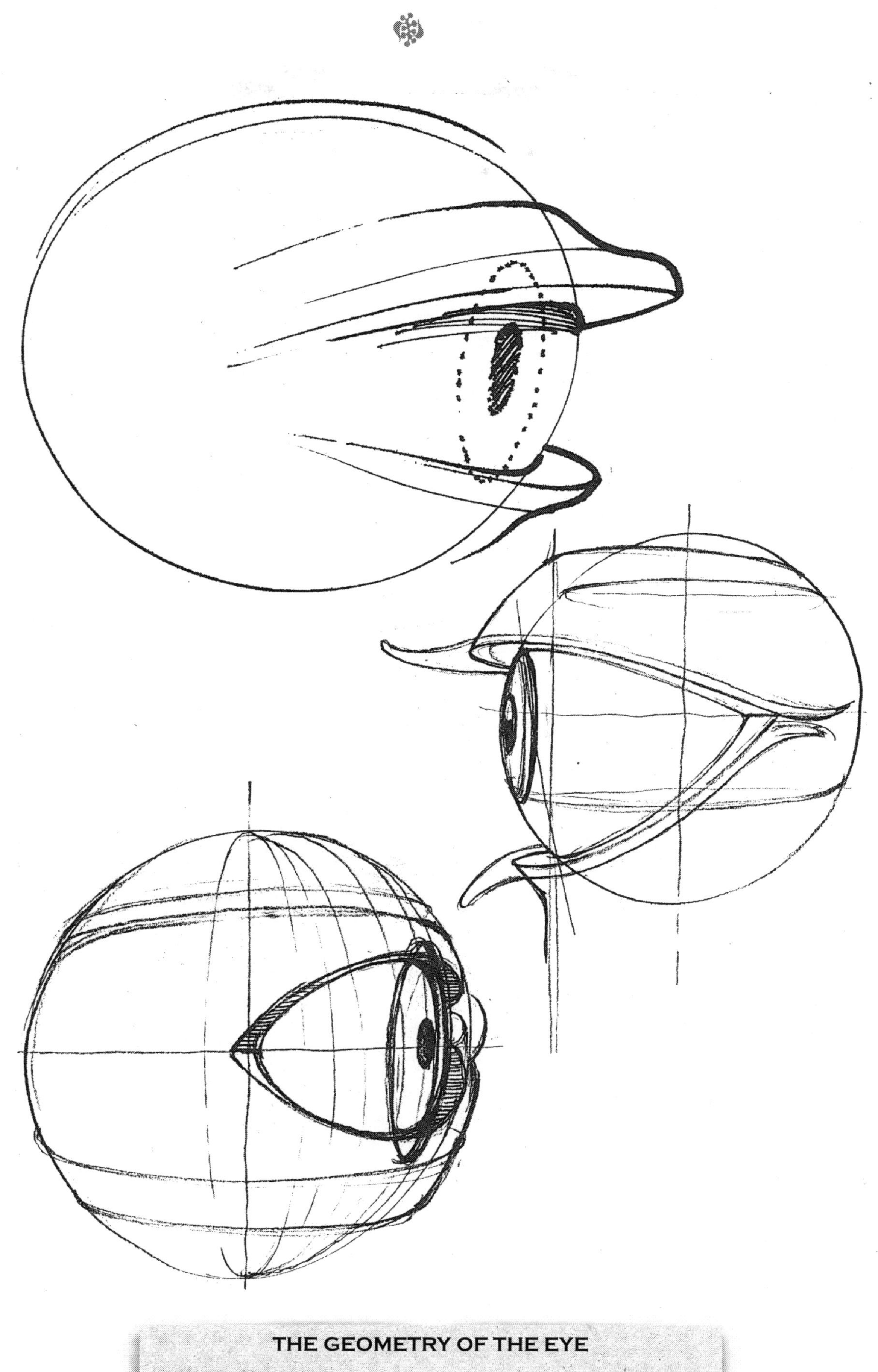

THE GEOMETRY OF THE EYE

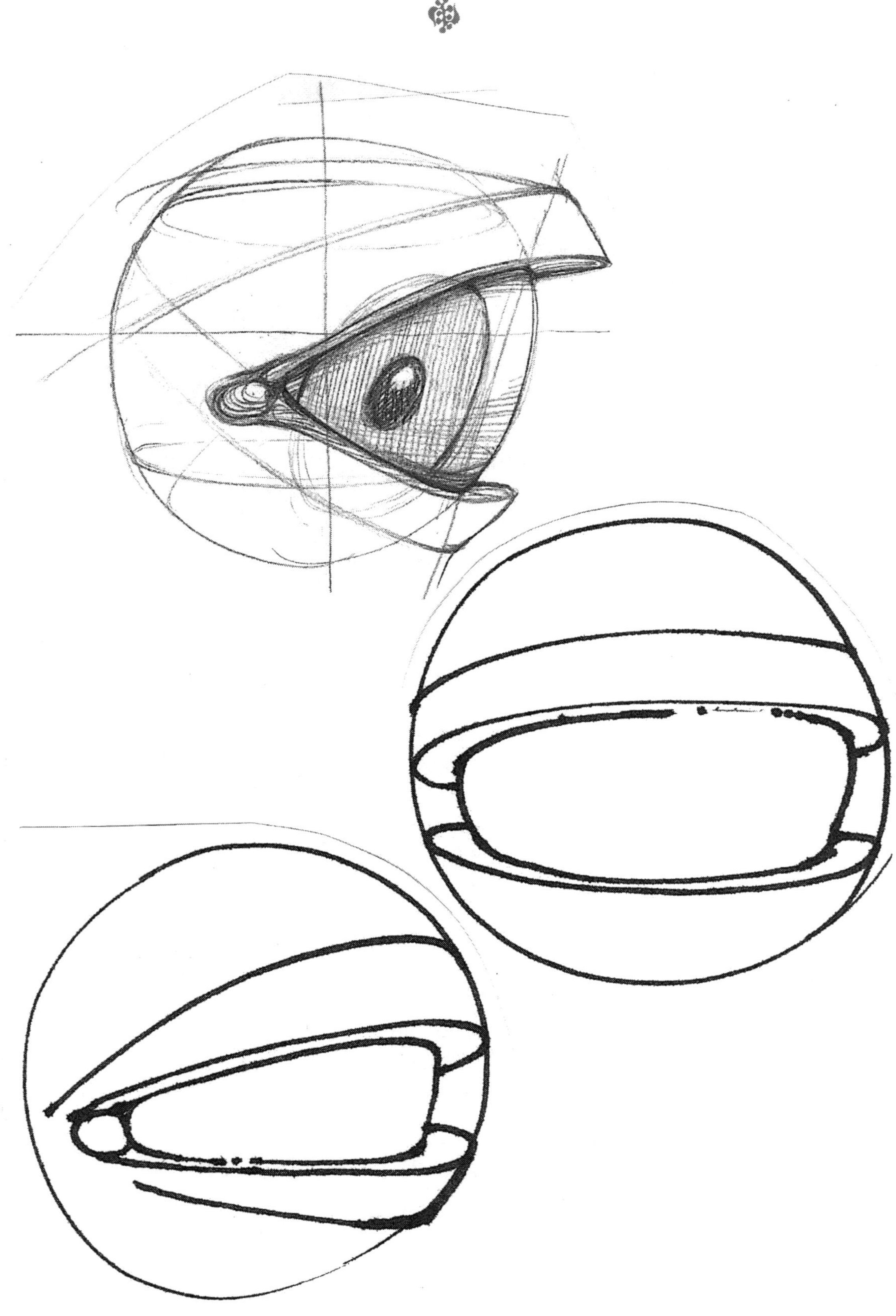

THE GEOMETRY OF THE EYE

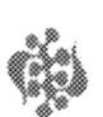

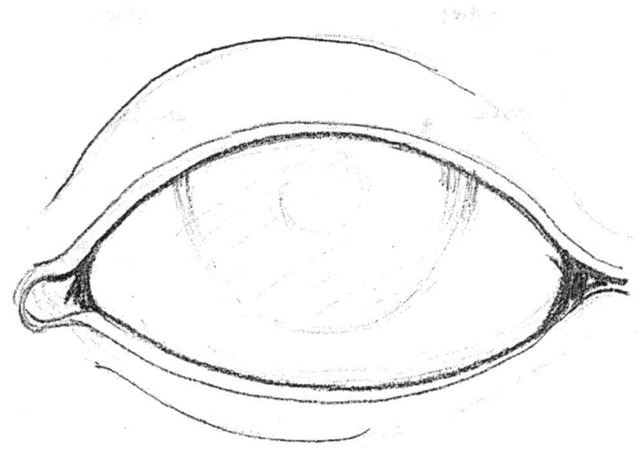

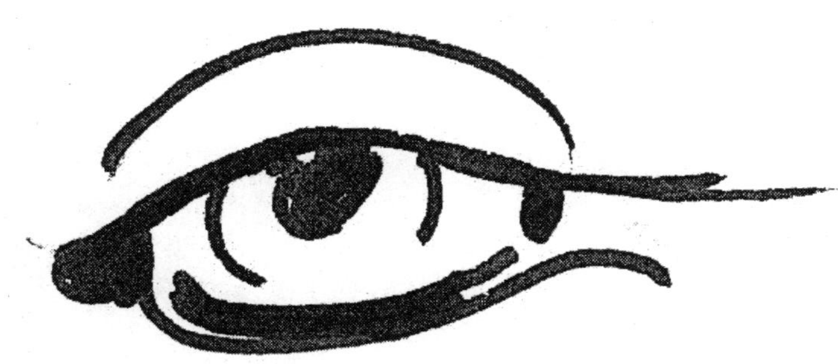

VARIOUS INTERPRETATIONS OF THE EYE

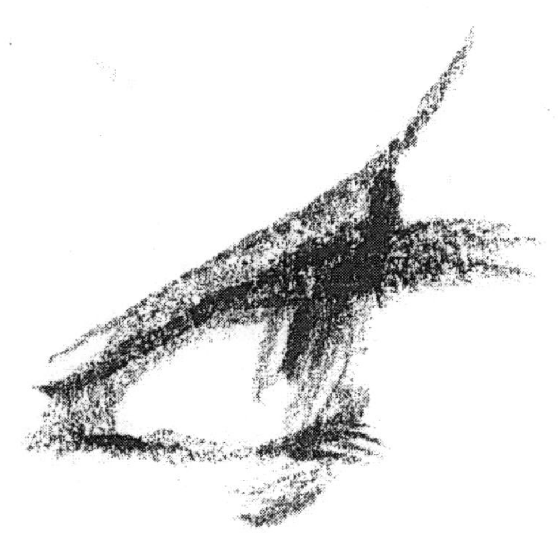

SIDEVIEW OF THE EYE

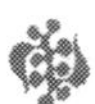

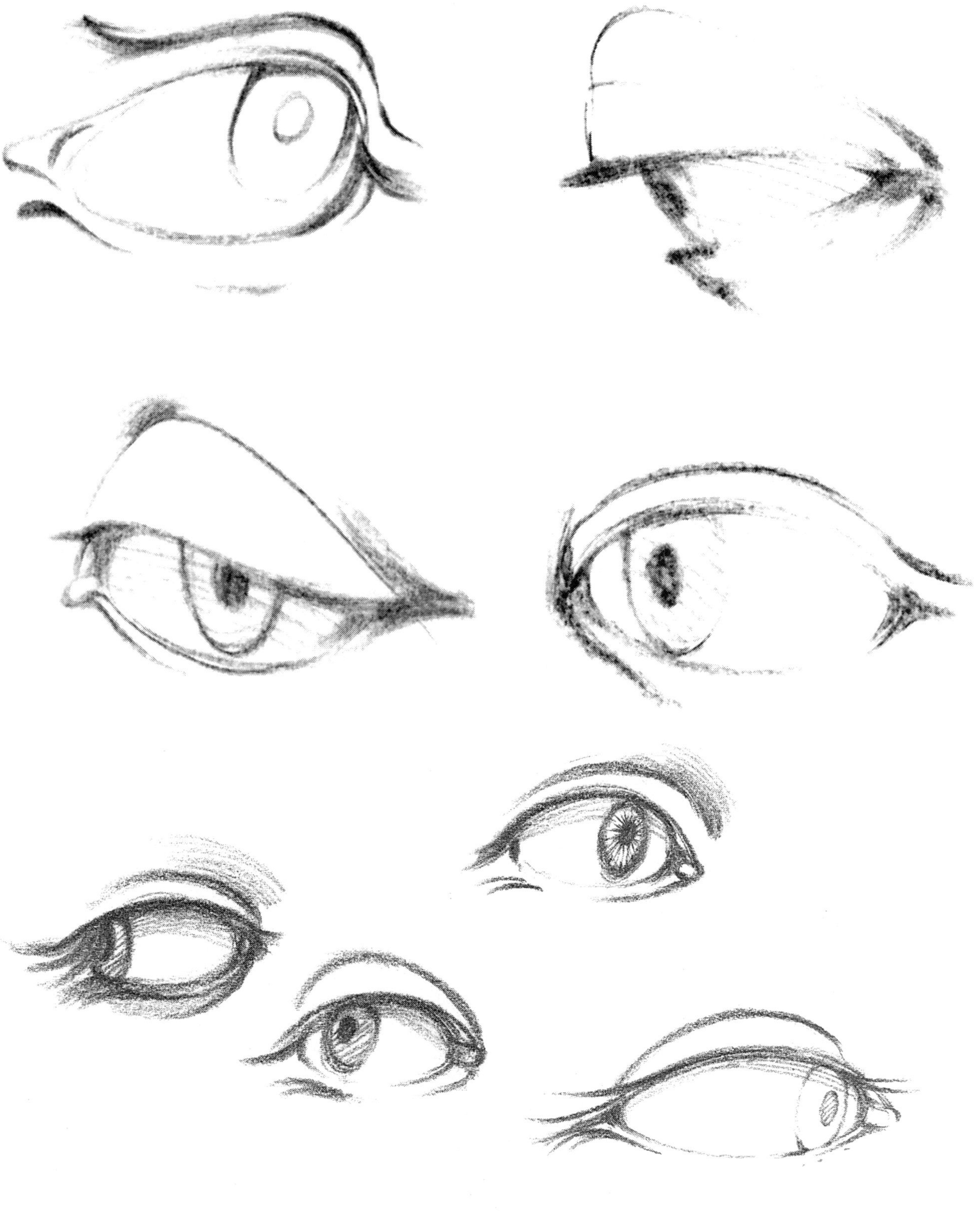

VARIATIONS OF THE EYE DIRECTION AND GAZE

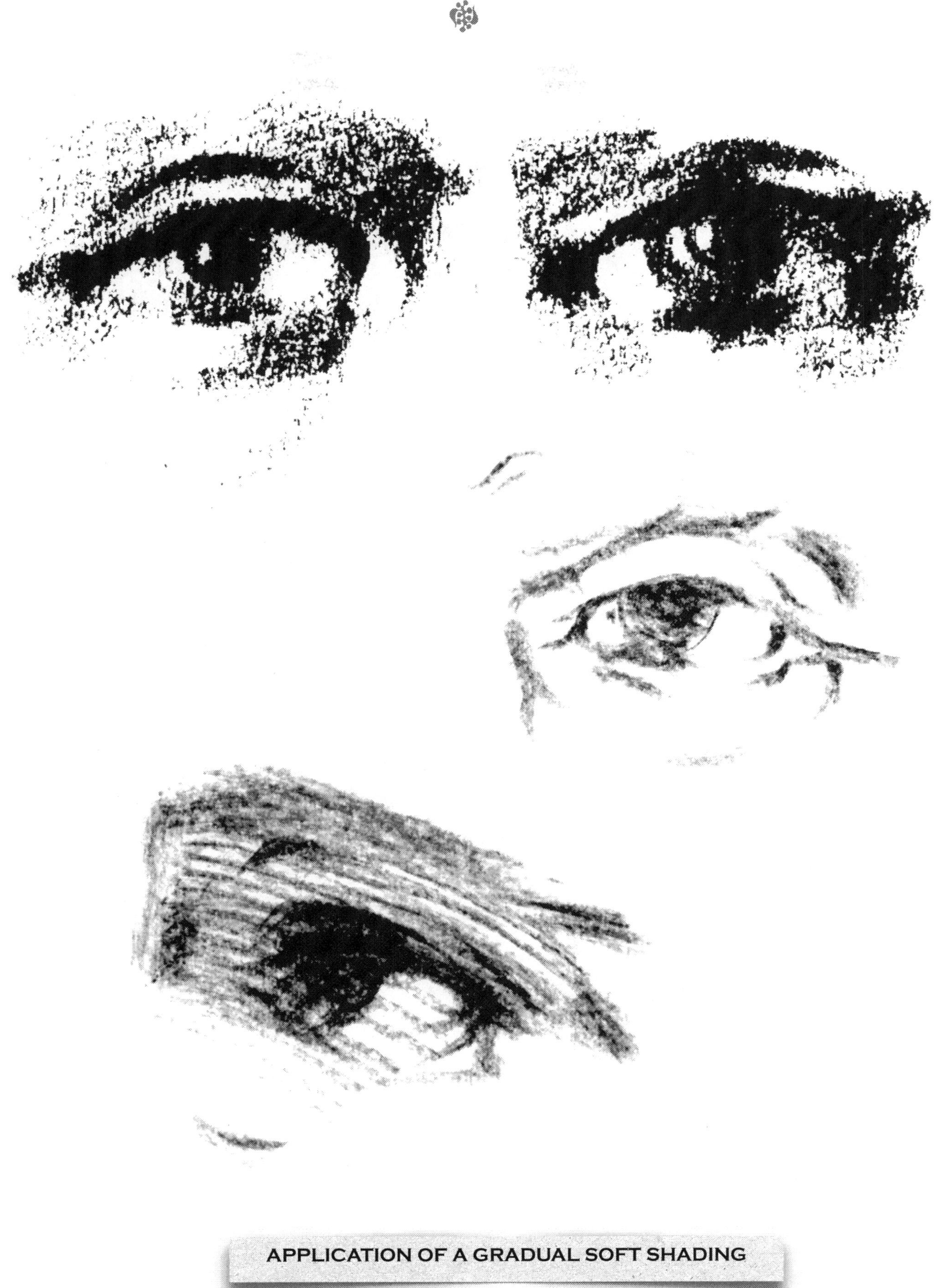

APPLICATION OF A GRADUAL SOFT SHADING

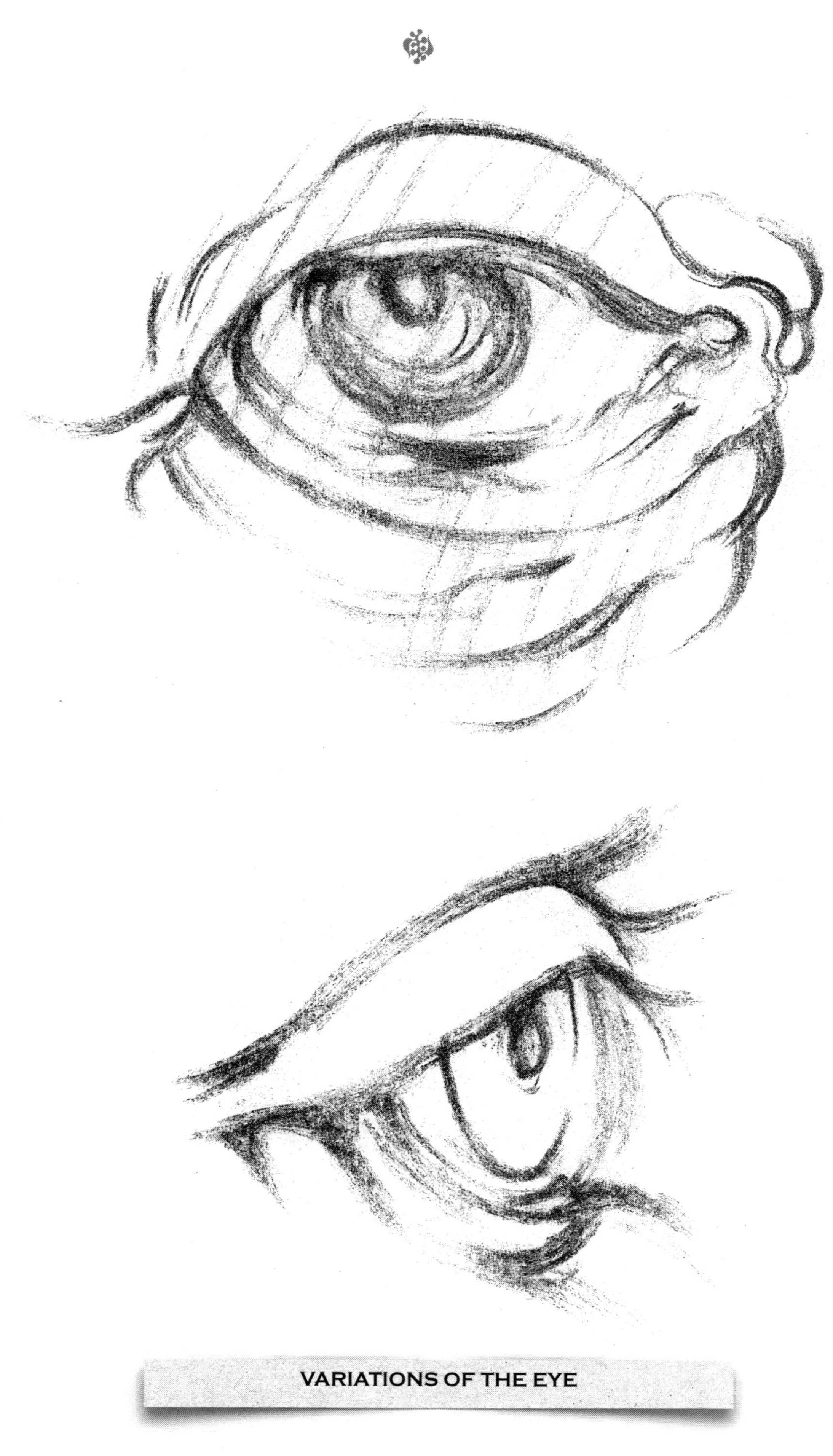

VARIATIONS OF THE EYE

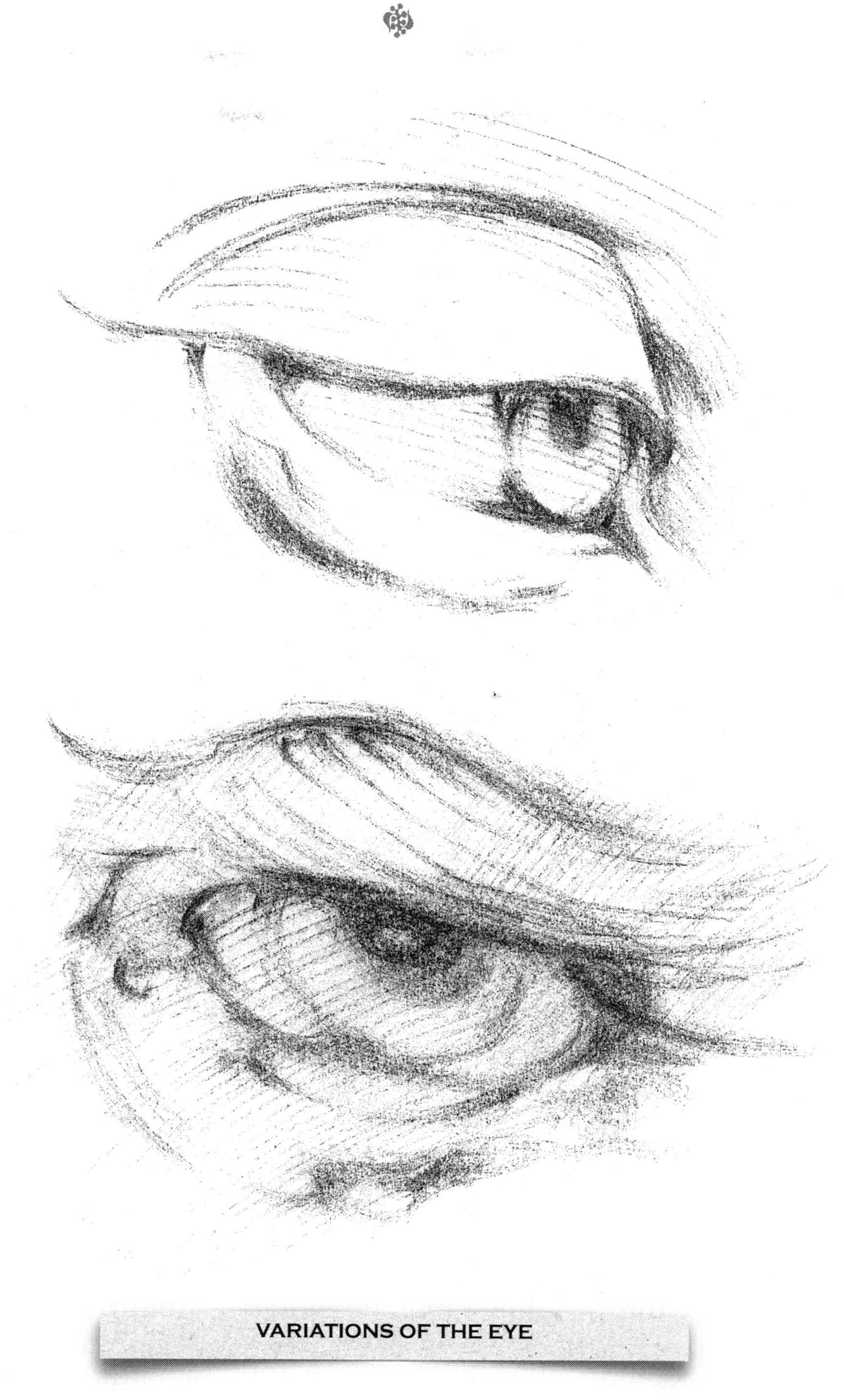

VARIATIONS OF THE EYE

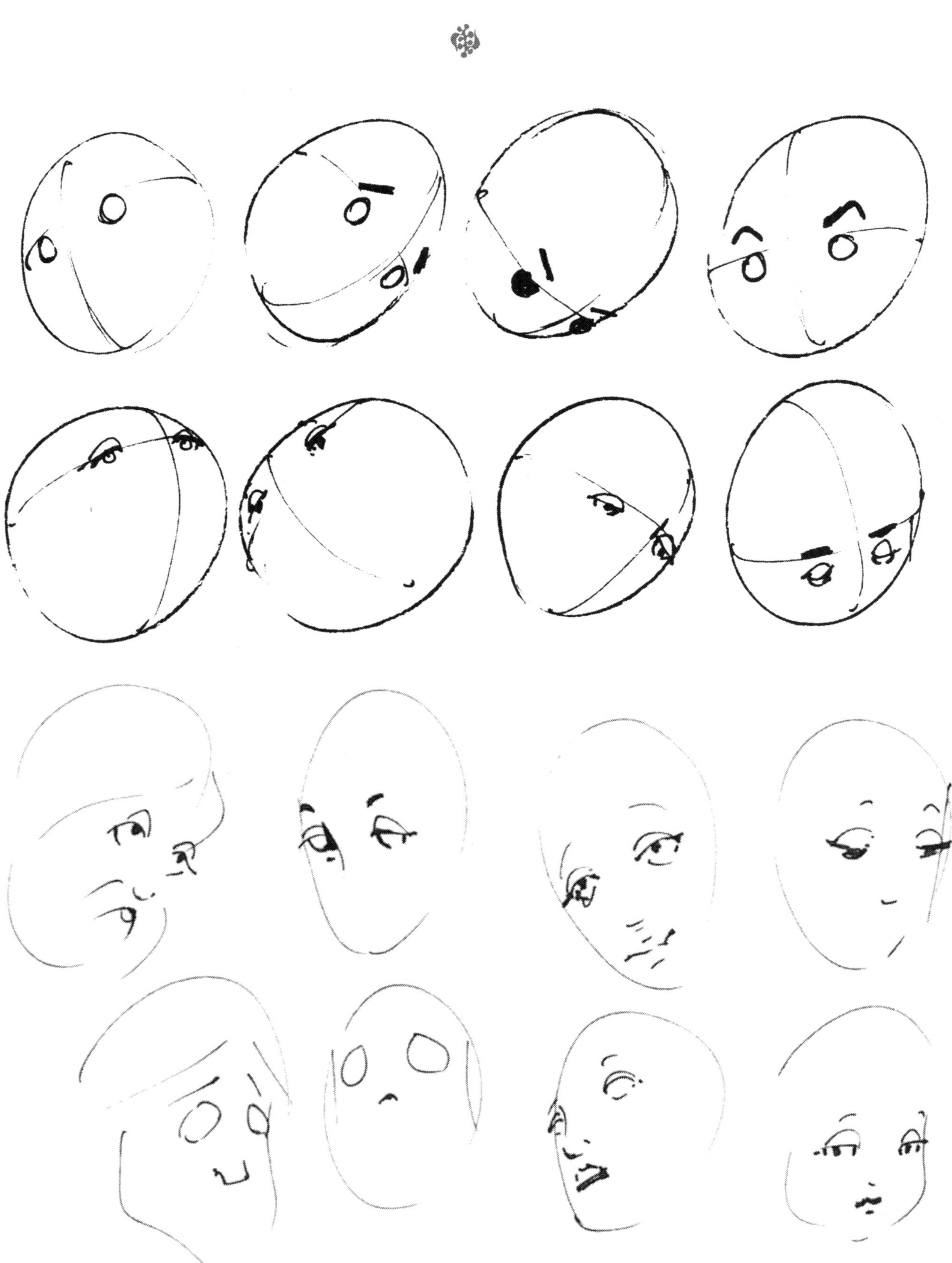

VARIATIONS OF THE EYE PLACEMENT IN HEAD

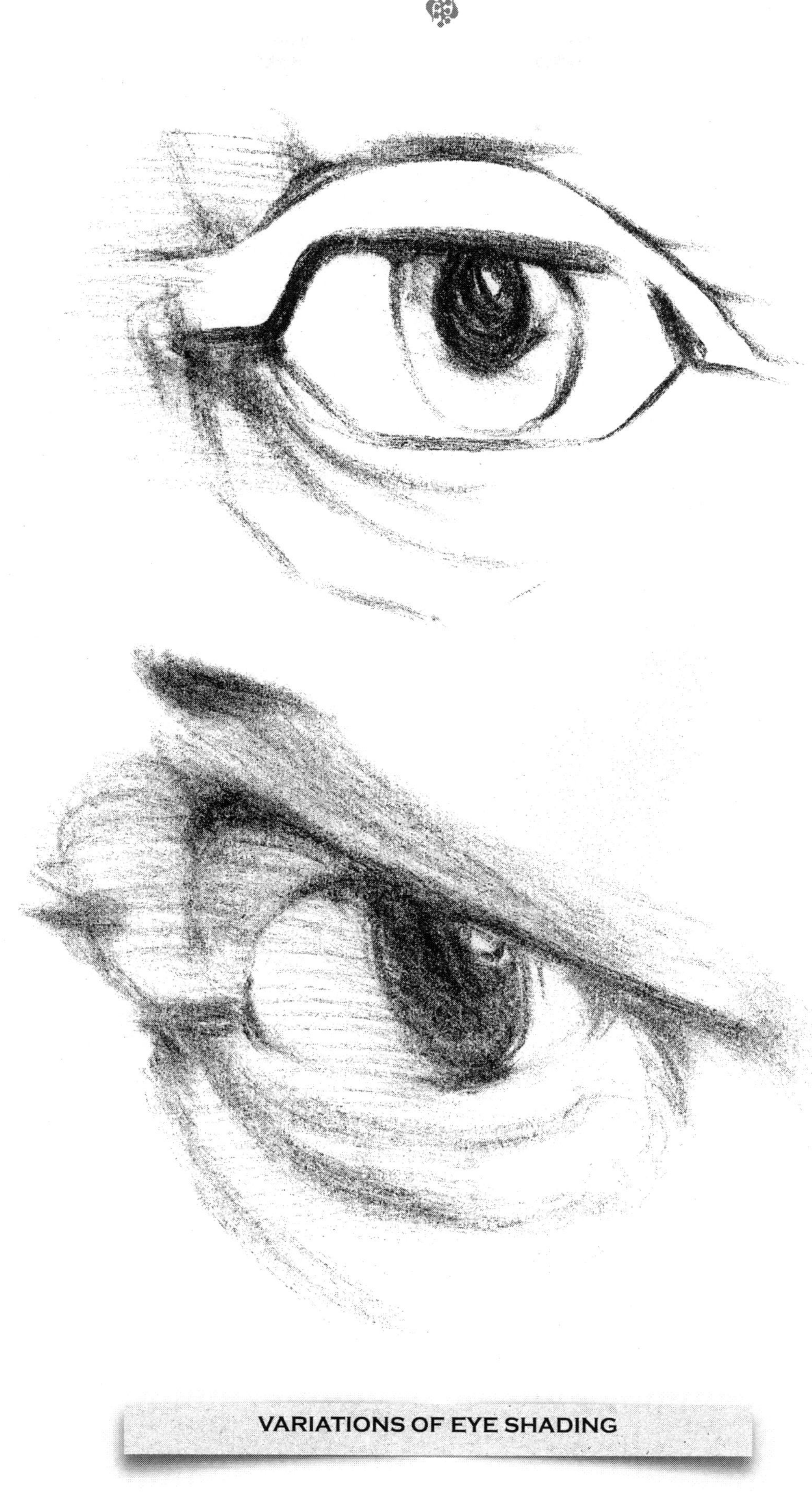

VARIATIONS OF EYE SHADING

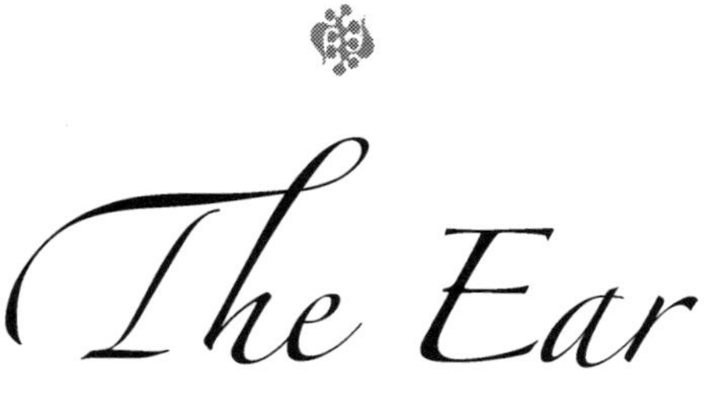

The Ear

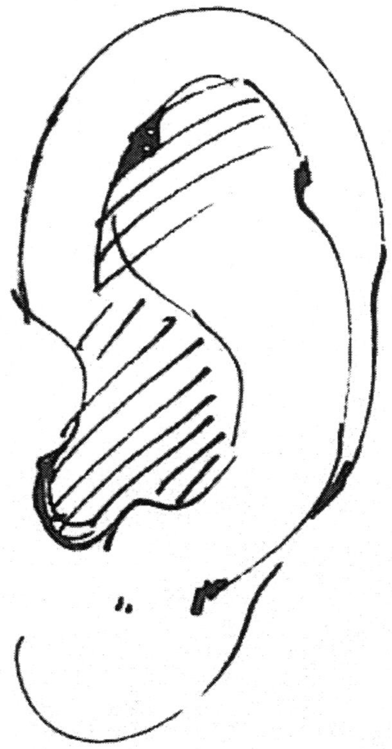

IT IS CHALLENGING TO ANALYZE the tangled complex of shapes that compose the ear. Oversimplification results in an unconvincing and cheapened illustration. In case we master the drawing of the ear, we land in a difficult position of how to interpret it in a painting. We cannot console ourselves with the fact, that even some of the great masters avoided this challenging task. They covered the ears with hair, appropriate cap or a hat. If you take the time and carefully explore this topic, you may find a few examples that are quite embarrassing.

We have to look at the ear as a result of four most visible parts:
- The top of the ear which can be more or less prominent, pointy or barely noticeable
- The largest, middle and wide part that contains central deepening
- The lower part, which gives the ear character with its size
- The entry into the ear canal that is closed off with a rounded harmonious shape

The difficulty lies in the fact that simplifying the ear is almost impossible. The answer is simple but demanding; practice and more practice, diligent drawing and observation.

The essence is in the first line which encompasses the entire silhouette. Next comes the decision about the central deepening and so on. Practice and give it a try.

All examples are made after following the best masters. In the beginning there are a few illustrative samples which are not exemplary, but only samplings.

We can categorically say that depicting the ear requires especial calligraphic quality. We can accomplish this with much practice. Remain encouraged by the fact that eventually you will playfully master drawing the ear. Stay persistent and keep at it.

TECHNICAL ADVICE AND SUGGESTIONS

FOR GEOMETRY EXERCISES PENCIL IS THE BEST. Try various levels of hardness. Experiment also your own possible geometric shapes and various size dynamics of each segment.

For all other exercises a pen is most useful. You may choose pens of various thickness. You may explore and combine various levels of thickness. Larger, darker surfaces can be presented with multiple lines in netlike forms.

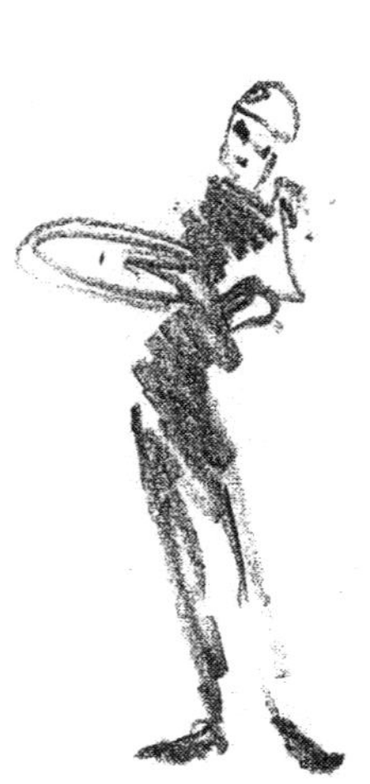

Reticulate lines do not represent modeling or shading. Reticulate lines present larger or smaller surfaces. Observing flat surfaces represents a painting style of the drawing.

The ear is the perfect example for discovering the difference between two styles of drawing:
- with lines as in shaping,
- by depicting surfaces, as in painting.

As the saying goes: a pen is the king of drawing. Explore and discover, if this is truly so. To draw the ear, its geometric qualities are primarily important, as well as the position in relation to the head: whether they are placed close to the head, or more or less protruding. Most important is the surface value of the ear, its positioning and axis in space.

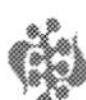

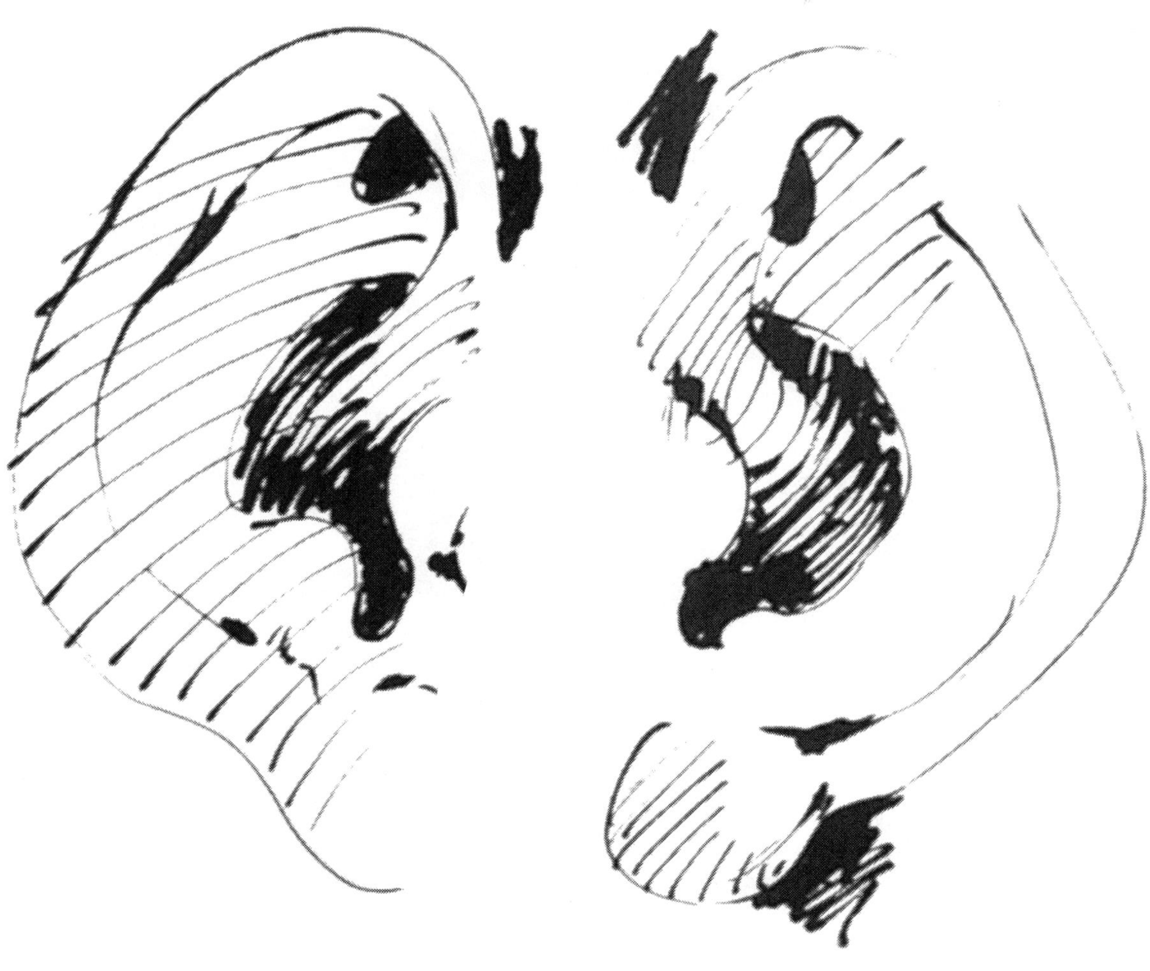

**ALWAYS EXPERIMENT WITH THE LEFT AND RIGHT SIDE
VARIATIONS OF THE EARS**

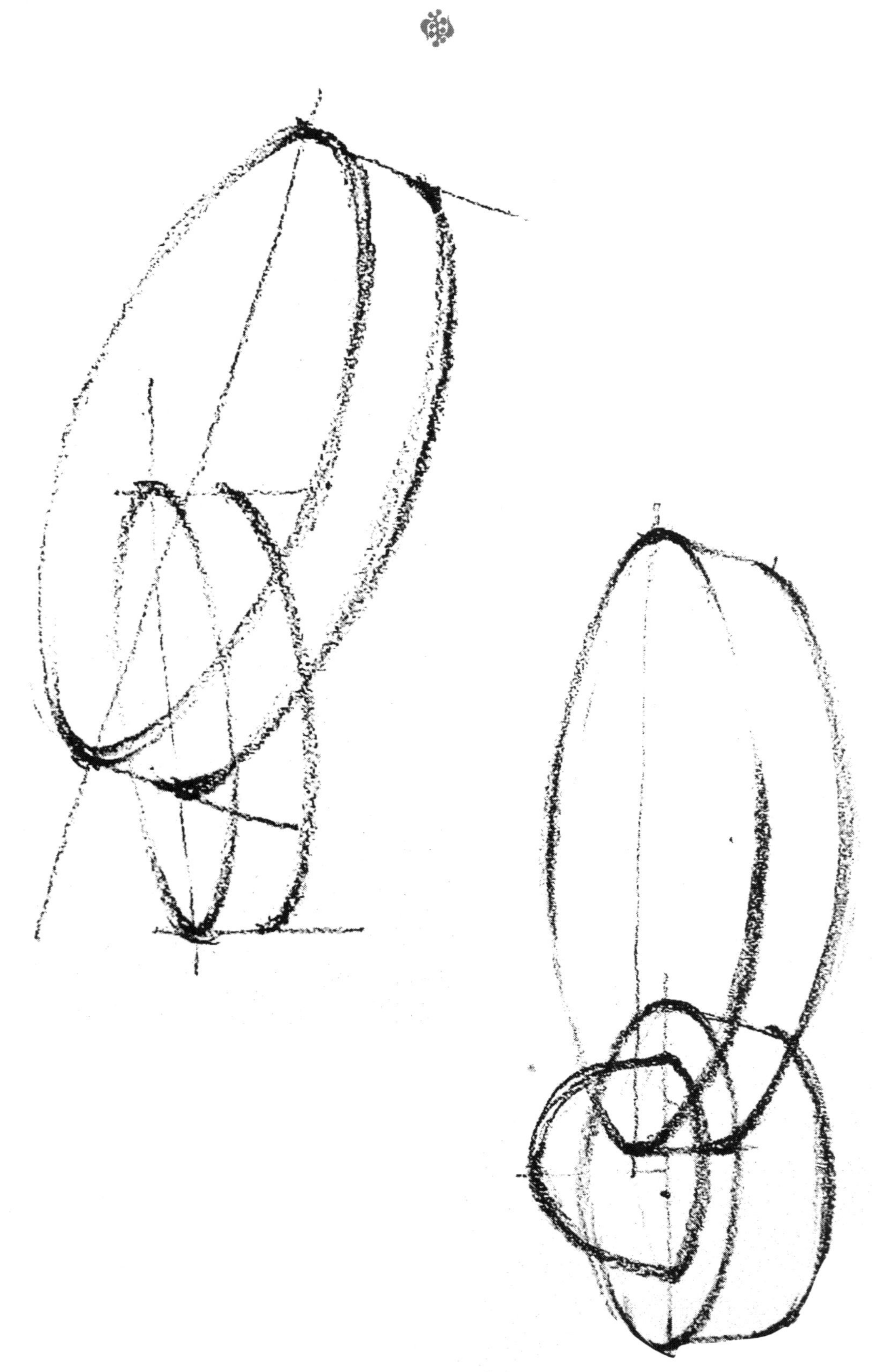

WHEN DRAWING AN EAR, GEOMETRIC APPLICATION MAKES SENSE IN EACH INDIVIDUAL CASE, NONE HAS A GENERALIZED VALUE

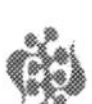

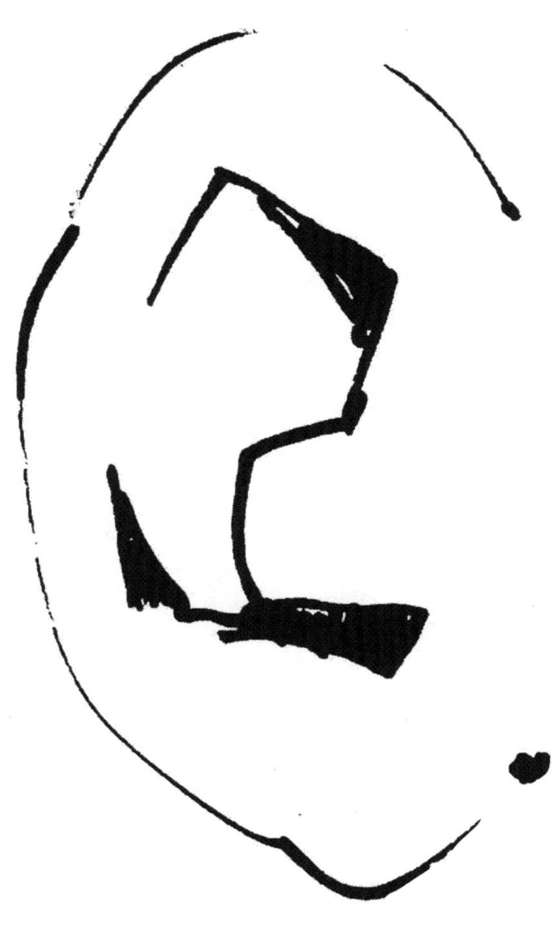

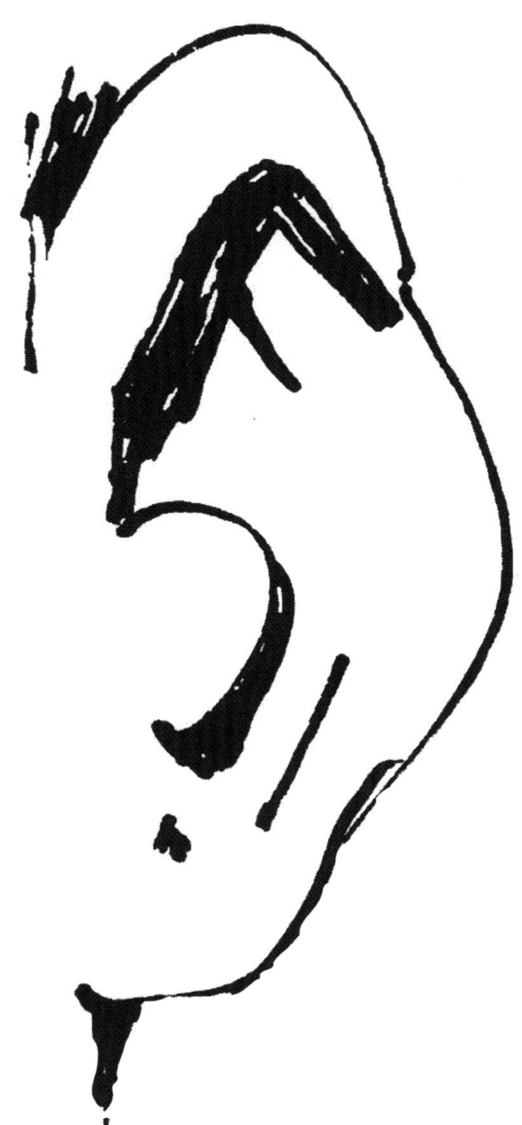

TWO VARIATIONS OF EAR ILLUSTRATION

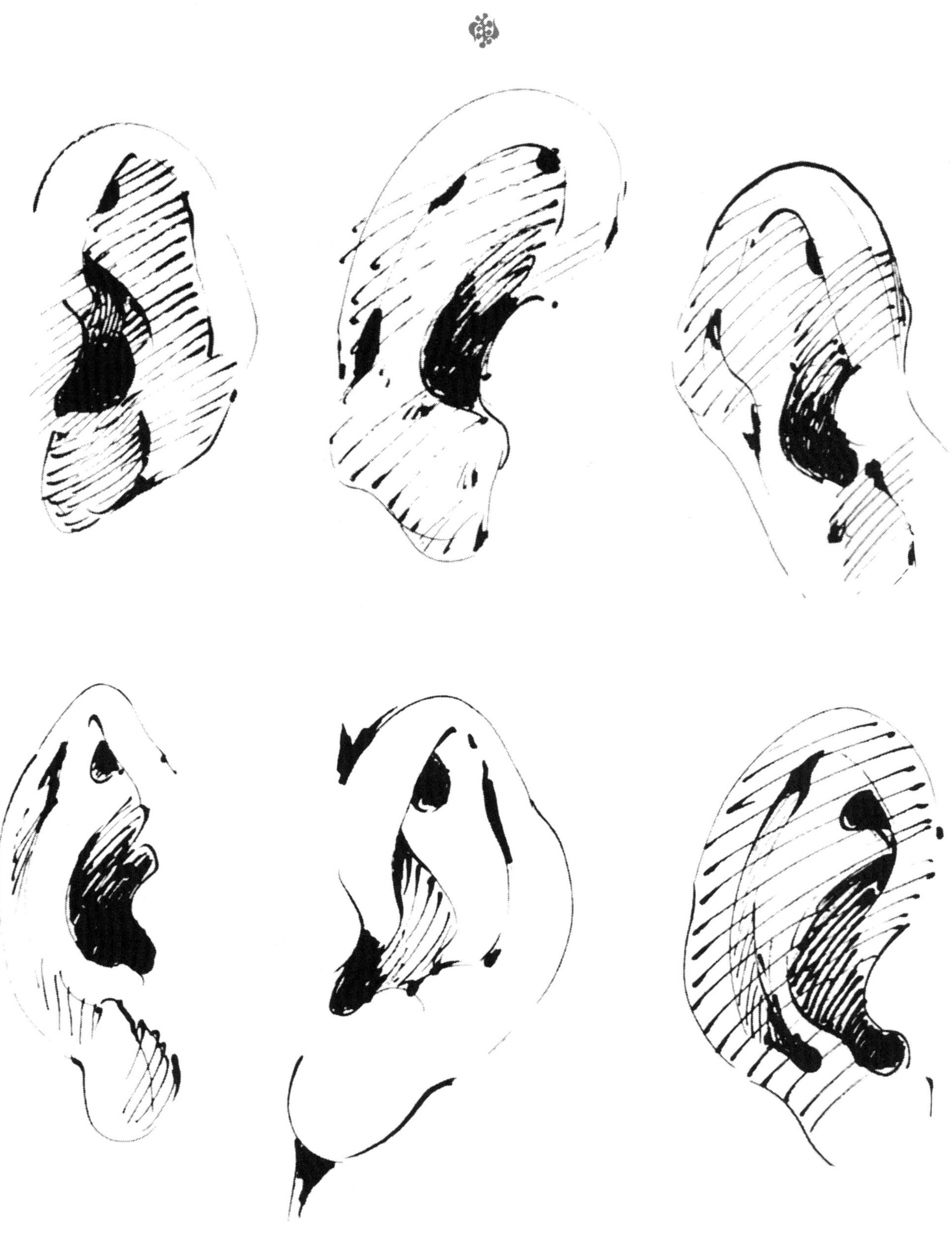

WHEN DRAWING AN EAR CALLIGRAPHIC EXECUTION IS OF GREATEST IMPORTANCE

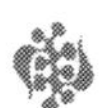

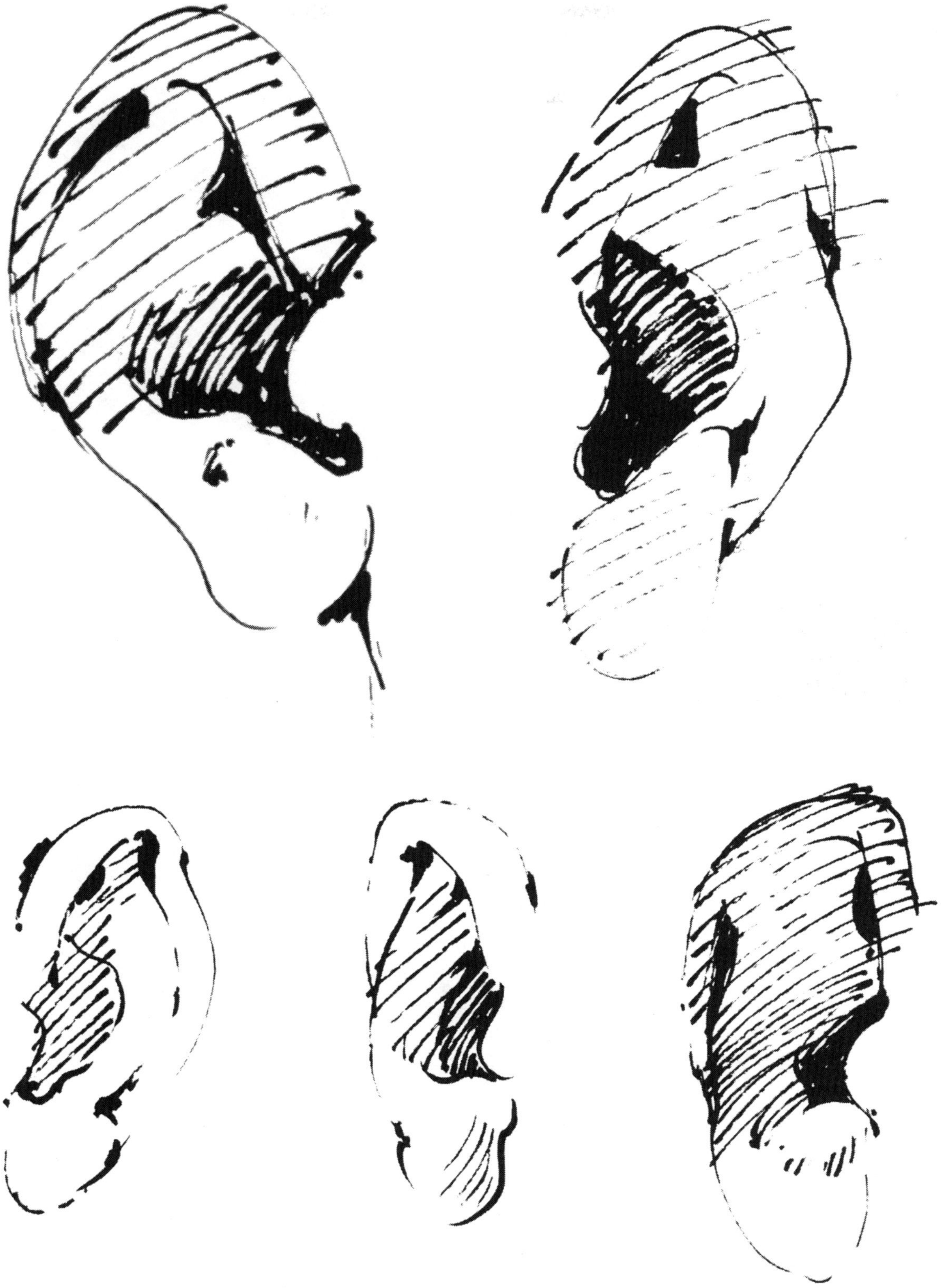

**WHEN DRAWING AN EAR CALLIGRAPHIC EXECUTION
IS OF GREATEST IMPORTANCE**

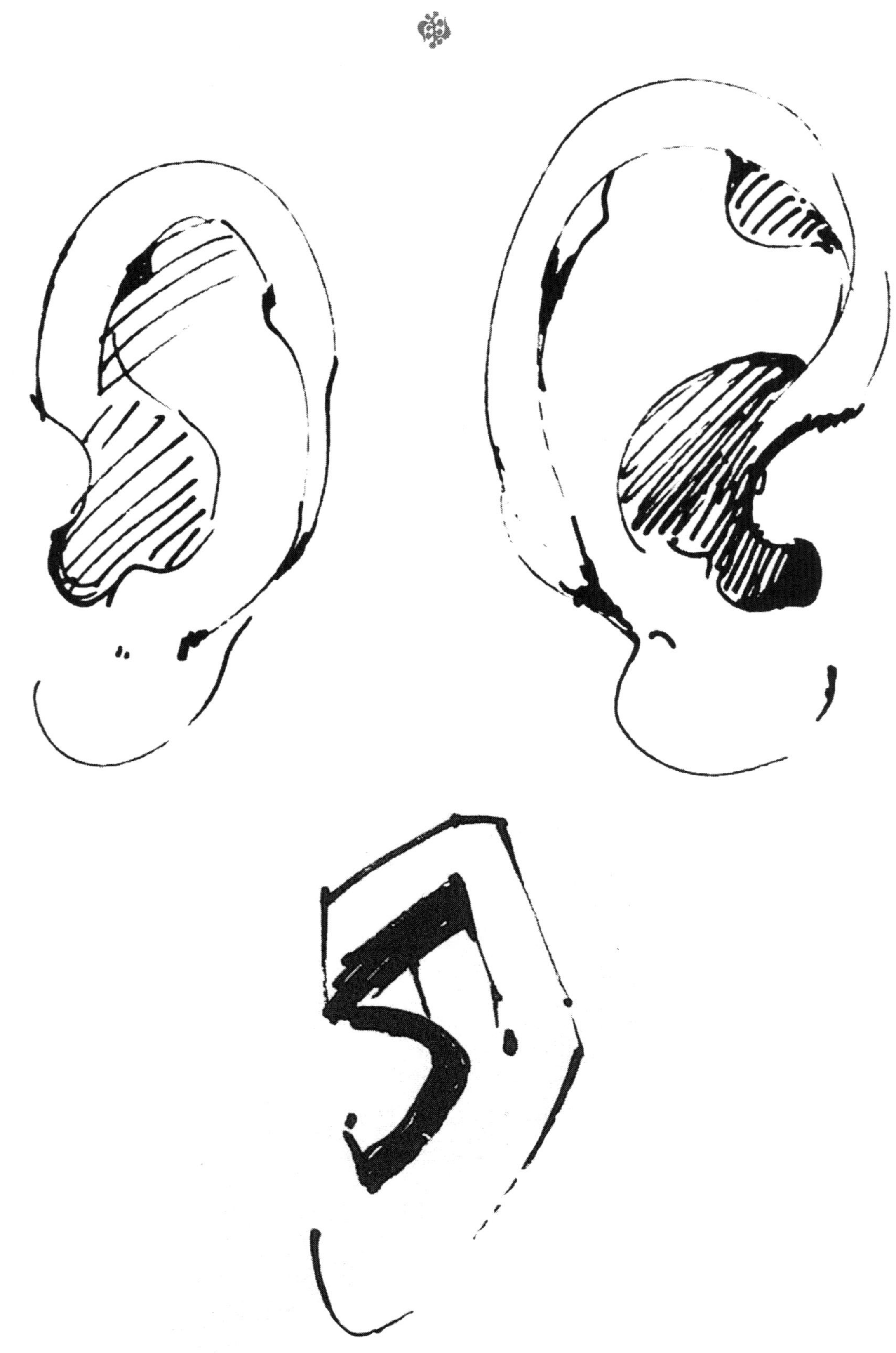

EXPERIMENT WITH STRAIGHT AND CURVED LINES

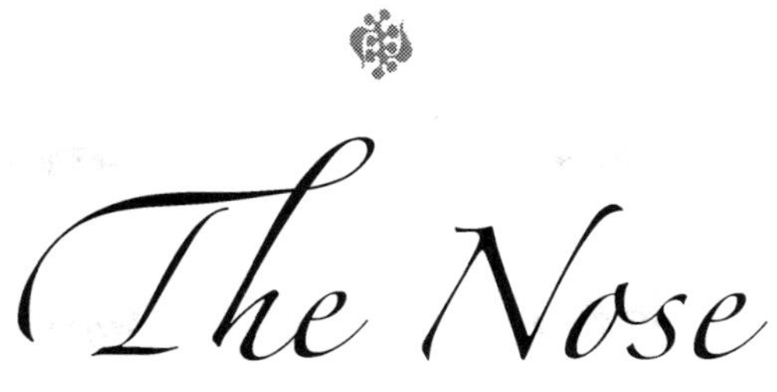

The Nose

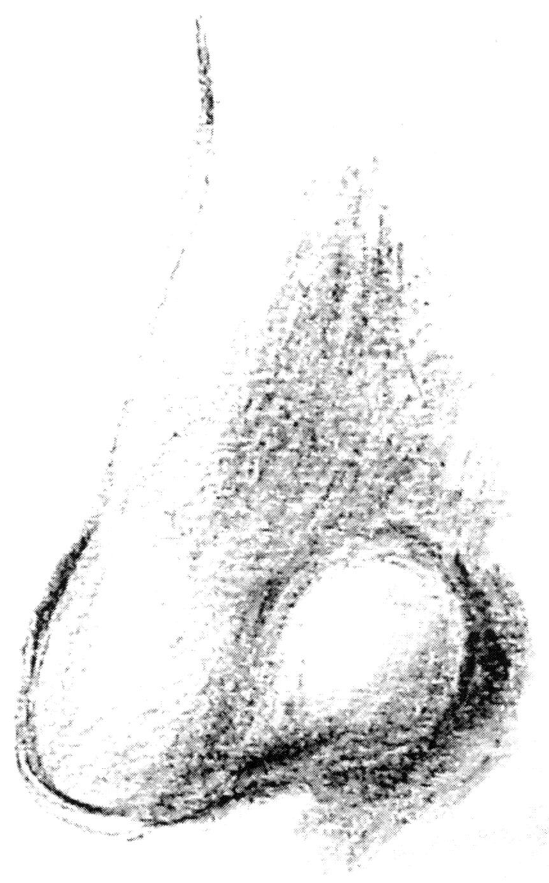

THE NOSE IS A SPECIALLY COMPLEX challenge for drawing or painting. It is a relatively small shape that sticks out with important geometry. In geometrical sense it has three values:

- Geometric value of separate parts; nostrils, nose point and nose bridge with nose root
- Symmetry, visible from various angles and sides
- Geometrical placement of the nose on the face

The best advice for masterfully drawing the nose is to carefully observe such work by great masters, and then studious redrawing. Similarly as one studies chess by repeating the moves of the best chess matches. We develop a sense of the essence.

It is interesting to recognize how it seems that when creating a portrait, there is very little knowledge of how to draw the necessary nose: as a geometrically established shaded spot of the lower part of the nose and an indication of the nostril openings.

We soon realize the challenge of drawing a nose on faces or figure heads that are looking upwards.

We realize that it makes no sense when drawing the nose from the frontal position, to specify and use shading for depicting profile character. It is not essential and may even disturb the final impression.

With a single line we don't accomplish enough, therefore it is important to pay attention to modeling and decision making regarding surface flatness. This is especially important, since it presents the basis for painter's interpretation.

TECHNICAL ADVICE AND SUGGESTIONS

TECHNICAL SUGGESTIONS are especially useful if you are in a dilemma and unable to realize your image. What matters is personal effort and persistent hard work that will help you earn valuable experiences.

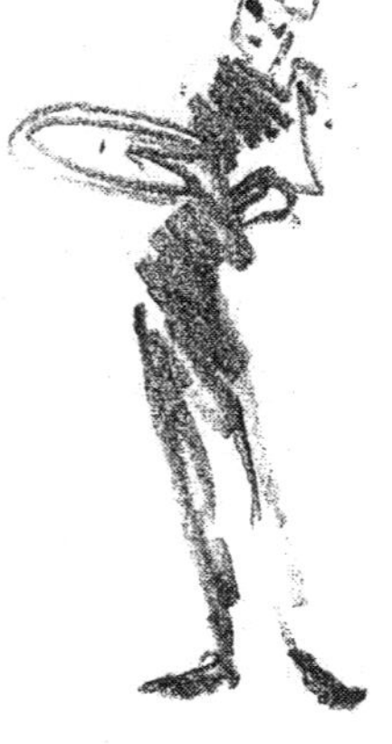

Geometric analysis is drawn with a hard and sharp pencil.

Begin with soft moves. Since the shape is not very demanding, the exercises are a kind of a drawing - calligraphy drill.

The following drawings are almost exclusively based on drawings of Leonardo da Vinci, Michelangelo, Rubens and paintings of Rembrandt, Hals and Velazquez.

Accordingly, select thinner pencils and writing pens for specific drawings. For picturesque patterns, use your own judgement when selecting softer drawing tools.

Experiment in various directions. Gather your own personal experiences. Most of all, learn to take risks.

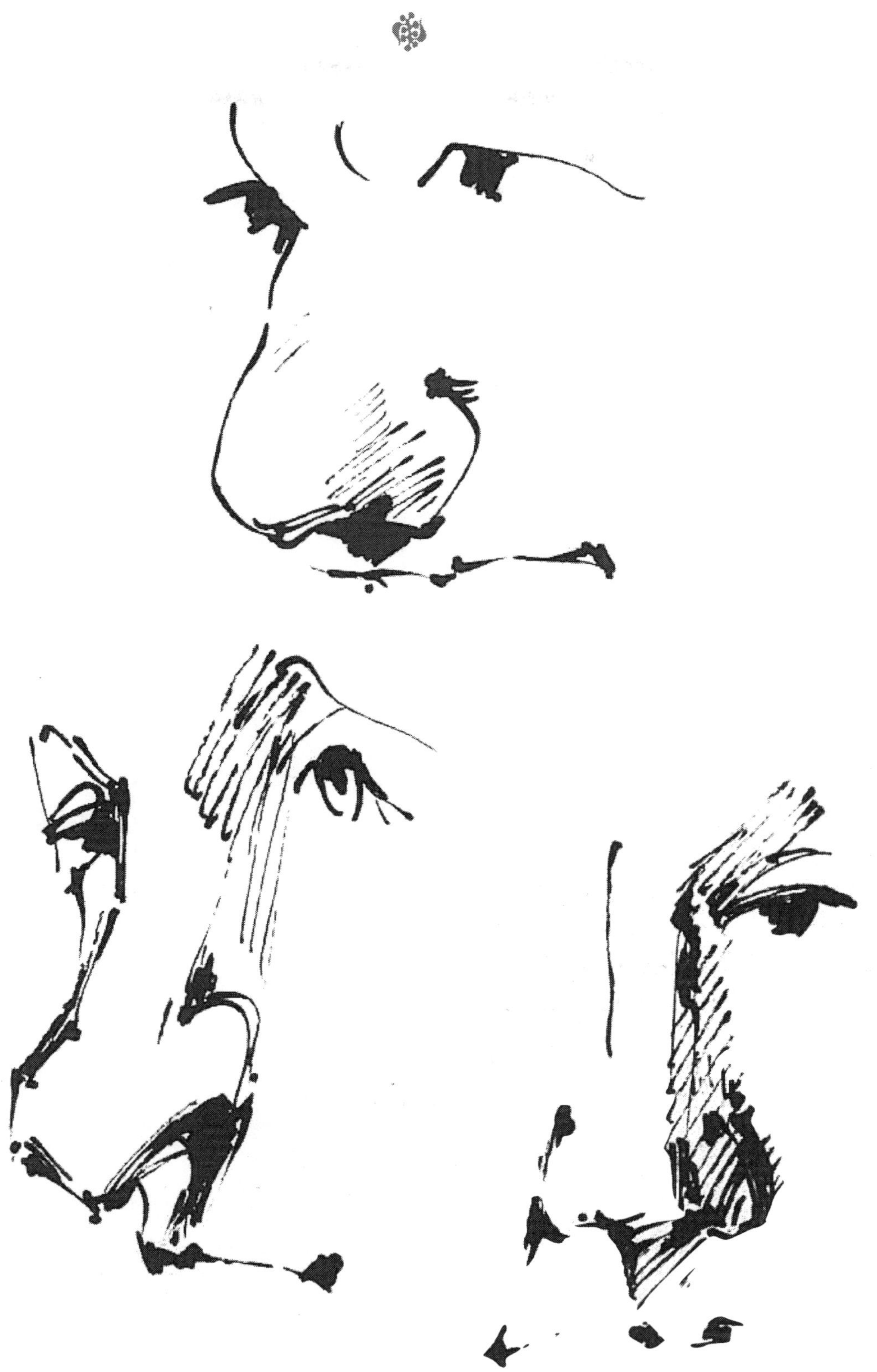

ALWAYS TAKE INTO CONSIDERATION THE SHAPE OF THE ENTIRE HEAD
OR AT THE LEAST FACIAL SURFACE,
WHEN DECIDING THE POSITIONING OF THE NOSE ON THE FACE

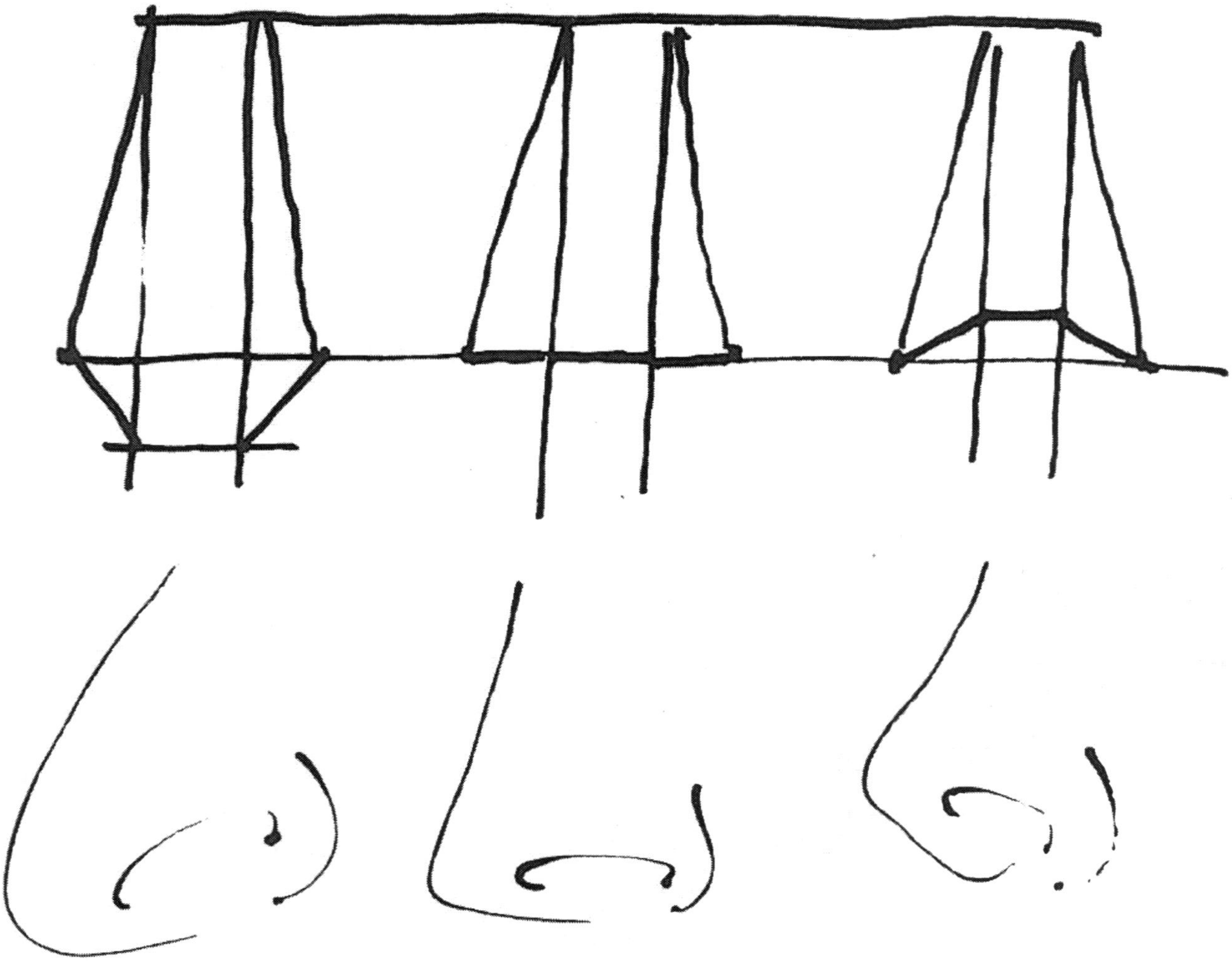

THE NOSE IS STRUCTURED WITH ROUND AND ANGULAR SHAPES,

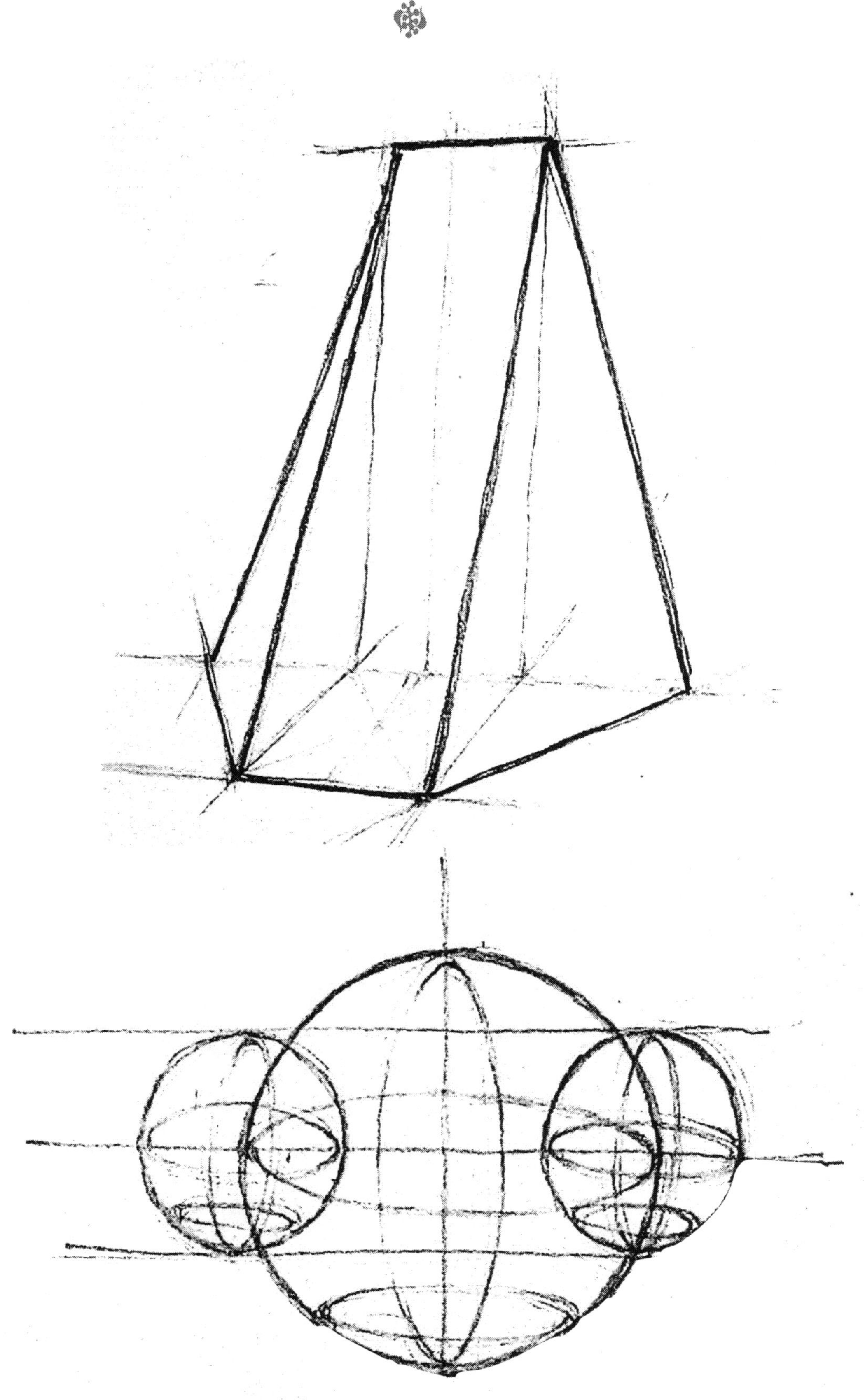

TWO EXAMPLES OF GEOMETRICAL ANALYSIS OF THE NOSE

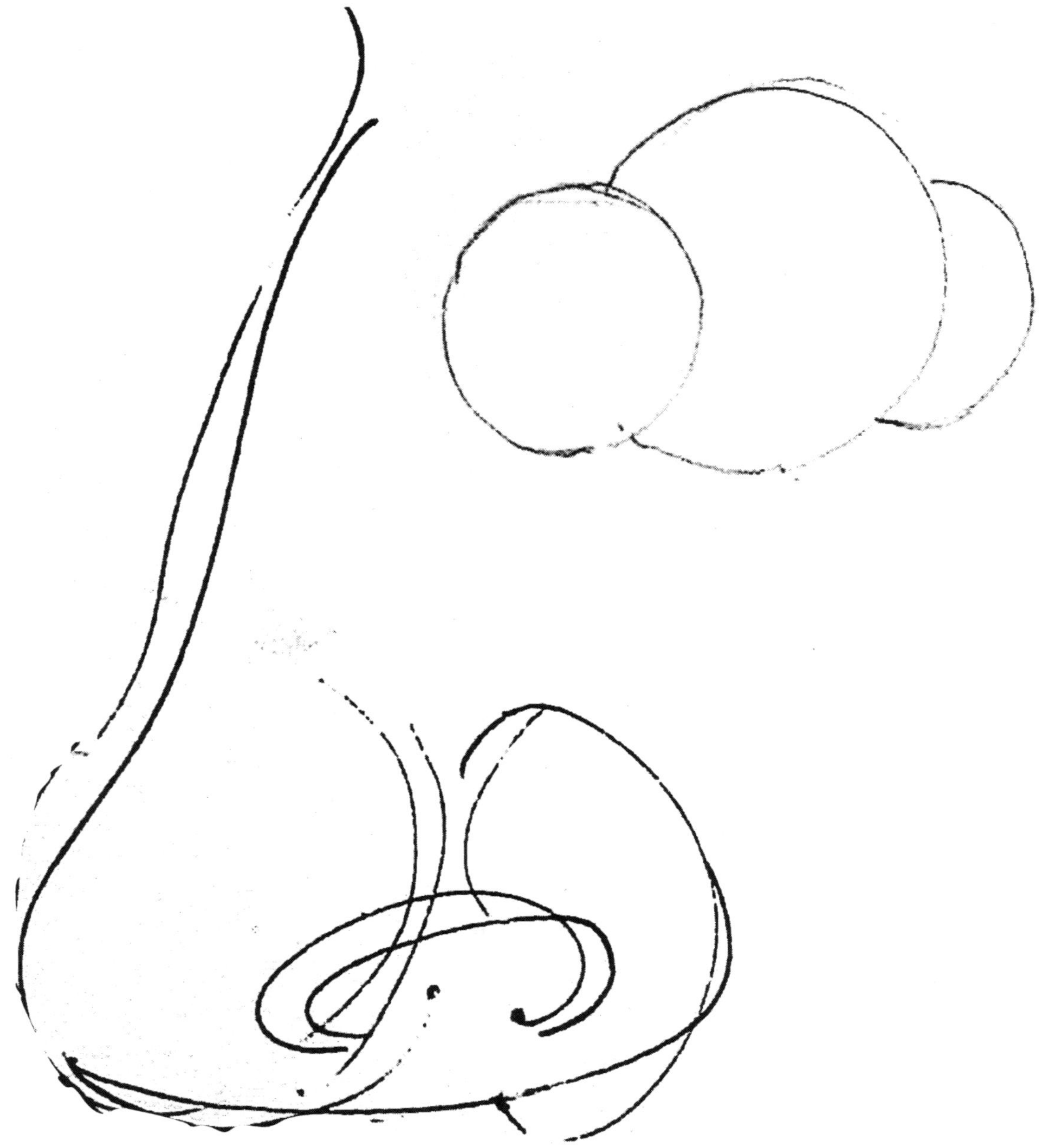

CONSTRUCTION OF ROUND SHAPES

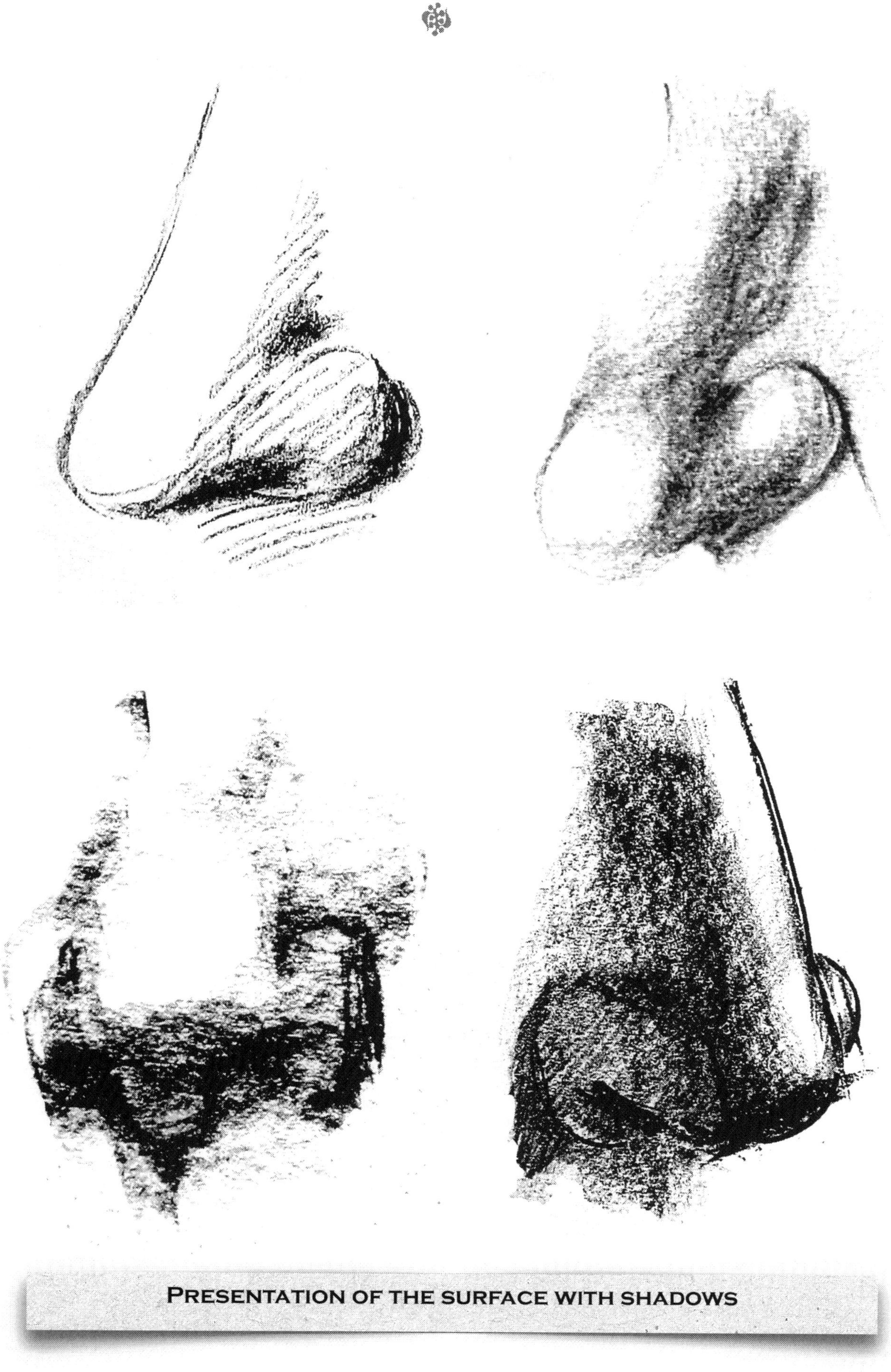

PRESENTATION OF THE SURFACE WITH SHADOWS

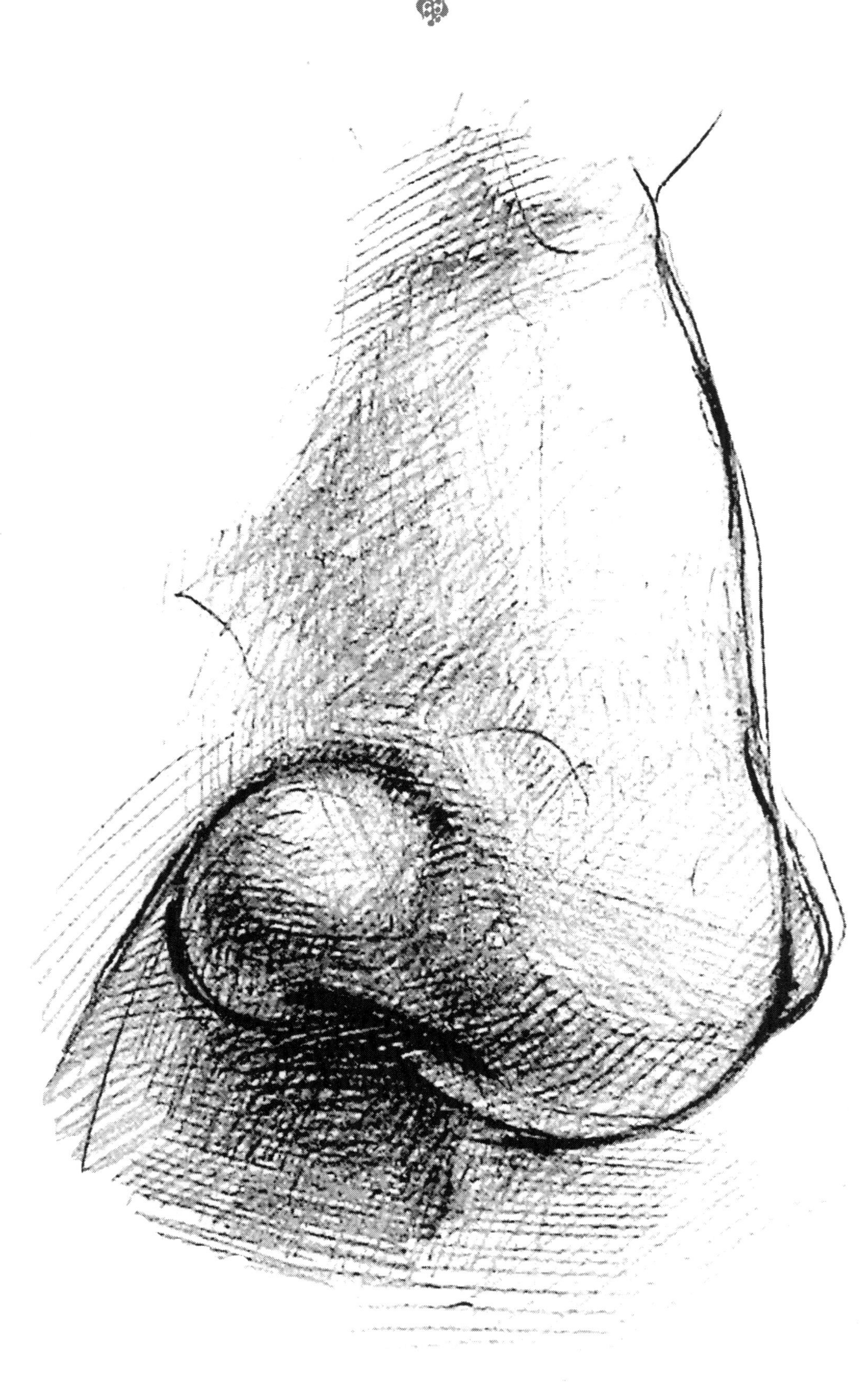

AN EXAMPLE OF SHADING WITH RICH TRANSITIONS

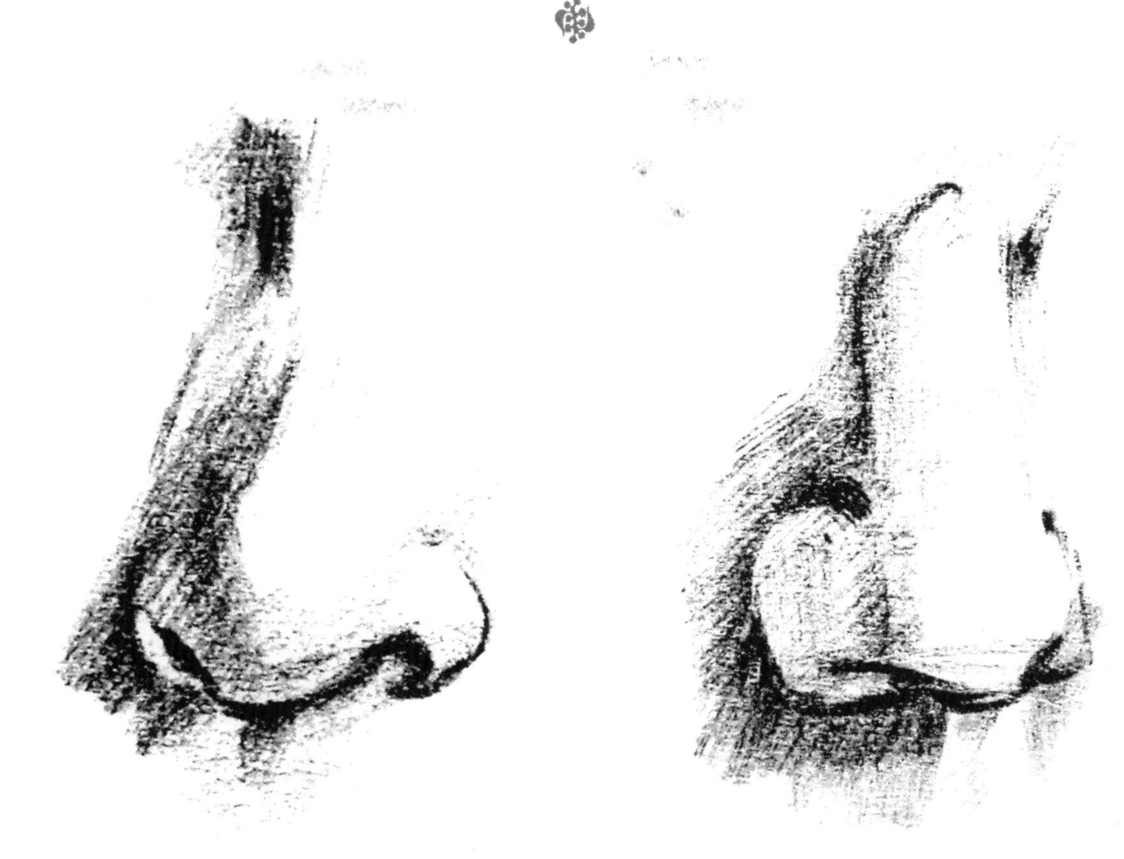

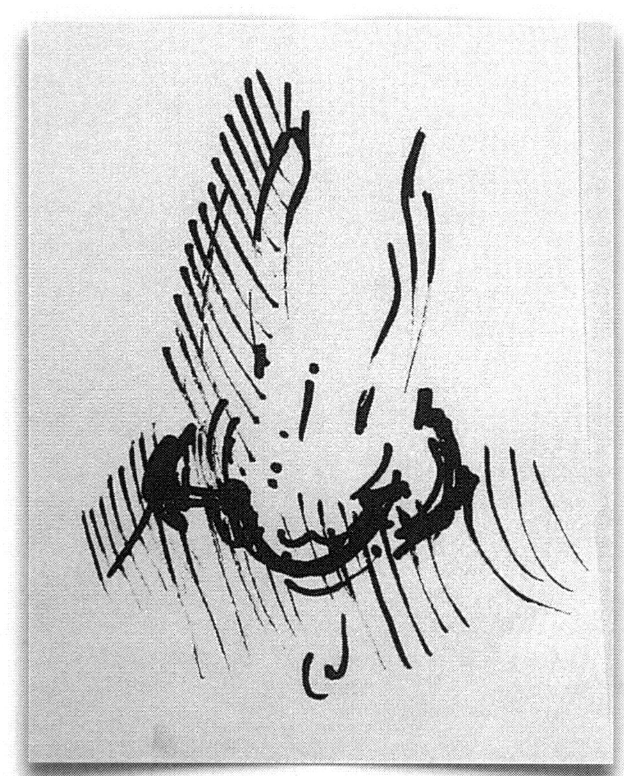

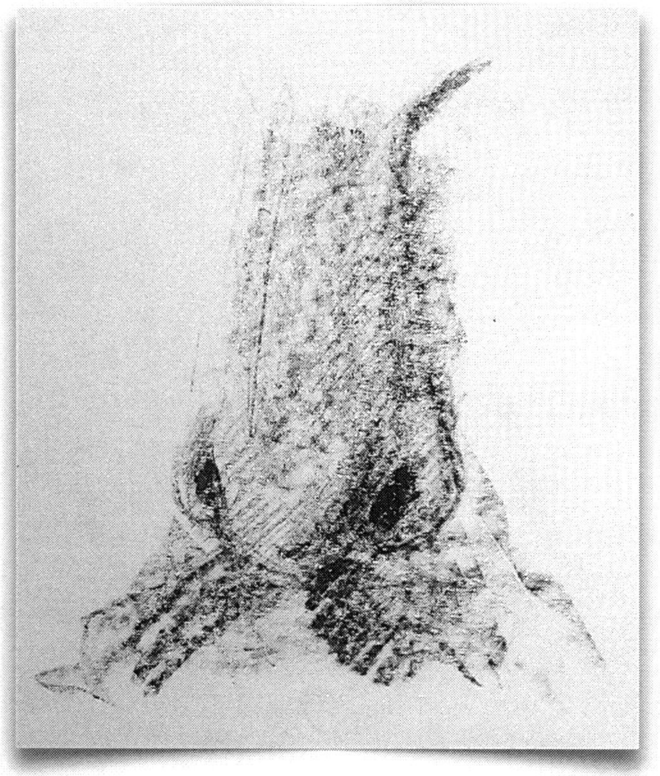

IF THE LINES DO NOT SUFFICE, SHADOWING WILL HELP

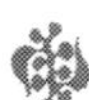

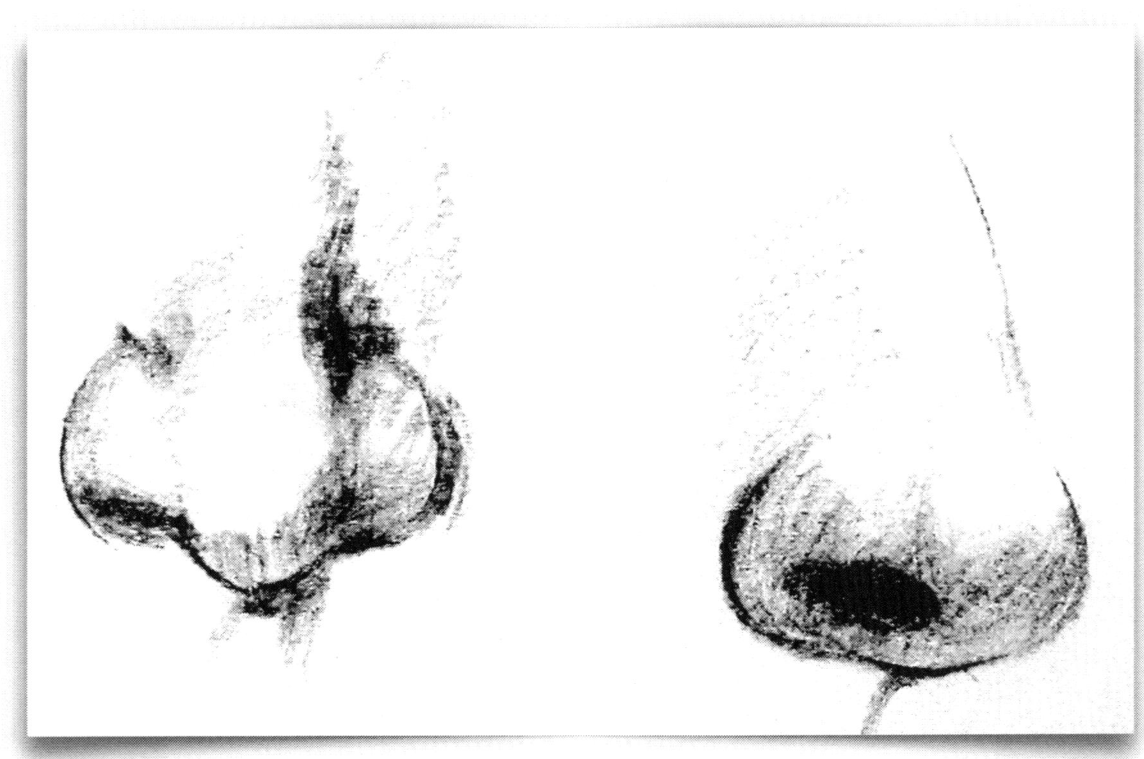

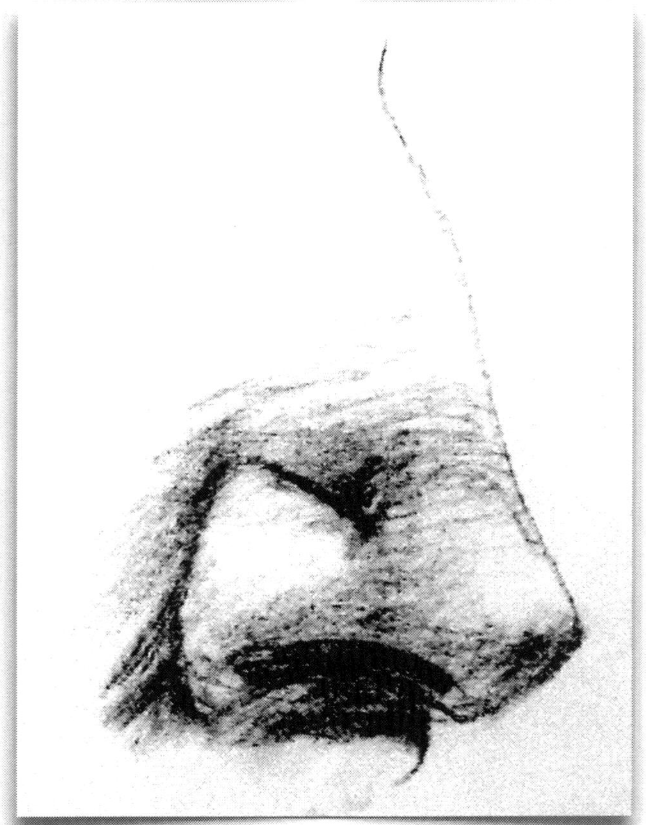

**IF THE NOSE IS VERY PROMINENT
IT REQUIRES DETAILED ATTENTION**

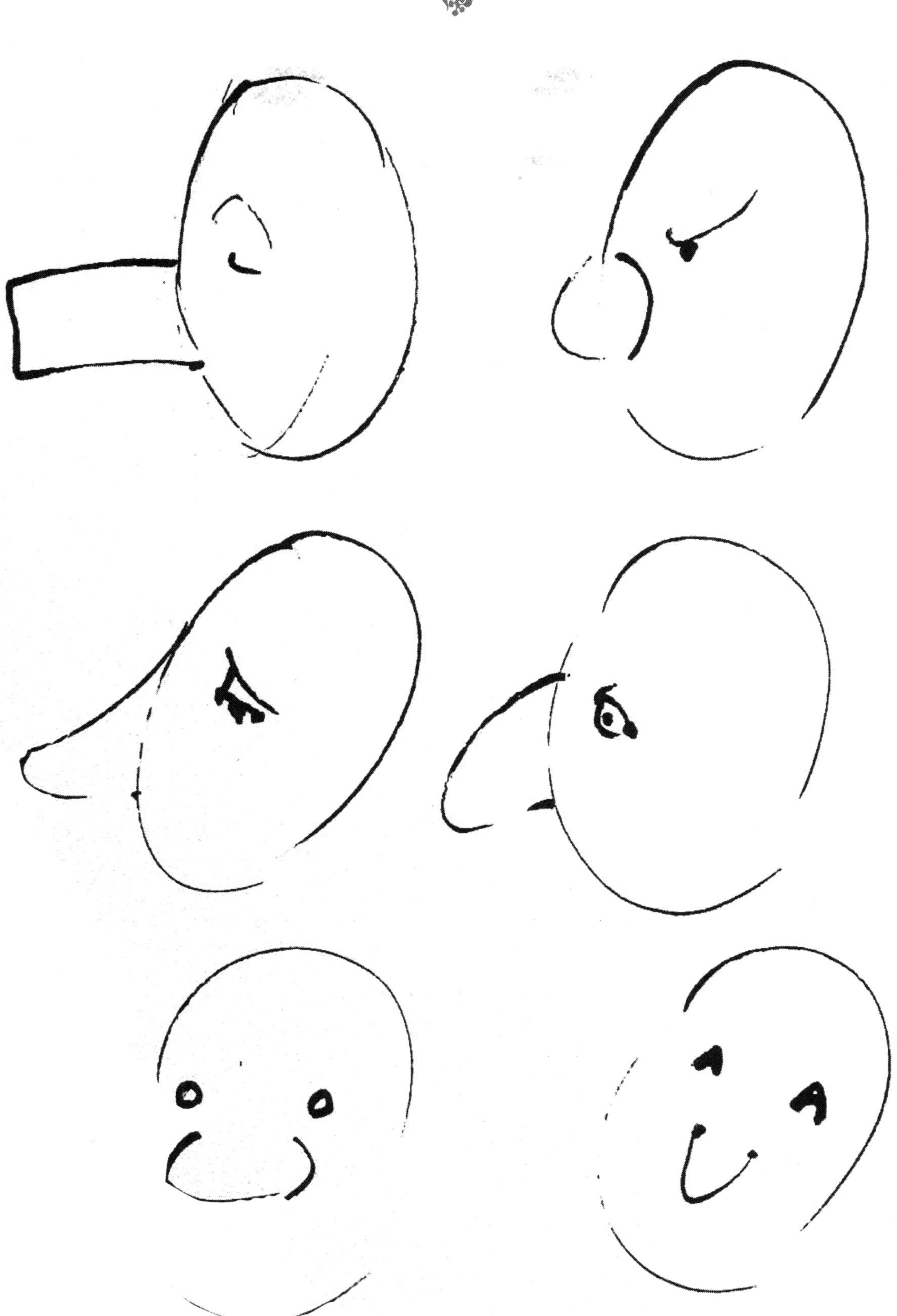

CARICATURED POSITIONING AND CHARACTER OF THE NOSE

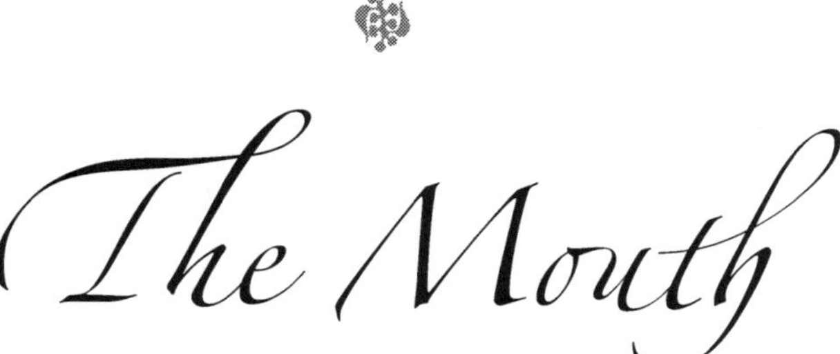

The Mouth

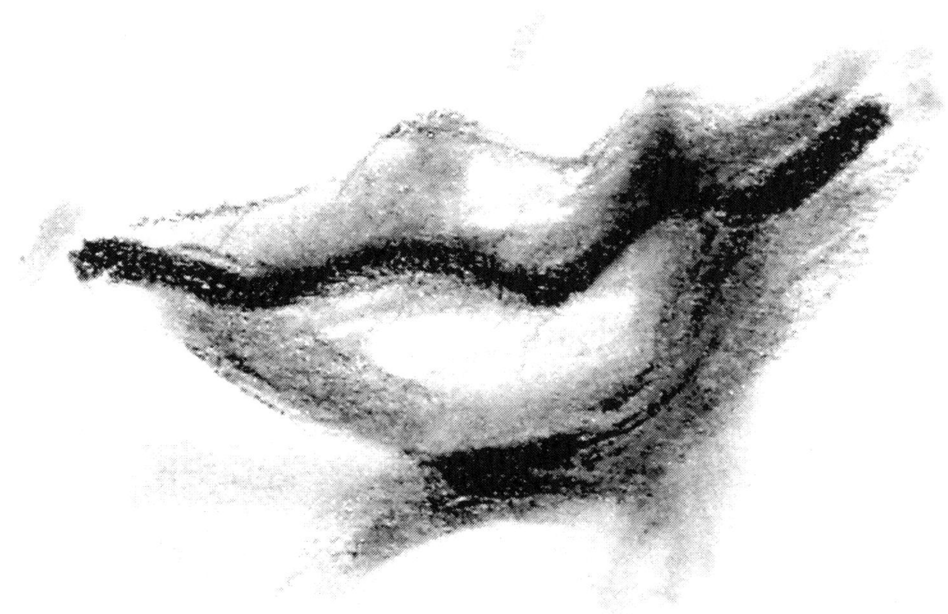

THE FORMAT ESSENCE OF THE MOUTH is the composite of two symmetrical shapes, the upper and lower lip. We can depict this composite with angular or rounded shapes. It is also possible to depict it with a simple line that represents the meeting of these two shapes. There're endless variations of the mouth, but always follow this principle.

In case the mouth is open or slightly apart, a redefinition of the newly created shape is needed. This represents a new challenge.

Especially demanding is drawing of the mouth from various aspects and angles.
You must take into consideration the perspective.
The roundness of the jawline plays an important part on this.
All of this, in addition to the fact that the upper and lower lip don't meet in a straight line but create a gentle wave.

Understanding these facts does not mean you have masters this complex problem. It is beneficial to know this especially when evaluating drawings and paintings of various masters, some good some better.

In order to gain and master the ability to draw, the decisive factors are hours and hours of persistent practice despite occasional failures.

While one can somewhat hide their inability or laziness to draw the nose or the ears, this is not possible with the mouth.

Especially in portraits the mouth is a true test of ones abilities and clear proof of ones drawing mastery. Together with the eyes, they play the main role in presenting a person's character.

TECHNICAL ADVICE AND SUGGESTIONS

W HEN DRAWING GEOMETRICAL REPRESENTATIONS, select a sharp-pointed pencil that offers accuracy and analytical style of drawing.

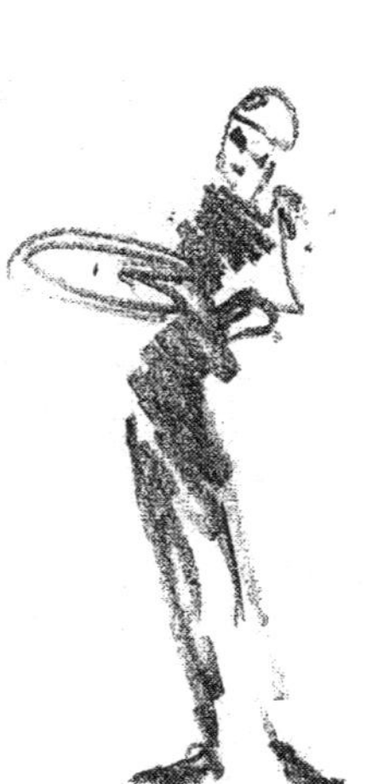

When practicing less accentuated geometry and representing the main depiction with simple scarce lines, you may use also very soft pencils or charcoal.

With changes to pencil pressure at mouth corners and mouth's center, you will achieve interesting effects. Observe this new value.

When practicing, chose between two options:
Shaping and shading or interpretation of flat surfaces.

Using a pen may also prove very interesting. You have a choice to try various thicknesses.

Especially demanding is the mouth's view from the side. Don't shy away from it.

With regular and dedicated practice you will master also these drawing test with ease.

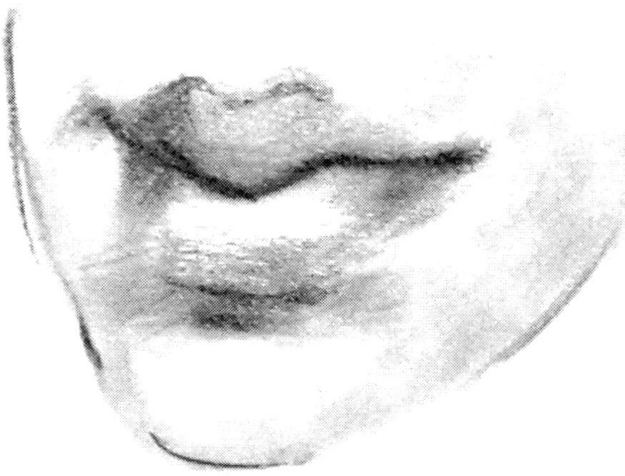

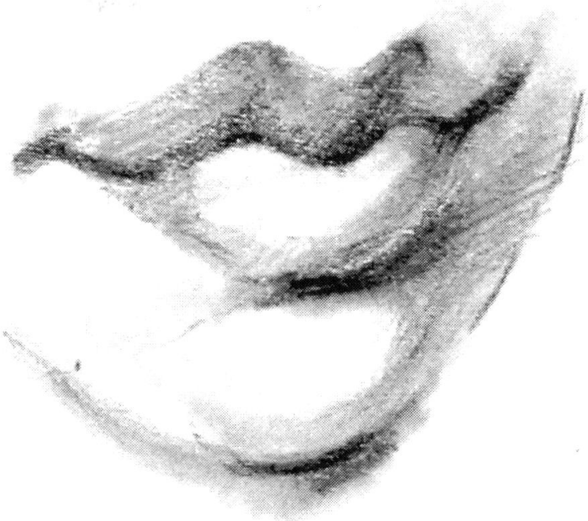

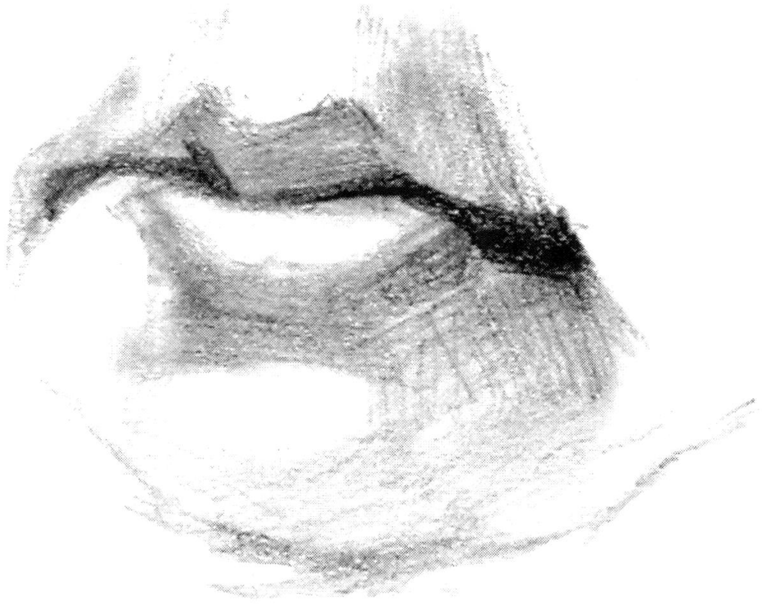

THE MAIN GEOMETRIC VALUE OF THE MOUTH, REPRESENTED WITH SOFT SHADING AND CLEAR SURFACES

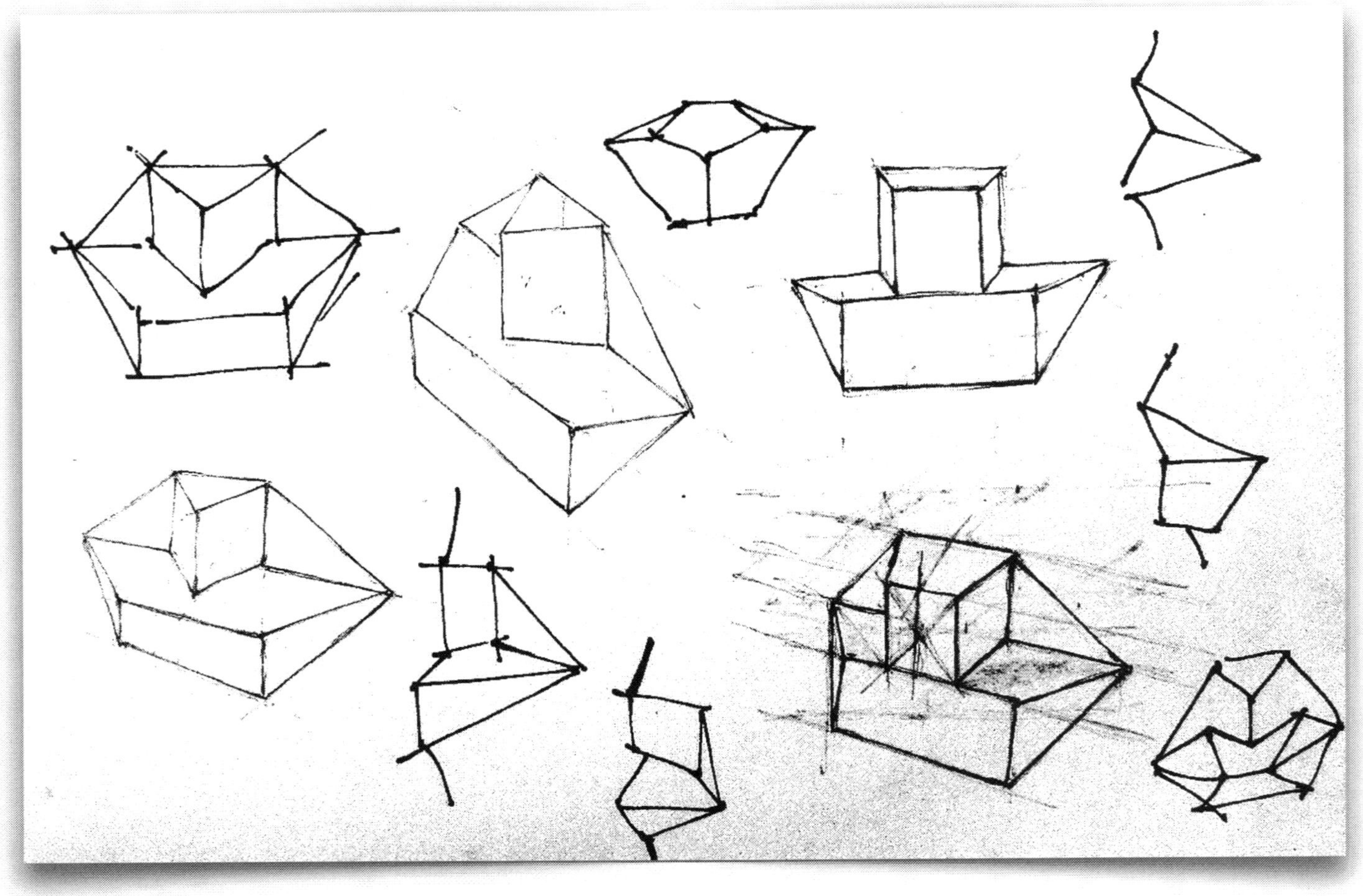

VARIOUS GEOMETRIC ANALYSIS OF THE MOUTH

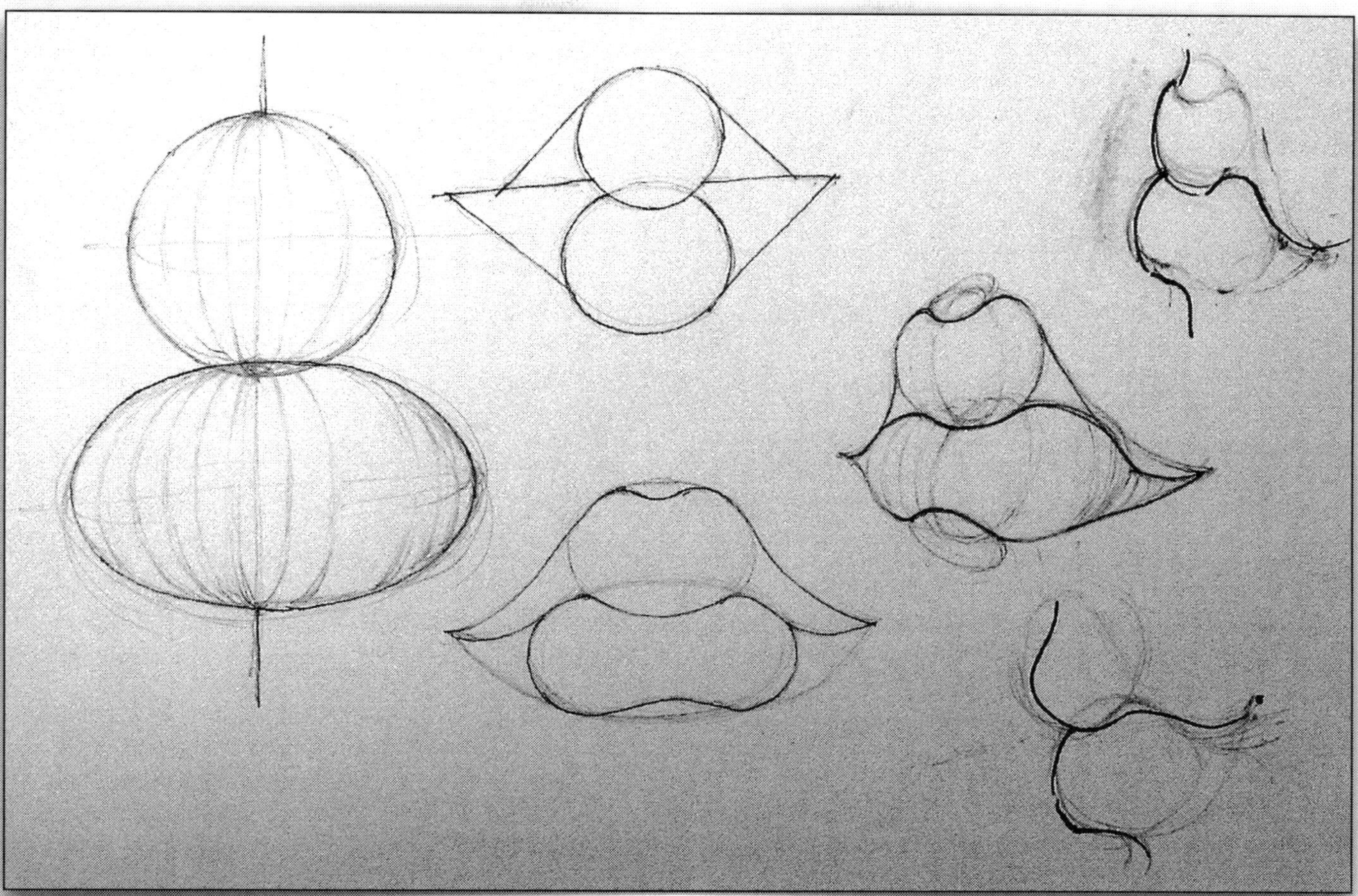

ANALYSIS OF THE MOUTH WITH ROUNDED SHAPES.
EXAMPLES OF FRONTAL AND SIDE VIEW

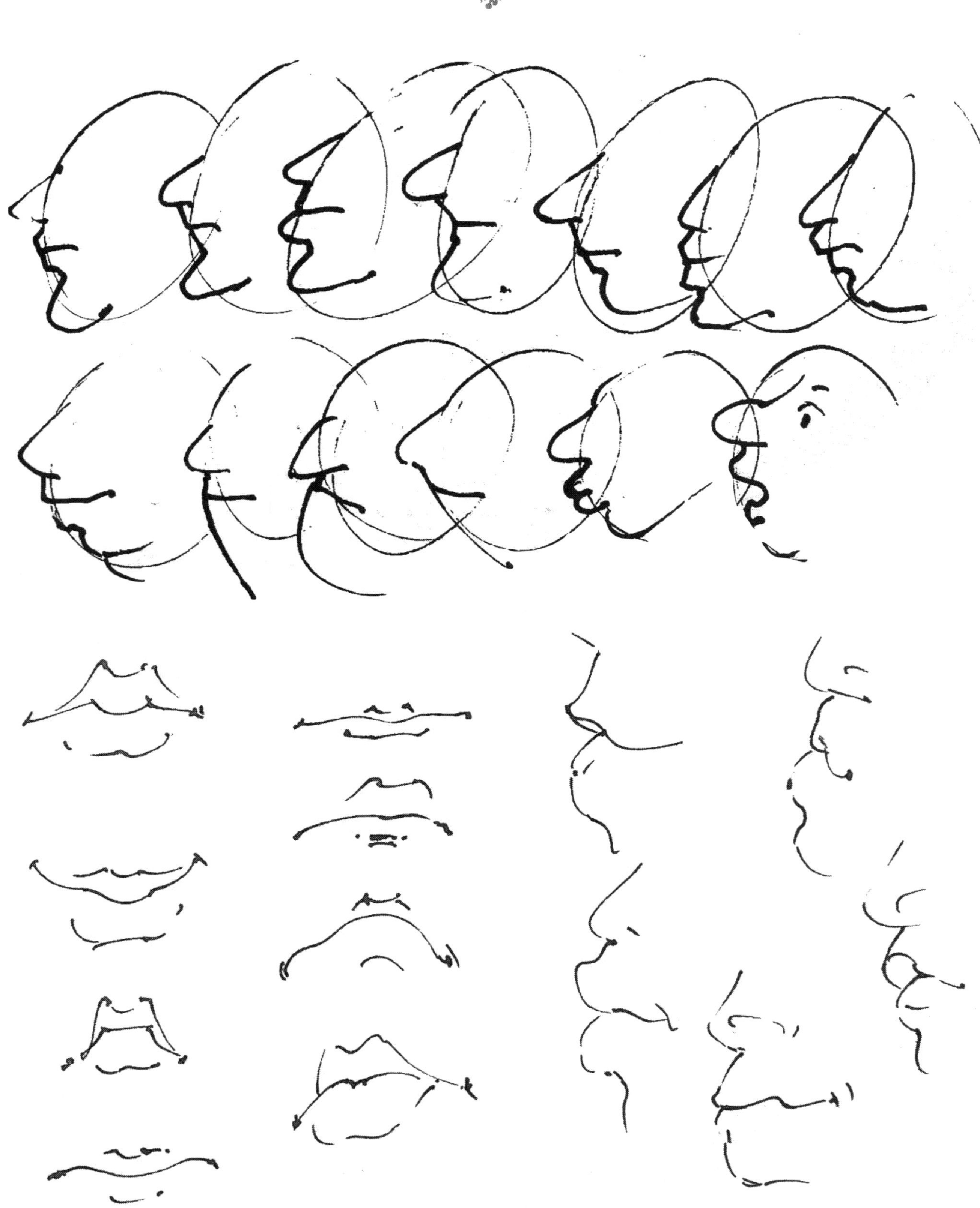

CARICATURED POSITIONING AND CHARACTER OF THE MOUTH

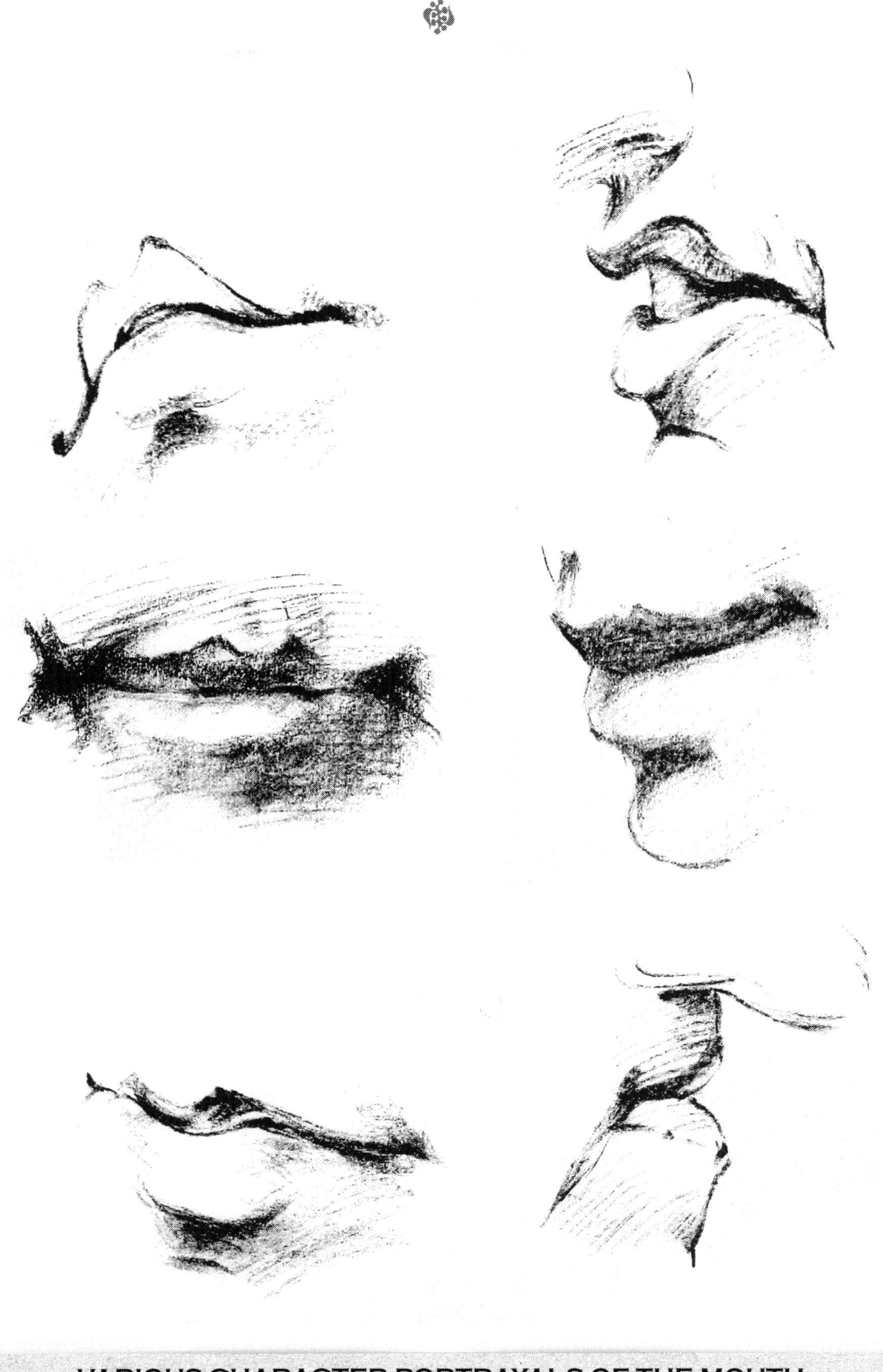

VARIOUS CHARACTER PORTRAYALS OF THE MOUTH

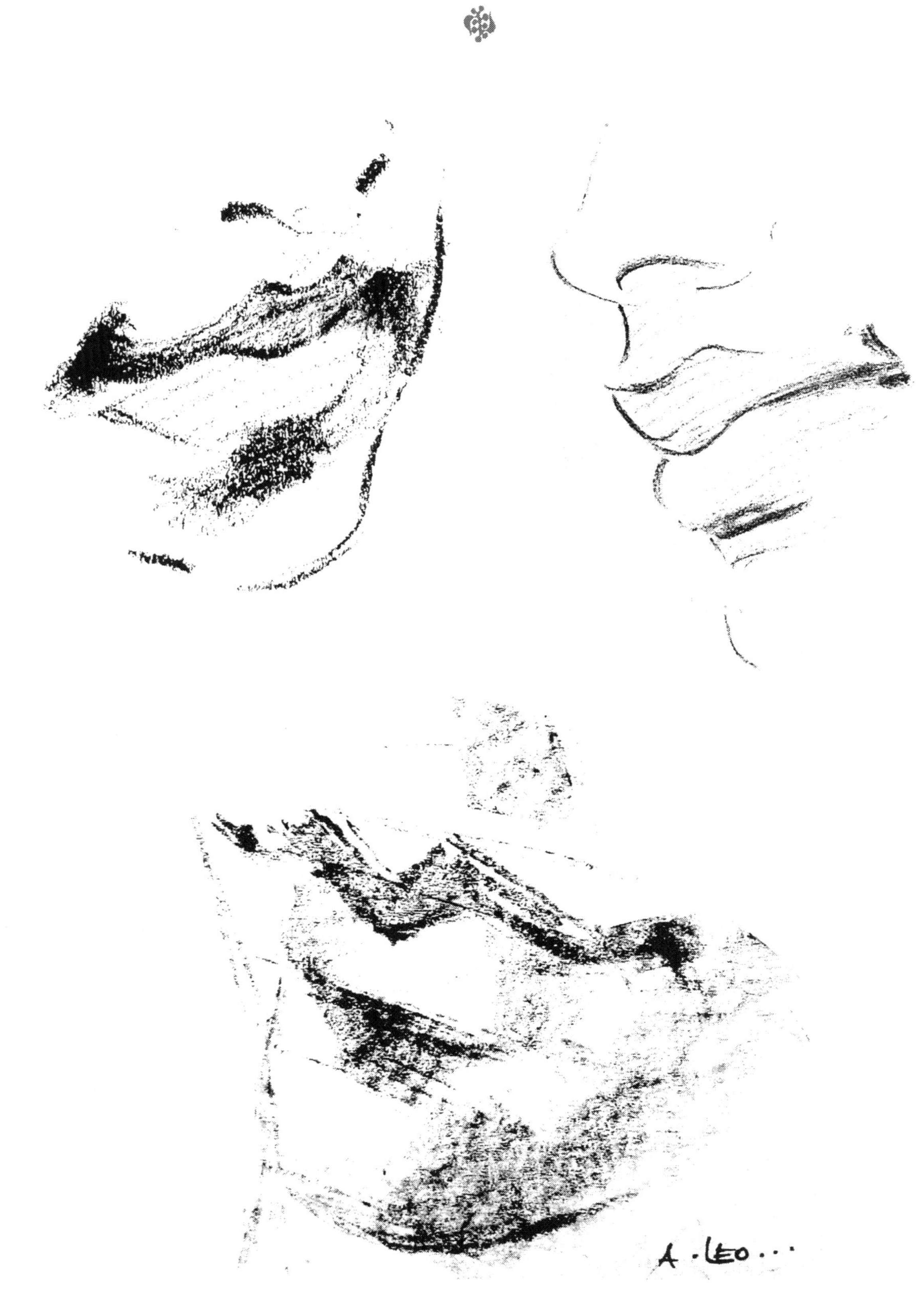

VARIOUS VIEWS OF THE MOUTH

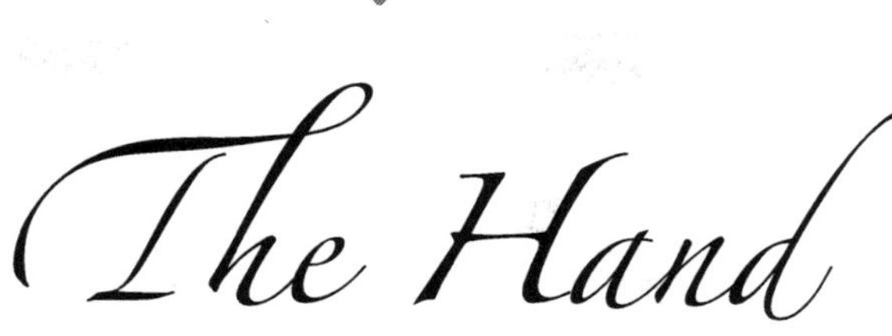

The Hand

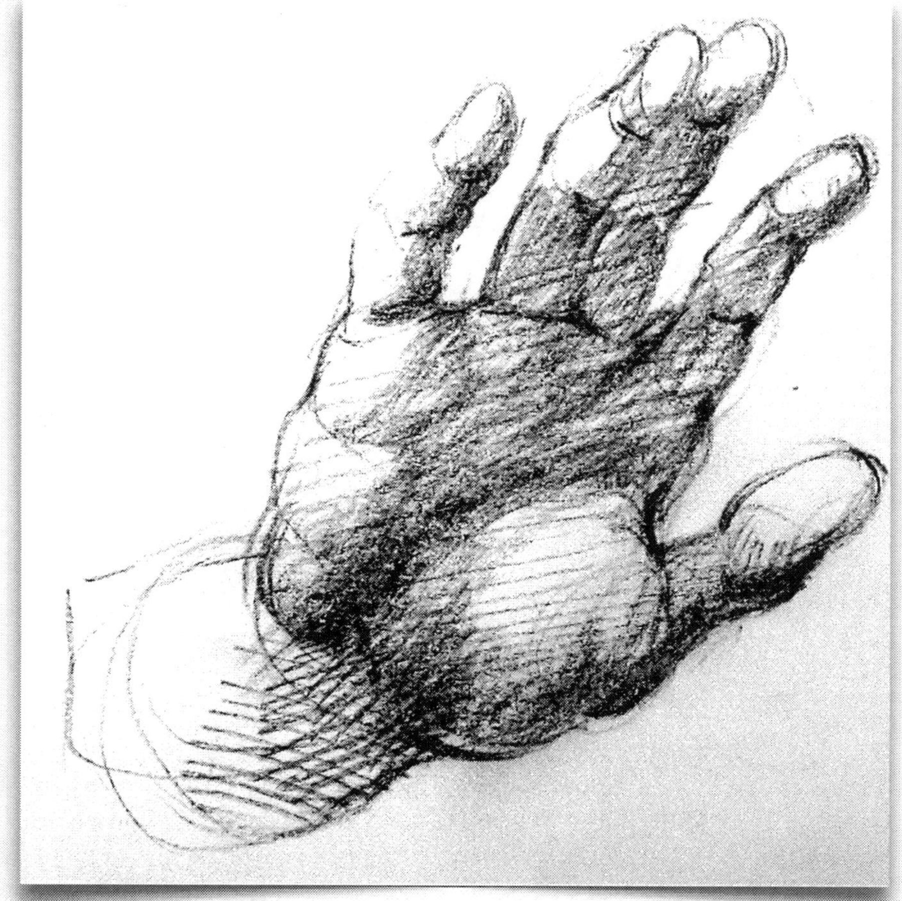

THIS IS THE MOST DEMANDING chapter for drawing and painting of human body. Nevertheless, don't underestimate yourself or overestimate the masters. The hand is a complex of shapes that are difficult to simplify. You have to take into consideration geometrical and anatomical interior values. The method of drawing a hand based on deep observation is successful only in case one has excellent drawing abilities. More reliable is the path of dividing it into separate geometrical shapes.

All my presented drawings of geometric and analytical character are from ,my past preoccupation with the drawing process. They rested in my attic for the last 45 years ,but are still quite useful. Surely you've heard of the old master Van Dyke. Take a look at his portraits especially the brilliantly depicted hands. He used the same hand model for most of them., so we see always the same hands in various poses. The artist obviously did not wish to appease the demands of spoiled and wealthy clients to accommodate the depiction of hands to their character. The hands reveal someone's character just like the face; such as beautiful, interesting or unattractive.

All the way to the beginning of the 17th century the same rule of great drawing applied also to painting of the hands, from virtuoso Botticelli, Leonardo, Michelangelo and Rubens. Excellent drawing completed with shaping and shading. Technically demanding, but risk free. After these seemingly unreachable ideals appeared Velazquez. He was a painter that mastered all technical secrets undisturbed, unaffected and unconfused by works of geniuses before him. He demonstrated the differences between various drawing values and their use in painting. Rembrandt was equally undisturbed in comparison to geniuses from the past, pure painting technique attracted him more than virtuoso drawing. Both of these artists represent interest in painting that were different from previous achievements. Not better or more advanced, just different.

The following drawings are patterned after paintings of acknowledged masters. Some are from the times of the "old guard." Others represent how the painting approach deals with drawing; flatness and the value of outline, and the shading qualities in drawing. All of them take into consideration the essential geometrical construction that was demonstrated in the first drawings. One needs to be familiar with this. Without knowledge of the essence - not just familiarity, but actual knowledge - it is useless to discuss quality or progress.

TECHNICAL ADVICE AND SUGGESTIONS

A LL PREVIOUS CHAPTERS accentuated the variety and diversity of drawing tools. Next emphasis was between differentiation of shading and shaping of round shapes and the flat interpretation of various forms.

It is important for understanding the difference between a line and flat kind of pictorial interpretation. Flat kind of pictorial interpretation facilitates so called values: the flat values of color and various degrees of light and shadow. These are the preliminary conditions for the painting of light and color. This is the condition for adding layers of opaque colors in the technique of oil painting. This is the basic difference between aquarelle and watercolor technique, which is available only in transparent colors.

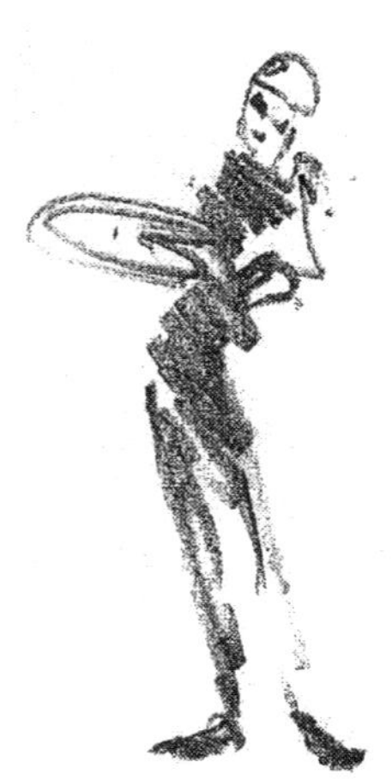

Interesting is also the value of shading in combined forms, such as the hands.
Experiment this value of shading as in silhouette; change the positions of your hands when lit from sideways and discover the structural value of the silhouettes. Try to do this with both hands. An exceptional example are the hands of Velazquez's court dwarfs. Of greatest value is the usual advice and encouragement for tenacious and repetitive practice, until you uncover your own satisfactory solution. If suggested solution feel insufficient, you may discover your own. Those carry the greatest value. The final piece of advice is almost a secret: even a well drawn hand in a painting doesn't suffice, it requires attention and depiction of the surface as well. Observe this aspect and give it a try.

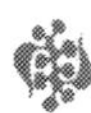

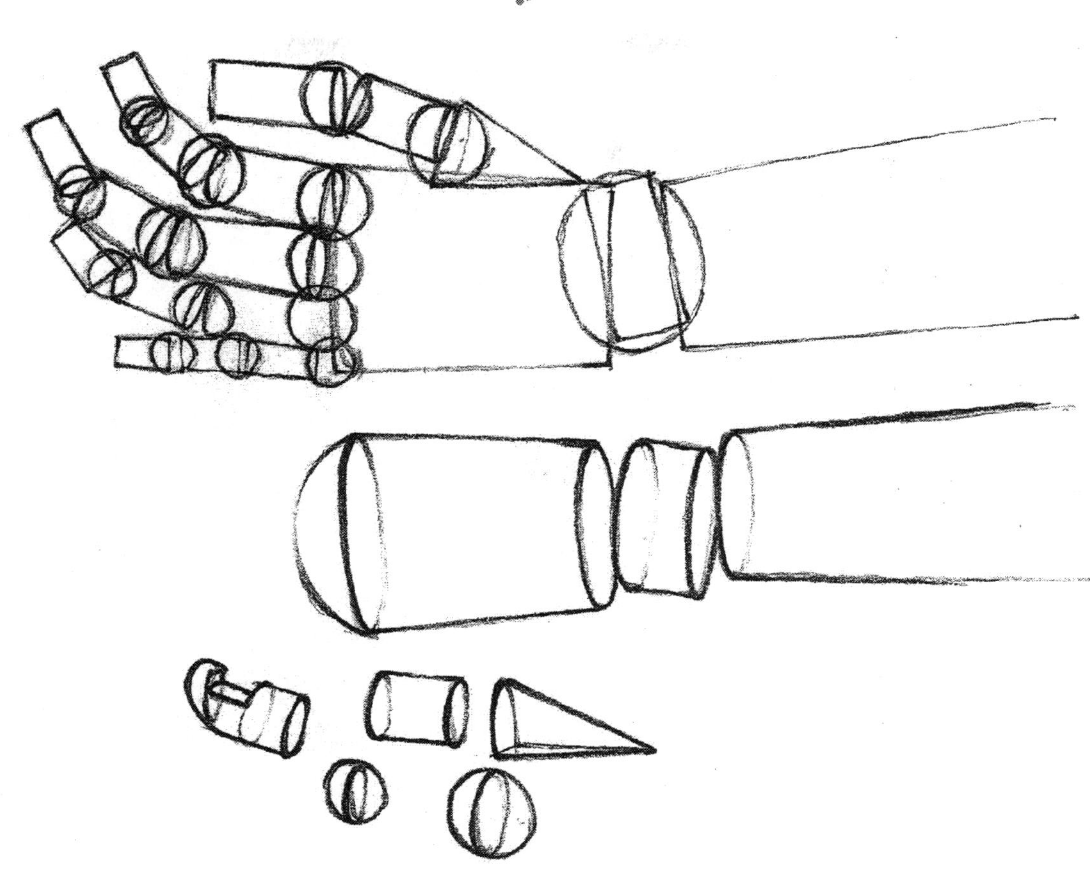

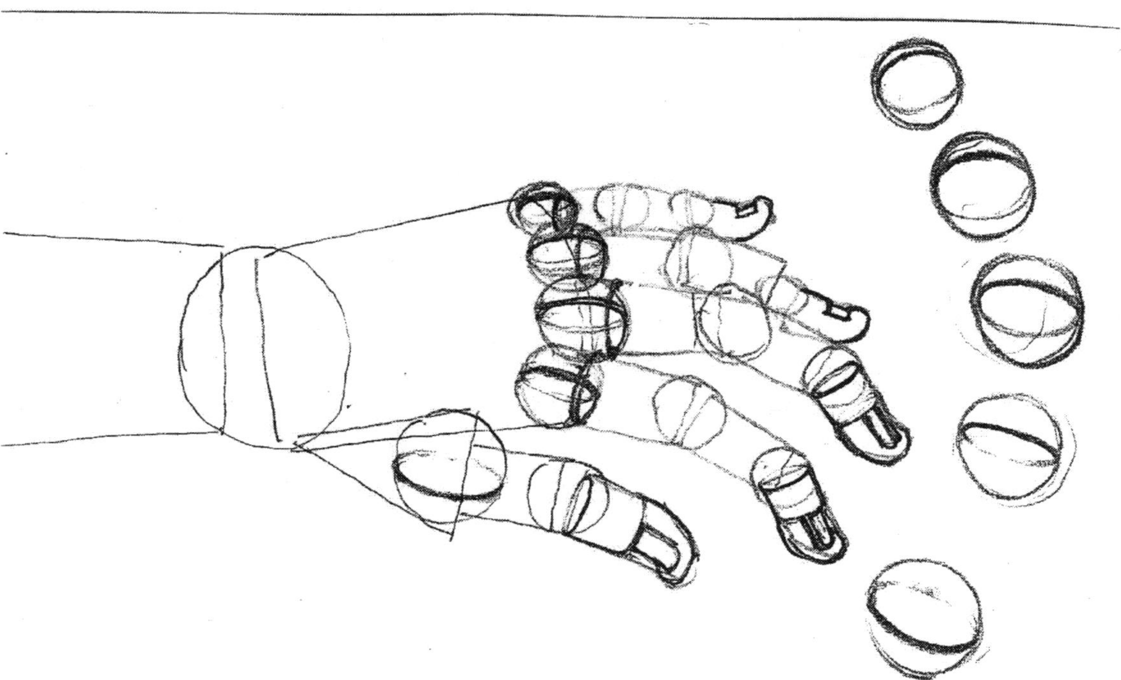

LARGE AND SMALL GEOMETRIC BASIC COMPONENTS OF THE HAND

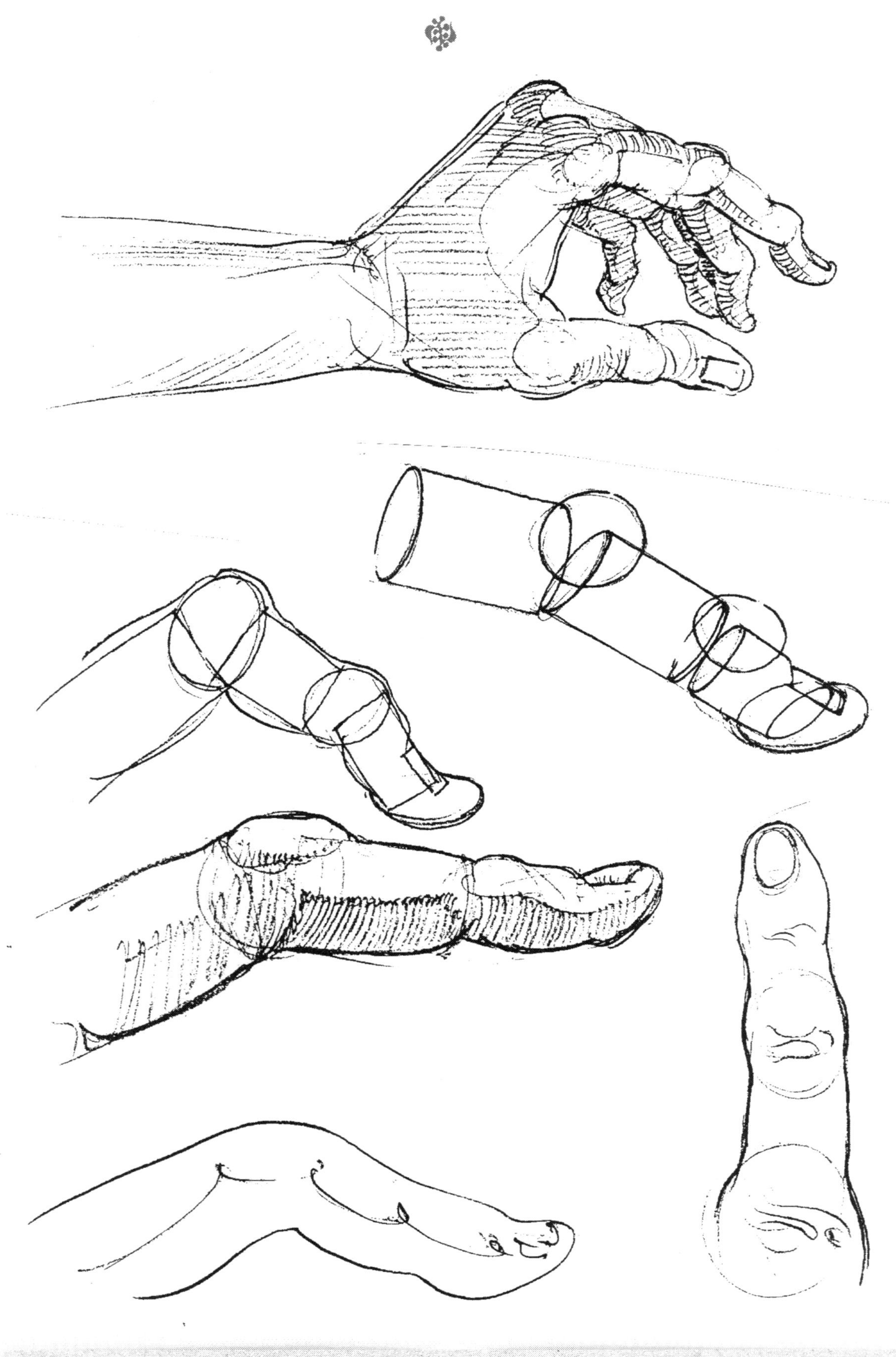

GEOMETRICAL BASIS OF ORGANIC SHAPES
OF HAND AND FINGERS

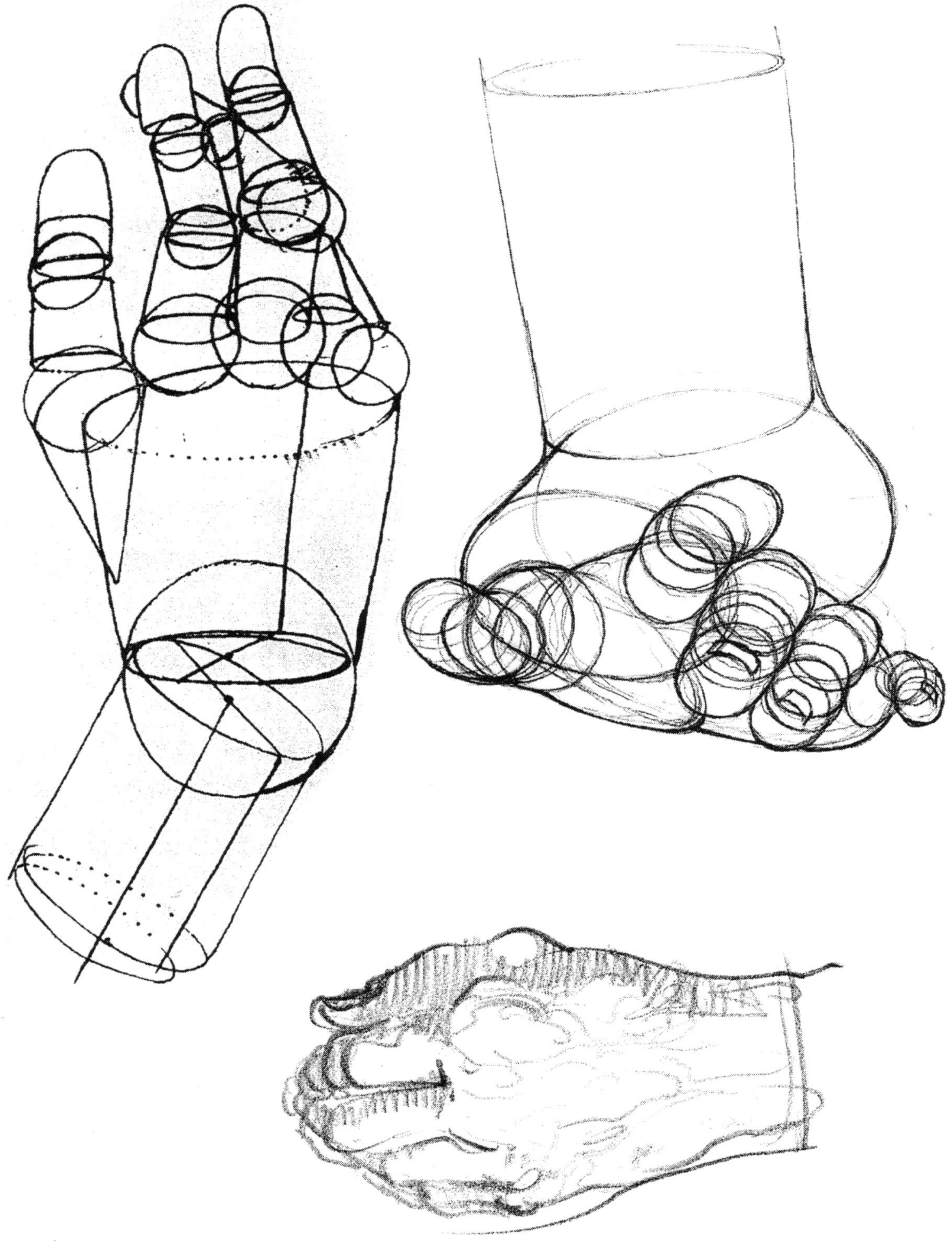

THE GEOMETRICAL ANALYSIS AND MOVEMENT OF THE WRIST AND ANATOMICAL INTERPRETATION

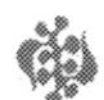

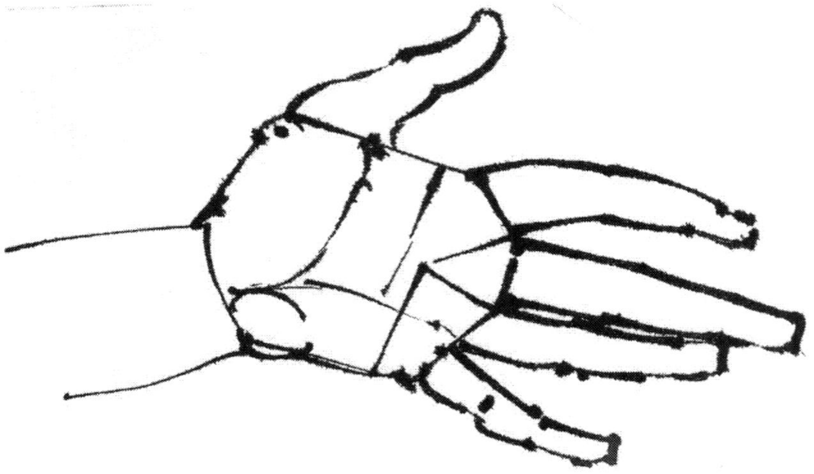

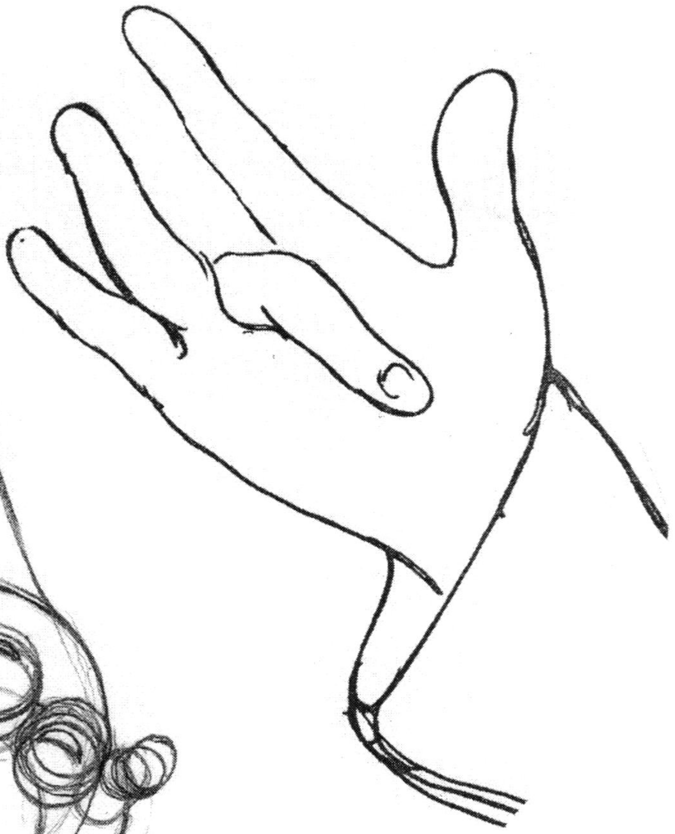

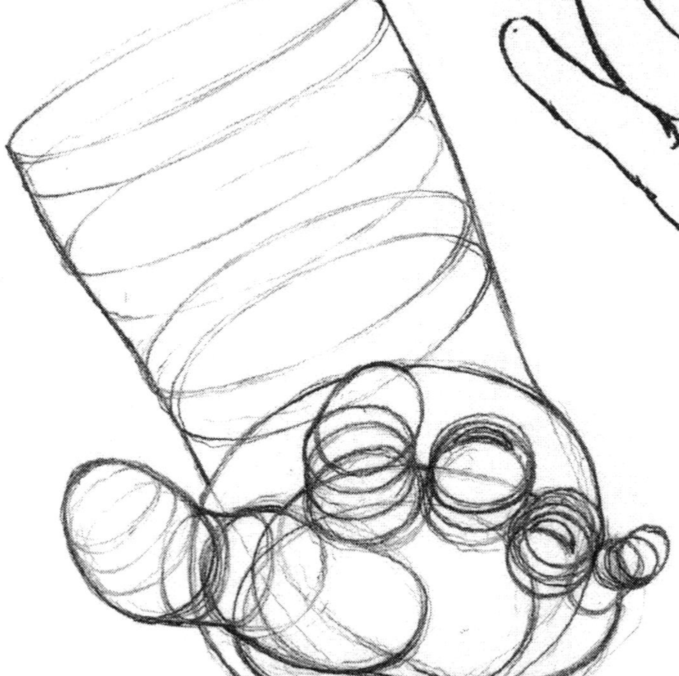

ANALYSIS OF MOVEMENT AND FLEXIBILITY

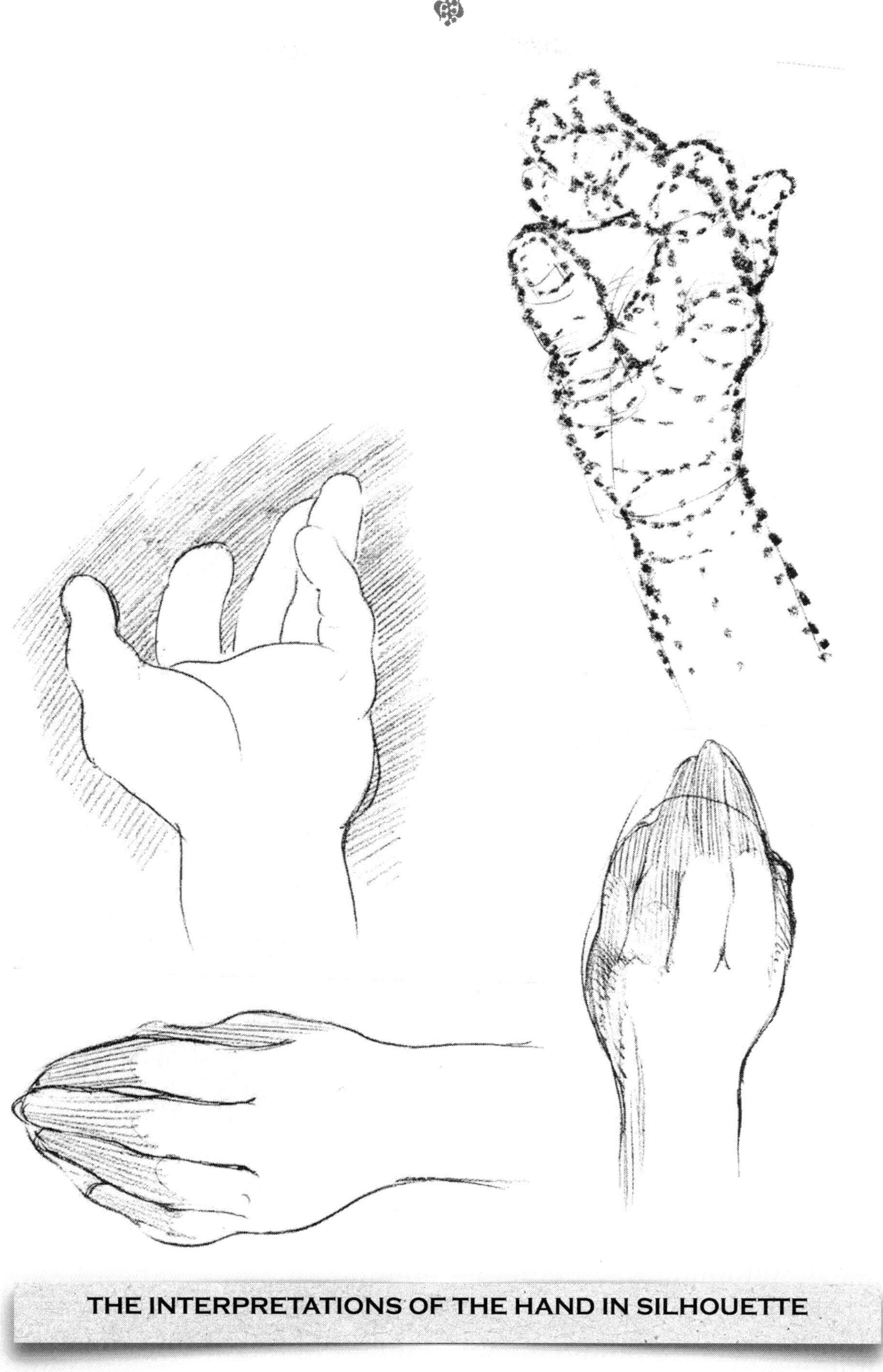

THE INTERPRETATIONS OF THE HAND IN SILHOUETTE

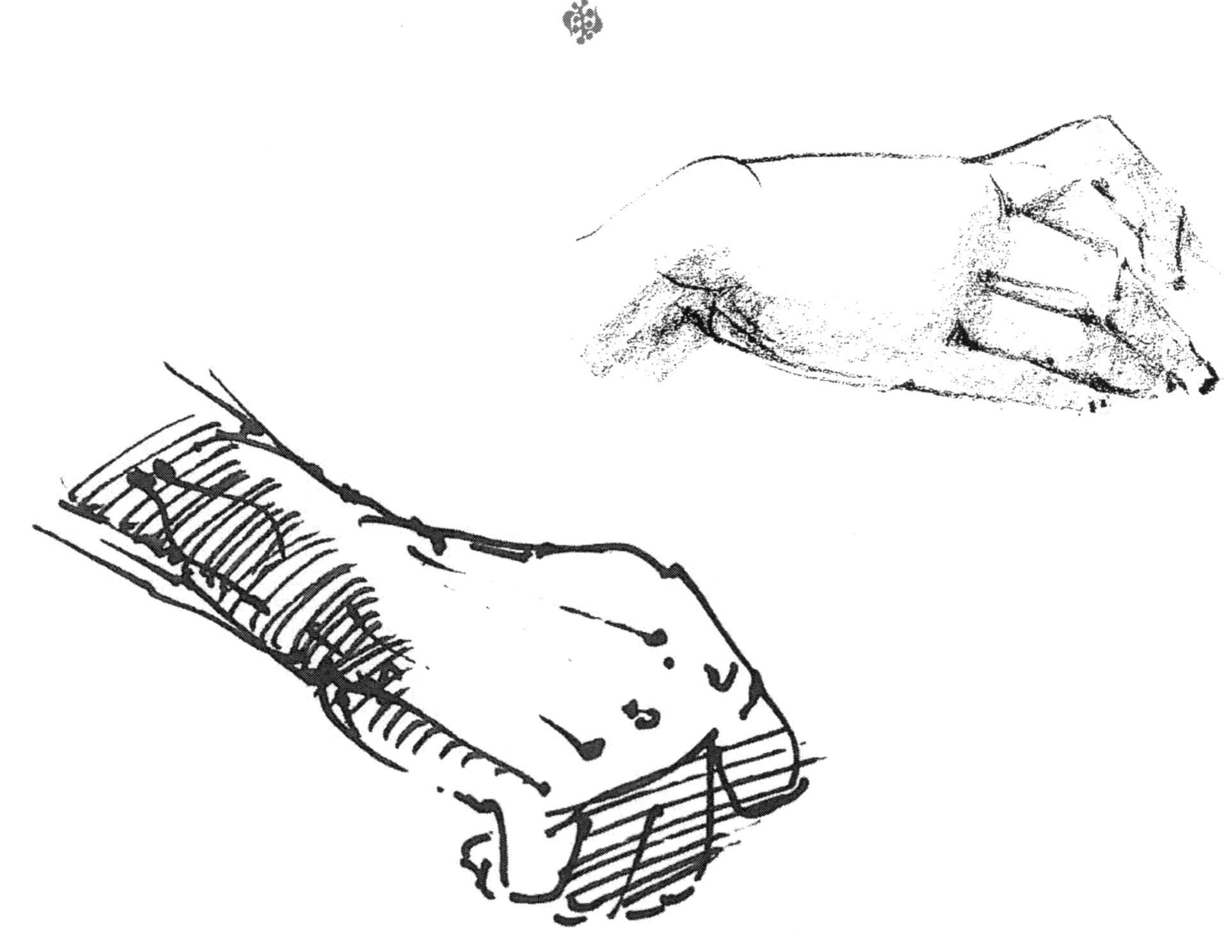

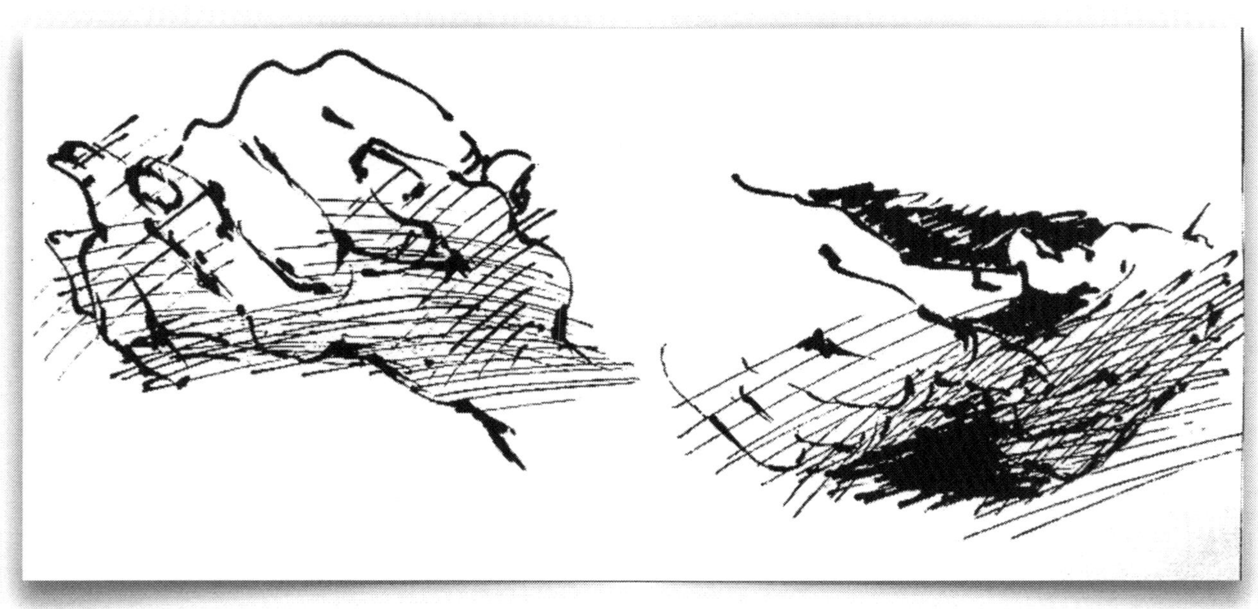

EXAMPLES OF A SINGLE HAND OR PAIR OF HANDS

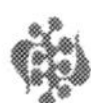

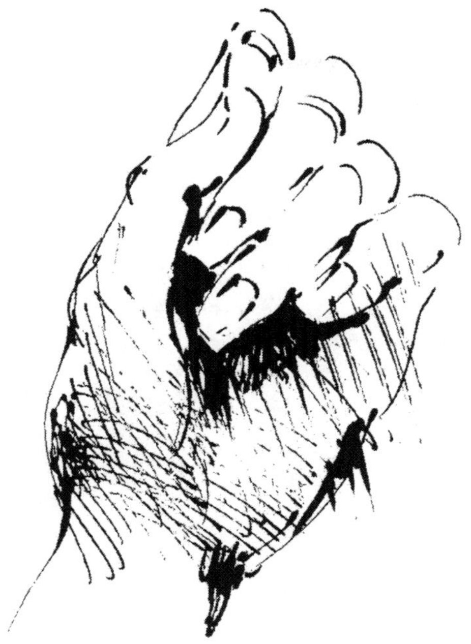

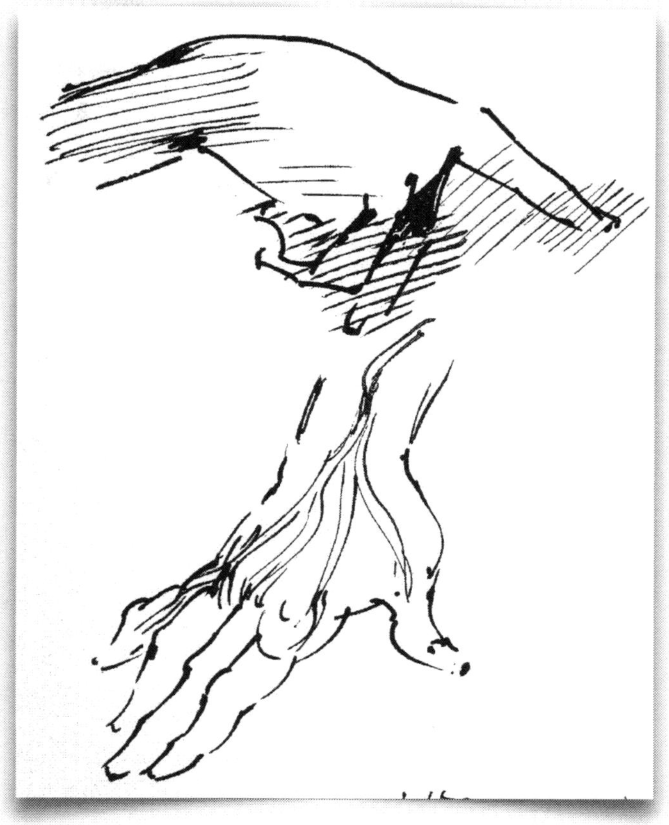

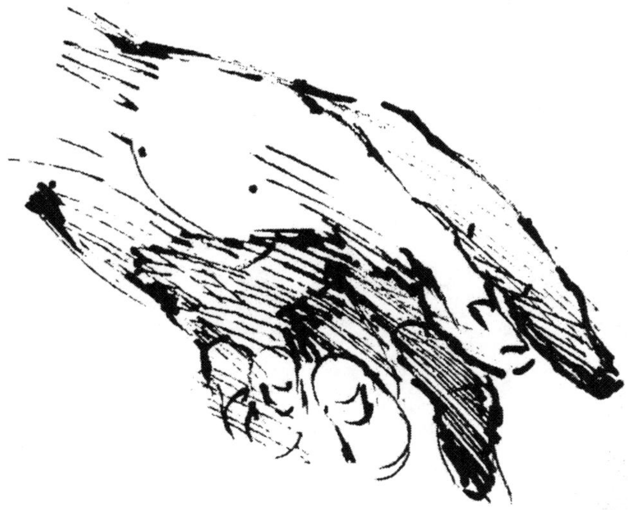

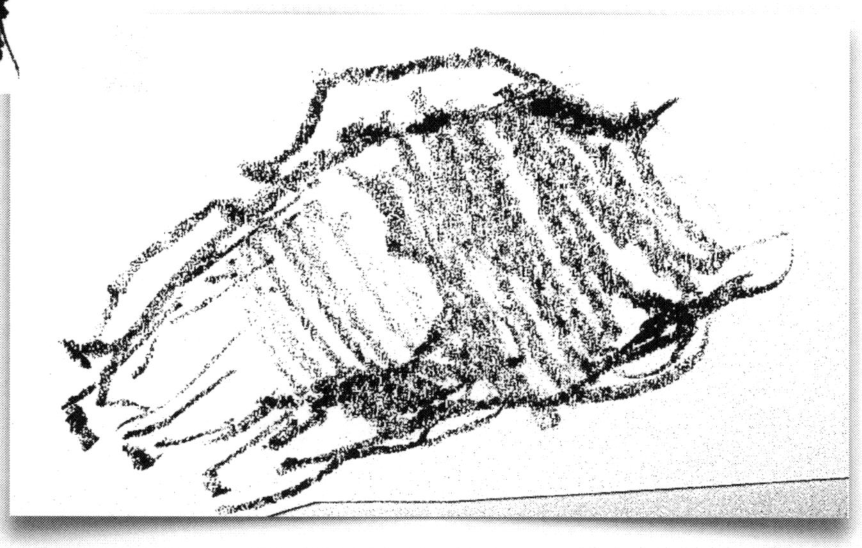

EXAMPLES OF HAND DETAILS

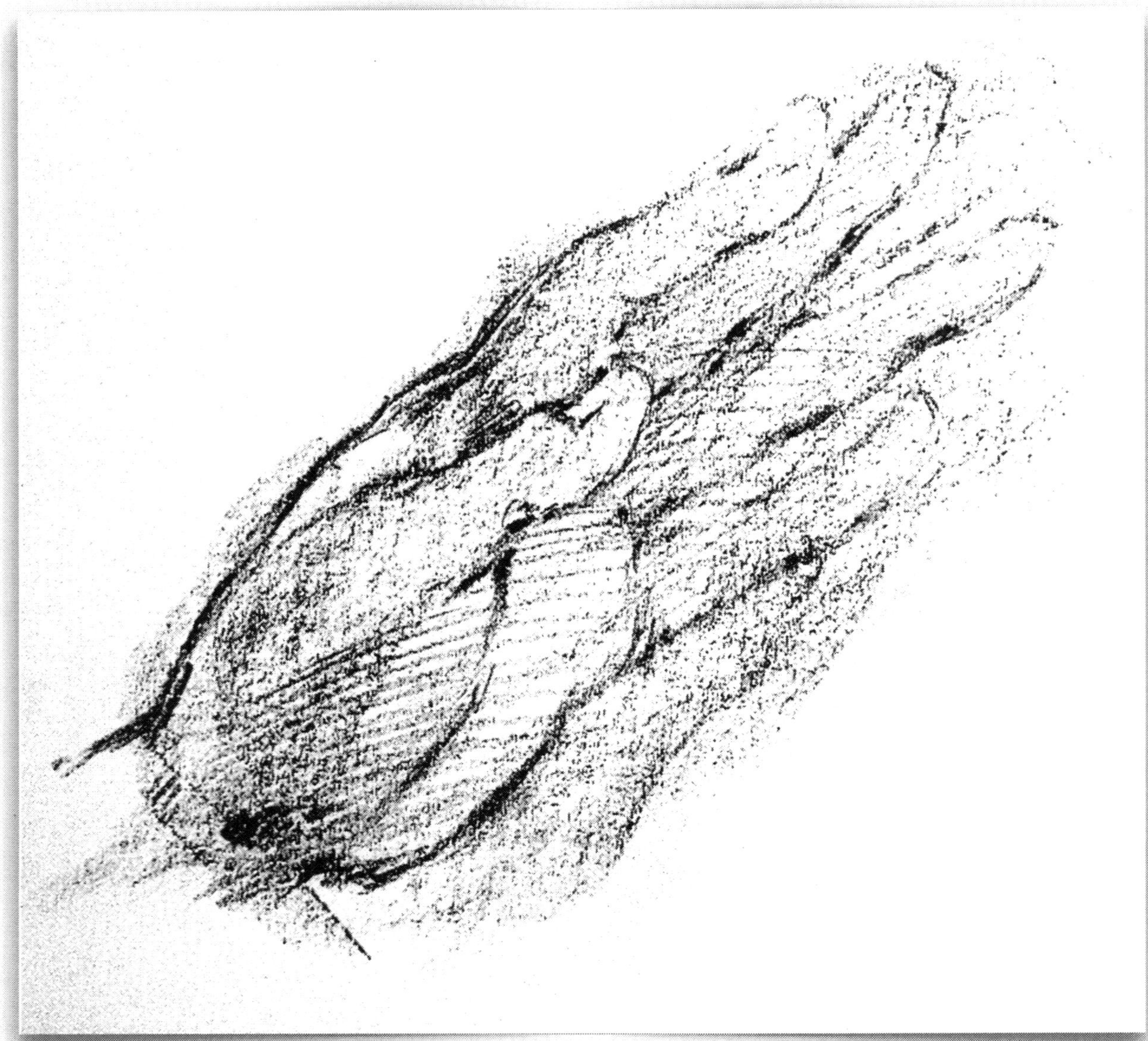

EXAMPLE OF HAND WITH SOFT SHADING

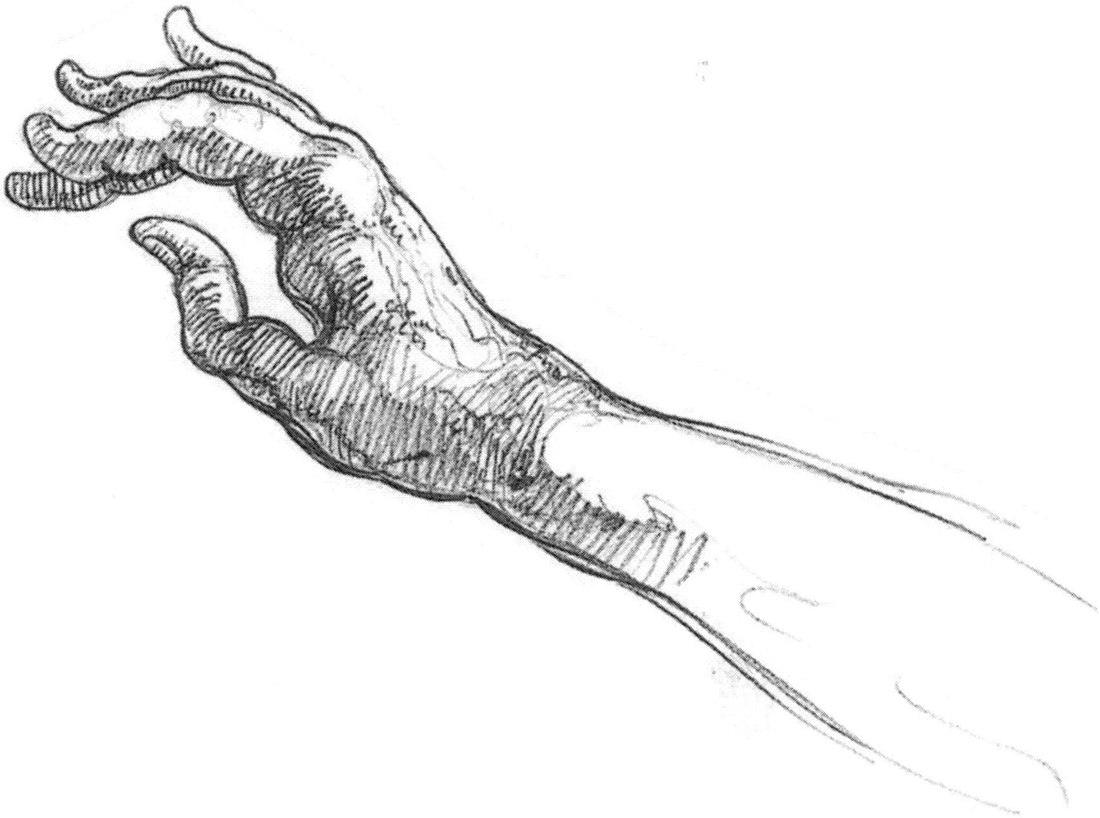

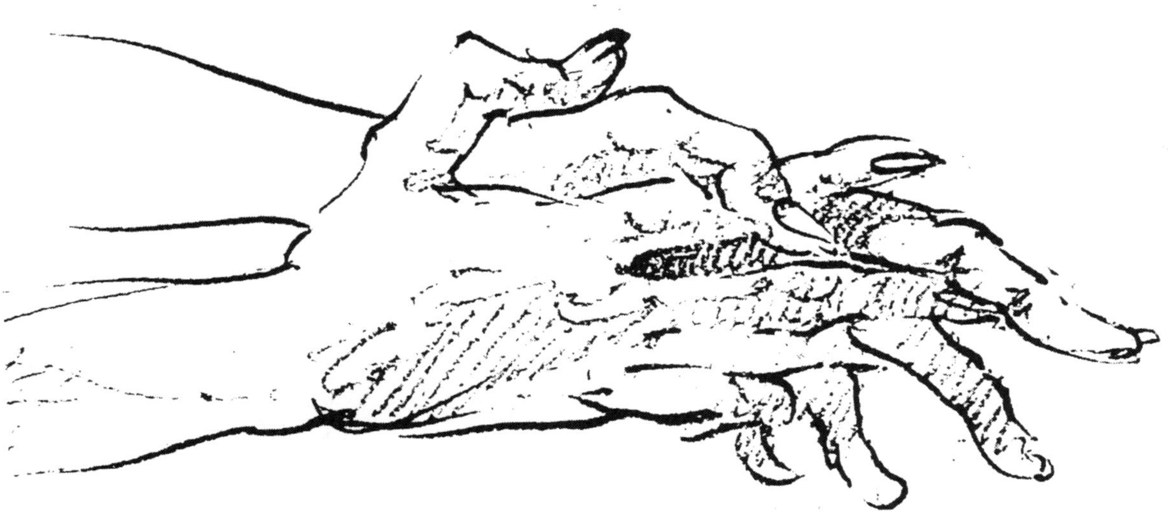

EXAMPLES OF HANDS WITH ACCENTUATED CHARACTER

The Arm

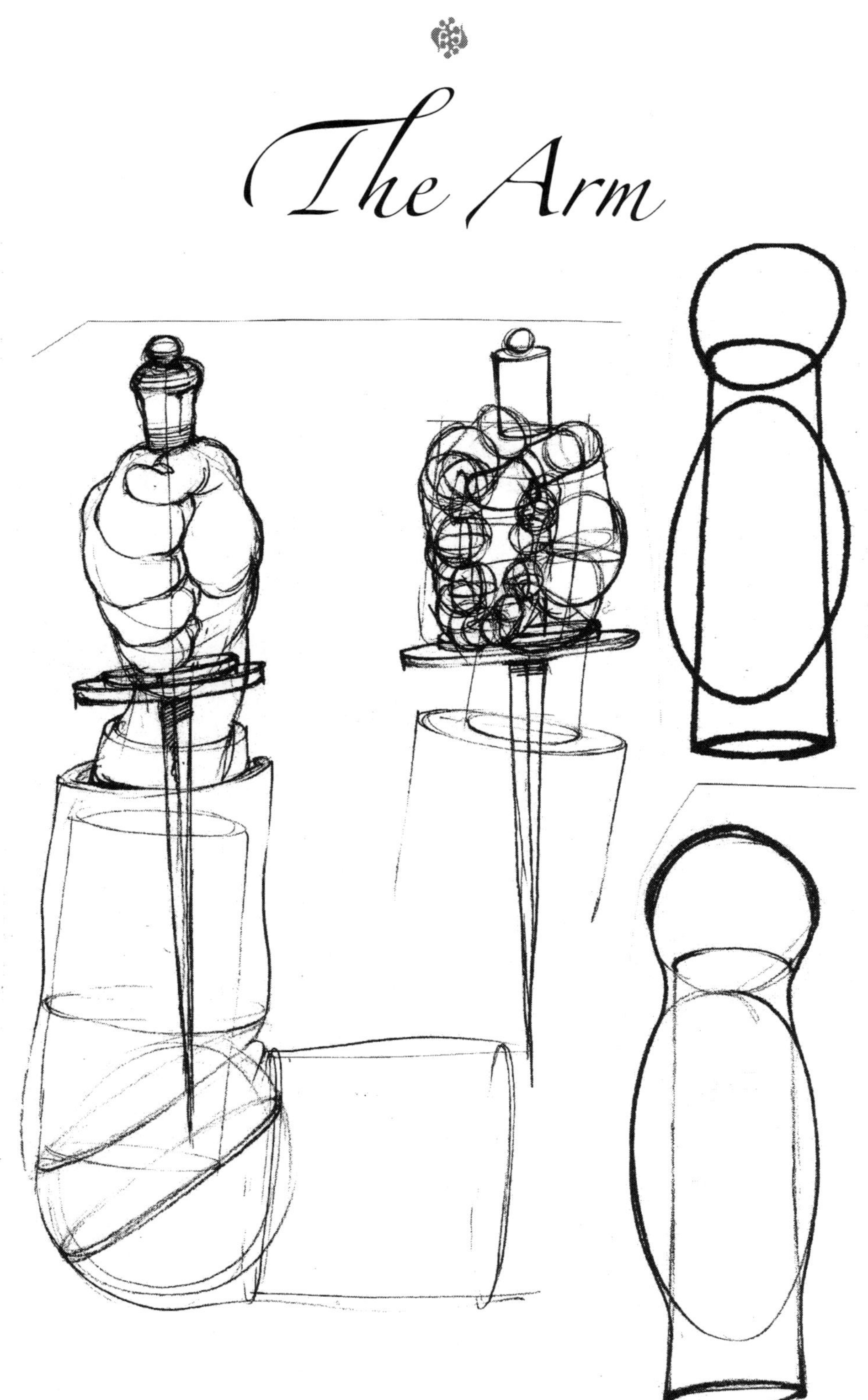

THE MAIN VALUE WHEN DRAWING AN ARM is not in tis geometry or anatomy. The main value is its mobility; from the point of the shoulder joint with the thorax , all the way down to the fingertips. Likewise, the main character of the arm in connection with the body is its flexibility in various directions and through a selection of turns.

Fundamental are the main component parts, clear in their geometrical and anatomical structure. Without that, every presentation remains two-dimensional, lacking in spacial depiction and unconvincing. This gives a rather amateurish effect.

Mastering the command of the human body in motion is a privilege of good painters that are not content with drawing from a live model or using photographs. For that we need only some imagination and courage with persistence. The arm is an excellent example of constructed shapes, similar to the wholeness of human body.

The arm is the most flexible part of the body. If we are familiar with its geometric structure, we can freely play with numerous variants. We can explore all kinds of movements and continuously authenticate the anatomic correctness. No medical education is necessary for this task, we can simply observe ourselves, that will suffice.

The shoulders, the elbows and wrists represent possibilities for rotation and bending. All this facts guarantee a wide dynamic of possibilities. Having all this abundance of movement possibilities must be preserved with harmony. Excessive embellishment will come across grotesque and give the impression of useless exhibitionism.

TECHNICAL ADVICE AND SUGGESTIONS

Y**OU MAY BEGIN** with geometrical presentations of arms. This is also conducive to experimenting with different types of drawing tools. Most of all, pay attention to correct shortening of arms. More open ellipses indicate a higher level fo shortening, as well as reduced length of the object or subject.

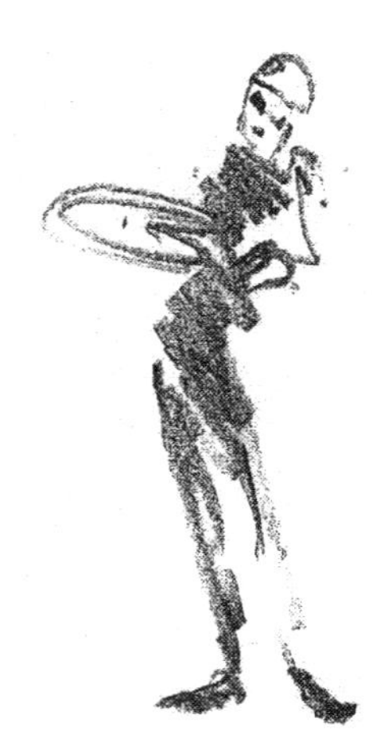

All possible movements can be completed with shading values as demonstrated in some drawings in this chapter.

For realization of this shading values you may choose various methods: lines, netlike woven patterns with pen or pencil. Surfaces can be depicted with a softer pencils, charcoal or even a brush. Do not forget the essence of presentation is a geometrical assessment of the arm.

Remember, the selection of the technique and drawing tools is yours to make. You can observe a few of your possible options and choices. Take into consideration the suggestions and advice, but never follow them blindly.

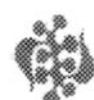

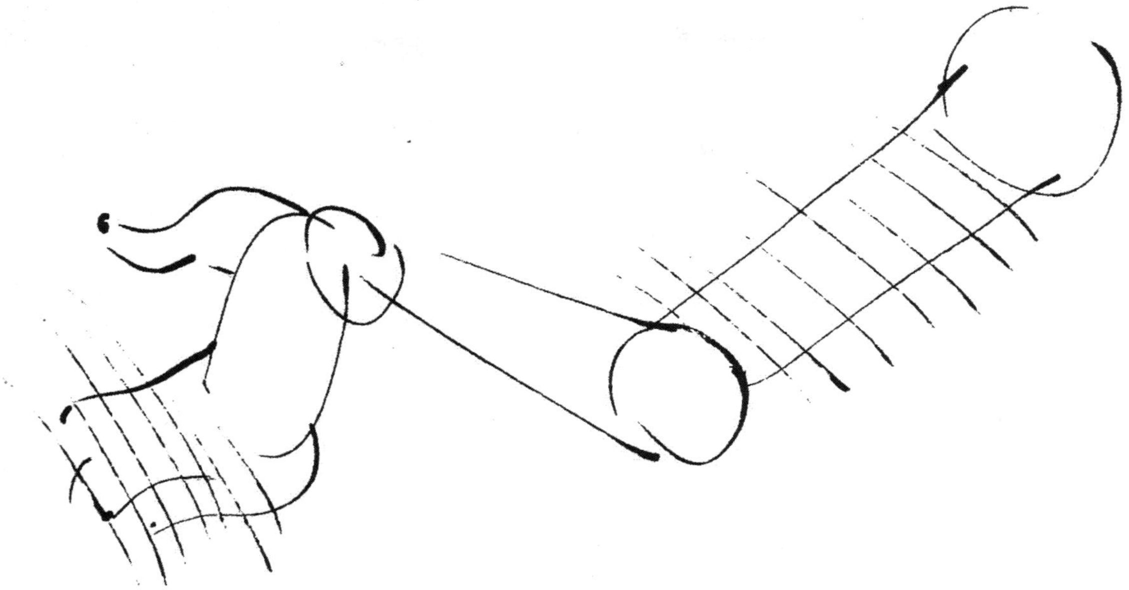

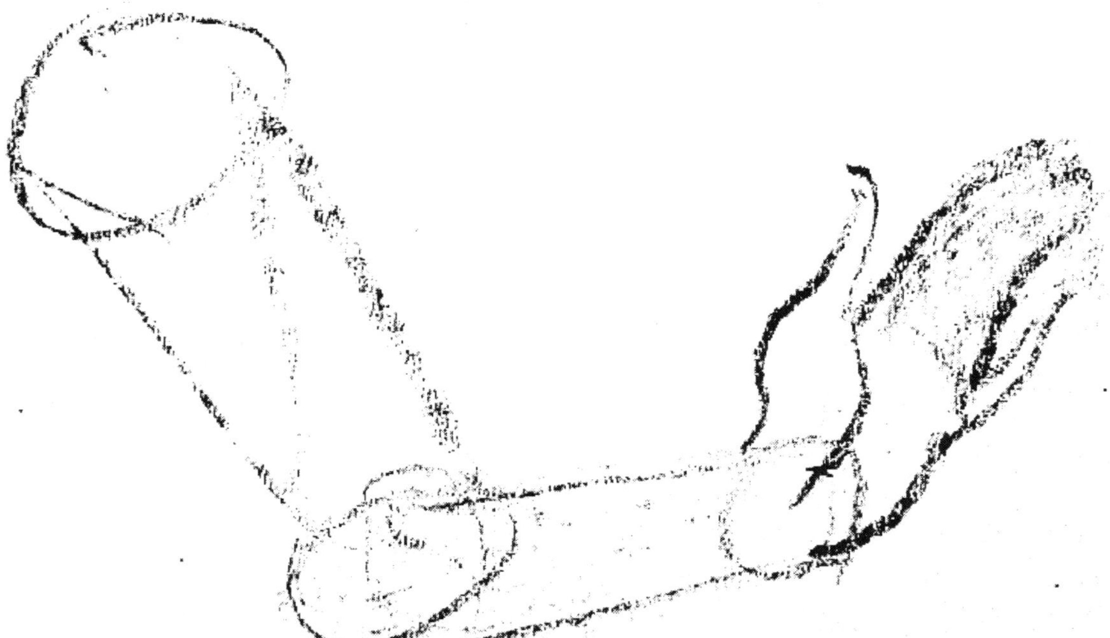

A RELAXED AND SKETCHY TECHNIQUE FACILITATES EXPERIMENTATION OF
VARIOUS MOVEMENTS IN ALL DIRECTIONS AND TURNS BEGINNING AT THE
SHOULDER ALL THE WAY DOWN TO THE FINGERTIPS

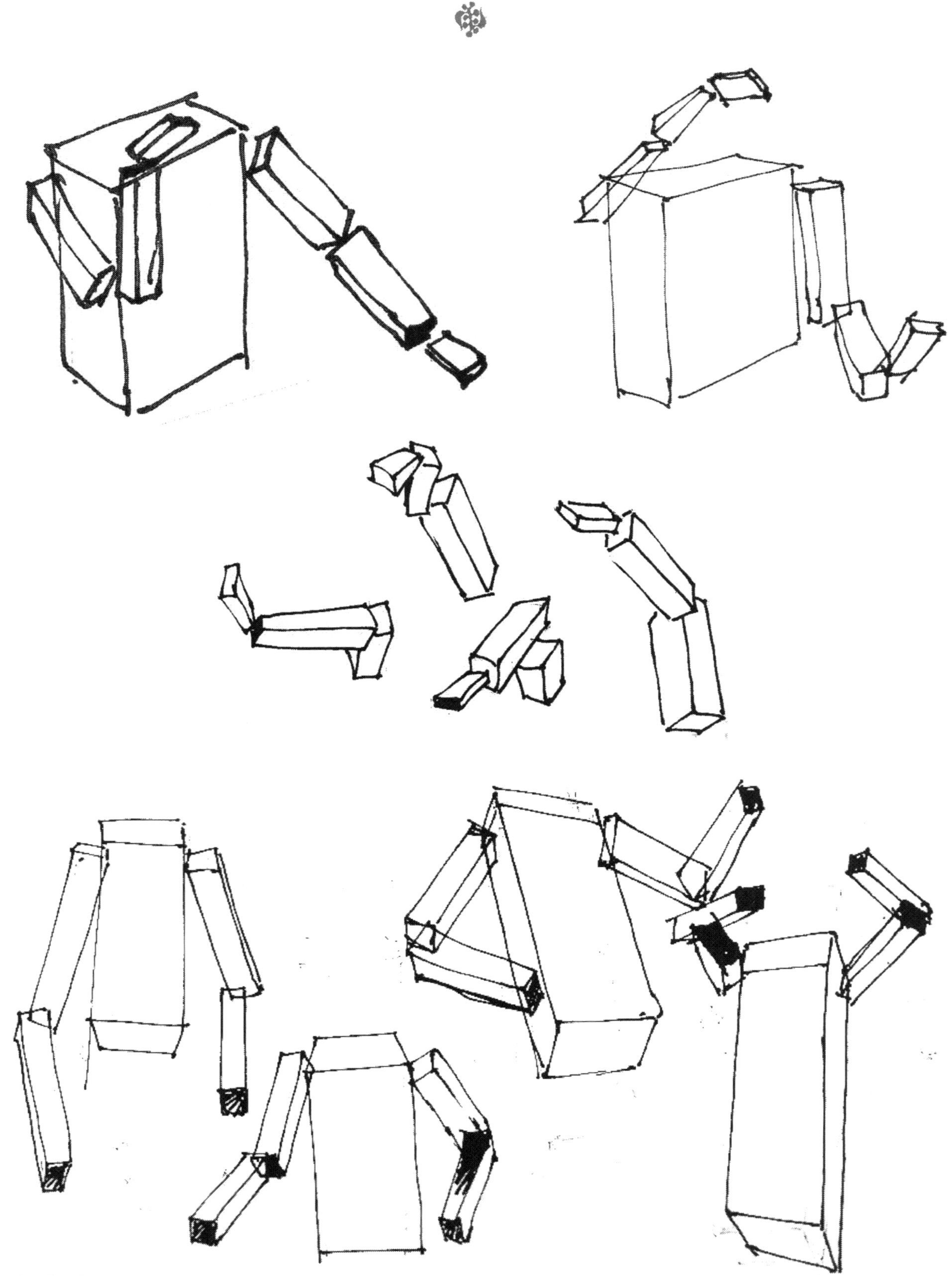

THE CONNECTION OF THE BODY, SHOULDER , ELBOW AND WRIST IS OF GREATEST IMPORTANCE. THE EASIEST WAY TO IMAGINE VARIOUS DIRECTIONS IN SPACE IS WITH THE USE OF ANGULAR SHAPES.

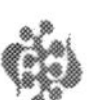

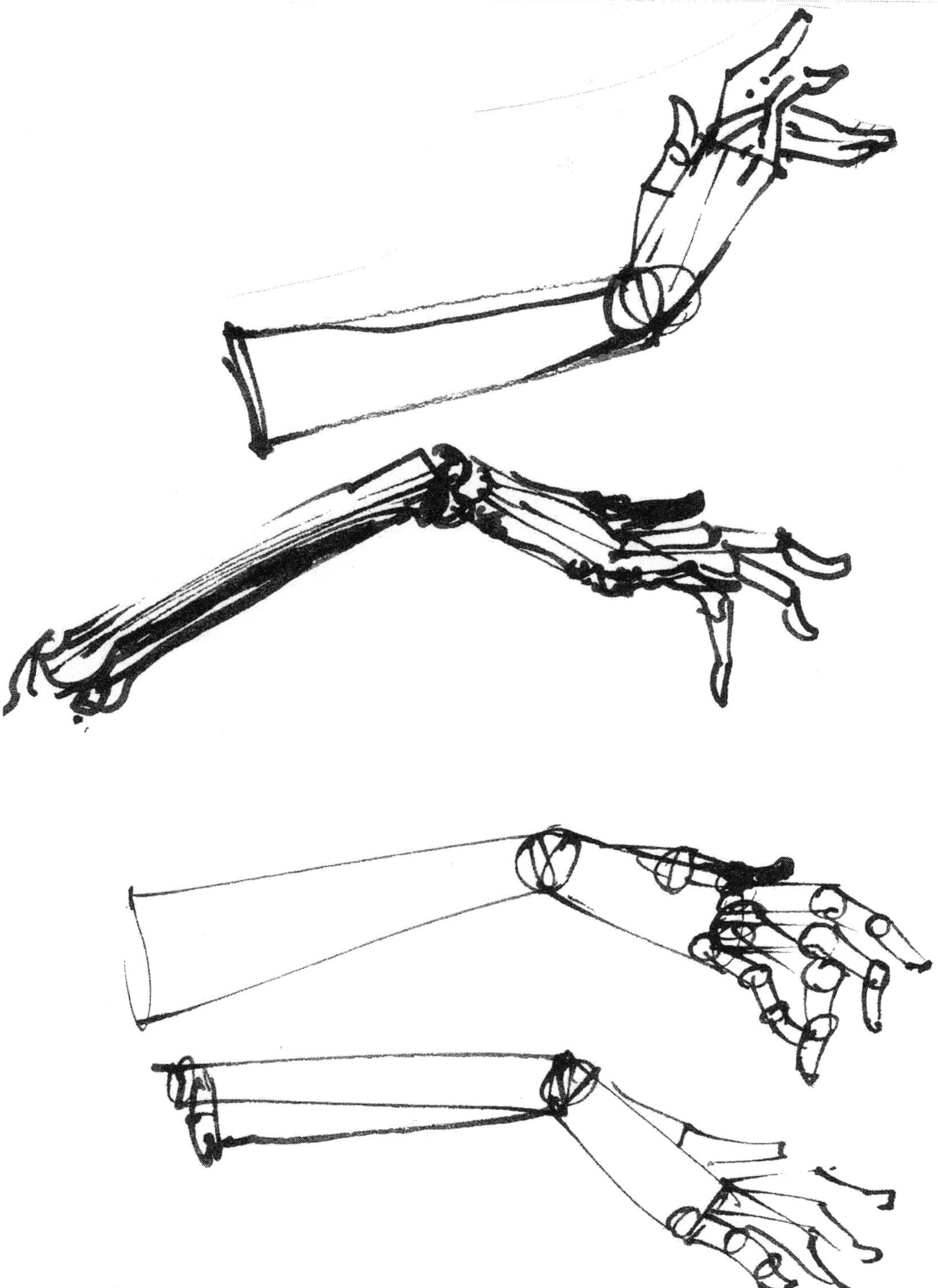

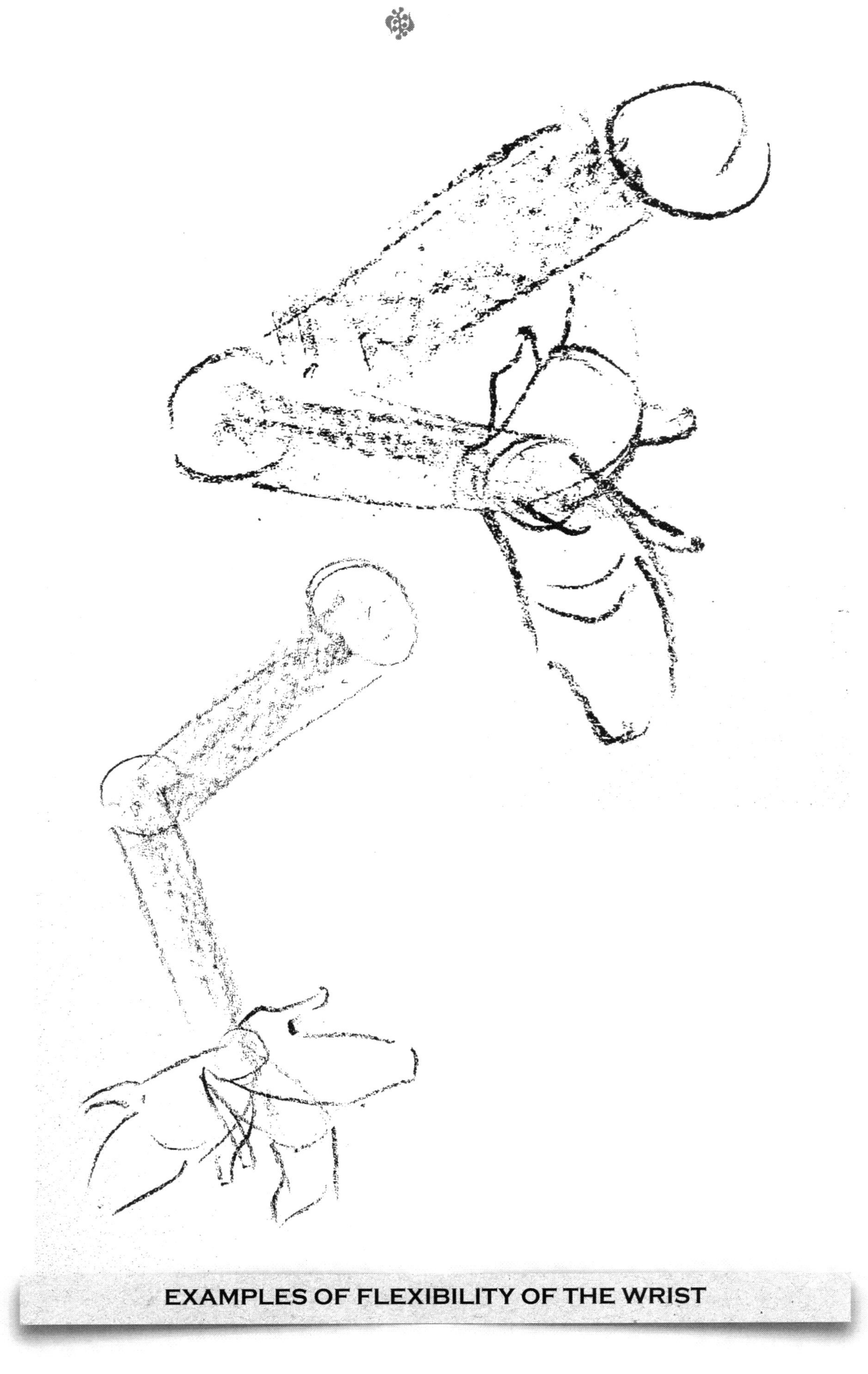

EXAMPLES OF FLEXIBILITY OF THE WRIST

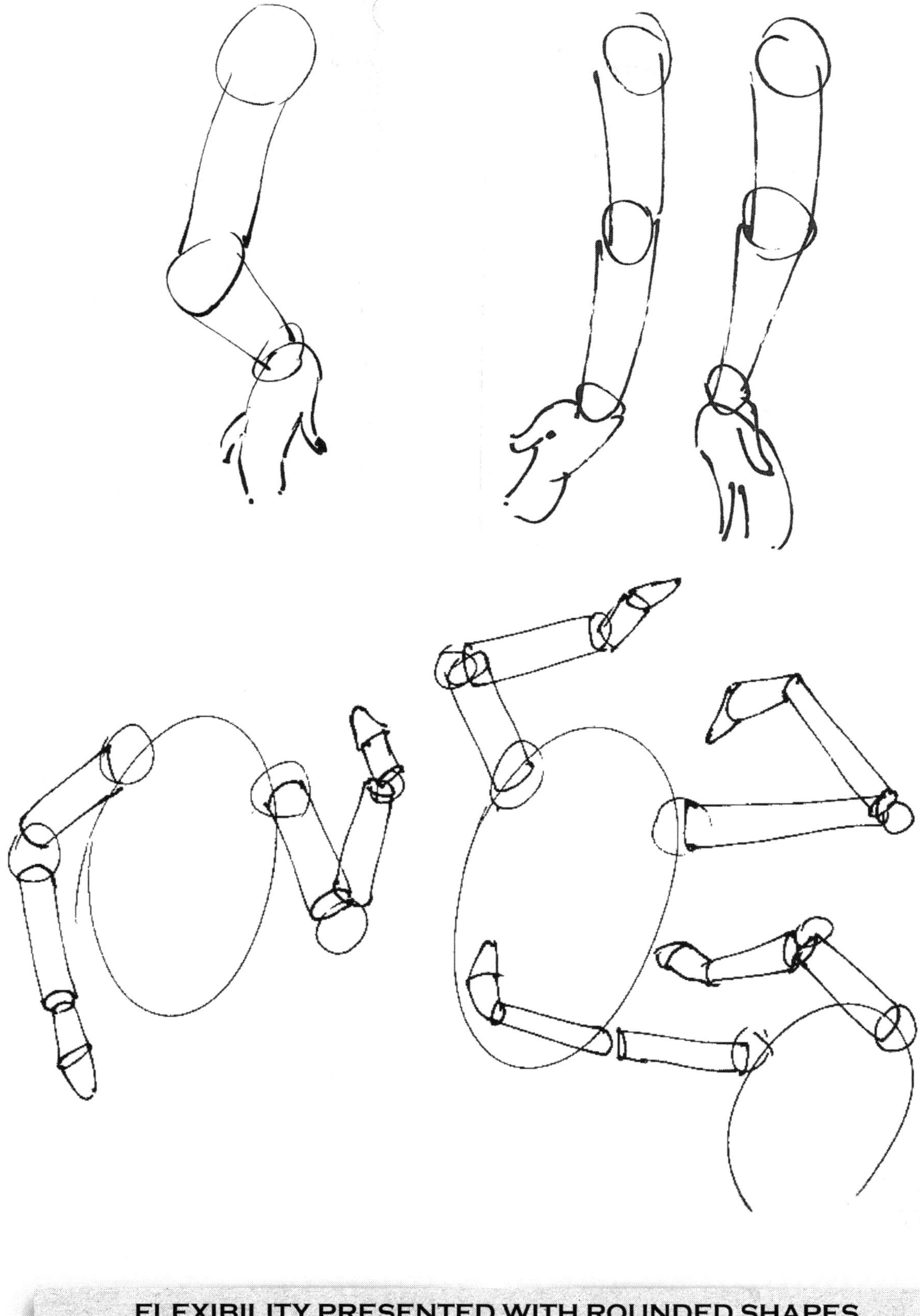

FLEXIBILITY PRESENTED WITH ROUNDED SHAPES

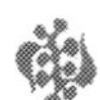

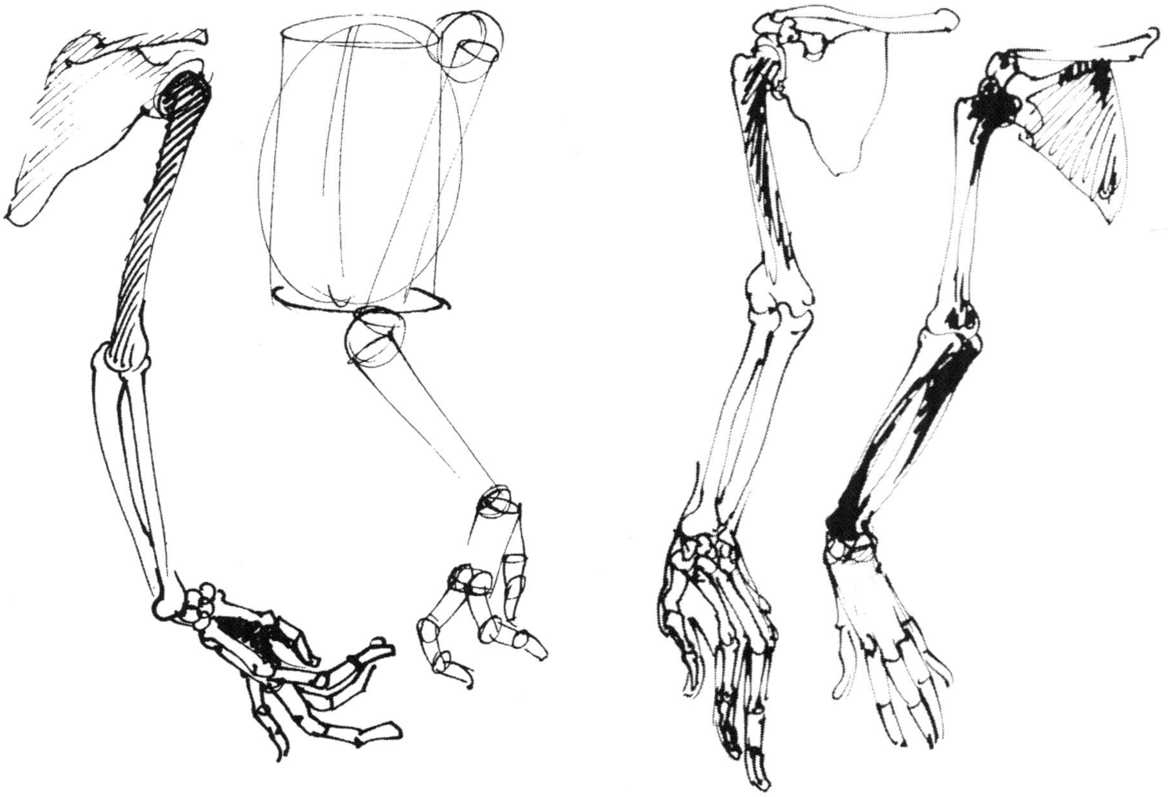

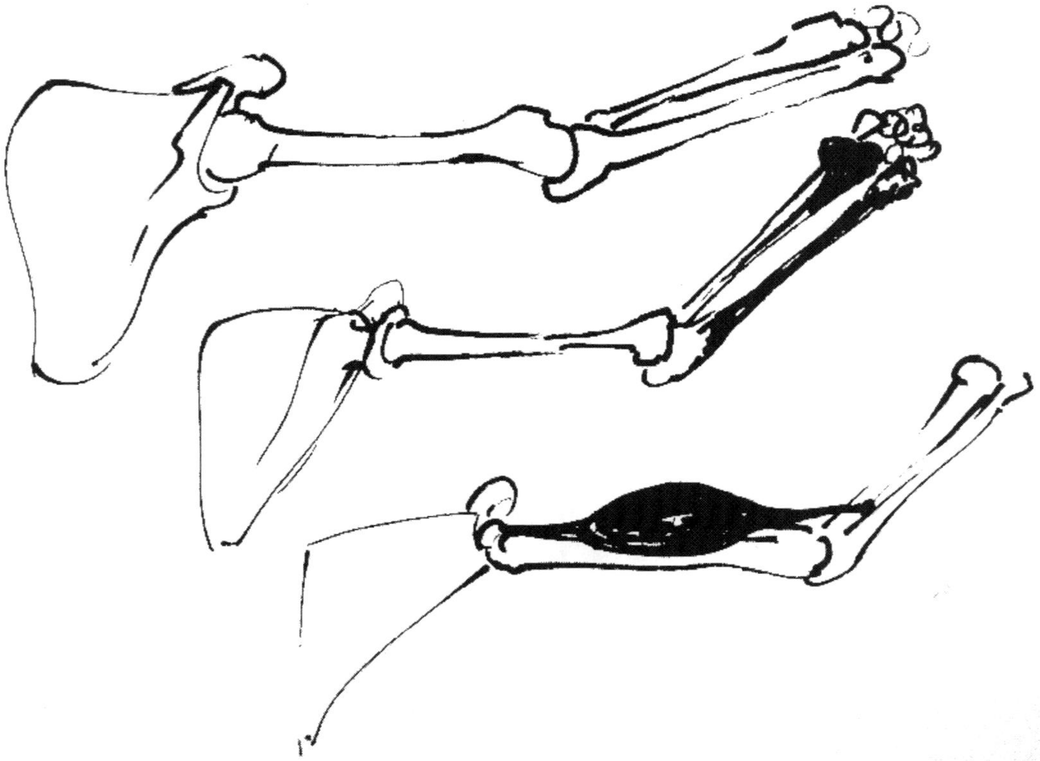

GEOMETRIC INTERPRETATION IS FOLLOWED BY ANATOMICAL BONE STRUCTURE AND FINALLY MUSCULAR ANATOMY

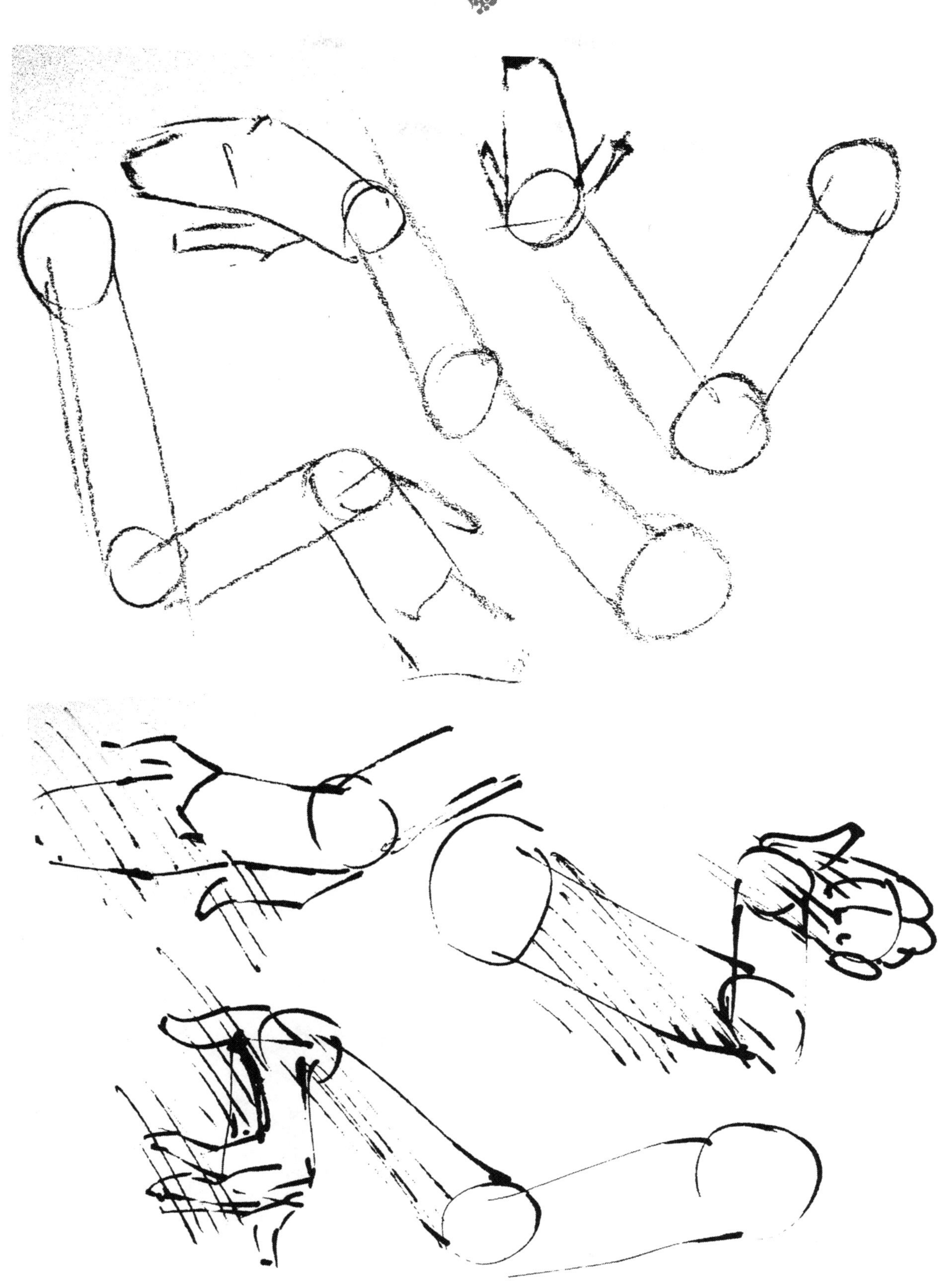

THE MOST SUITABLE IS THE USE OF ROUND AND CYLINDRICAL SHAPES

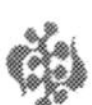

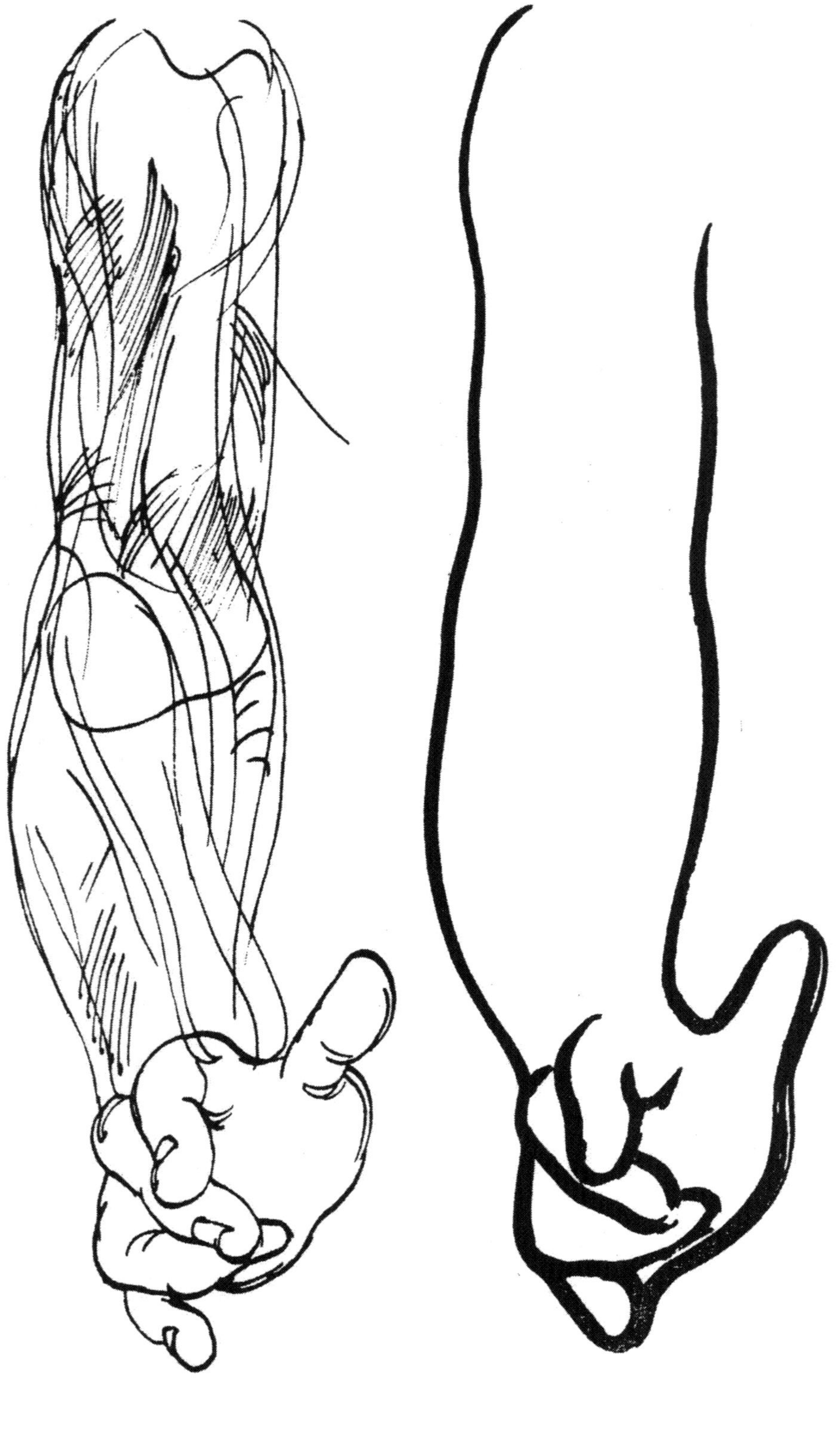

ANATOMICAL AND SILHOUETTE VIEW

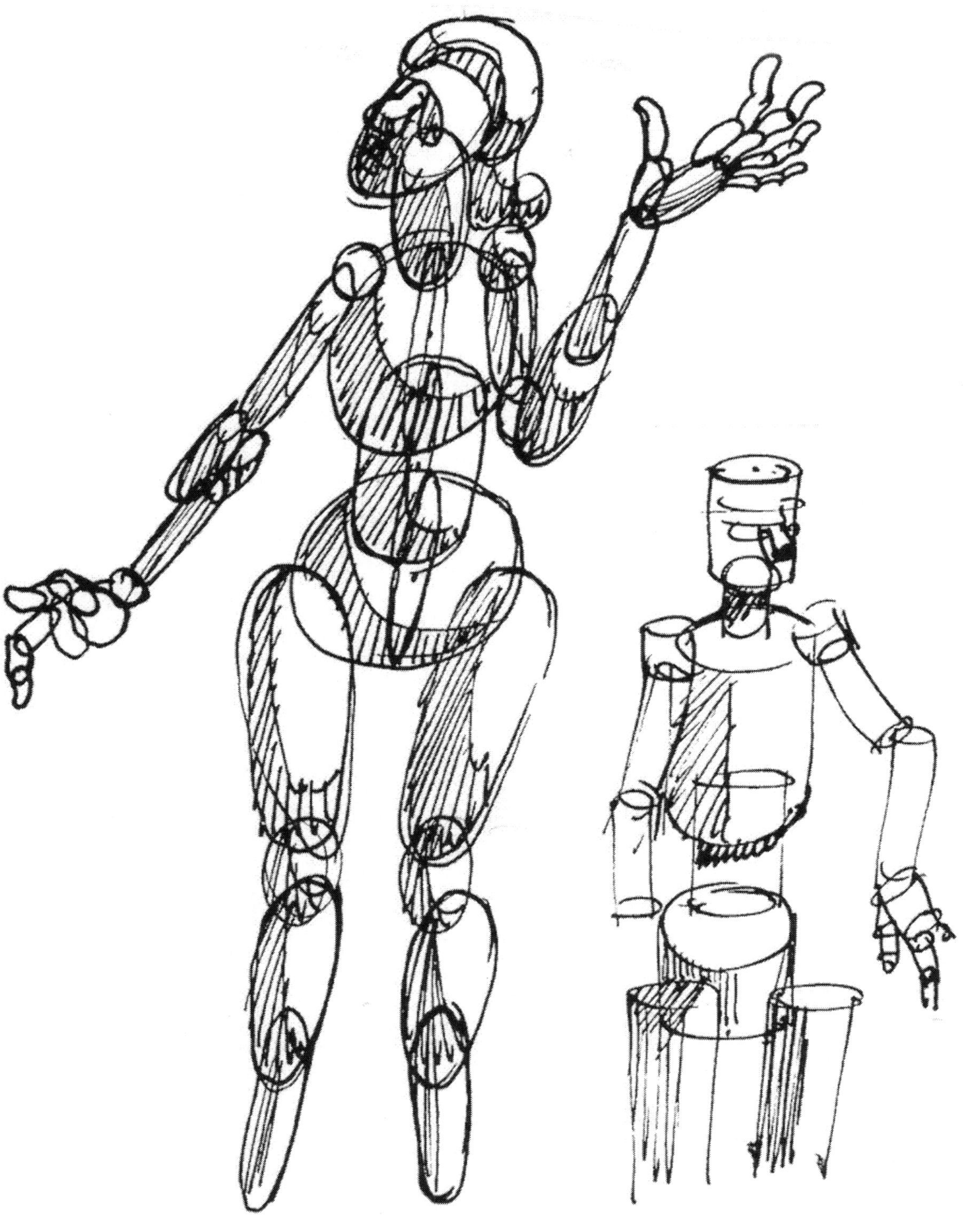

EXAMPLES OF INTERPRETATION WITH DIFFERENT GEOMETRICAL FORMS

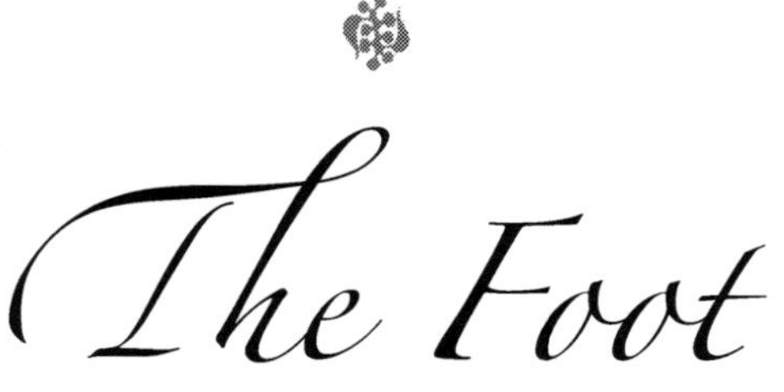

The Foot

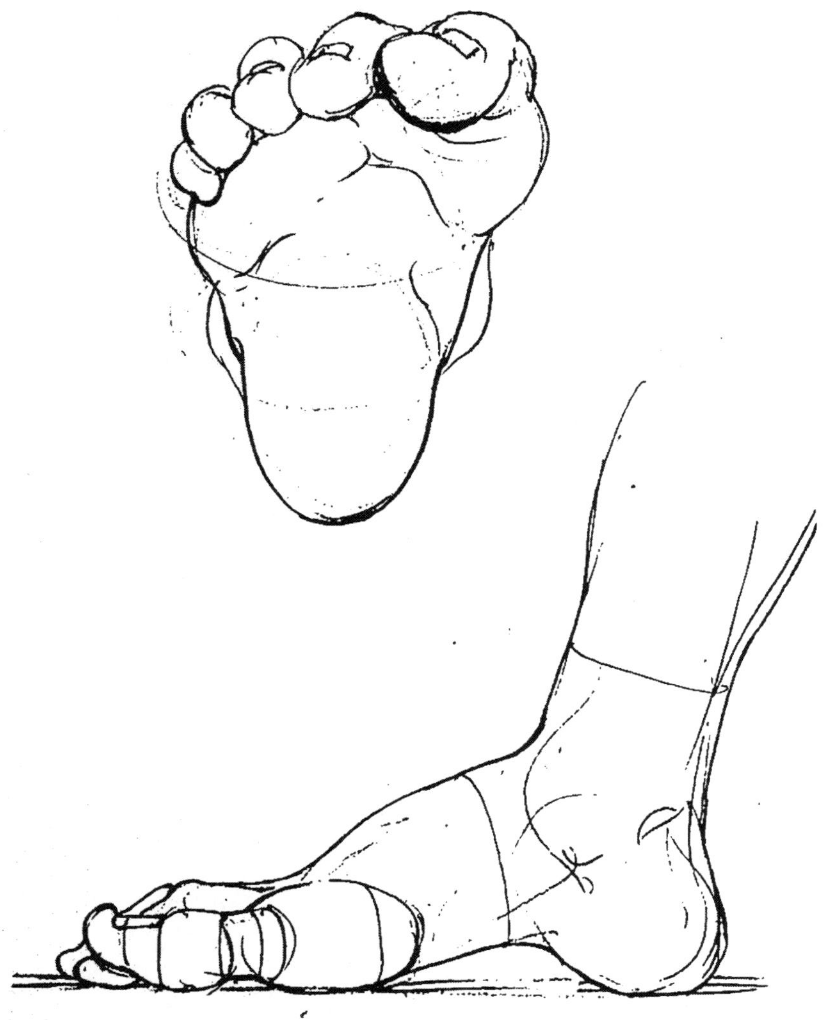

YOU MAY WONDER, who ever notices feet in drawings and pictures? But the fact is, the feet finalize a good drawing of the whole figure. The foot is an example of small secrets with a bigger meaning. On the feet stands the entire figure which determines its movement versatility, even if it hovers in space.

Drawing a foot is a certain kind of "final exam" for every artist. The geometric construction is very interesting, somewhat similar to the hand, but in most cases tightly connected to the level and surface of the ground it stands on.

A foot's anatomical construction reveals the importance of the ankle. The demanding level of drawing skill is evident in dynamic positions of the figure, when feet are lifted off the ground while walking, running or dancing. It demonstrates possible variations of direction and as consequence, unusual shortenings and aspects.

In case of footwear, these challenges seem to disappear, but it becomes soon evident that boots or shoes alone without geometrical or anatomical values do not contribute to a good drawing. This goes for dancers as well as warriors.

The times of drawing and painting nude figures are a thing of the past. Who needs paintings of barefoot saints, plump cherubs or playful coquettes? Nowadays very few differentiate between a foot of a baby, old greek goddess or a shipyard laborer.

Good painters in classical style can sustain themselves only in an environment, where old Greek and Roman cultural values still matter. Today we call this the Western culture. This is a rarity, worthy of special care.

TECHNICAL ADVICE AND SUGGESTIONS

DRAWING FEET REQUIRES EXPERIENCE. This can only be gained with a great number of various exercises and experiments.

Often our drawing efforts can be limited because of seeming unimportance or lesser value of objects we draw. The best advice for this is to change the format size. Simply select smaller paper This way you will eliminate the feeling that you are uselessly wasting great paper for your seemingly unimportant efforts. More important is the fact that a smaller paper format brings more attention to the essence of the whole shape. A smaller format will also discourage you from useless and exaggerated meticulousness.

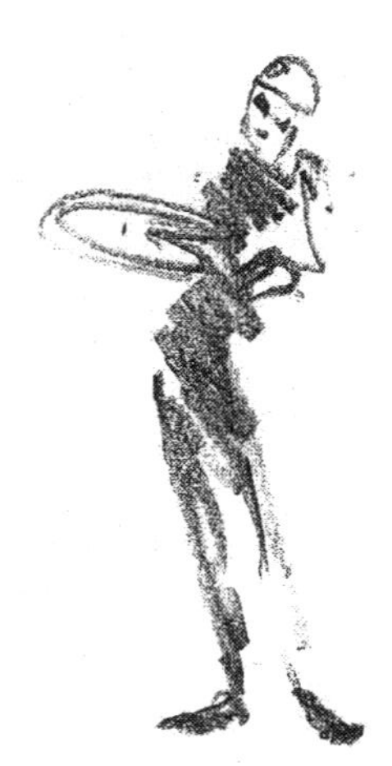

In addition, a smaller format also changes the functionality of drawing tools; with a softer pencil we get charcoal like results, they allow increased gradation from fogy grayness all the way to deep black. With a thicker pen we can achieve effects similar to the stroke of a brush.

Everyone relies on their own personal choice. This is why it is very important to cultivate your own ability to hold your vision also in the technique of execution of a drawing exercise, concept or idea.

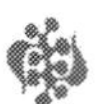

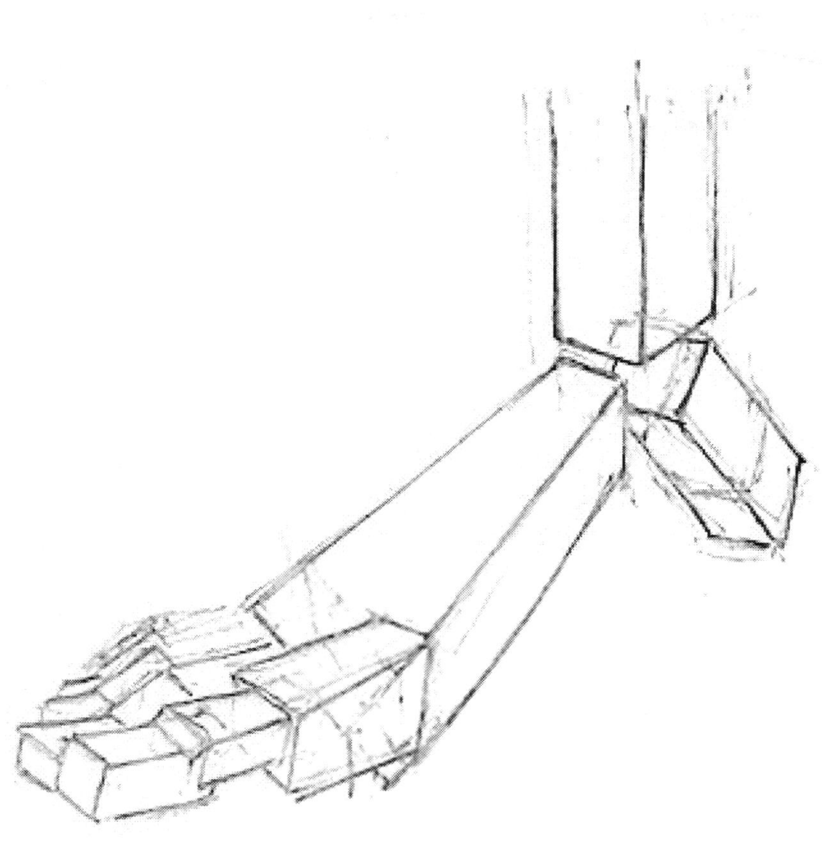

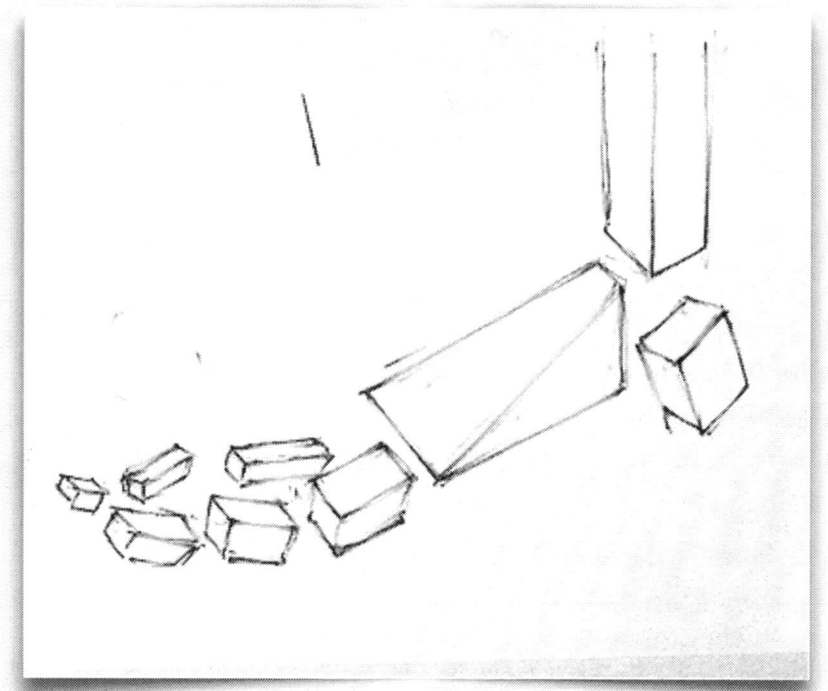

THE FOOT DEPICTED WITH ANGULAR GEOMETRIC C SHAPES

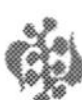

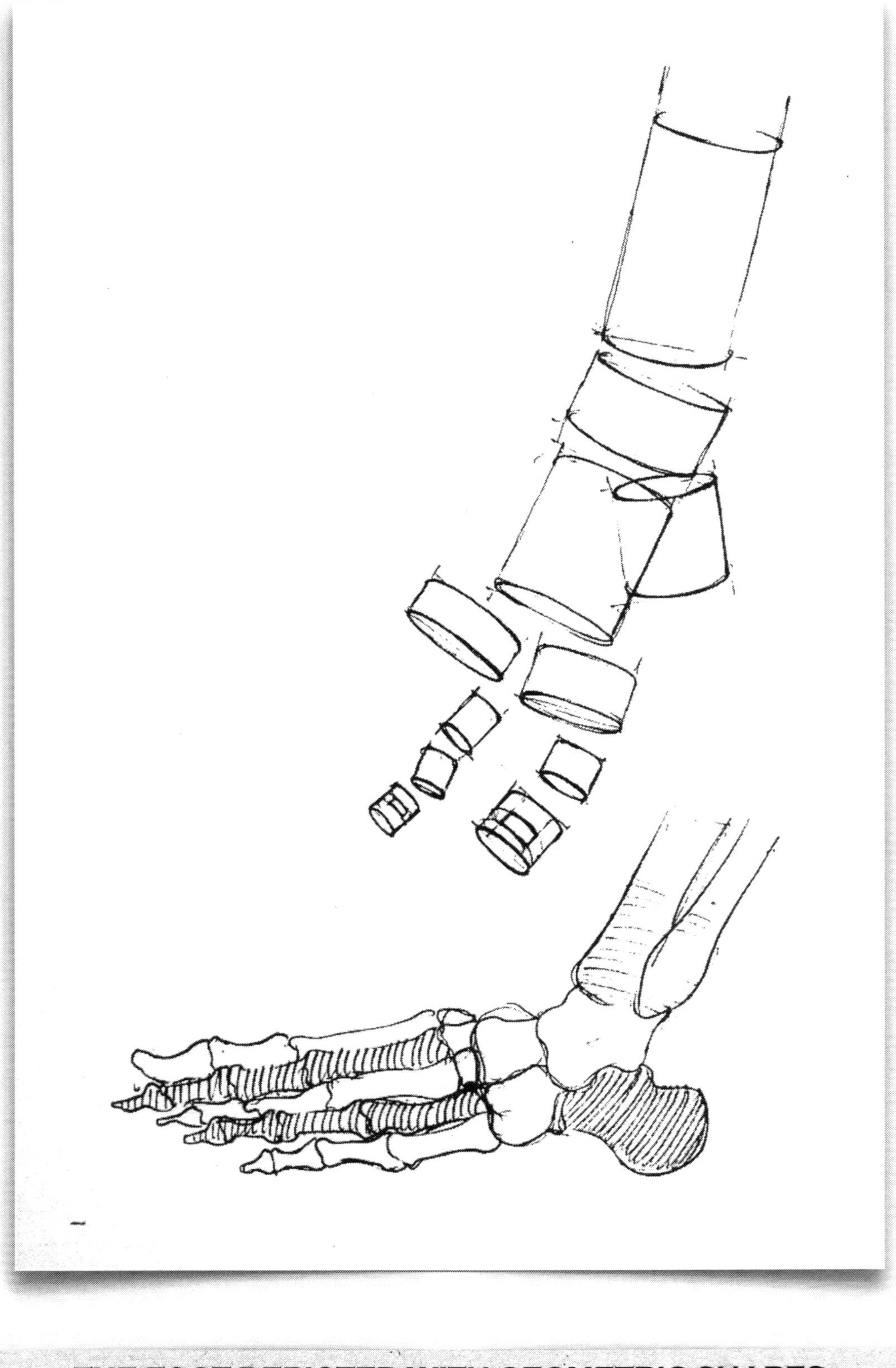

THE FOOT DEPICTED WITH GEOMETRIC SHAPES AND ANATOMICAL STRUCTURE

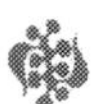

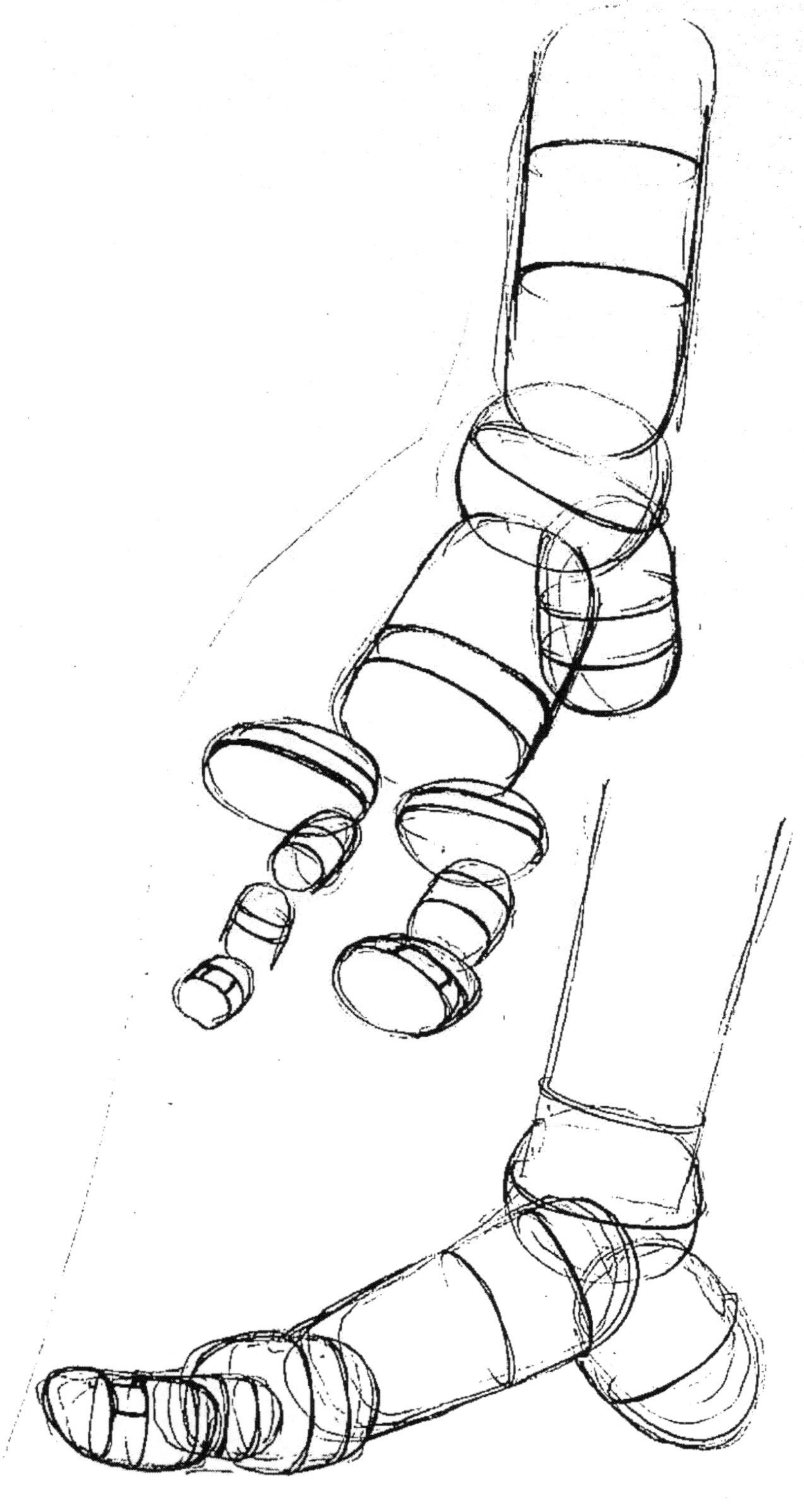

ANALYSIS OF THE FOOT WITH ROUNDED GEOMETRIC SHAPES

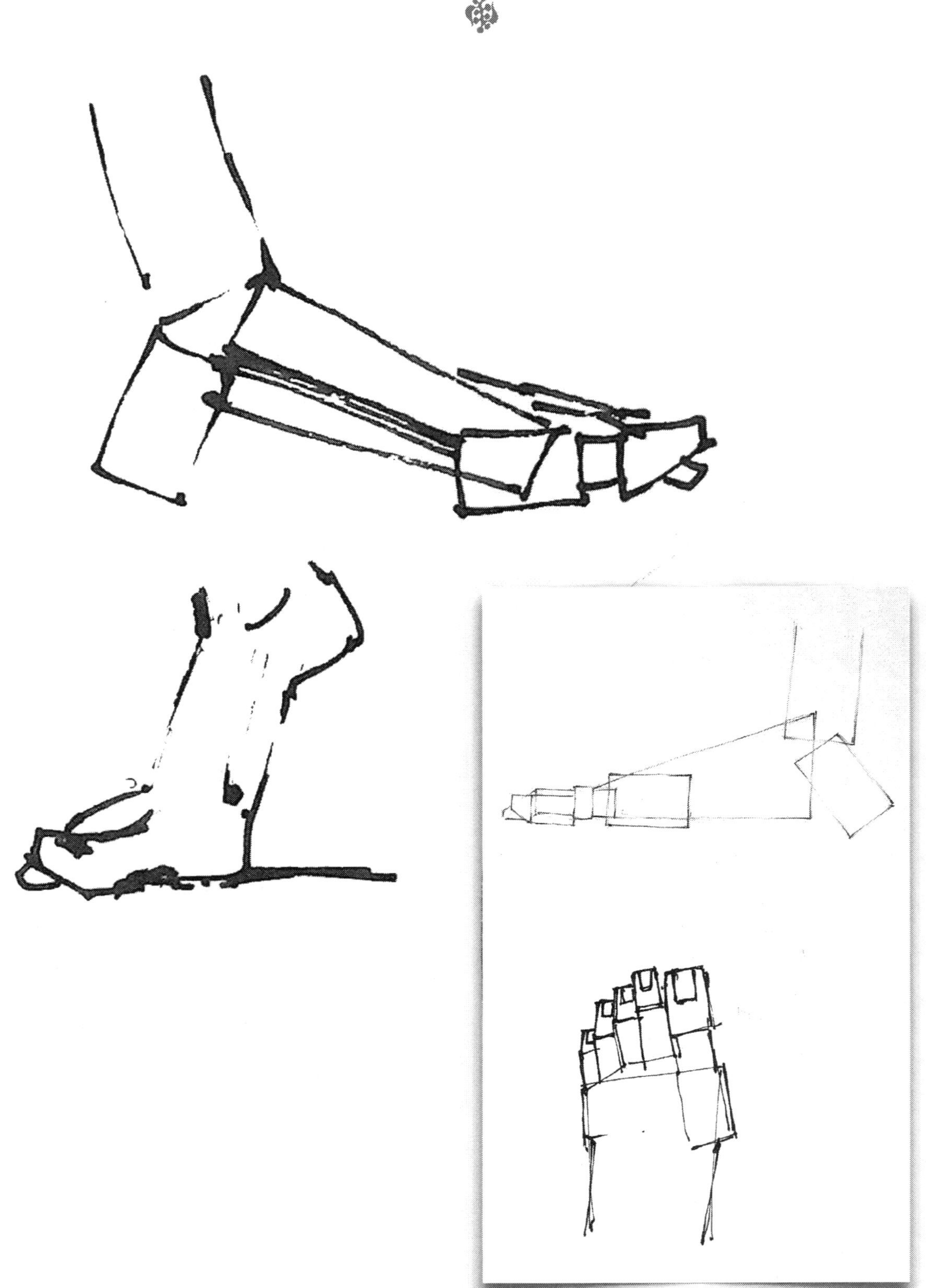

THE BEST STARTING POINT IS FOLLOWING GEOMETRIC PRINCIPLES WITH VARIOUS EXAMPLES OF THE FOOT IN CONTACT WITH THE FLOOR

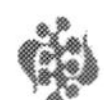

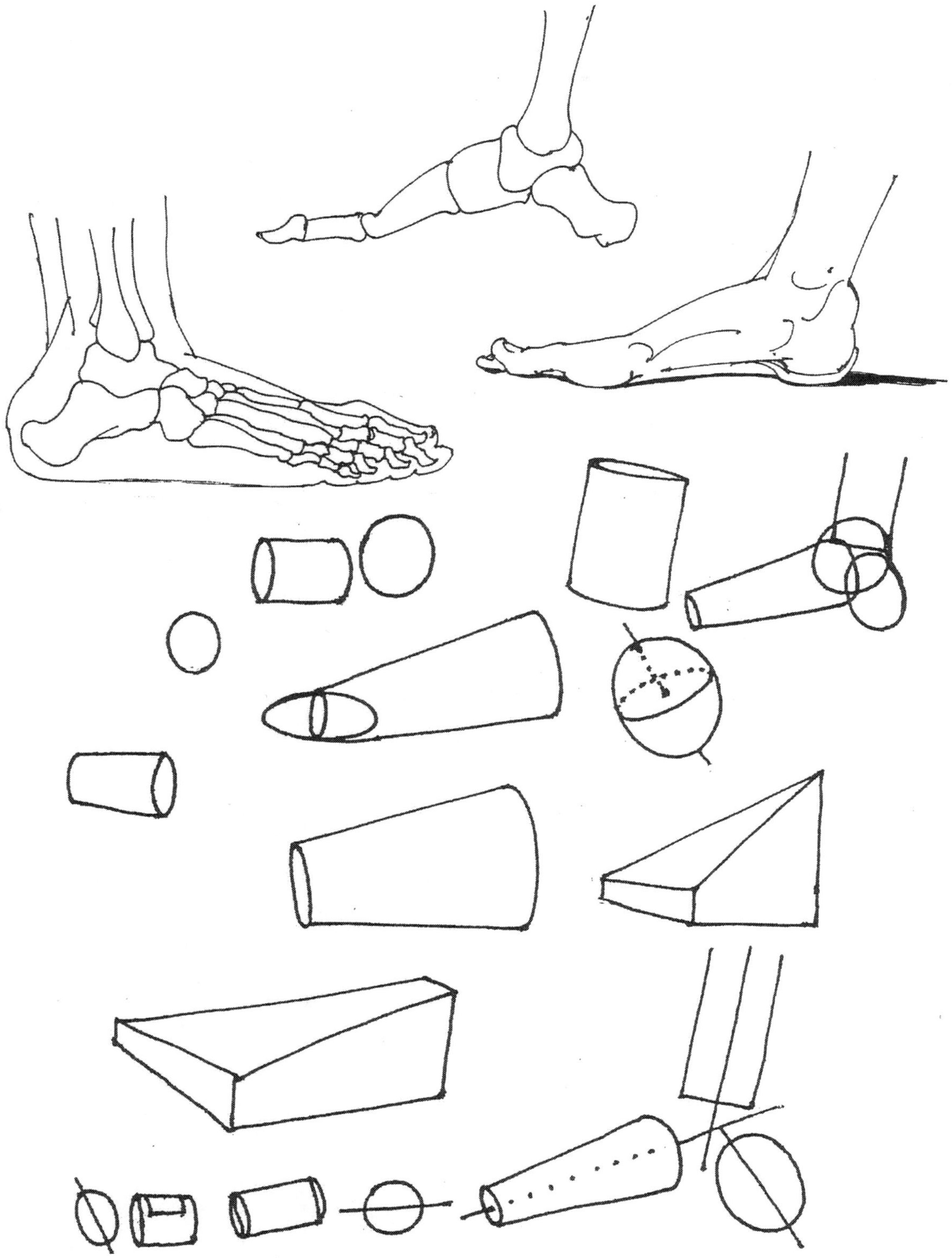

**WITH GEOMETRIC ANALYSIS WE CAN UNDERSTAND
THE STRUCTURE OF ANATOMICAL SHAPES.**

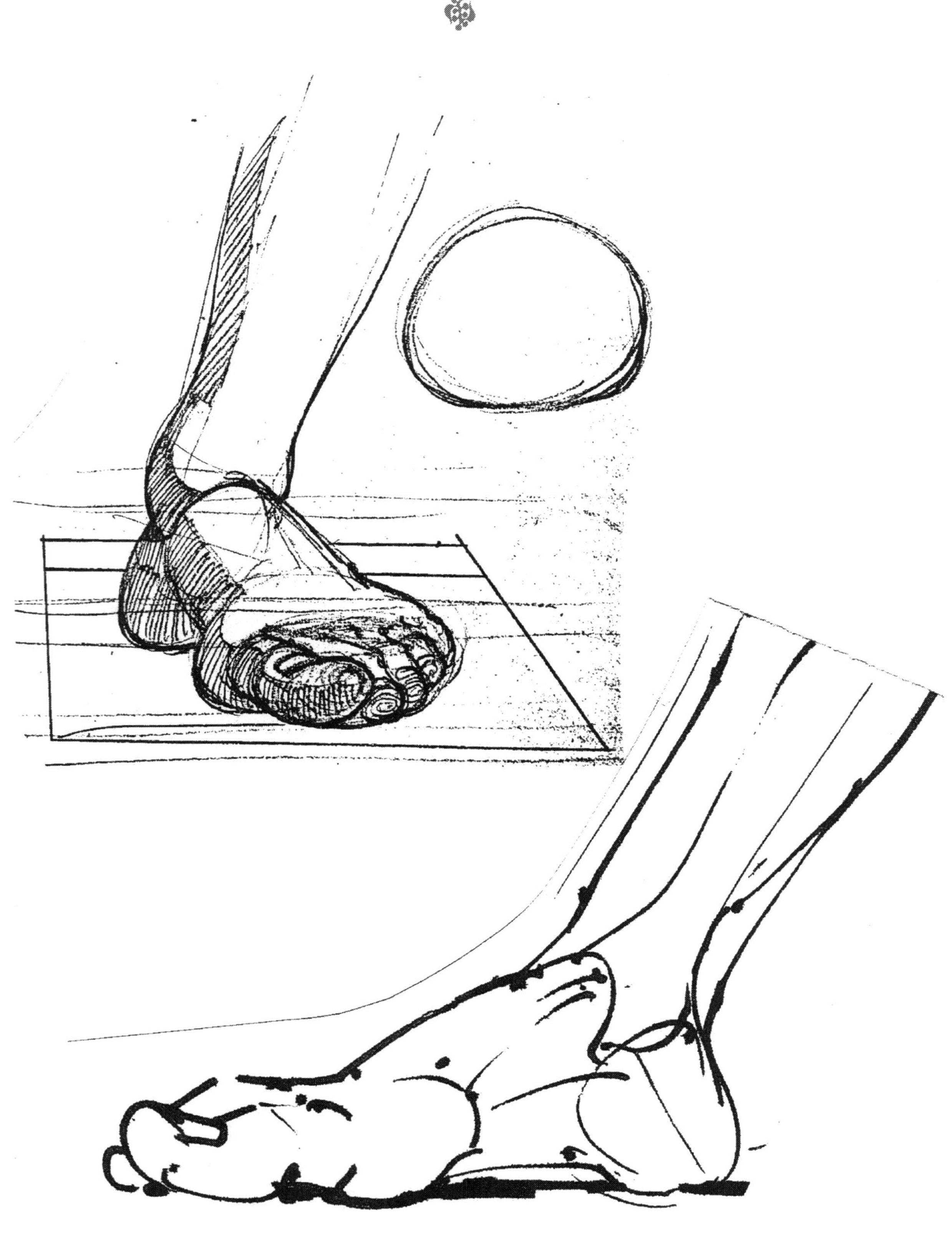

THE PRESENCE OF A BALL WITHIN THE HEEL OF THE FOOT

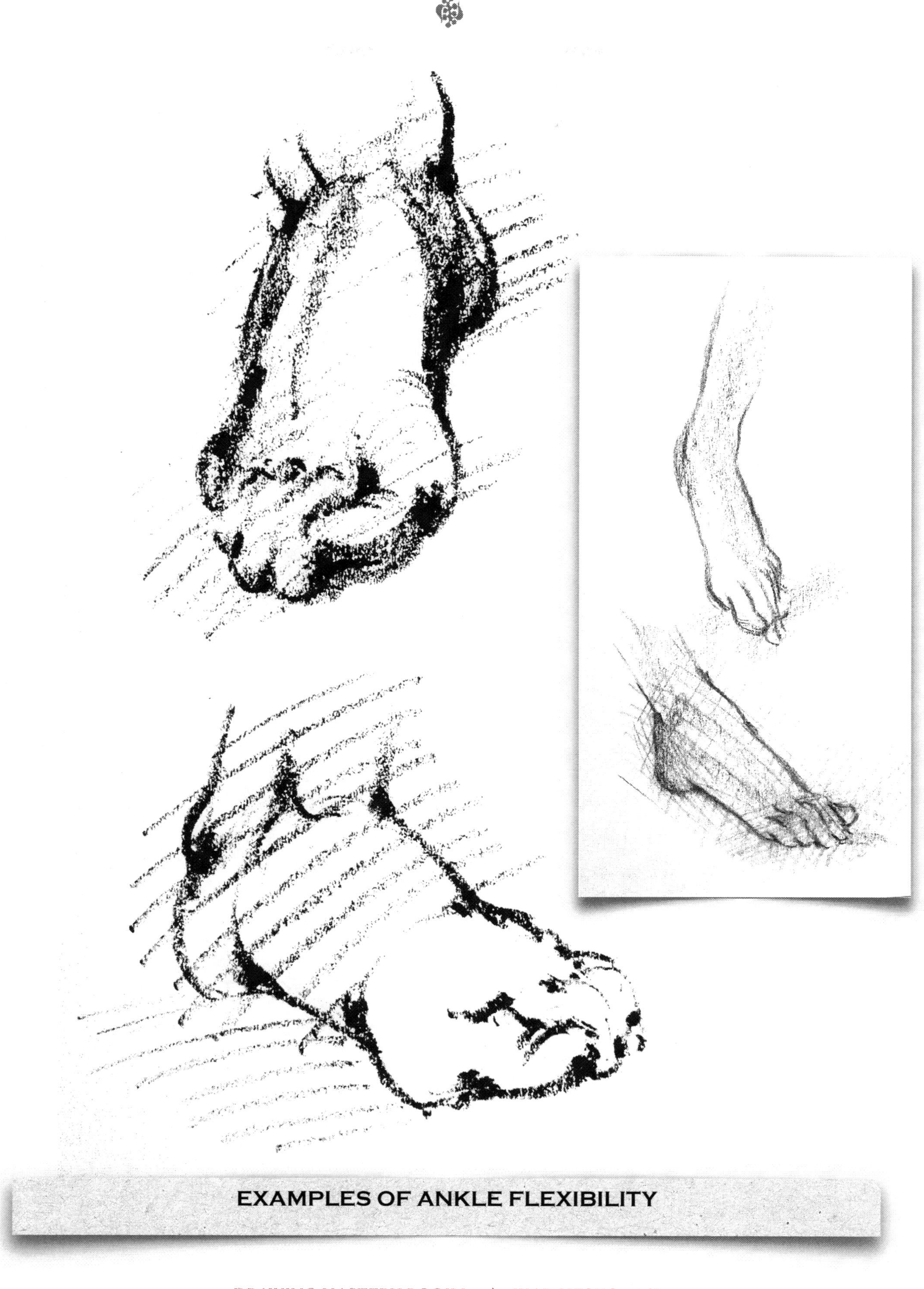

EXAMPLES OF ANKLE FLEXIBILITY

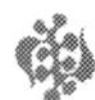

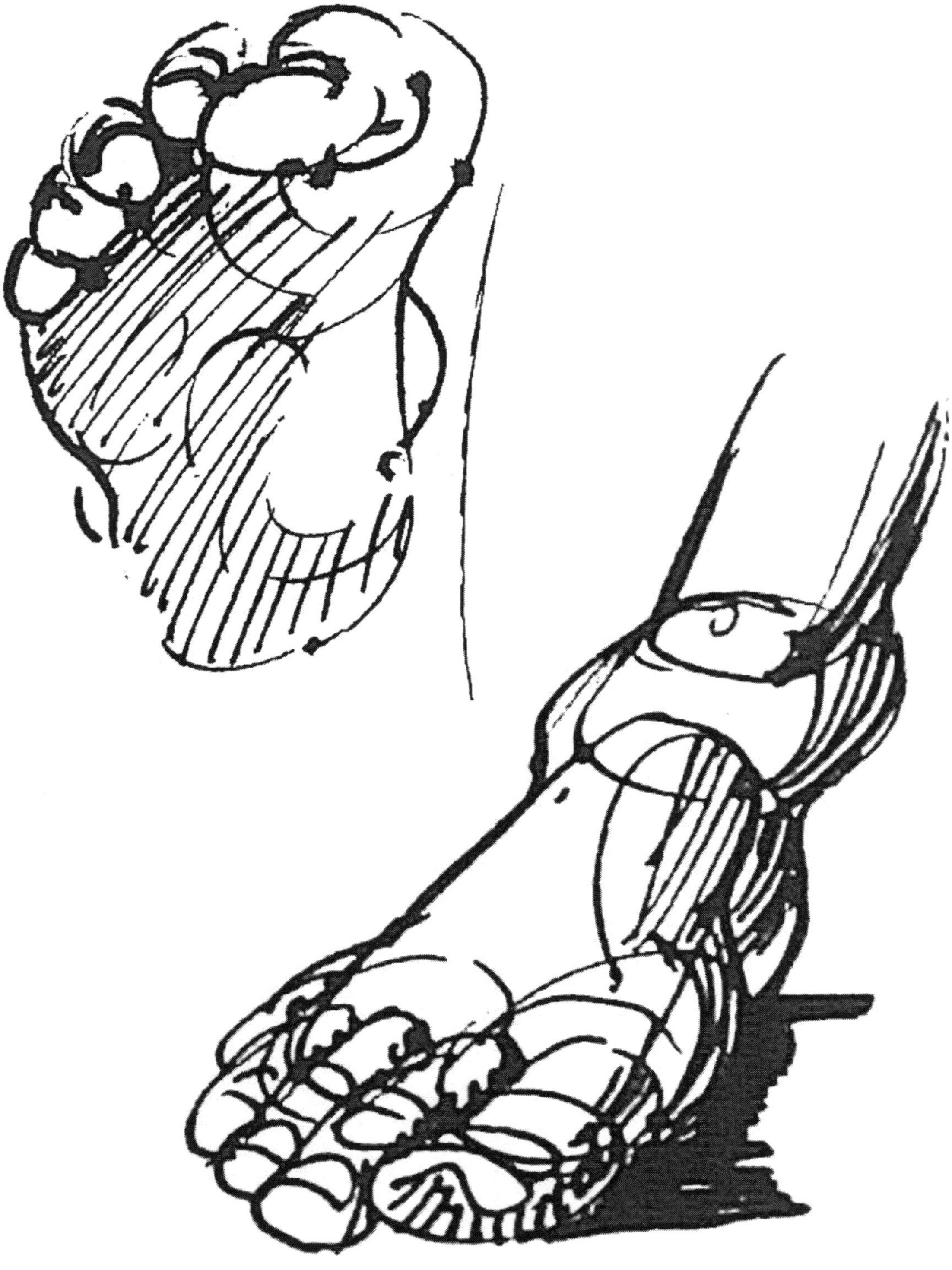

A CALLIGRAPHIC CONCLUSION SOFTENS GEOMETRICAL HARDNESS

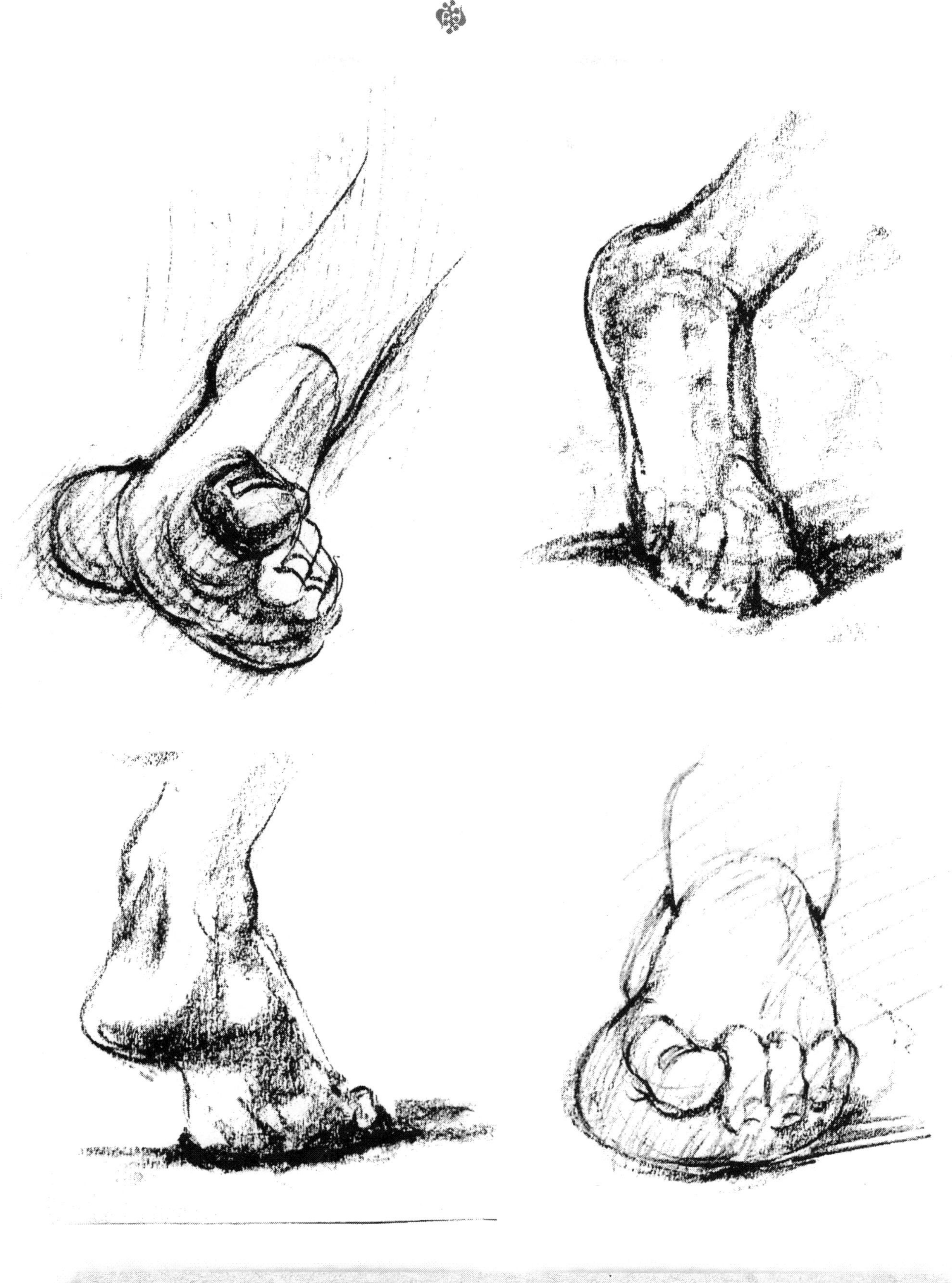

EXAMPLES OF VARIOUS SHAPES TRANSITIONING INTO EACH OTHER

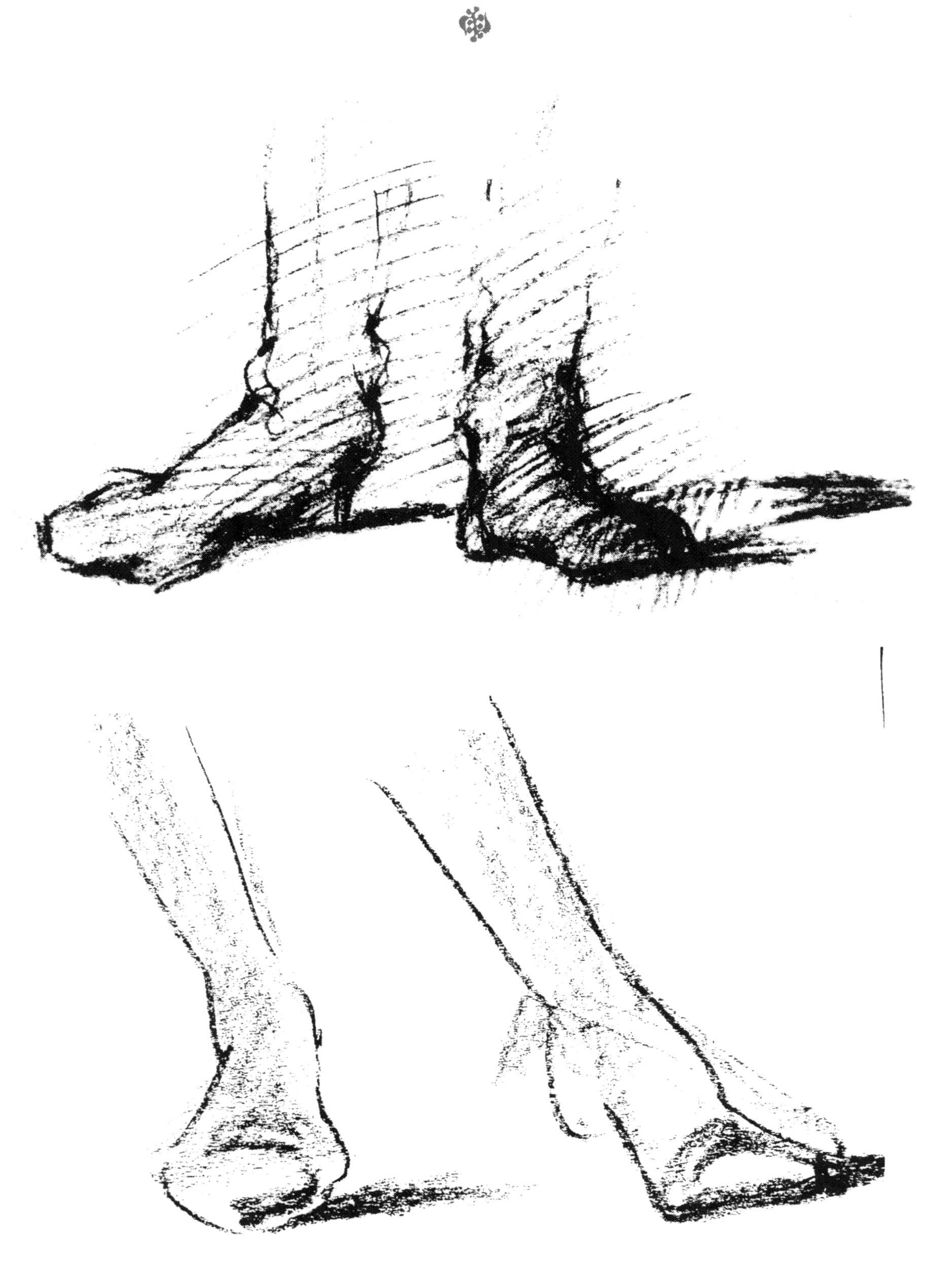

FOOTWEAR SIMPLIFIES THE SHAPE OF TOES

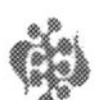

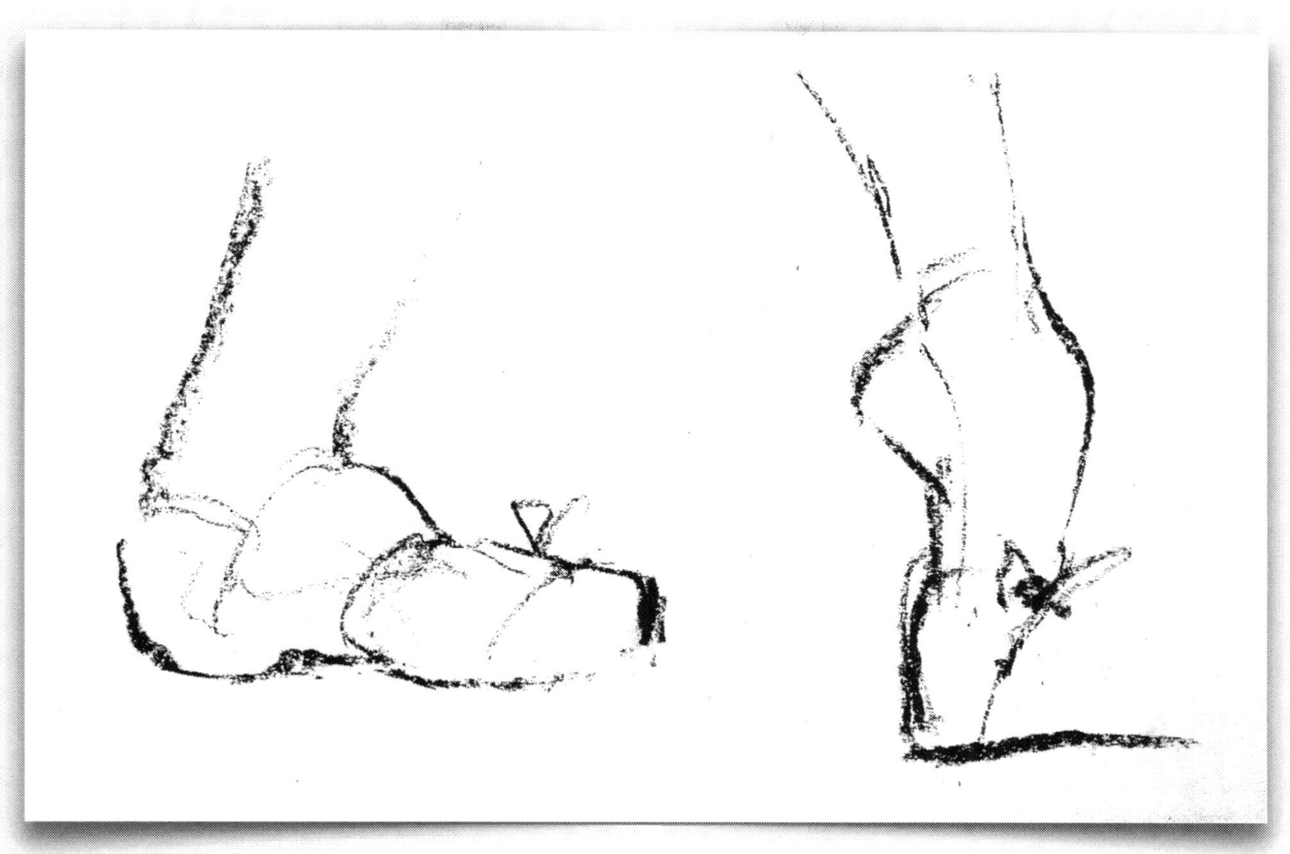

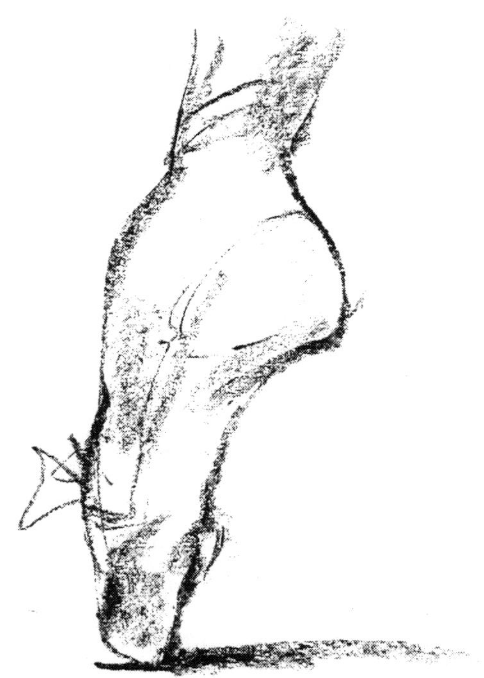

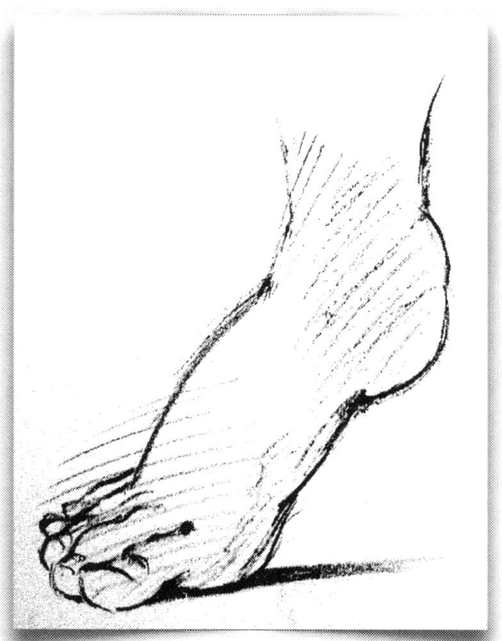

TOES HIDDEN WITHIN FOOTWEAR TRANSFORM
INTO A UNIFIED SHAPE

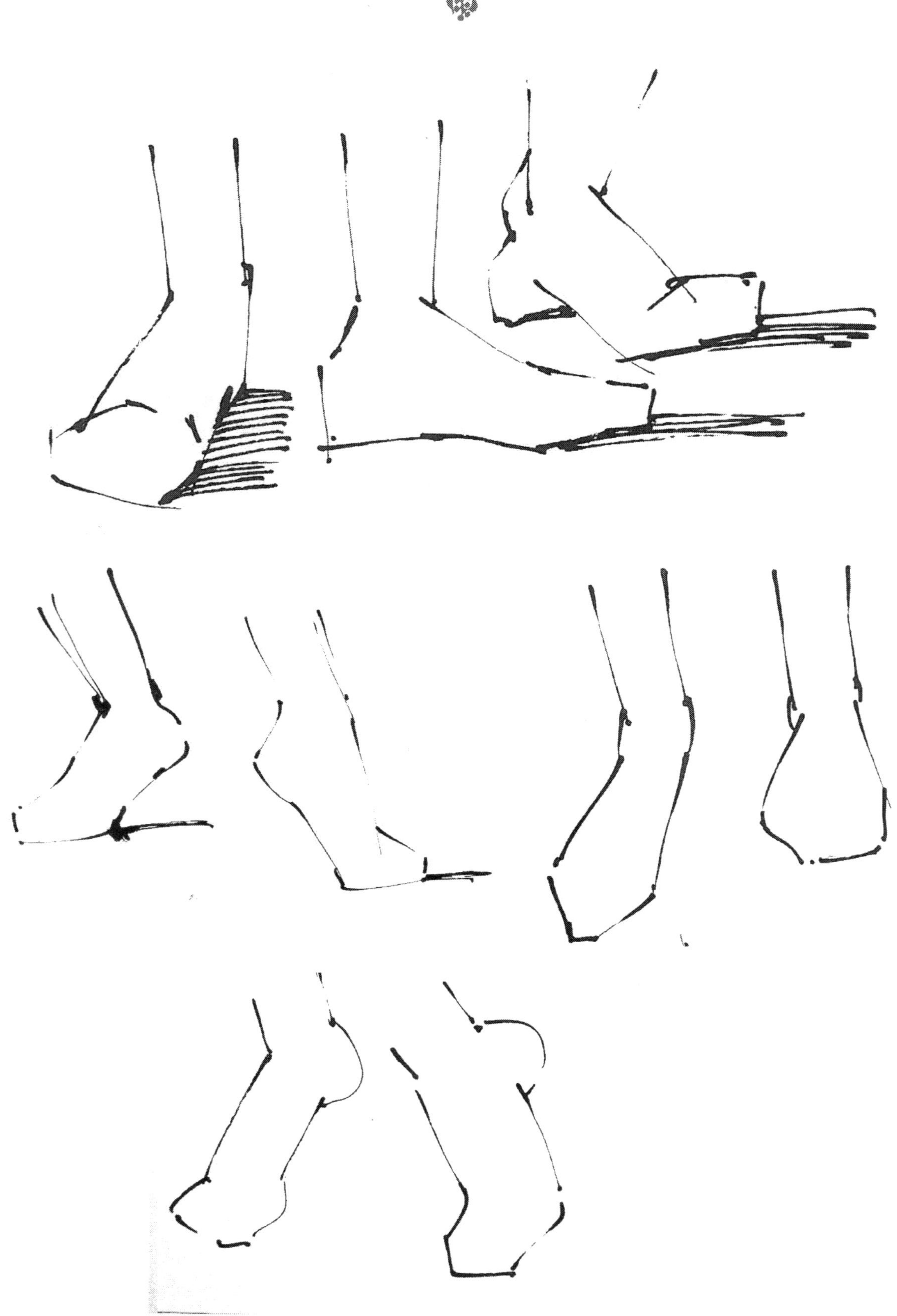

VARIOUS EXAMPLES OF THE DIRECTION OF THE FEET

The Leg

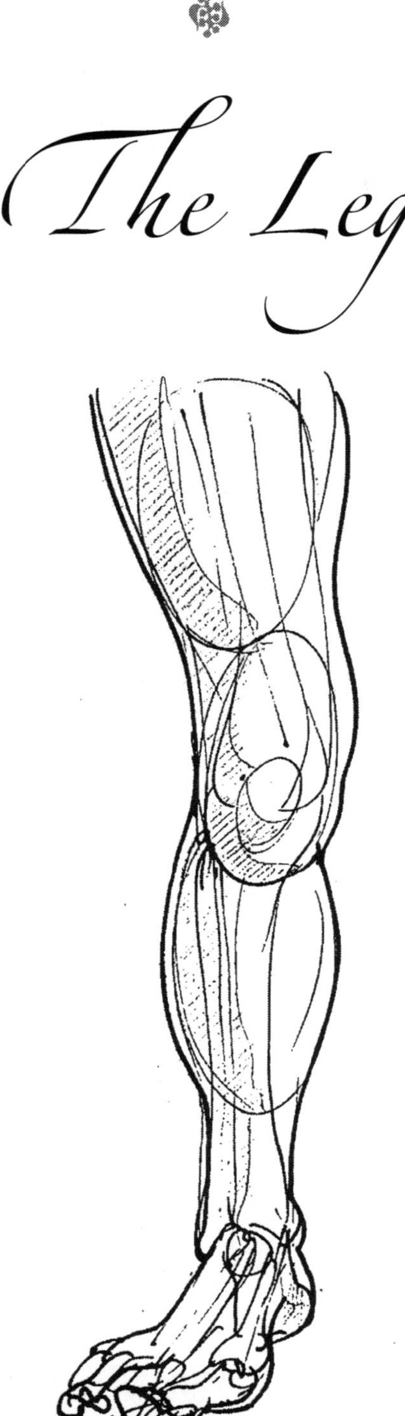

L IKE THE HAND, THE LEG PLAYS A SIMILARLY IMPORTANT ROLE as an element of dynamics. As a separate combination of shapes, the leg is not especially demanding. It becomes interesting in two ways: with interaction of both legs, and in relation to the whole body. With each leg we imagine its pair. The same leg with a different profile, different joint movement and distribution of weight. Always the same, long or short, weak or strong, even harmonious or rough. From knee upwards or from hip downwards all the way to the toes.

There are essentially three static phases of the body; sitting, standing or lying position. Each one of them can be in itself demanding to depict, however the sitting position offers the greatest dynamic. Take a look at various poses of Michelangelo's figures in the Sistine Chapel. They exemplify such extreme level of complex and difficult positions, that they earned even a public review by the artist N Benjamin Haydon in Encyclopedia Brittanica 1838!

The conviction that it is easy to draw the legs in a lying down position is also quite deceptive. Despite the small number of variants, the selection is subtle and therefore demanding, specially when depicting a woman's beauty. We come to the unexpected realization, that drawing dynamic body positions and interactions is a most rewarding endeavor. The only catch becomes the level of one's ability to draw. All the luxury that a good drawing ability to capture legs offers, requires hours of practice and studious drawing. That is the required sacrifice. It is not the question of perfect drawings , but the pursuit of serious sketches of various positions and shortenings.

The order of sequence begins at the junction of hip and the thigh, next comes the thigh with the knee, the calf, the ankle and finally the complex of the foot. The rotation possibilities around the vertical axis are of the most importance. All these possibilities can only be explored with geometric analysis and drawings, partially also when drawing anatomical and skeletal structures. The muscle anatomy can prevent the effectiveness of spacial form and may mislead you from your principal interest and goal.

TECHNICAL ADVICE AND SUGGESTIONS

WHEN DRAWING THE LEGS, do not forget your knowledge of feet. Now you can observe the real value of geometry and return to the previous chapter. Very important is equal consideration of all the knowledge you've gained. Large shapes oblige us to respect smaller parts, so they do not become mechanical simplifications.

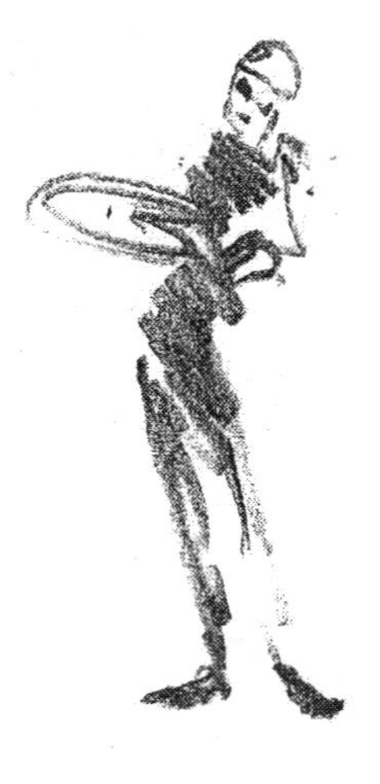

When drawing the legs the changes in direction of longer shapes is crucially important. The leg is not stiff or immobile when perceived form head on or a side view. The knee also has its own direction. When drawing a leg always imagine the position of the other leg as well, the left or right one. This way you will understand the depiction of the human body as one unified form. The examples in this chapter serve as a point of departure for improved and detailed interpretation of intricate clear lines or shading, shaping, the gradation of darkness and light when depicting surfaces.

Remember all the technical suggestions and principles that we've learned up to this point, they continue to hold value. New knowledge always offers an opportunity to add to your framework of deeper understanding.

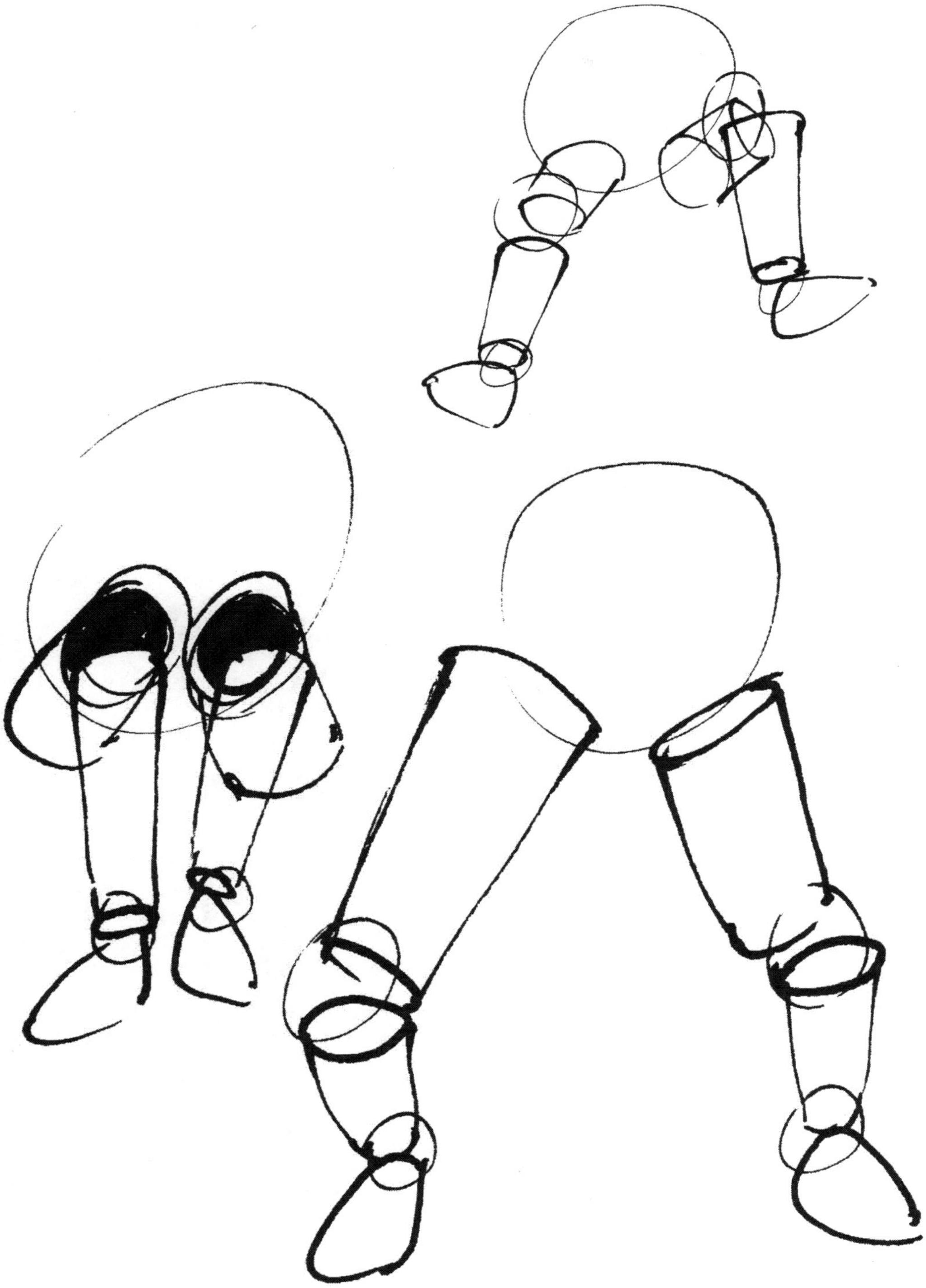

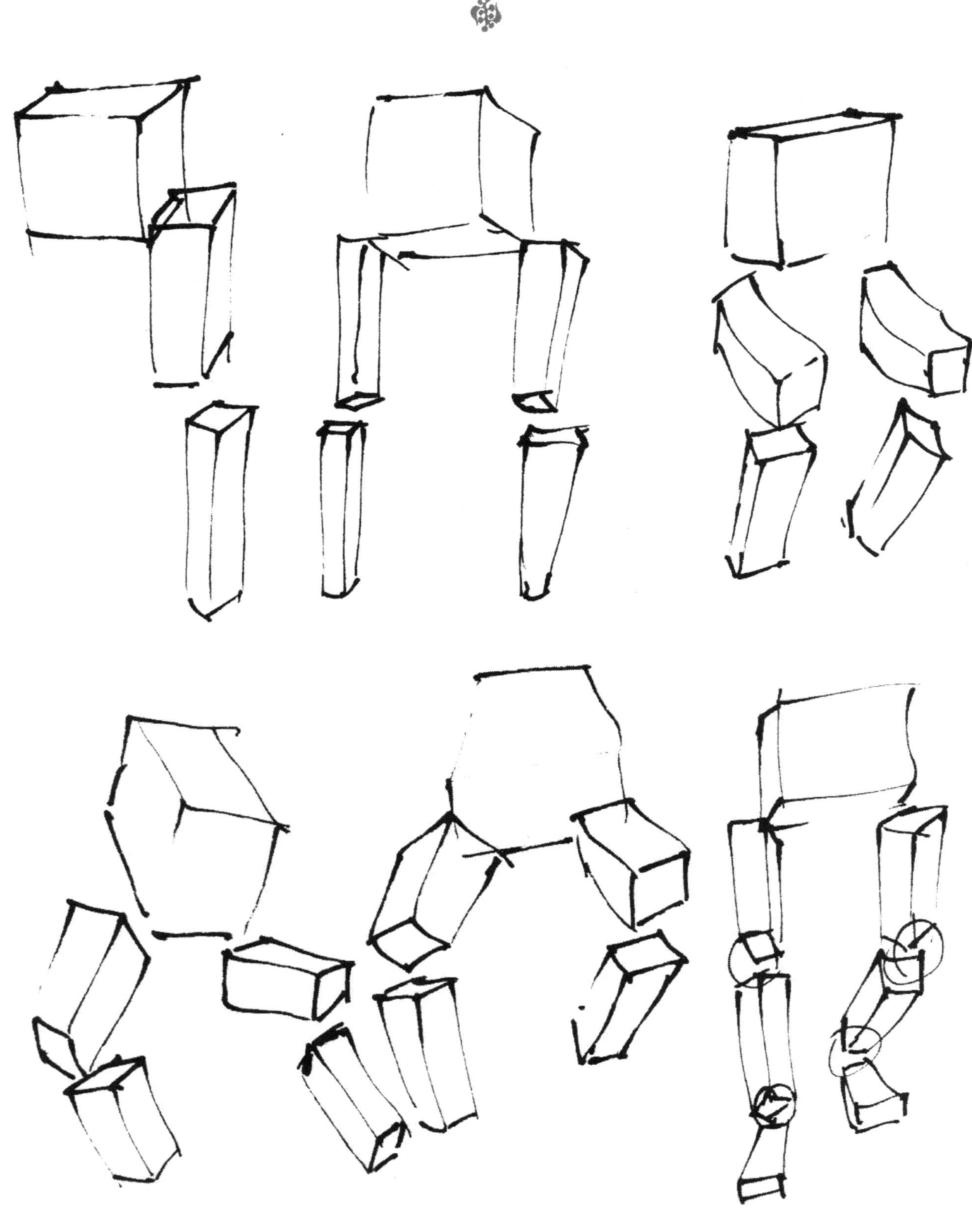

ANGULAR GEOMETRIC BODES REPRESENT CLEAR DIRECTION
OF ROTATION AND TURNS

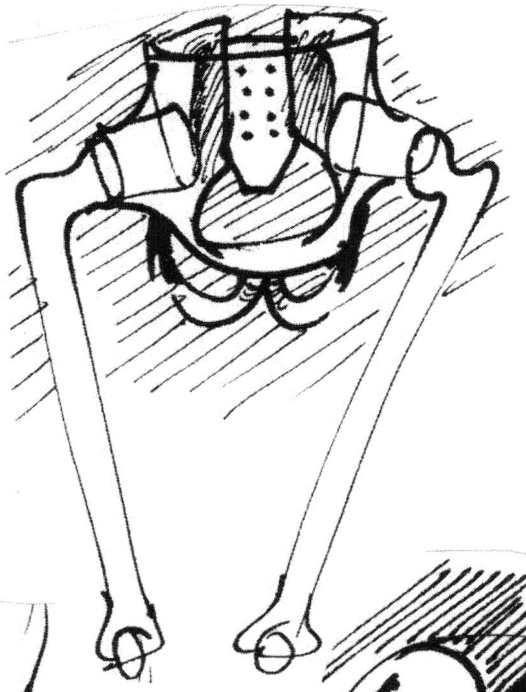

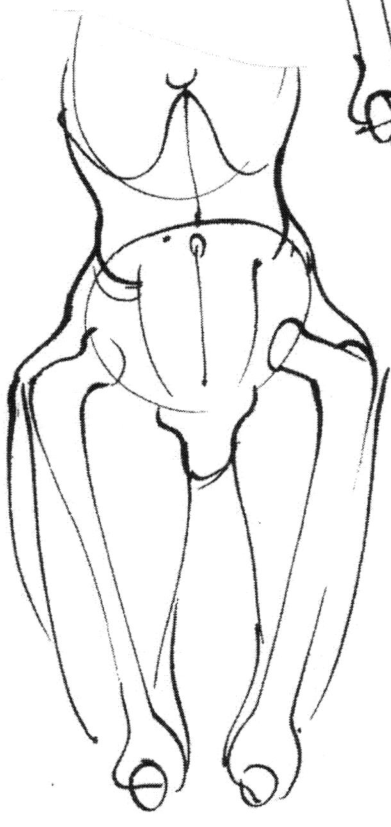

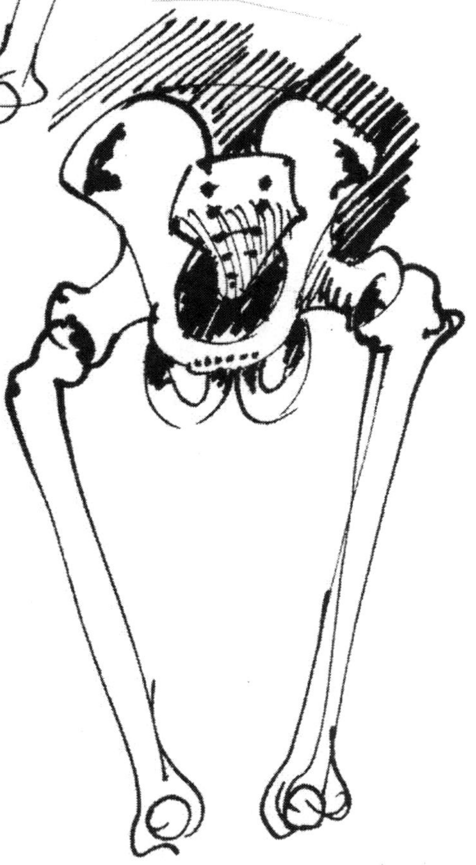

COMPLICATED BONE COMPLEX OF THE HIP AND ITS PRESENTATION
IN A RELAXED BUT ACCURATE DRAWING

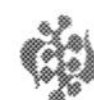

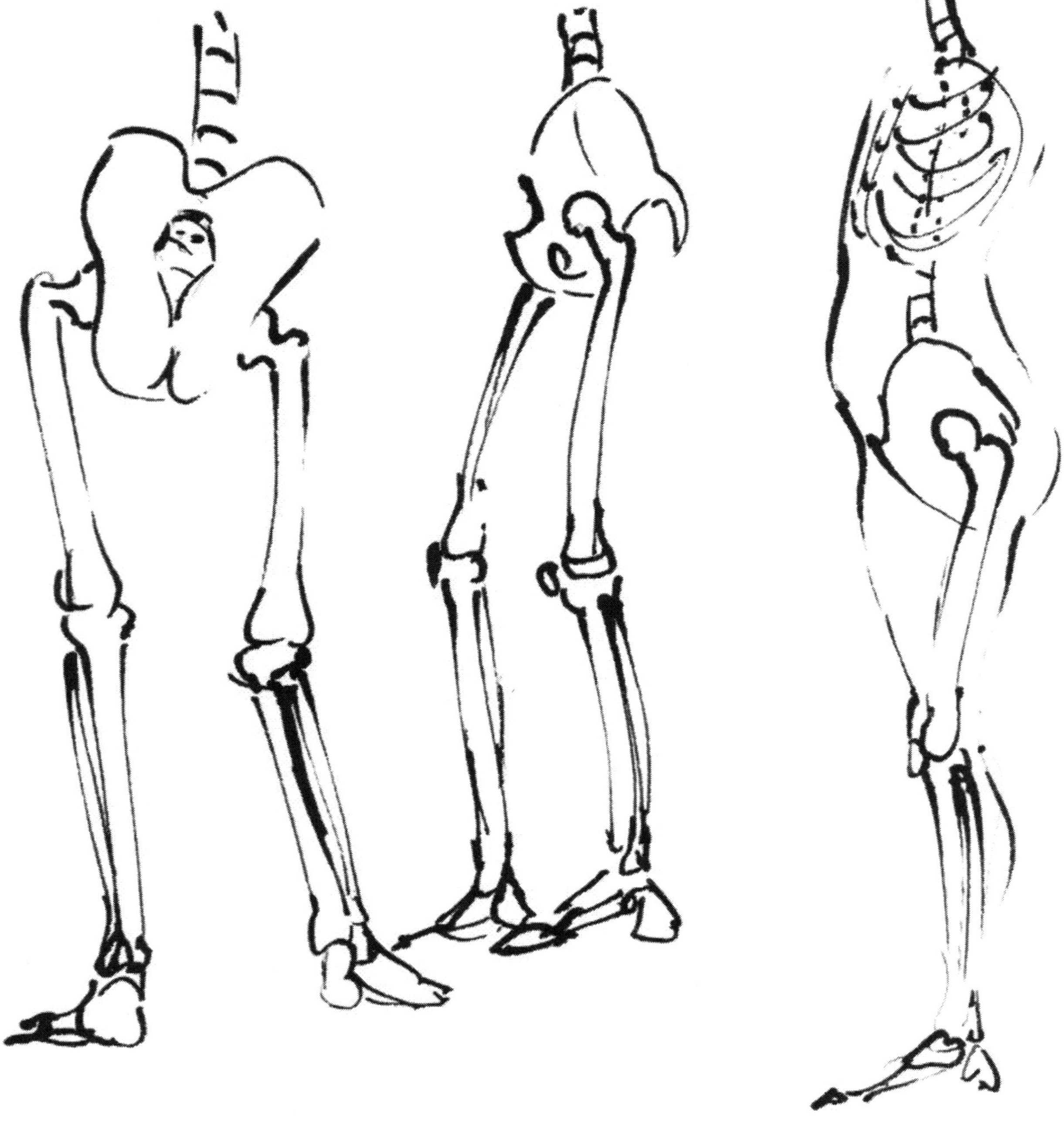

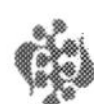

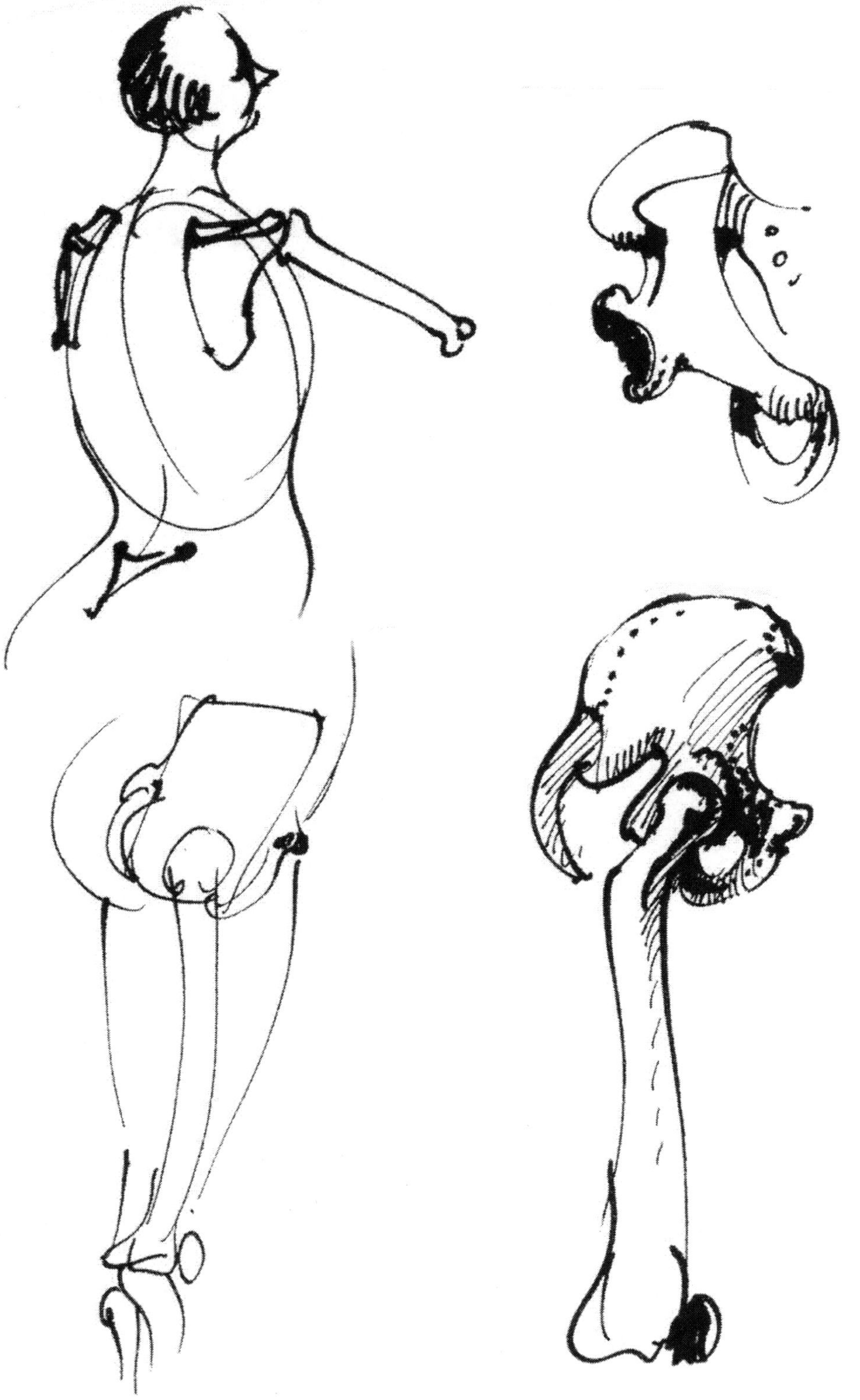

ANATOMIC VIEW FROM THE SHOULDER, OVER THE HIP ALL THE WAY TO THE KNEE

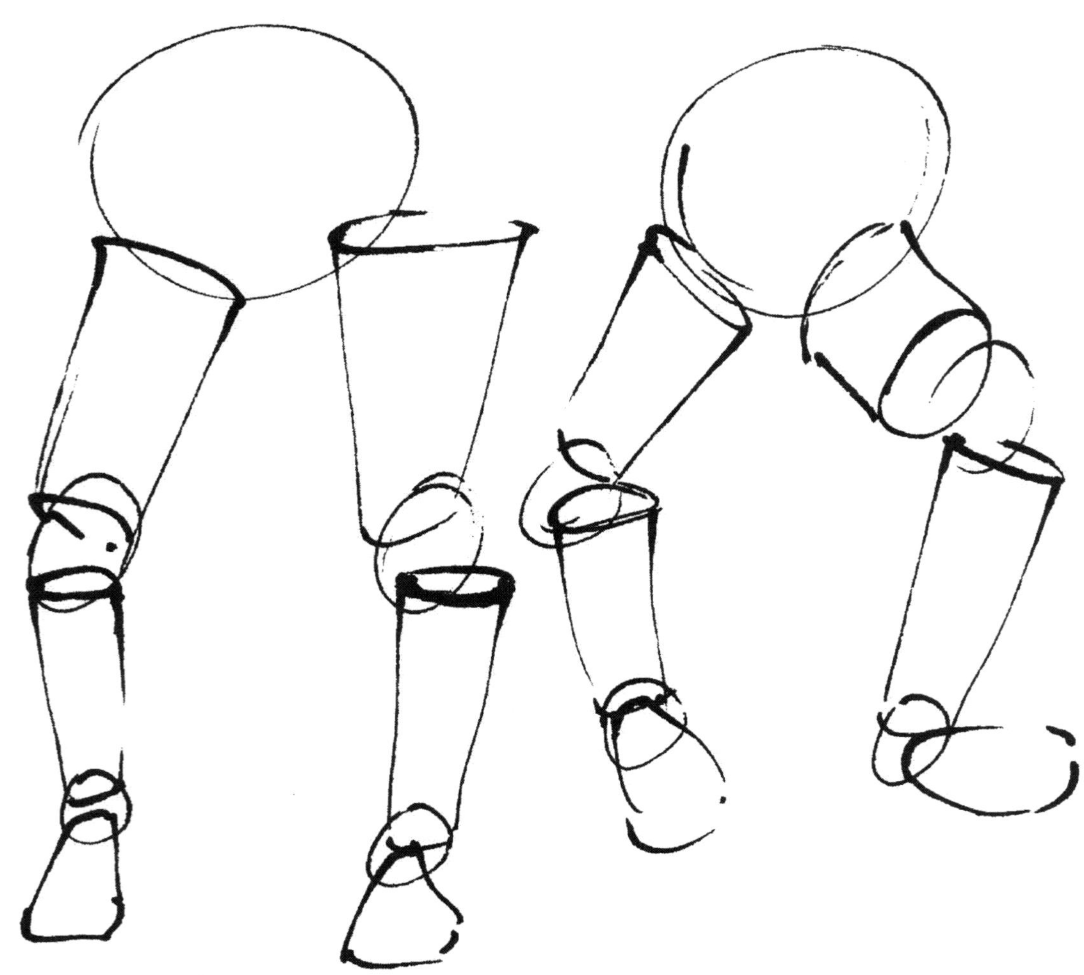

**CYLINDRIC SHAPES FACILITATE THE BEST DEPICTION
AND CLARITY OF THE DIRECTION OF LEGS**

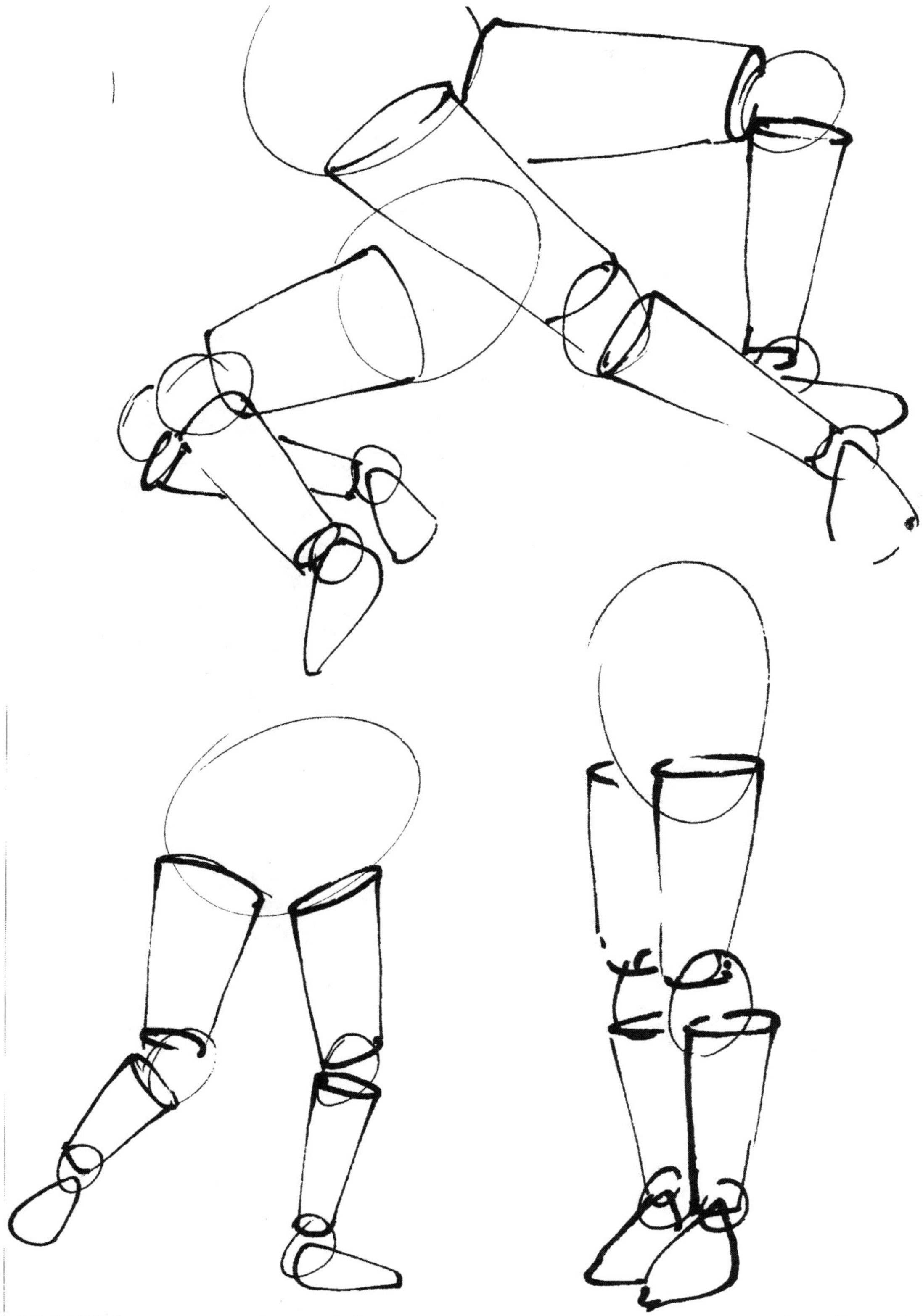

CYLINDRIC SHAPES FACILITATE THE BEST DEPICTION AND CLARITY OF THE DIRECTION OF LEGS

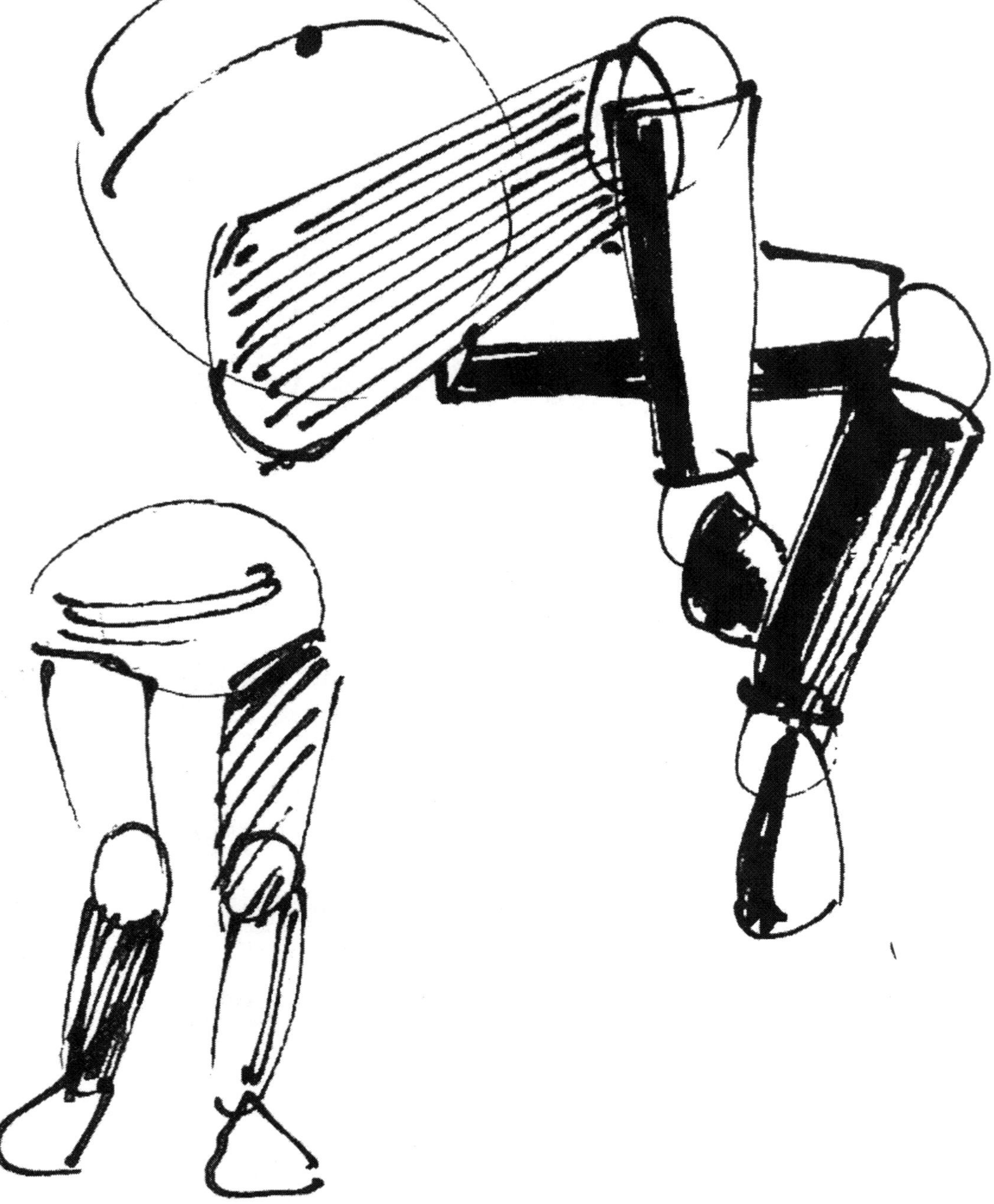

WITH SHADING WE CAN AMPLIFY THE DIRECTIONS OF THE SHAPES

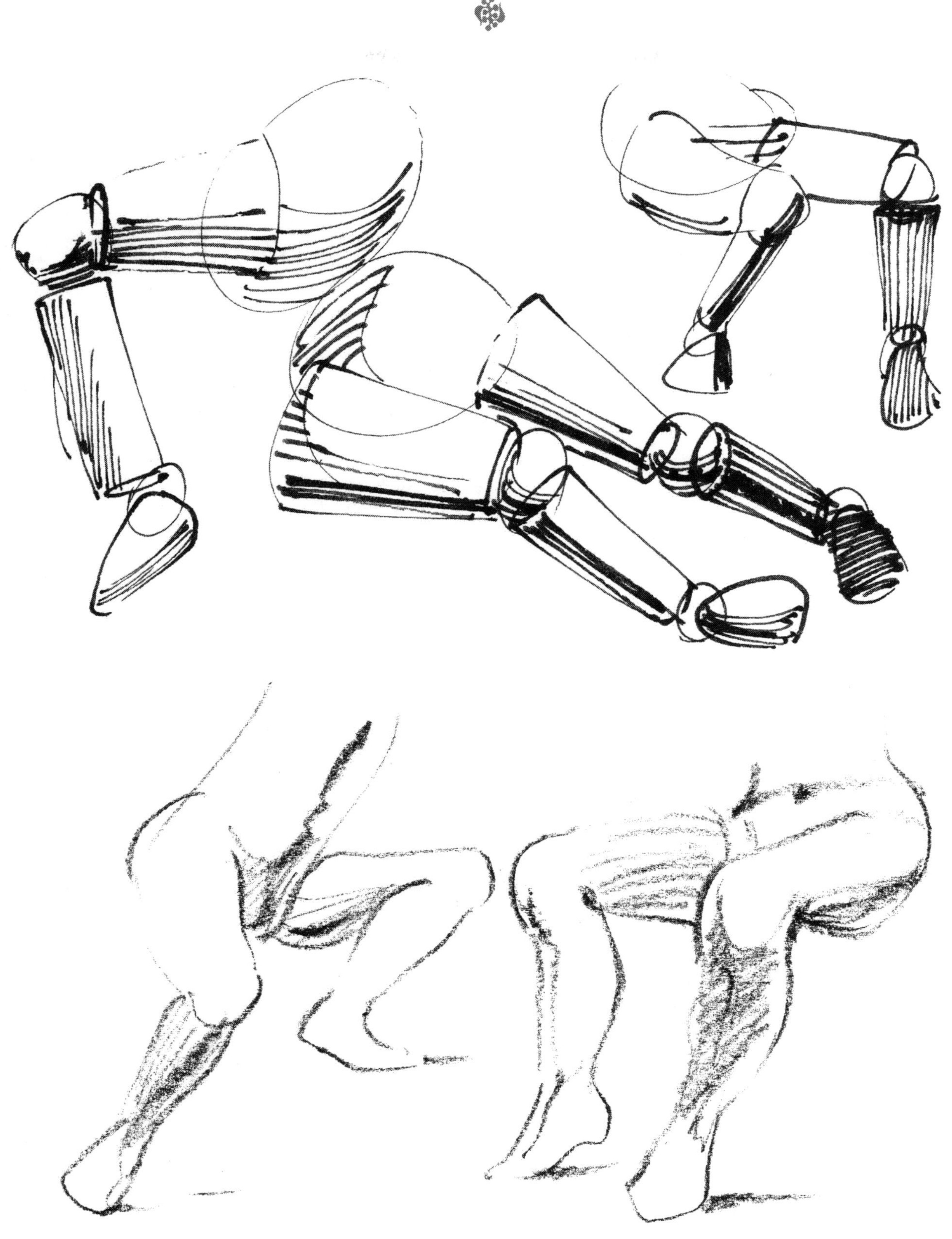

SHADING OF GEOMETRIC SHAPES AND
SHADING OF ORGANIC SHAPES

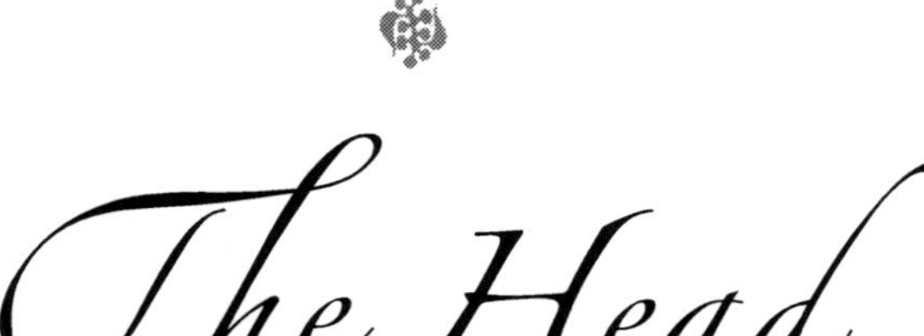

The Head

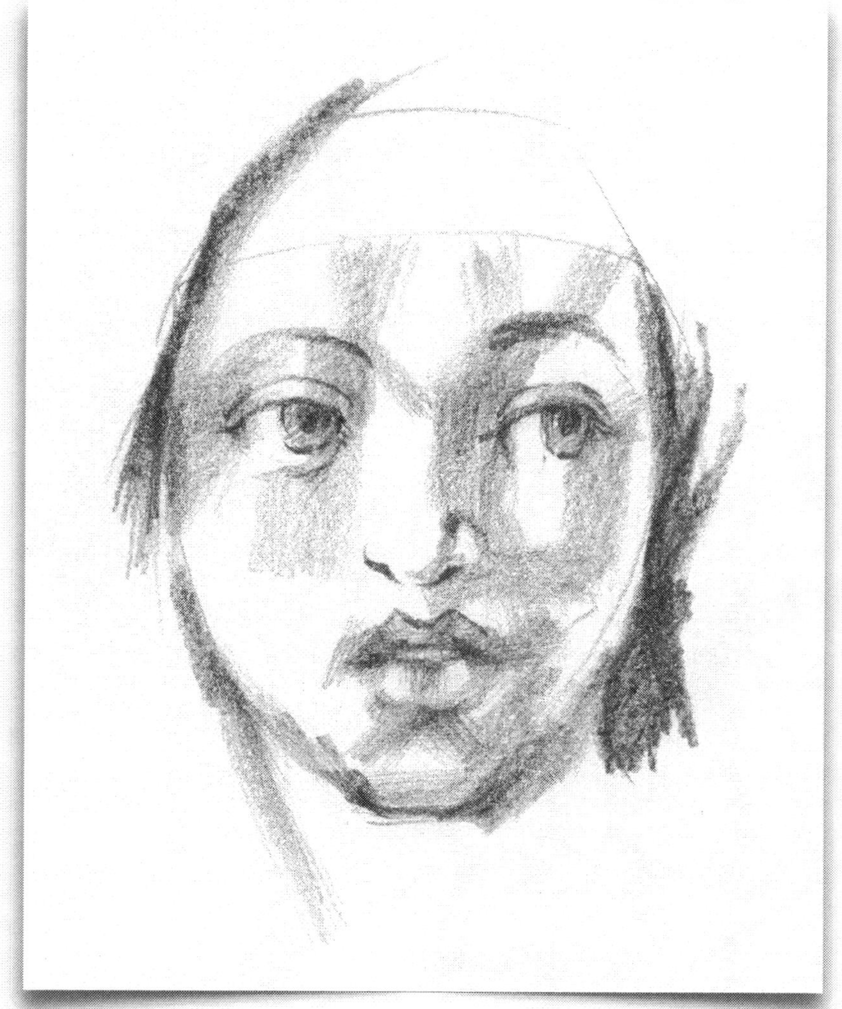

THE DRAWING LESSON USUALLY BEGINS WITH THE STUDY OF THE HEAD. It seems simple enough: we set up a model, and then the students should show what they can do. They receive only some basic suggestions. Second option is to draw after a pattern: we select an appropriate drawing or painting, that the student should faithfully copy. There are other, similar variations.

But the head has a multitude of demanding qualities that are well hidden even to a skillful eye. The special shape characteristics of the head are best expressed in a portrait. In such case the question of likeness plays a decisive part, which may outweigh the quality of execution. By this evaluation a caricature can present a higher level of drawing ability, as opposed to a well defined shape presentation of the face. The head consists of a large number of demanding geometric elements. The main point of drawing is an objective presentation of actual forms and shapes.

At first glance less important aspects seem essential. Which are these essential , less noticeable values when drawing a head?

Perspective. Symmetry. Proportions. Geometric clarity. Plasticity of the details. The changing axis of the three largest shapes: the chest with shoulders, neck and the head. The changes in angle, inclination and leaning of these three largest shapes. Take into consideration the rounding of the facial surface and placement and depiction of details. In connection to these elements take into consideration the general perspective. It is important to know the value of the gaze in each case of a portrait and how to adapt the shapes to the character of the subject, wether they are a child, a woman or a man, or more specifically a baby, a beauty or a warrior…

When professionally observing the portraits in most prominent galleries of the world, the artist's pure knowledge is the most valuable criteria. Even works from most admired masters are often humble in regards to real quality. More than what is represented was never demanded or even expected. What was expected was a psychological and decorative effect. That is the reality. It can occur that we unexpectedly discover a seemingly humble portrait that has it ALL.To recognize everything that it entails is true luck. It is worthwhile to study and test your knowledge in order to gain the ability to recognize and know a high quality drawing or painting. We can take a moment to think and reflect upon the value of the ability to draw and paint. Only with this knowledge and tested hands on experience can we reach the highest possible level. Therefore only the highest objectively proven level of handcraft and skill can be considered art.

TECHNICAL ADVICE AND SUGGESTIONS

THE FOLLOWING DRAWINGS demand reflection upon their essential value. For the most part, they are derived from the materials prepared for my students. It remains useful and is supplemented with new ideas. I suggest you simply use the free style redrawing approach using all techniques and tools we discussed in previous chapters.

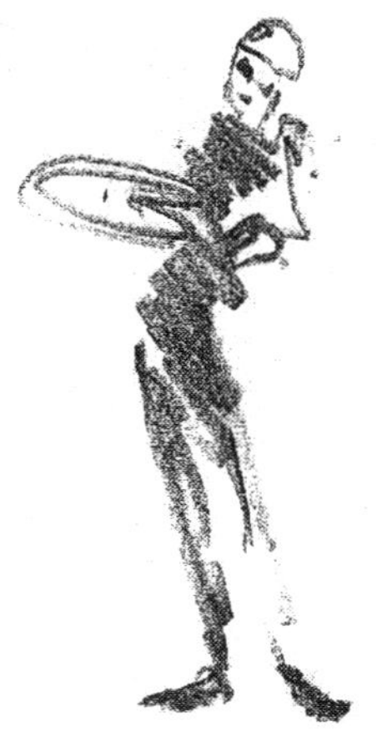

Take into consideration the suggestion about changing the size of studious drawings; try the same drawing in smaller and larger formats. Test your knowledge of drawing the eye, nose, ears and mouth when drawing the head in various positions. You will soon discover how very demanding this business truly is. Try t add the head sketches also the neck and shoulders. All other drawings of heads are various interpretations of the great masters with a comment that they are not careless, but each line is well though out, even if it appears as a careless, coincidental scribble. Observe the combination of charcoal - or soft pencil - and pen. Try these options and possibilities in more examples. Examine how far you can go with a loose stroke and how much concentration requires a seemingly relaxed and loose stroke. We can also create a calligraphic effect with supposedly less important lines by using the method of repetitive light strokes. Never underestimate simple hard work, sometimes it is our only choice.

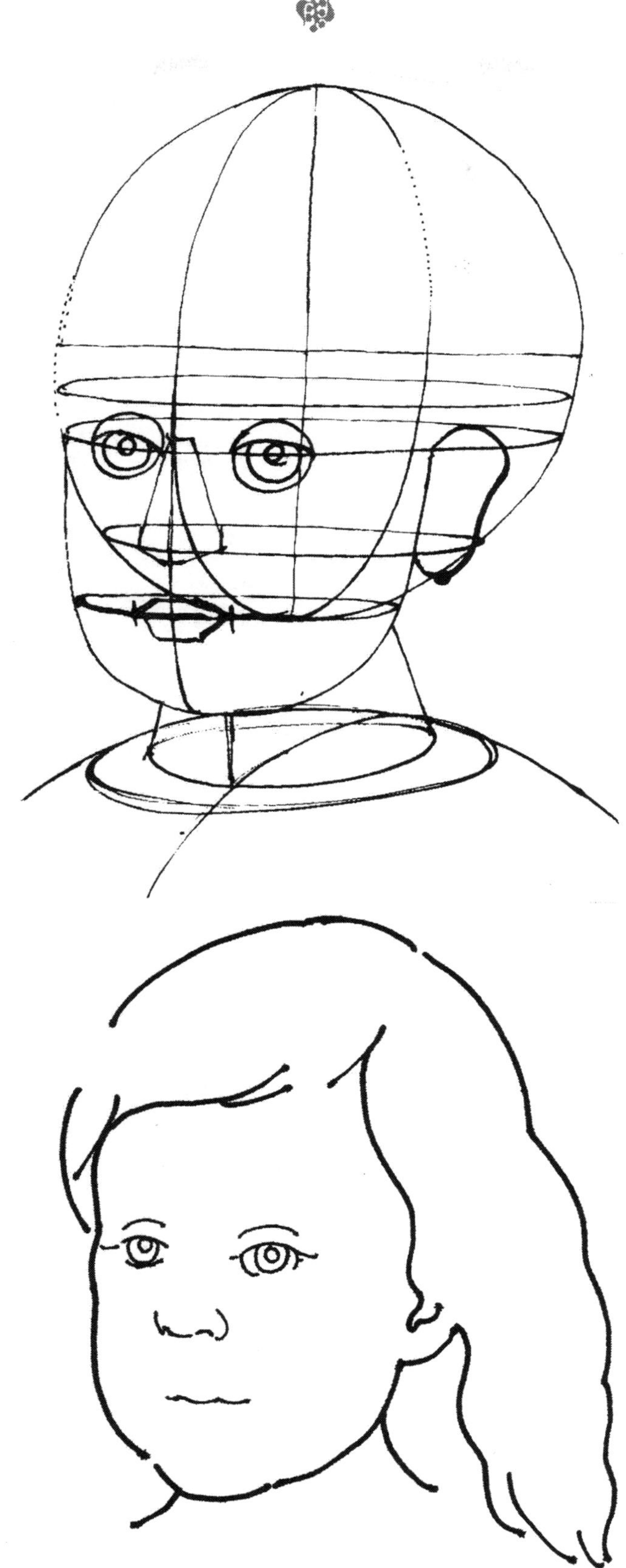

OBSERVATION OF GEOMETRY OF THE HEAD

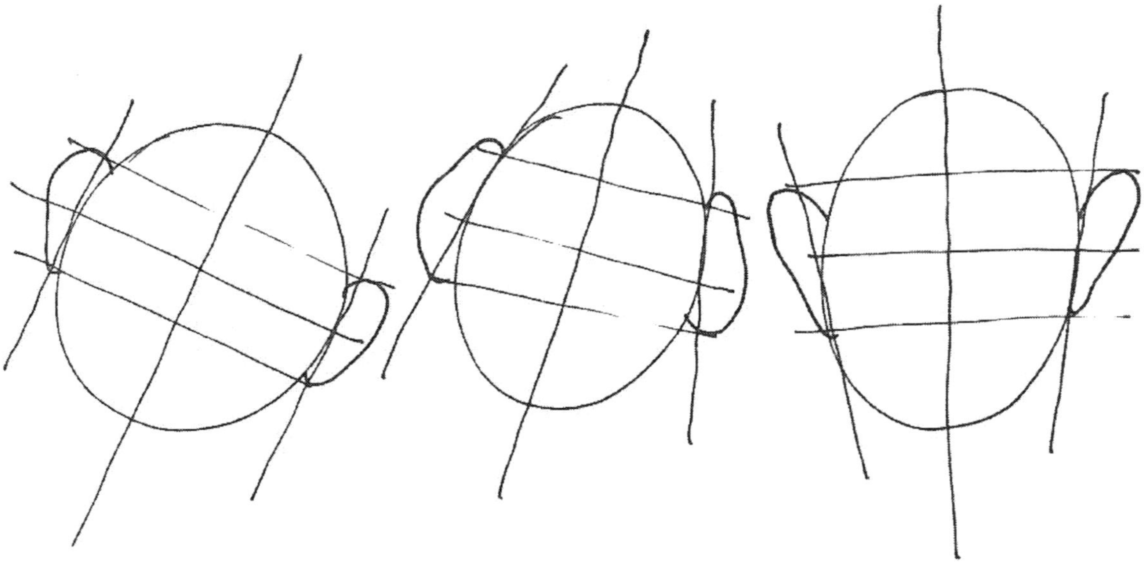

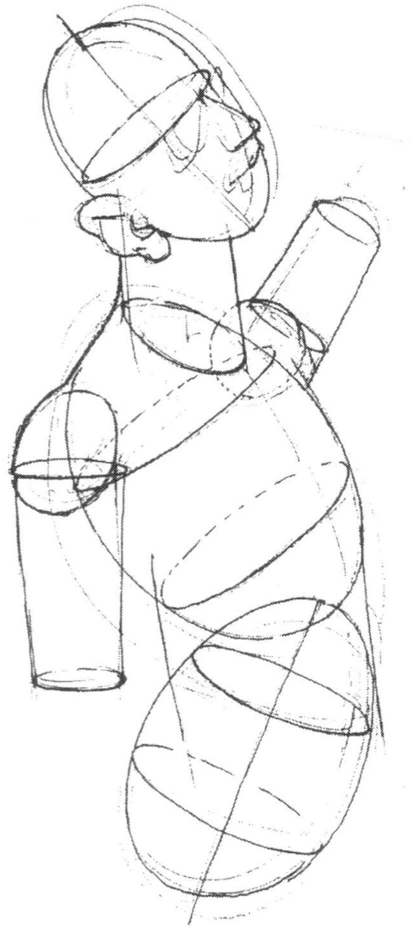

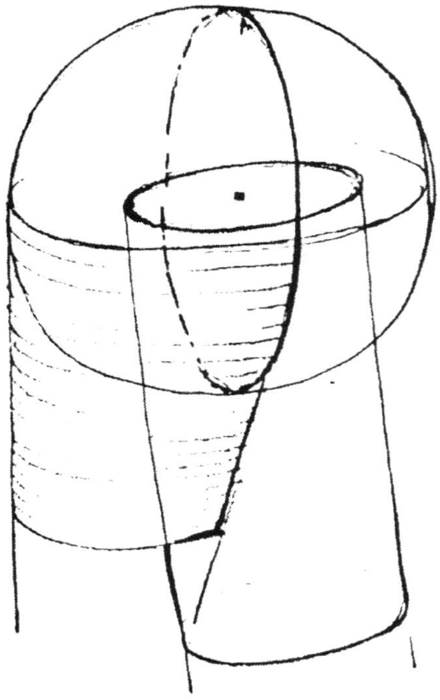

THE DIRECTION OF THE HEAD IN RELATIONSHIP WITH THE DIRECTION OF THE BODY

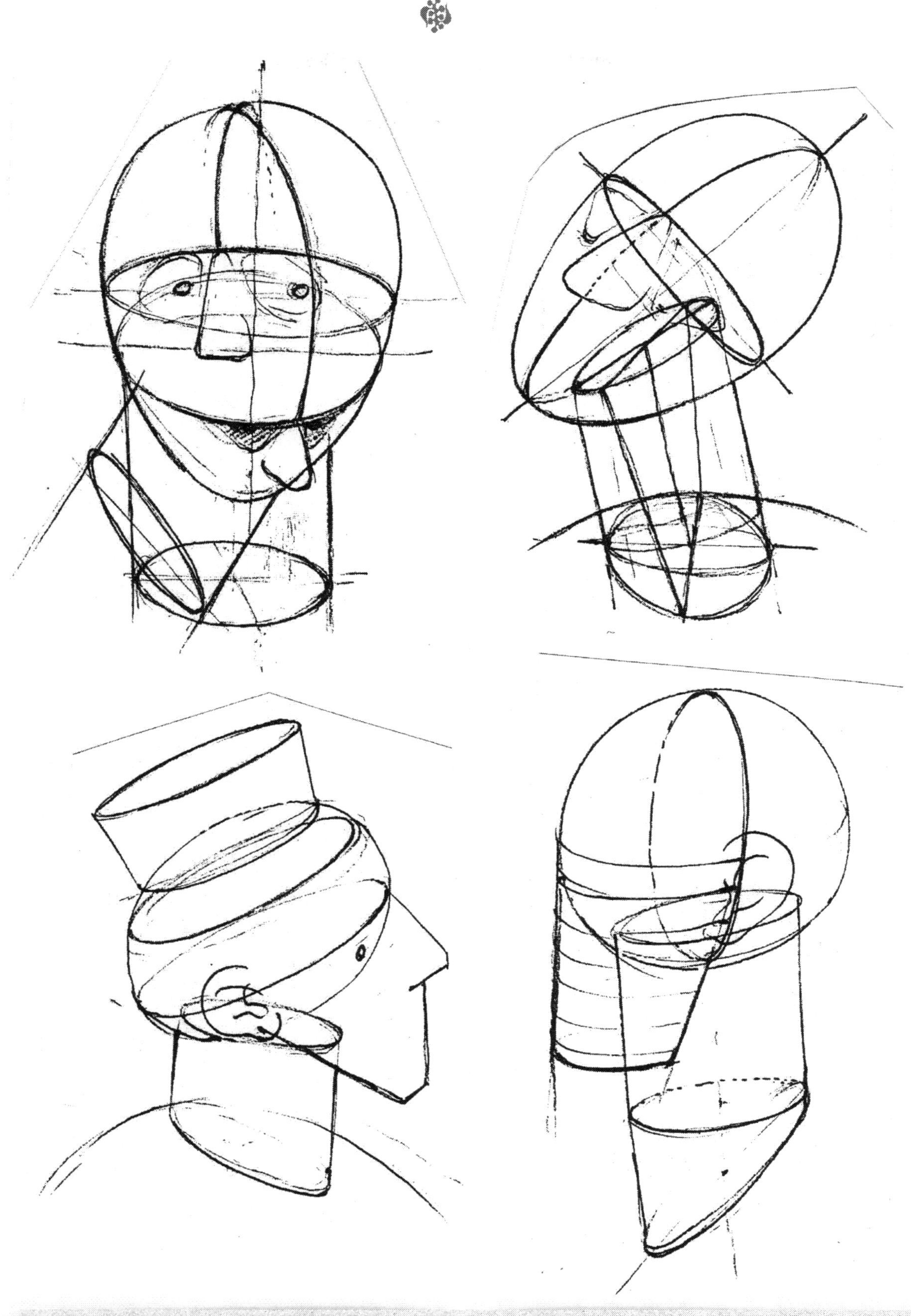

THE BASIC GEOMETRY COVERS THE COMPONENTS OF THE SKULL, FACIAL PART, THE NECK AND CONNECTION WITH THE SHOULDERS.

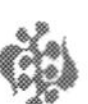

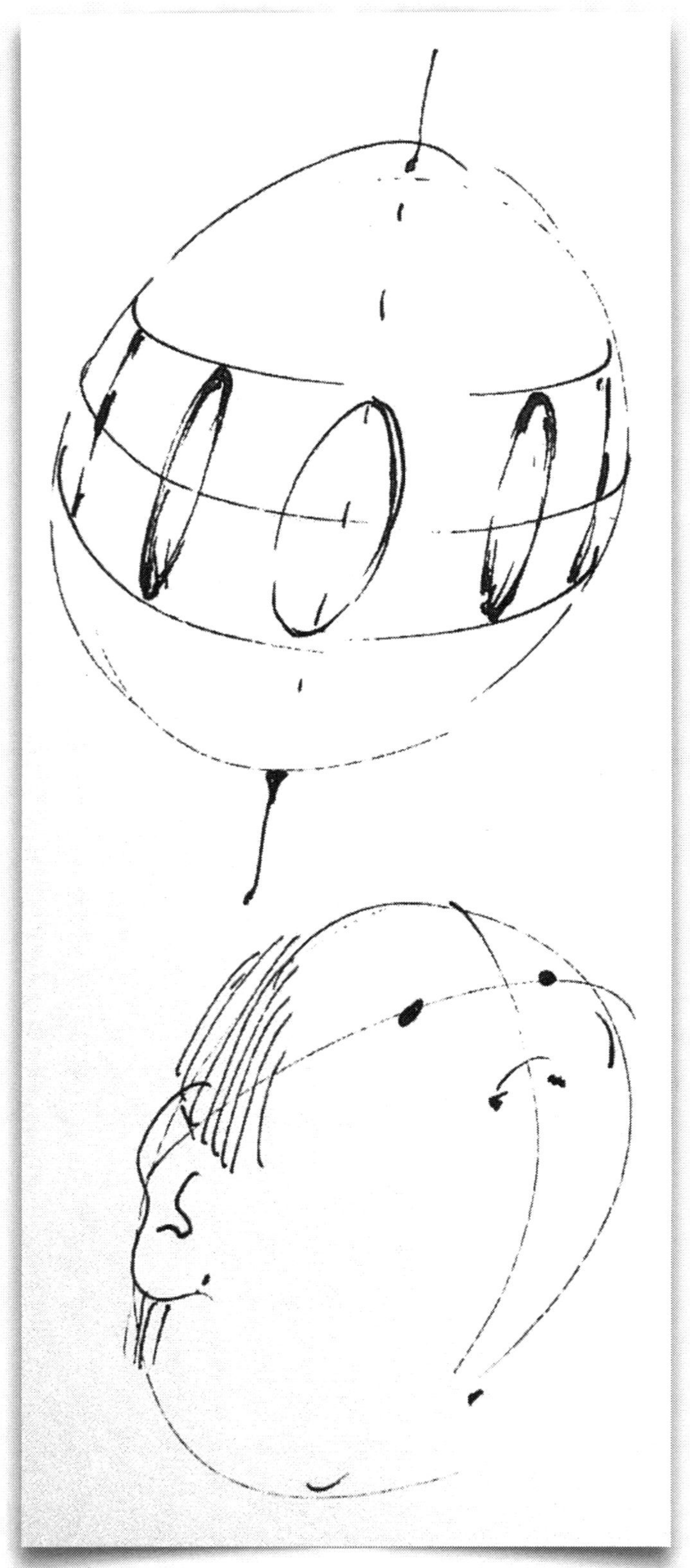

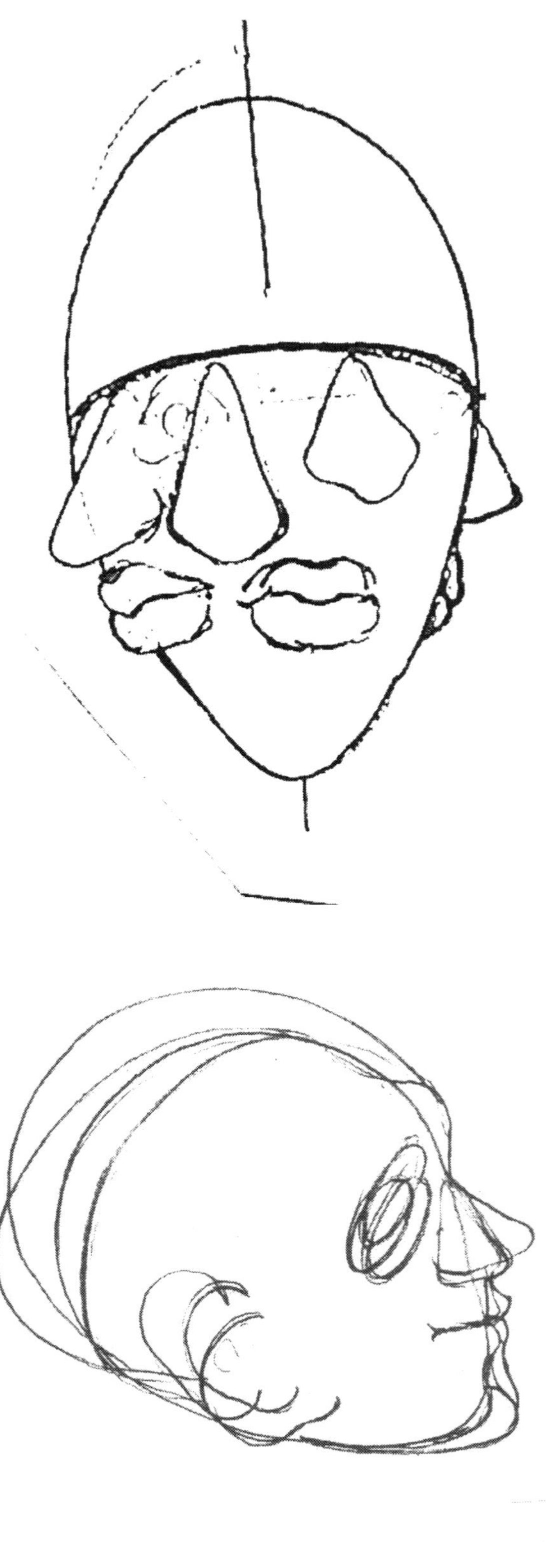

DIRECTIONS OF SMALLER SHAPES ON THE HEAD

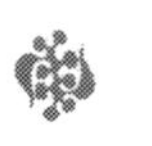

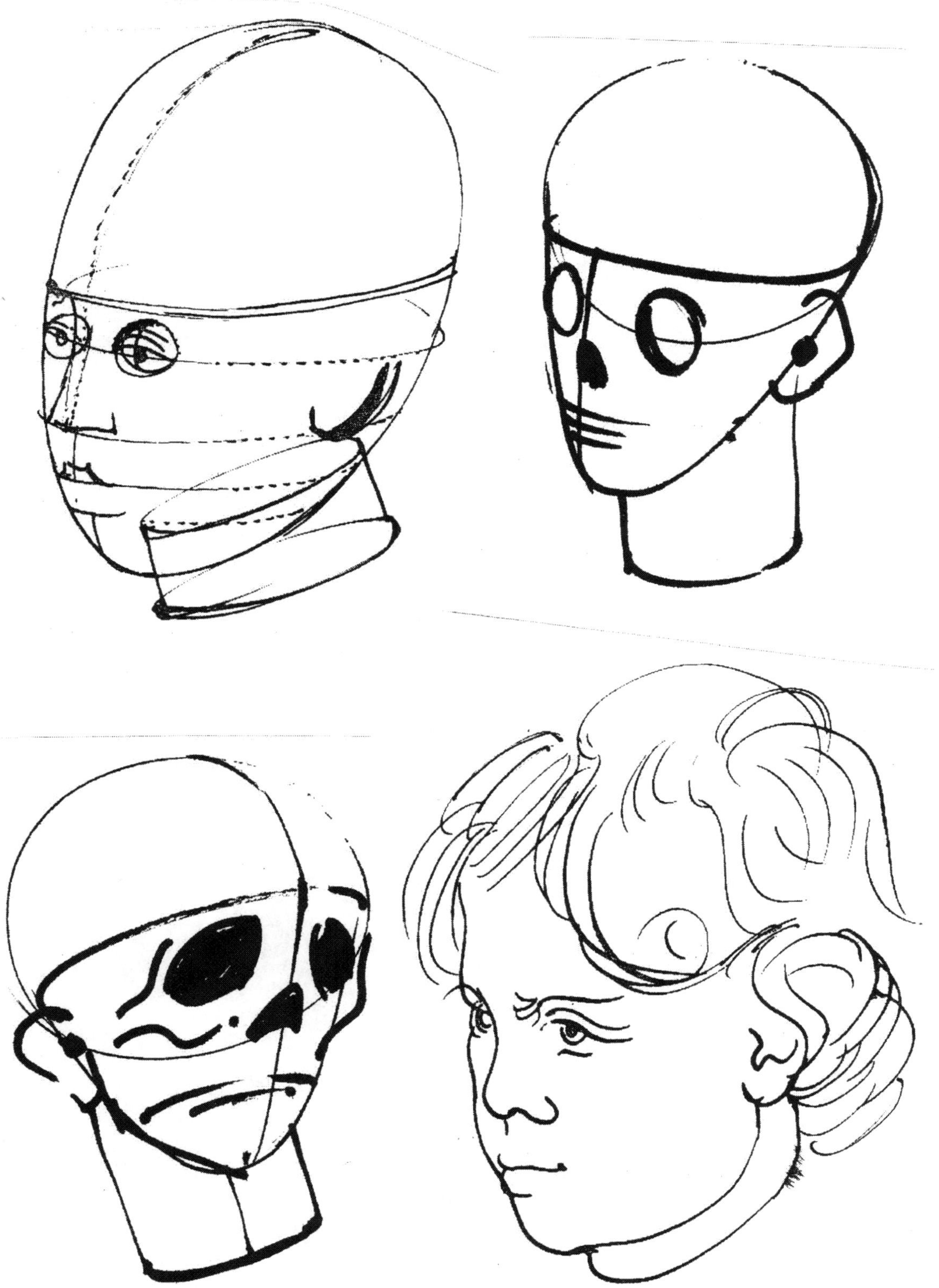

GEOMETRIC AND ORGANIC PRESENTATIONS OF THE HEAD

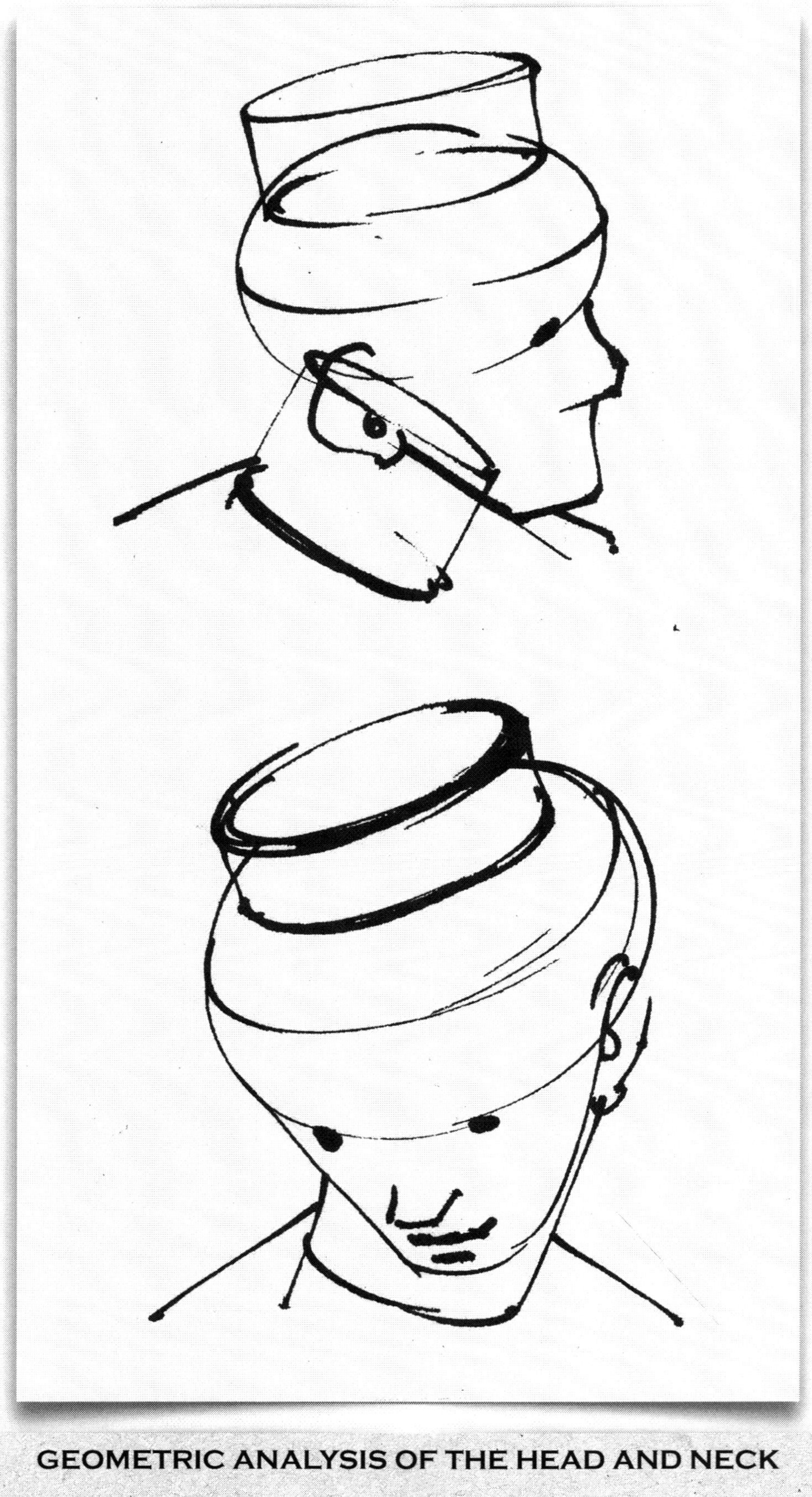

GEOMETRIC ANALYSIS OF THE HEAD AND NECK

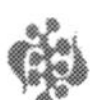

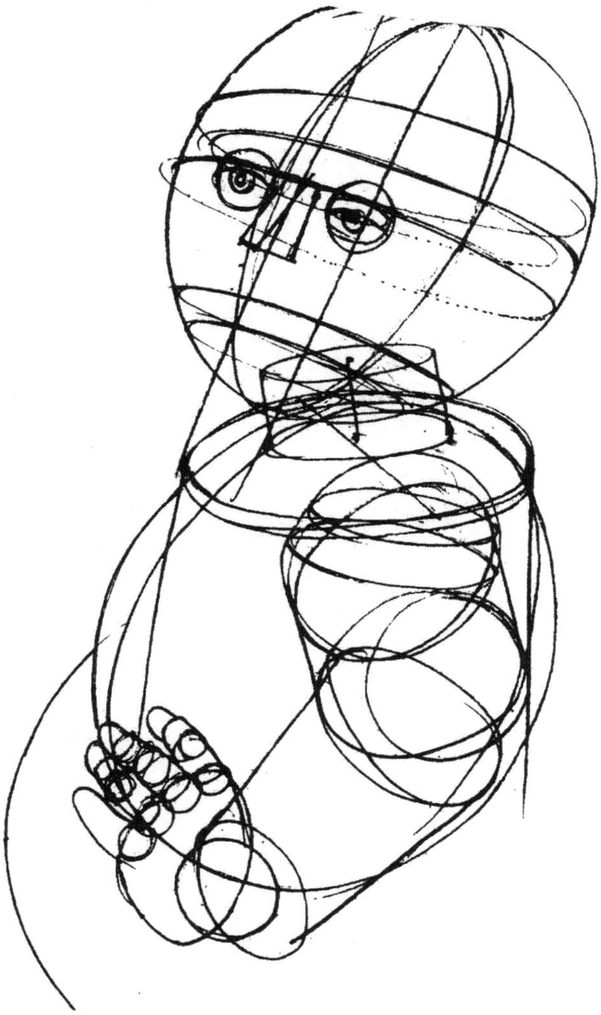

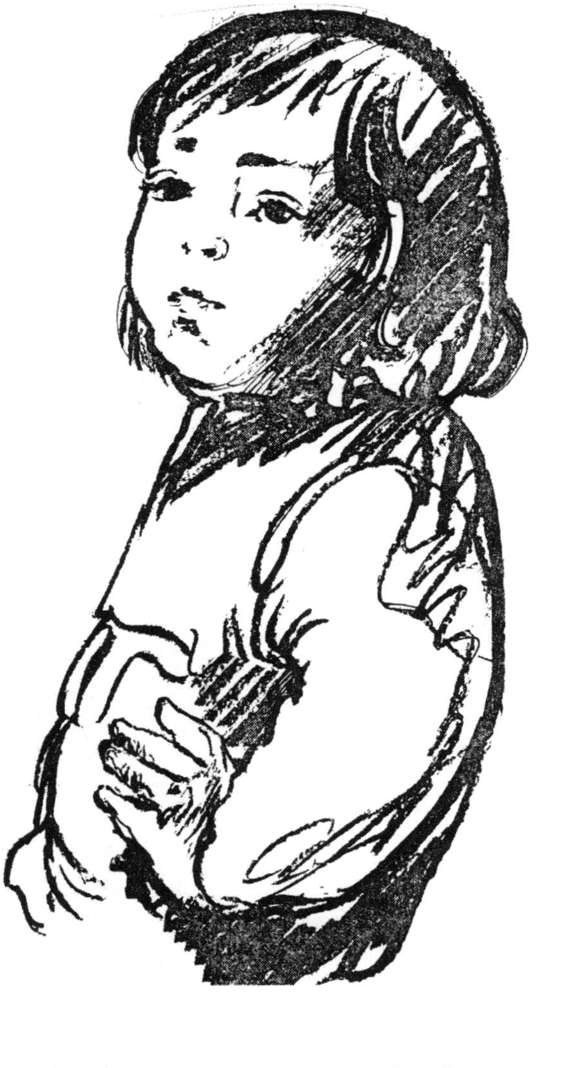

GEOMETRIC ANALYSIS OF THE HEAD, SHOULDERS AND BODY

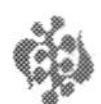

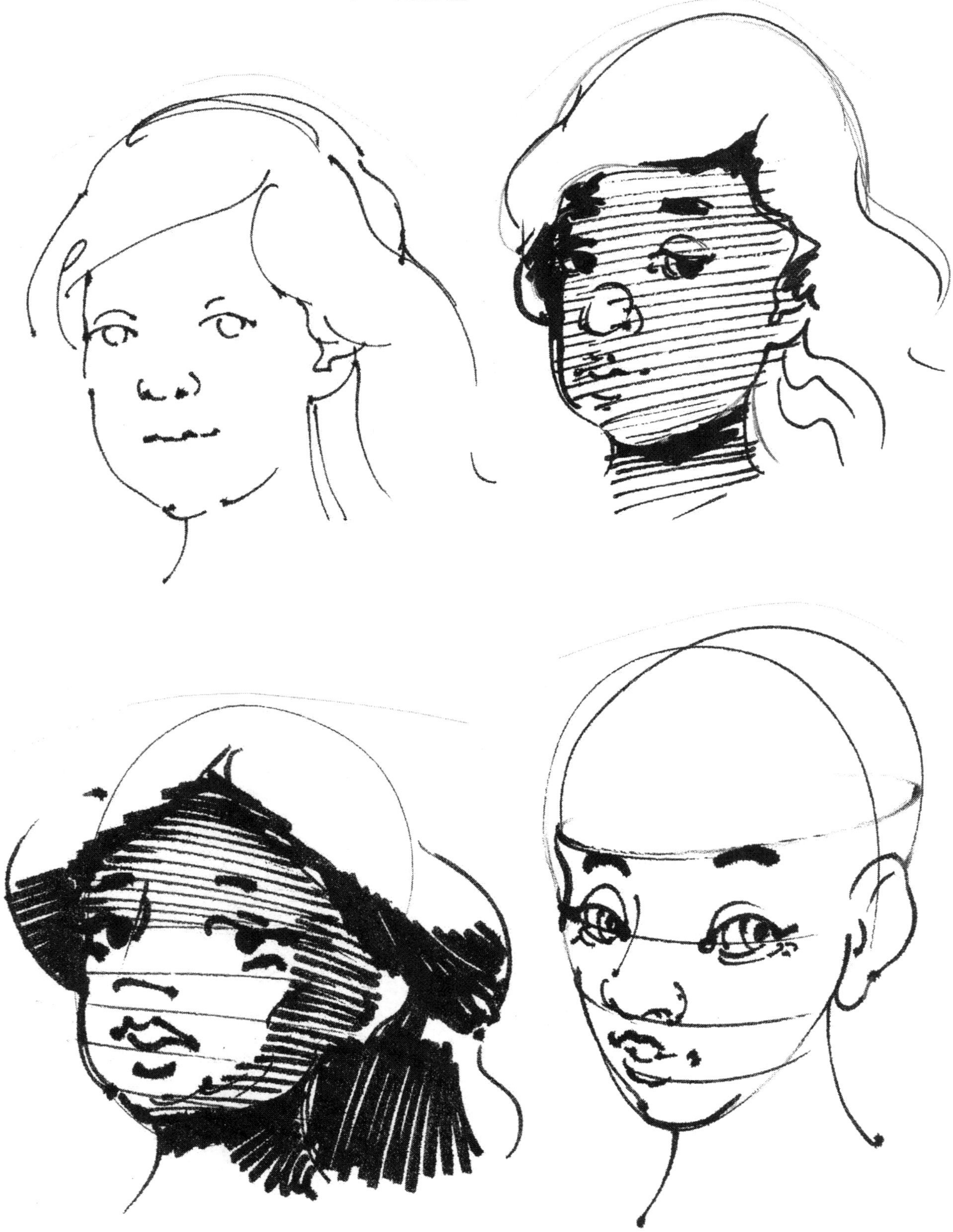

EXAMPLE OF PLASTICITY CREATED WITH SHADOWING.

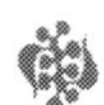

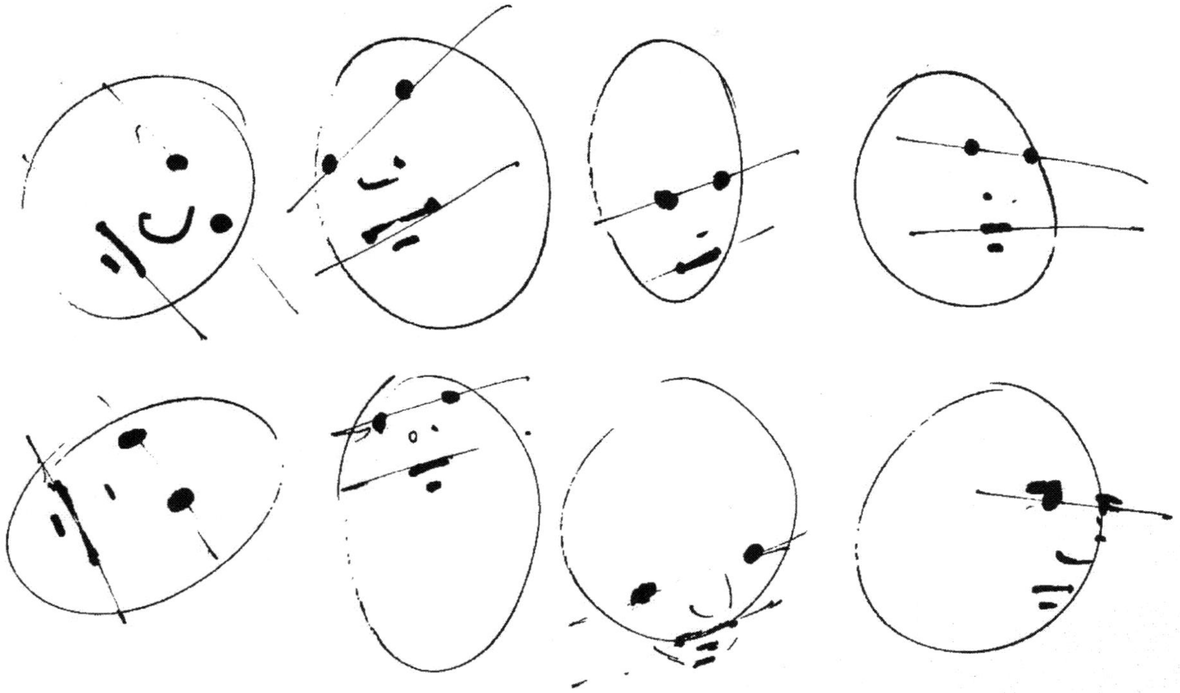

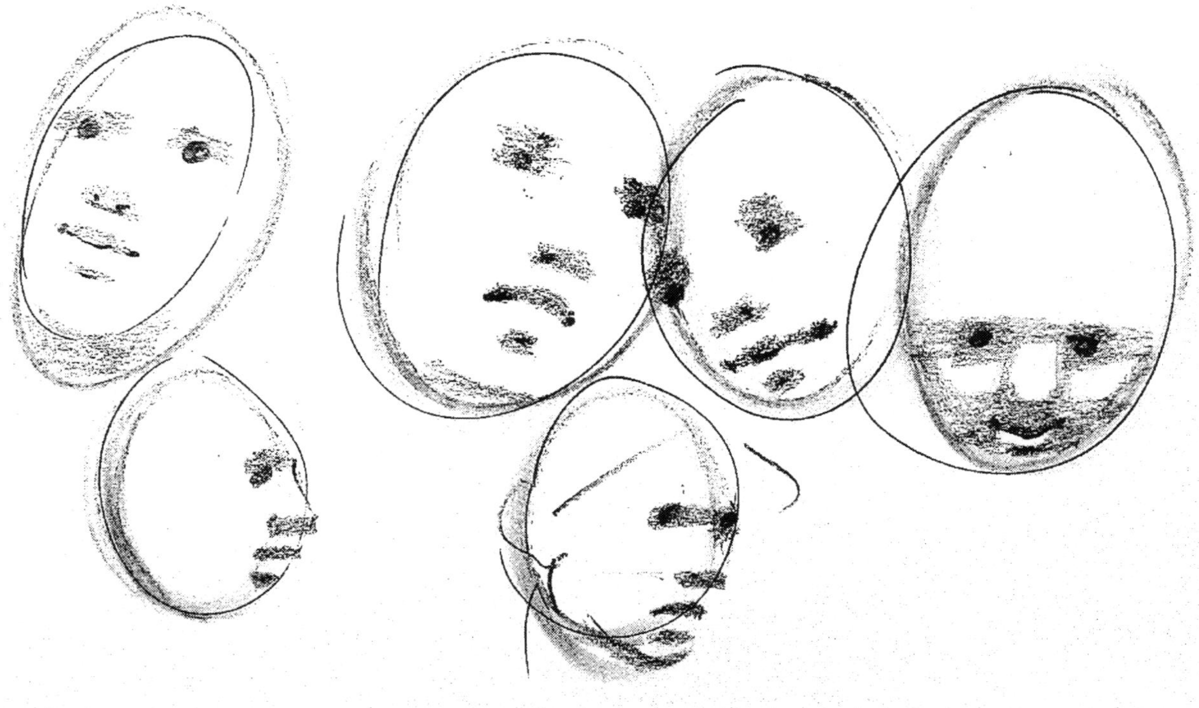

EXAMPLES OF VARIOUS HEAD DIRECTIONS

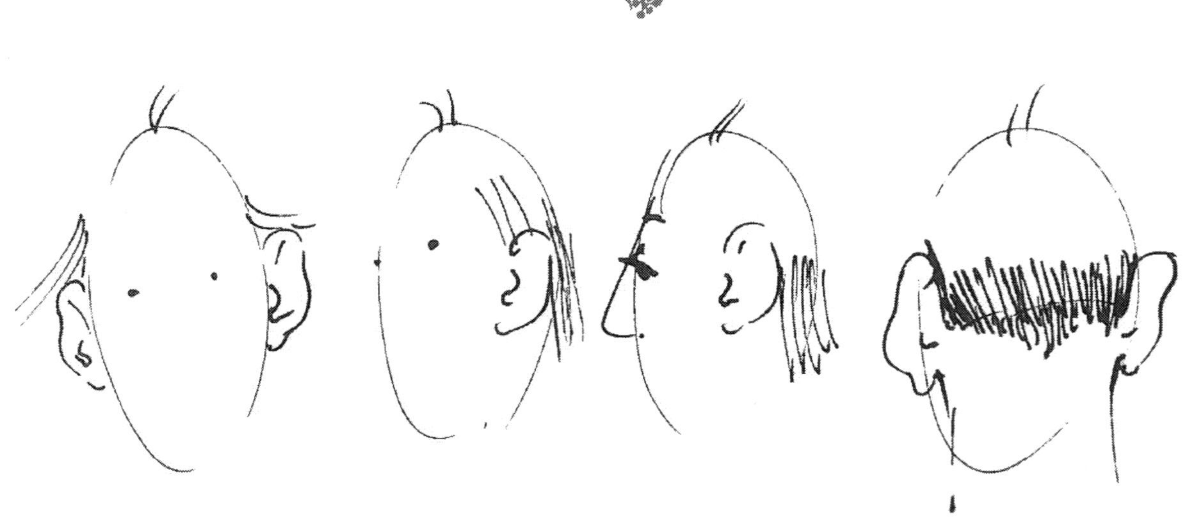

VARIOUS POSITIONS OF THE HEAD

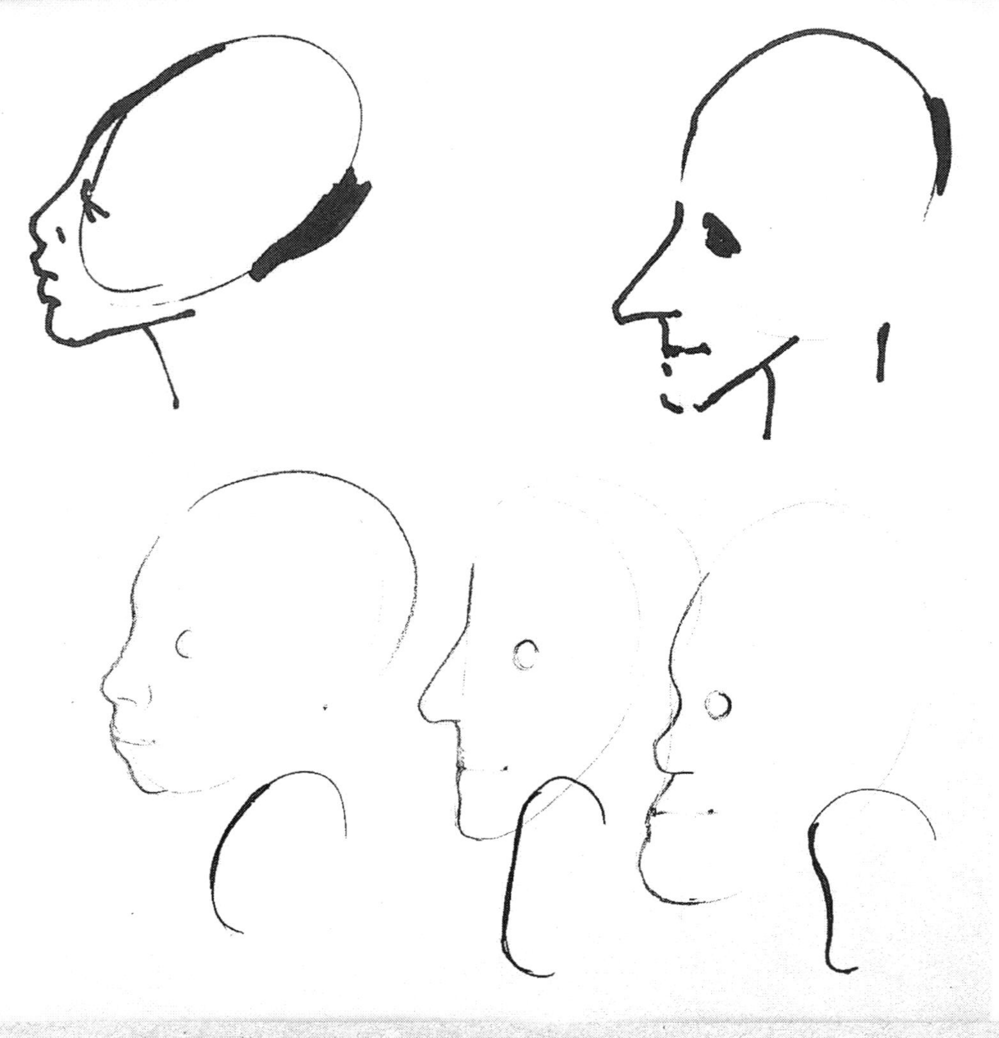

VARIOUS FACE PROFILES

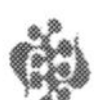

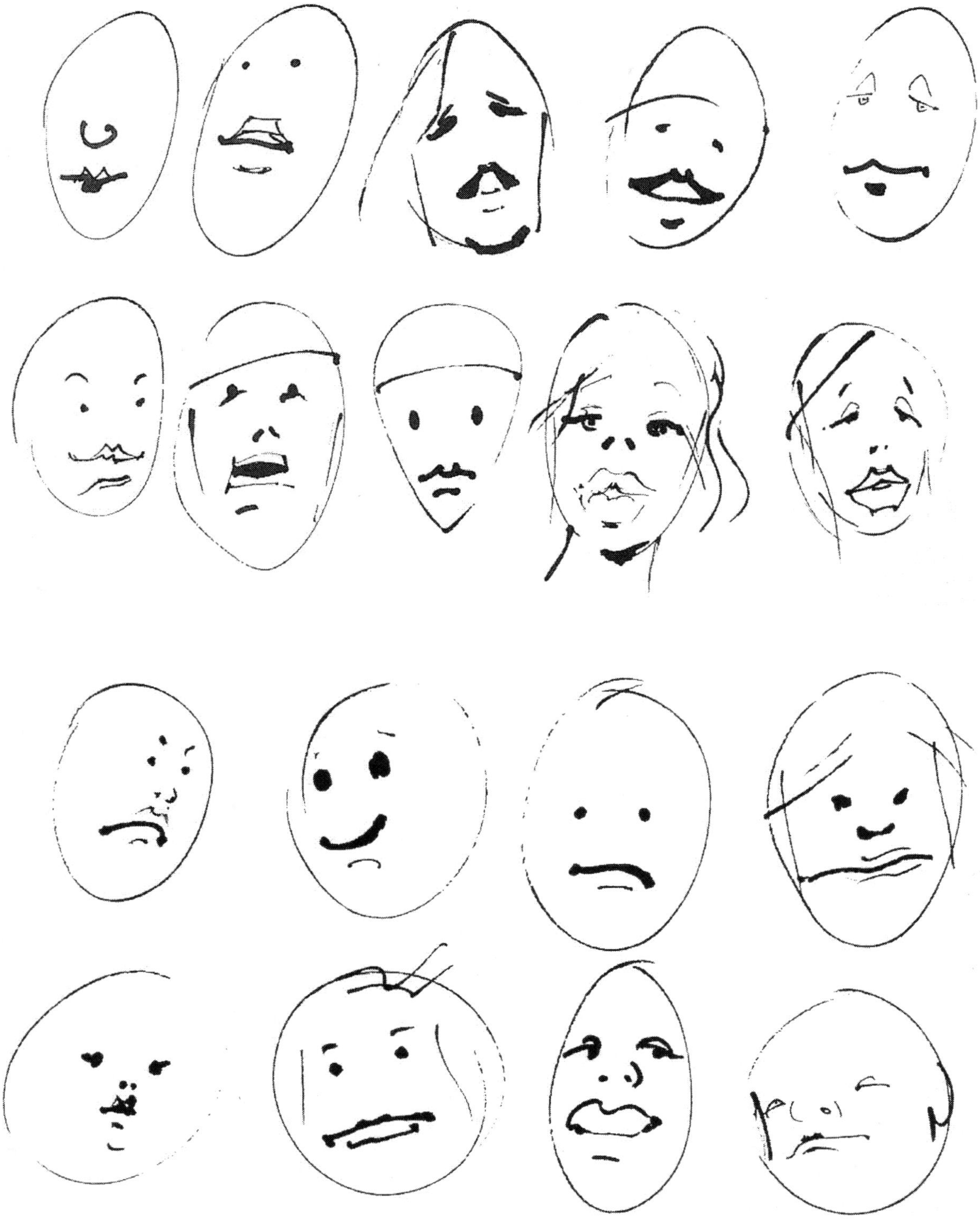

STUDY OF VARIOUS FACIAL EXPRESSIONS

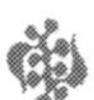

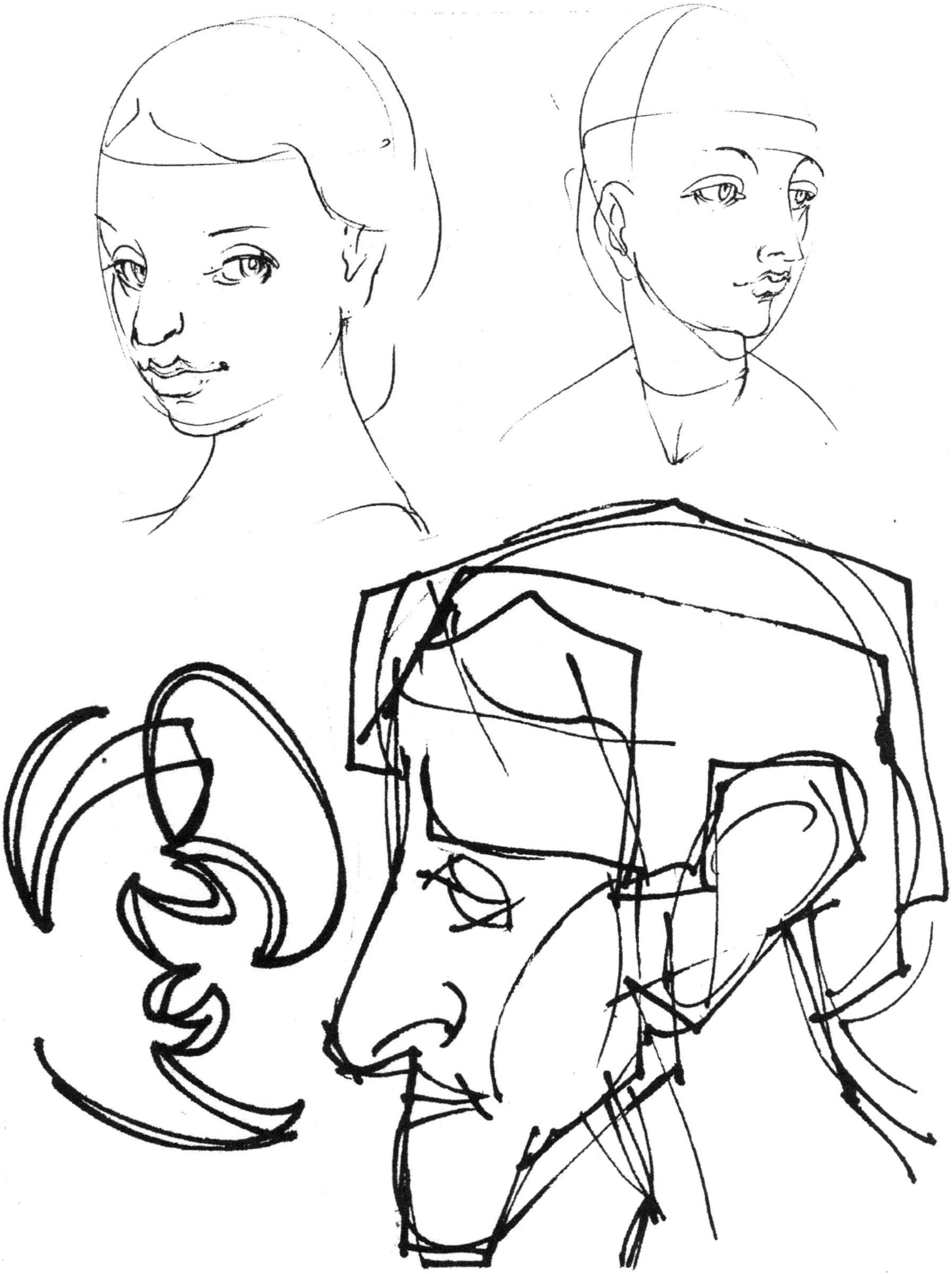

EXAMPLES OF GEOMETRIC AND CALLIGRAPHIC DEPICTIONS OF FACE

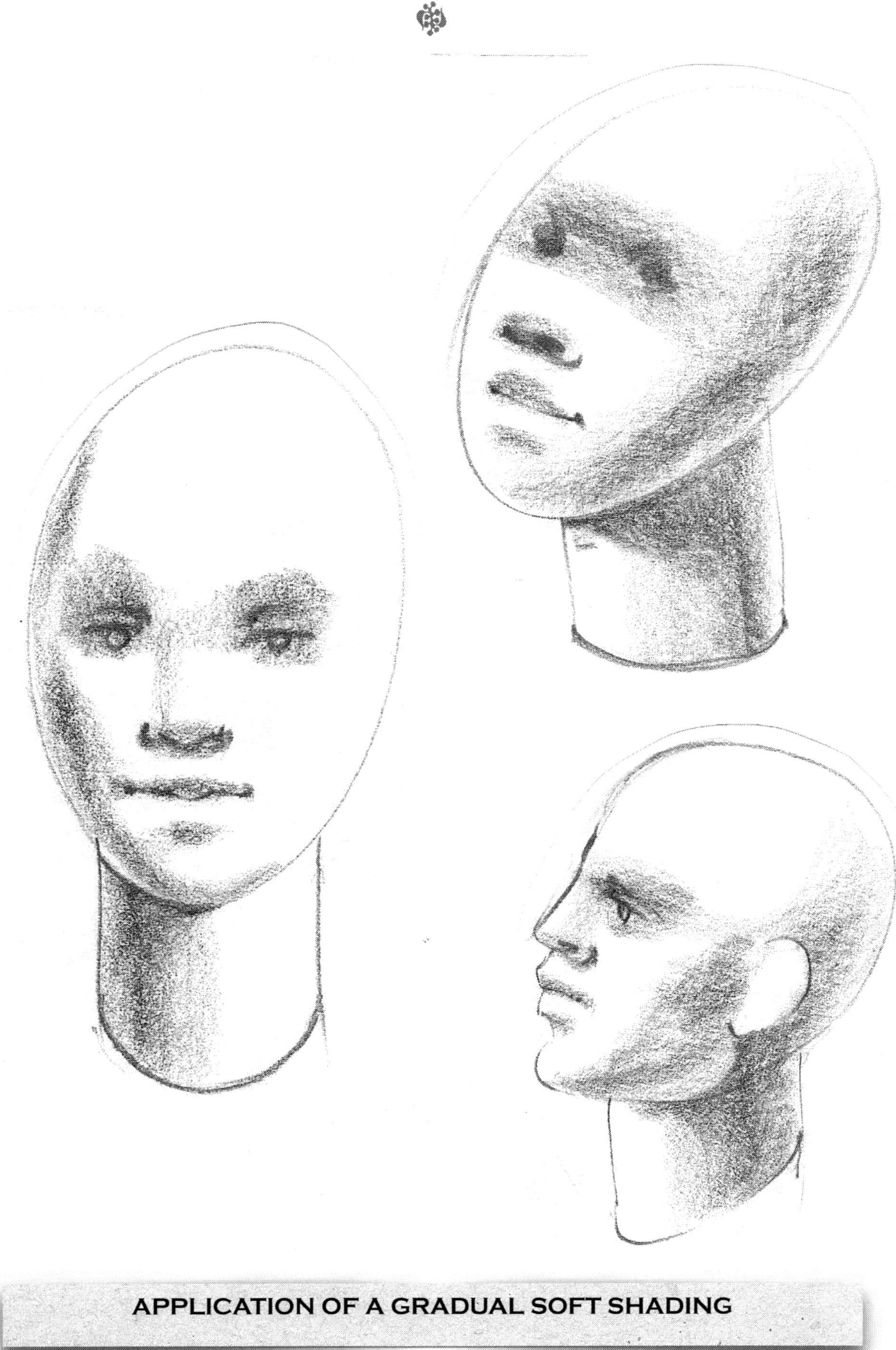

APPLICATION OF A GRADUAL SOFT SHADING

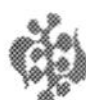

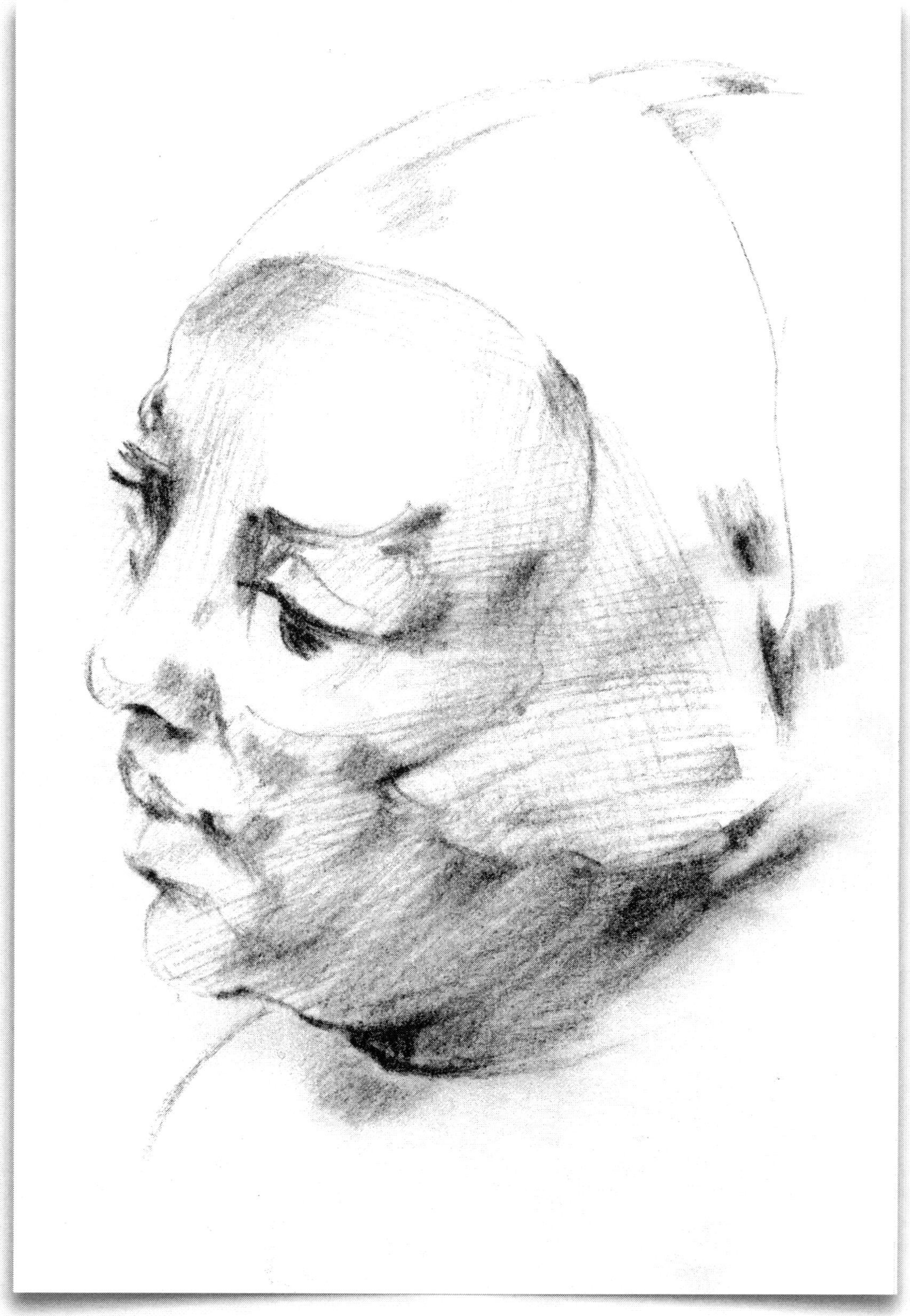

APPLICATION OF A GRADUAL SOFT SHADING

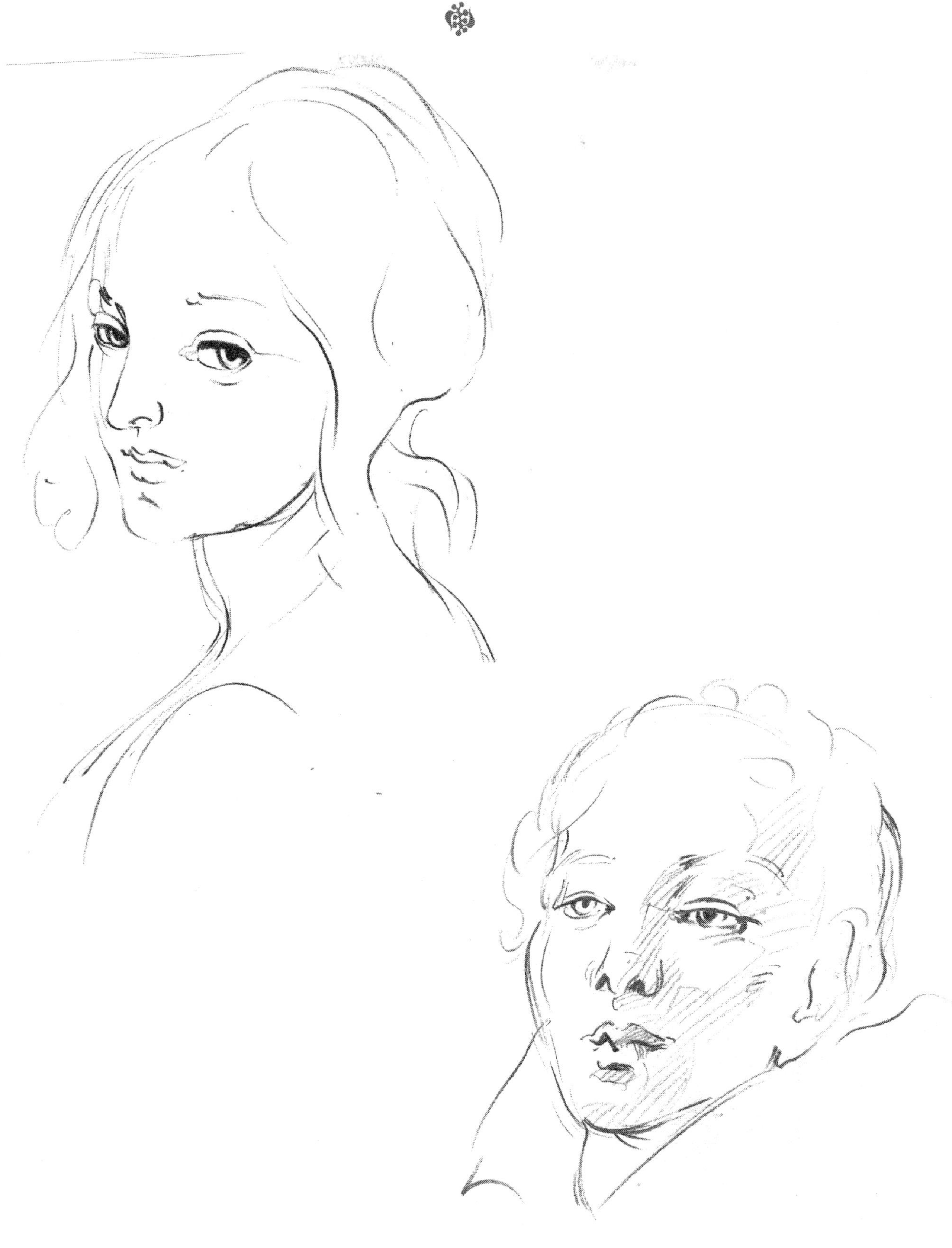

AN EXAMPLE OF SHADED AREAS ON FACE

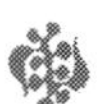

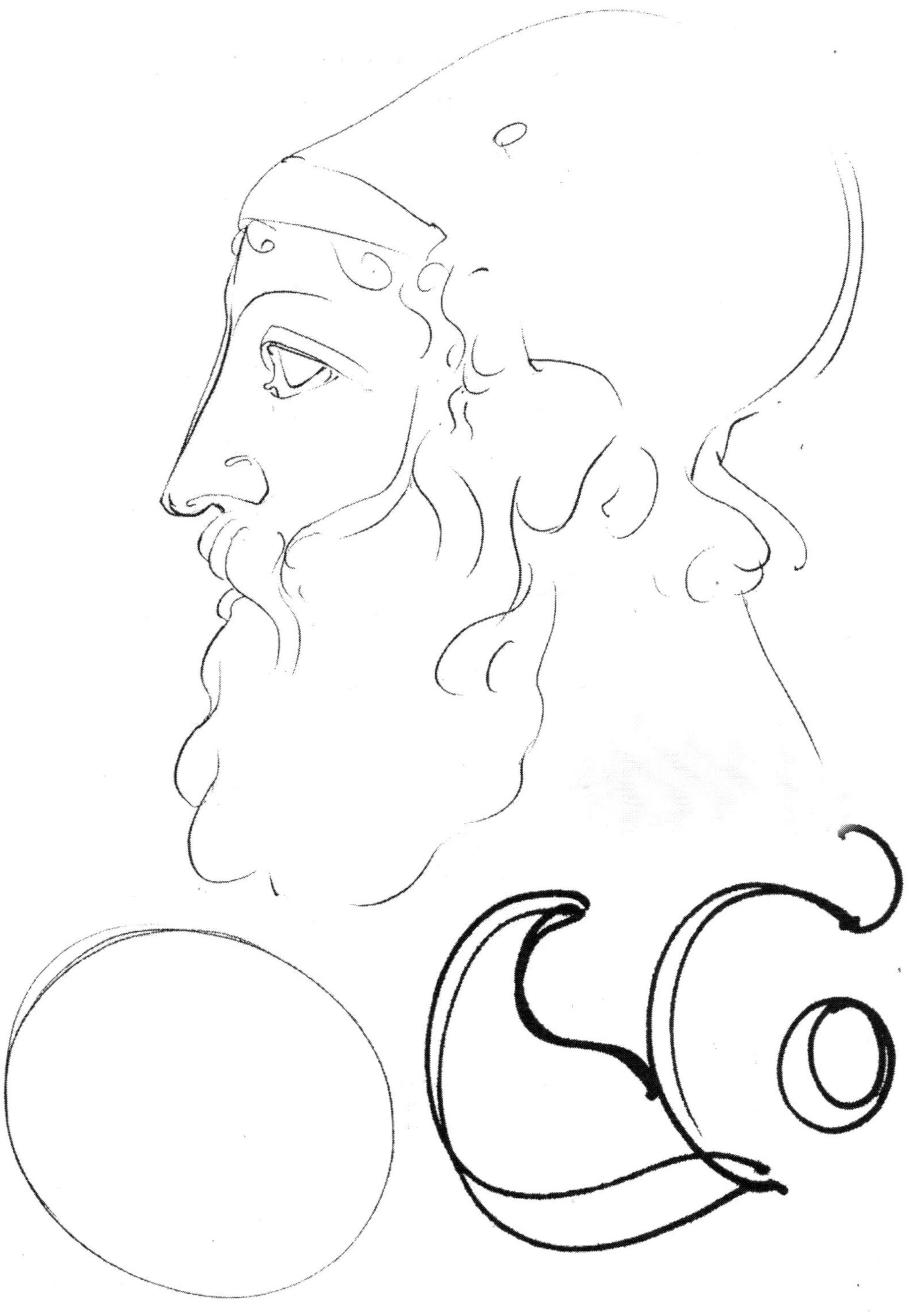

CALLIGRAPHY OF THE HEAD

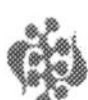

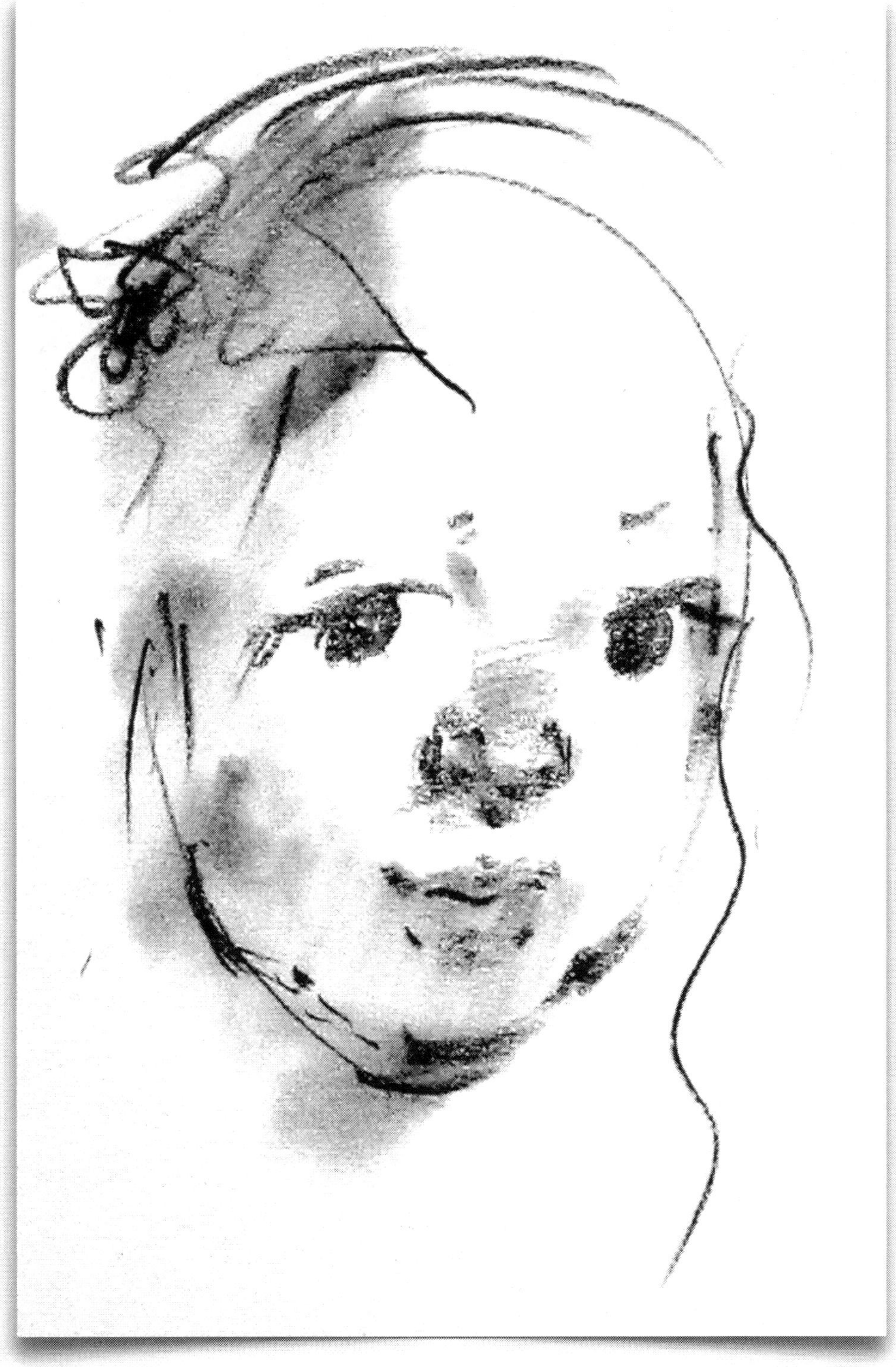

FIND THE PARALLELS BETWEEN THE DIRECTION OF THE EYES,
MOUTH AND THE SMALL SURFACE OF THE NOSE.
OBSERVE THE HARMONIOUS COMPLIANCE WITH THE SKULL.

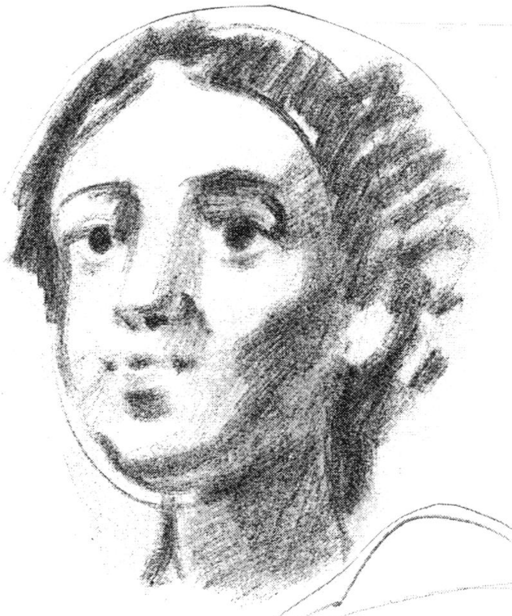

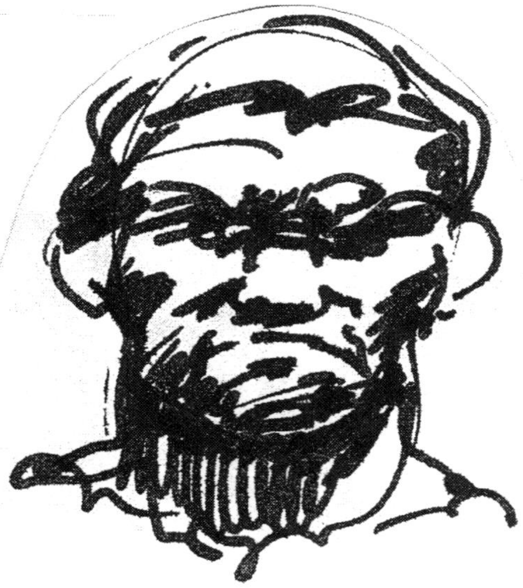

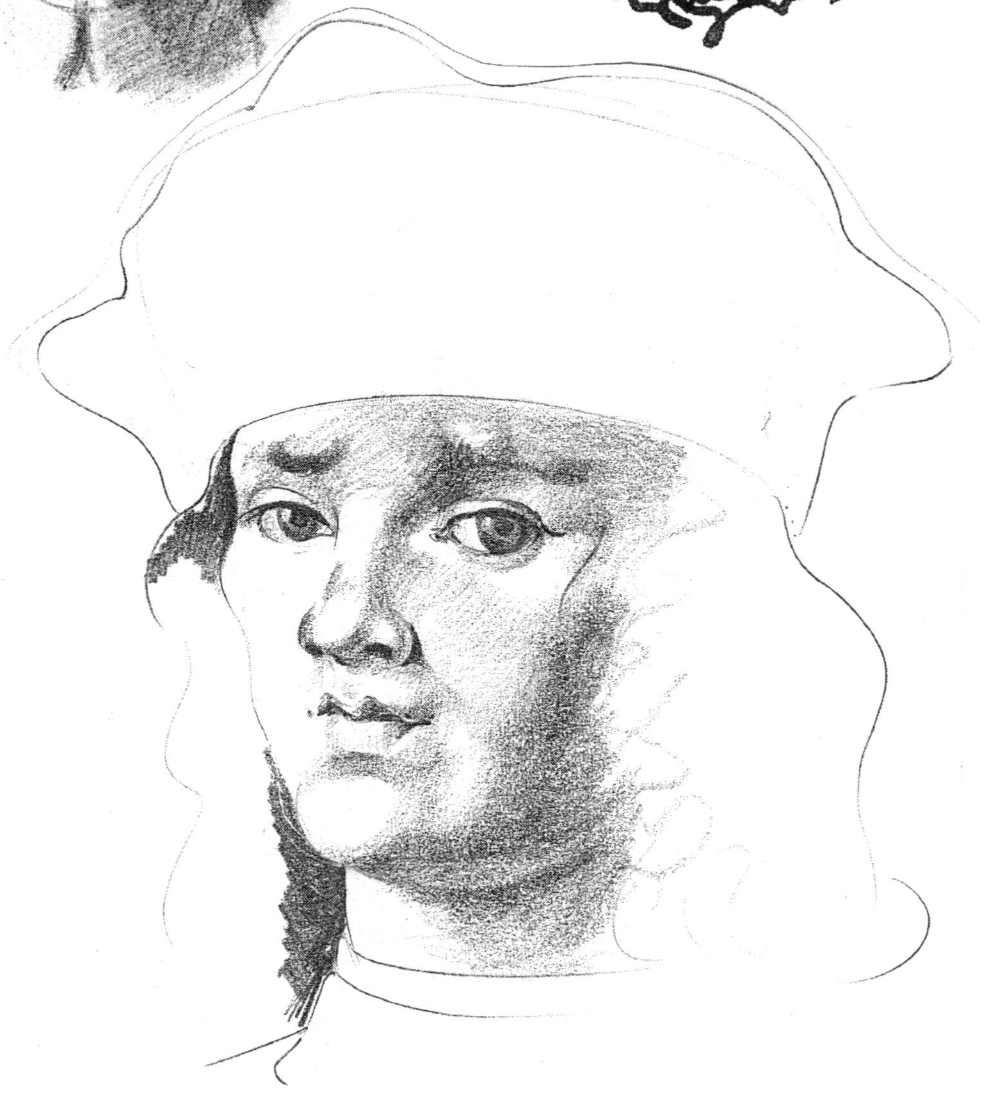

SOFT AND SHARP TRANSITIONS BETWEEN LIGTH AND SHADOW

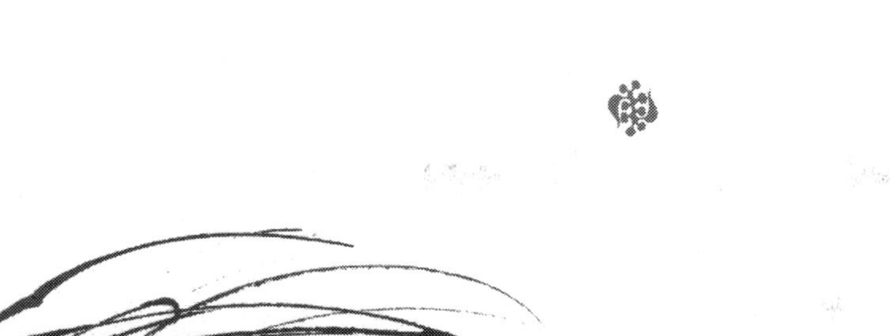

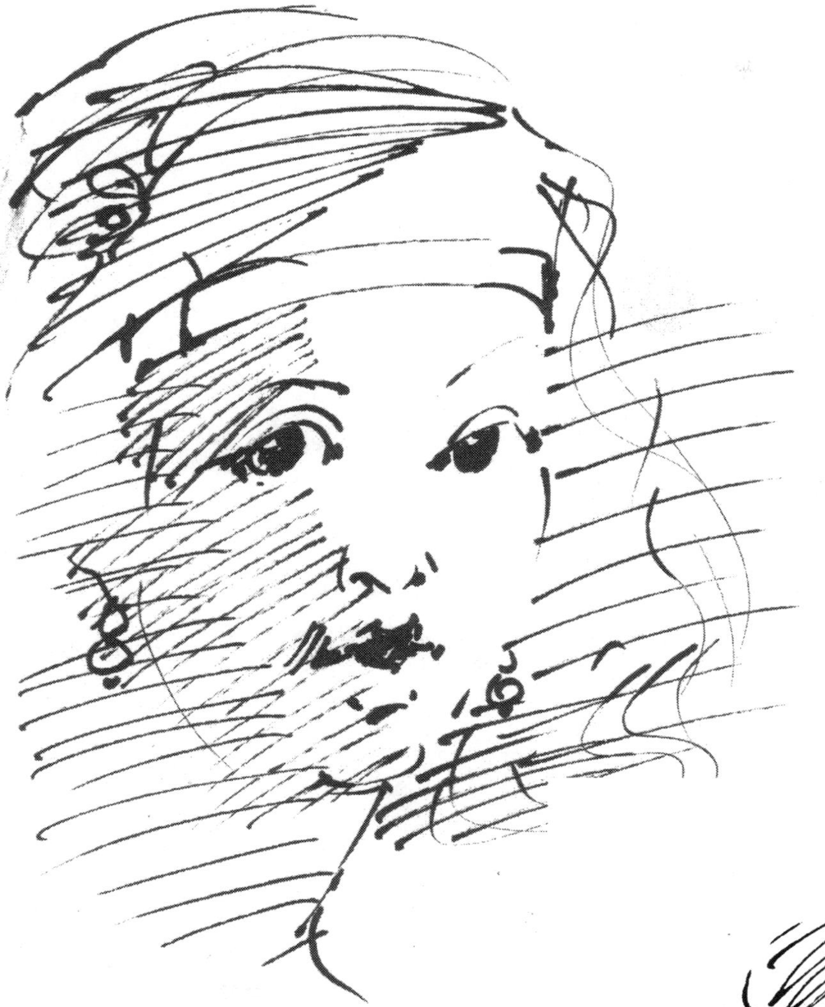

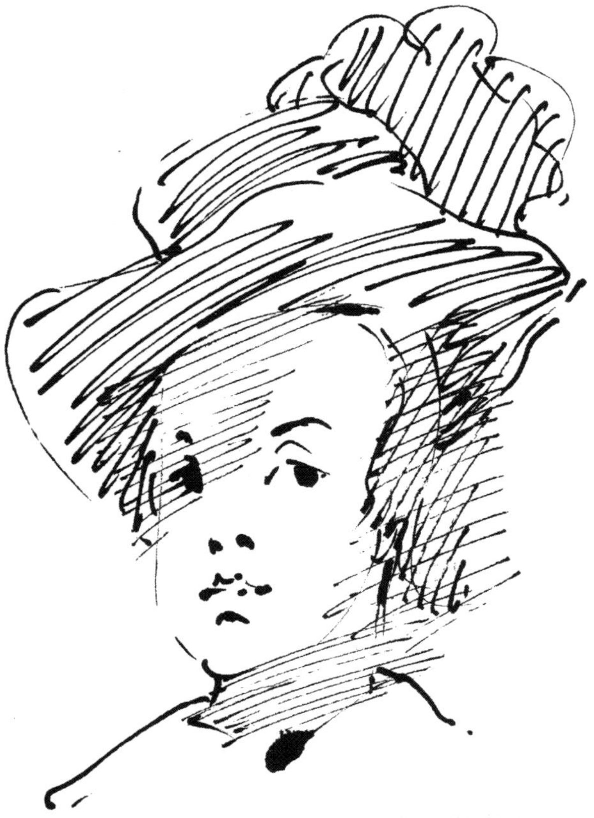

SHADOWS PRESENTED WITH LINES

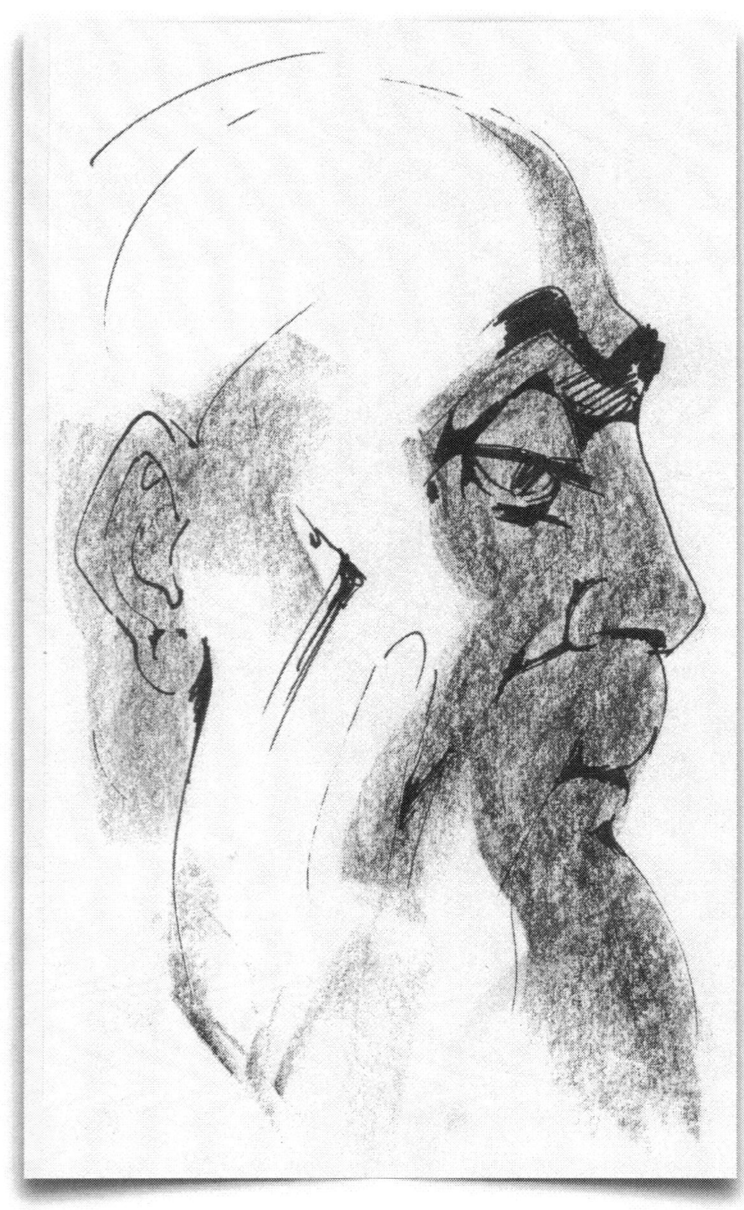

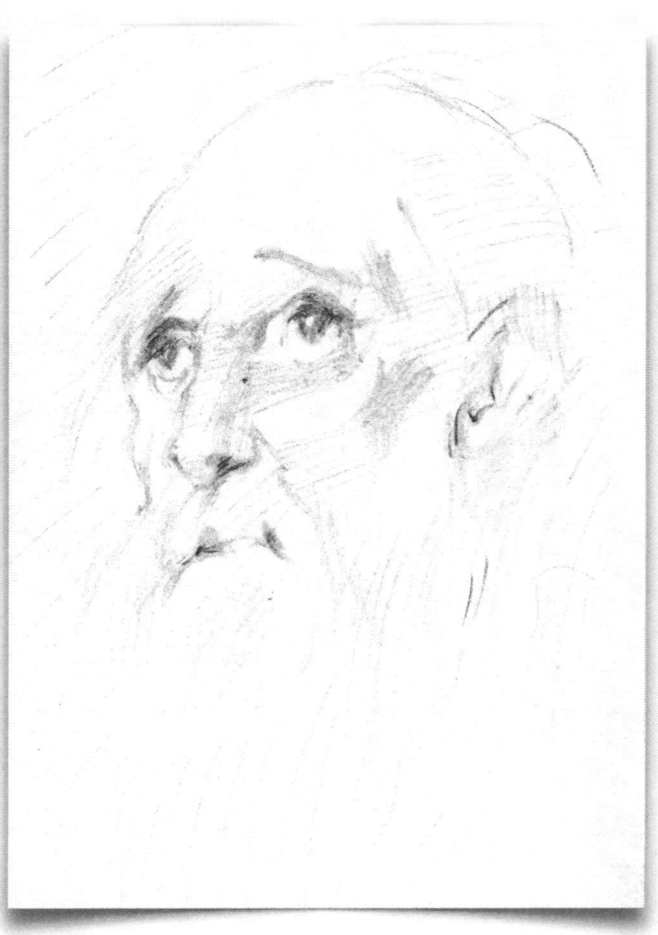

SHAPES IN LIGHT AND SHADOW

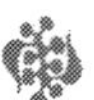

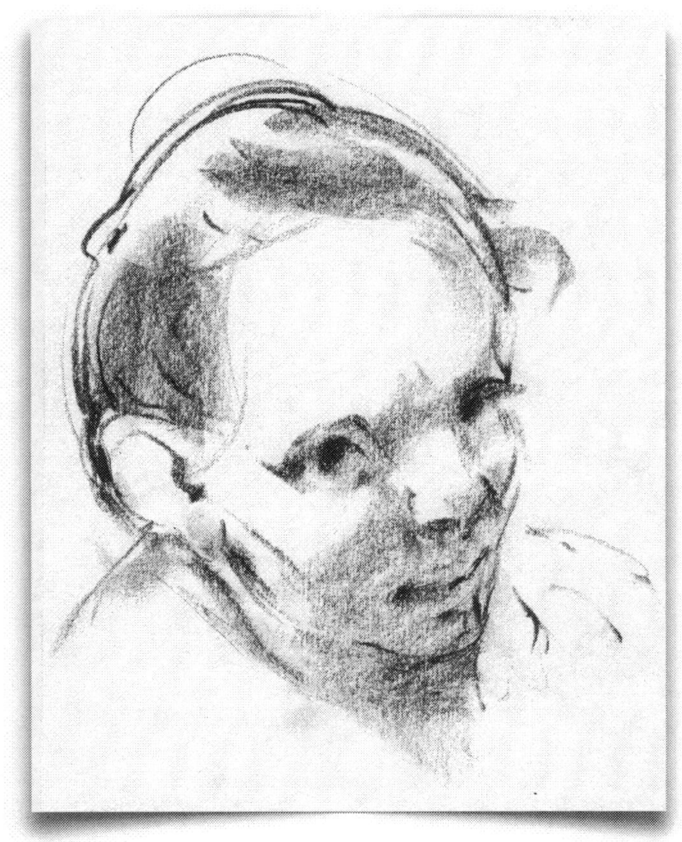

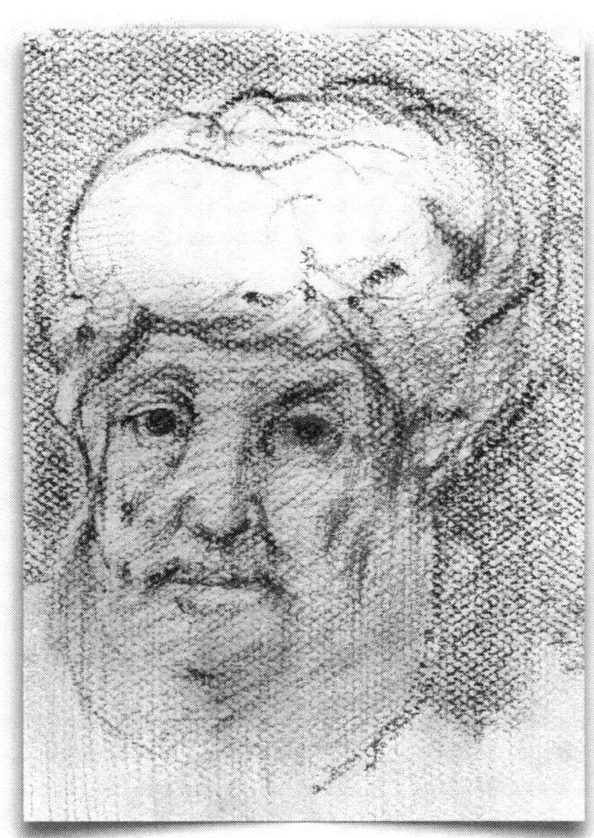

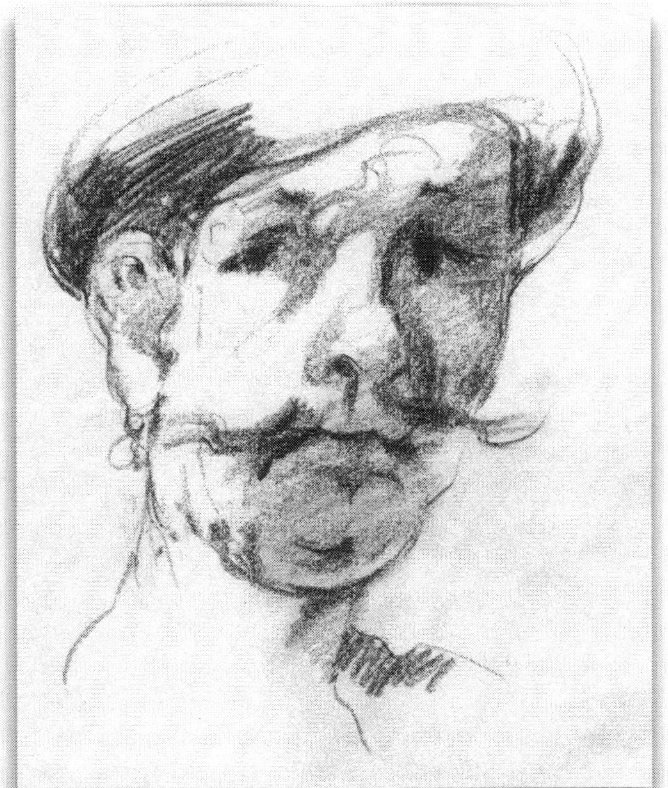

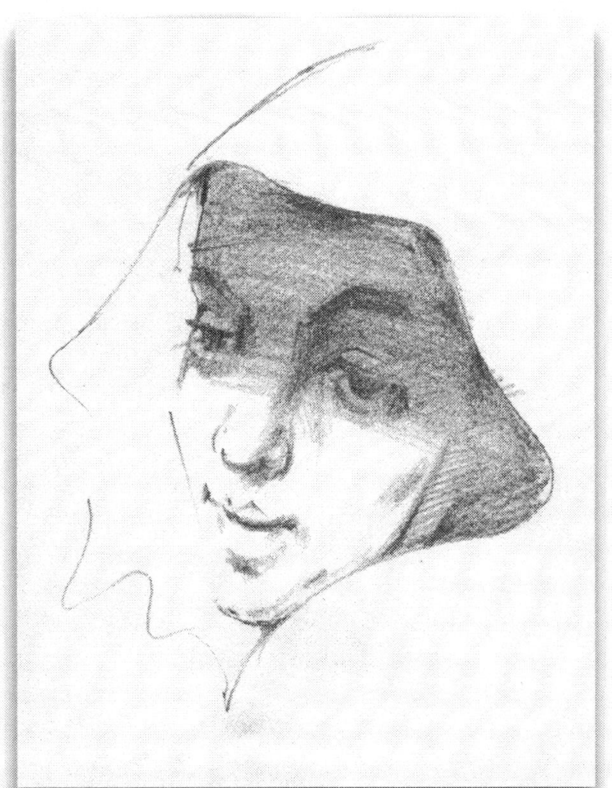

THE HEAD AS AN ENDLESS EXAMPLE
OF VARIOUS SHAPES AND SHADOWS

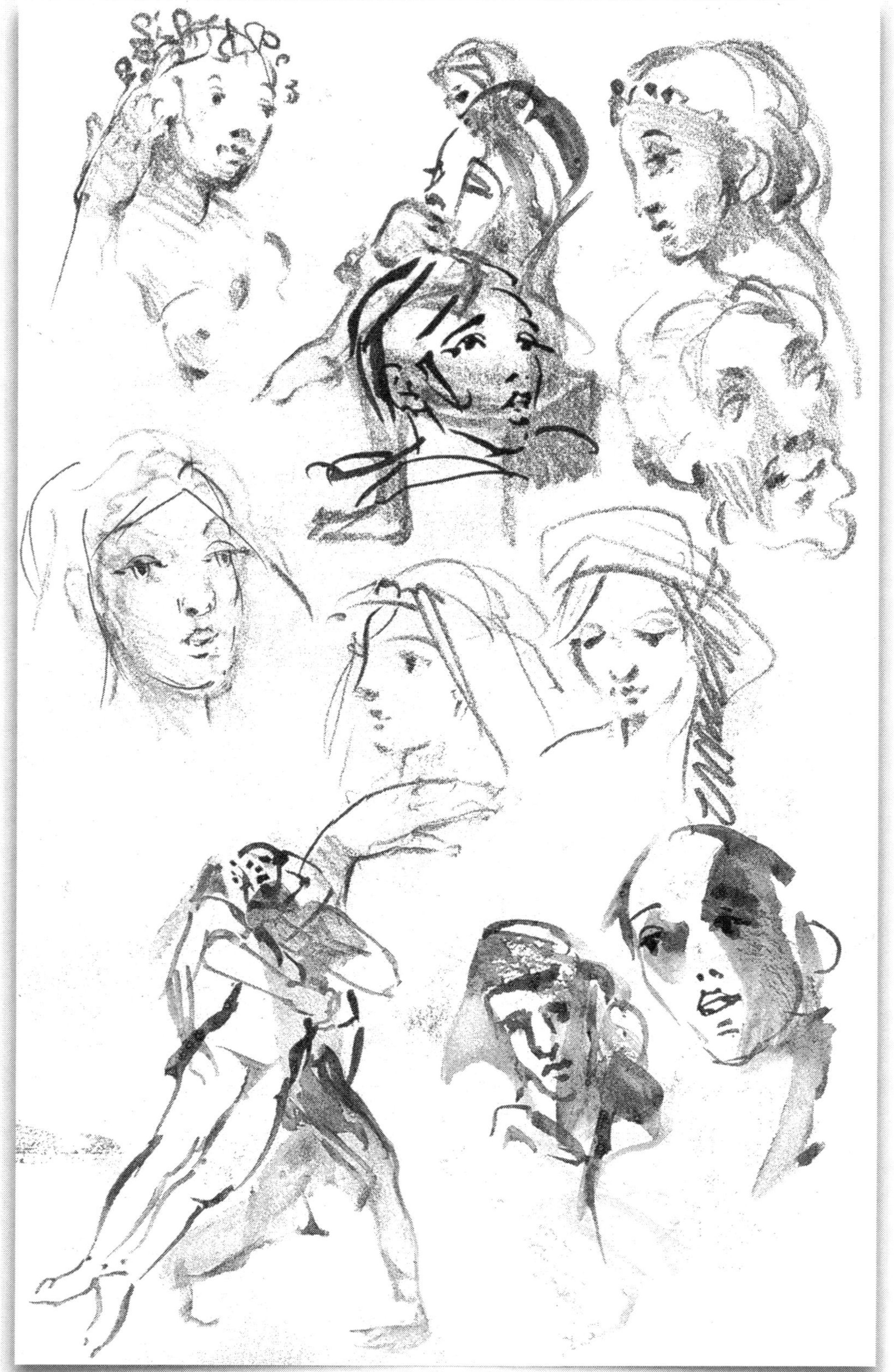

VARIOUS SKETCHES

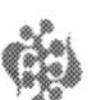

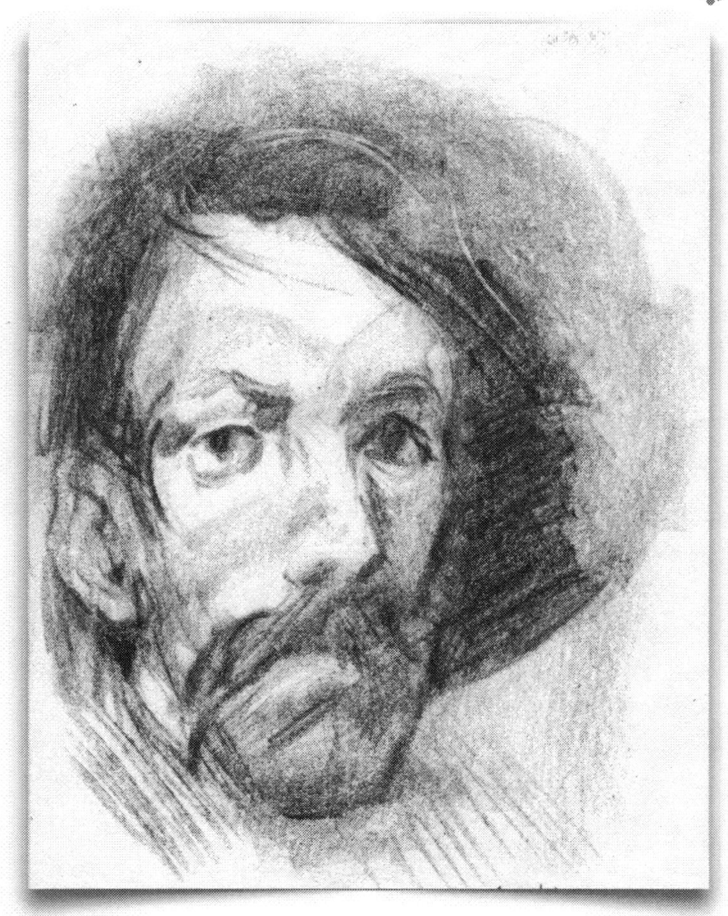

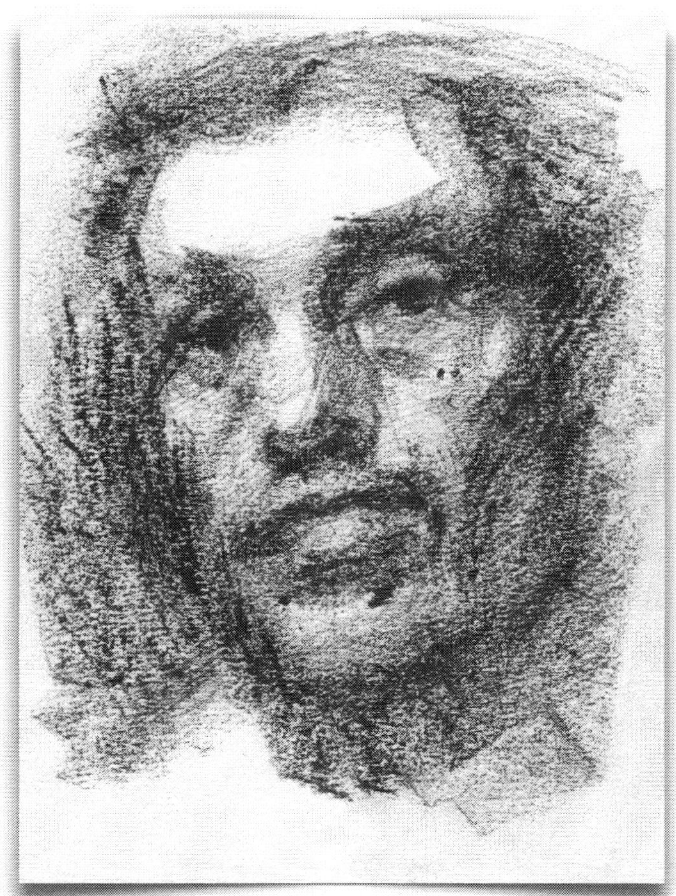

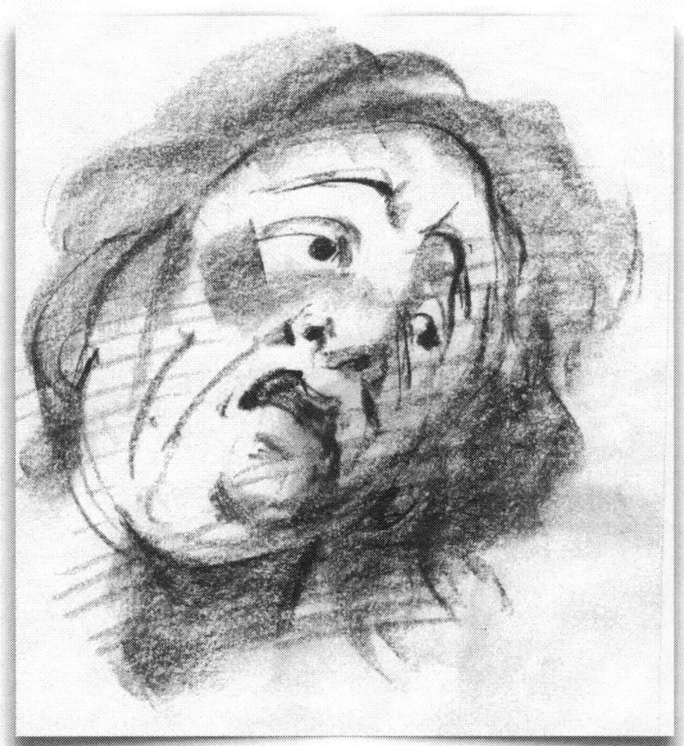

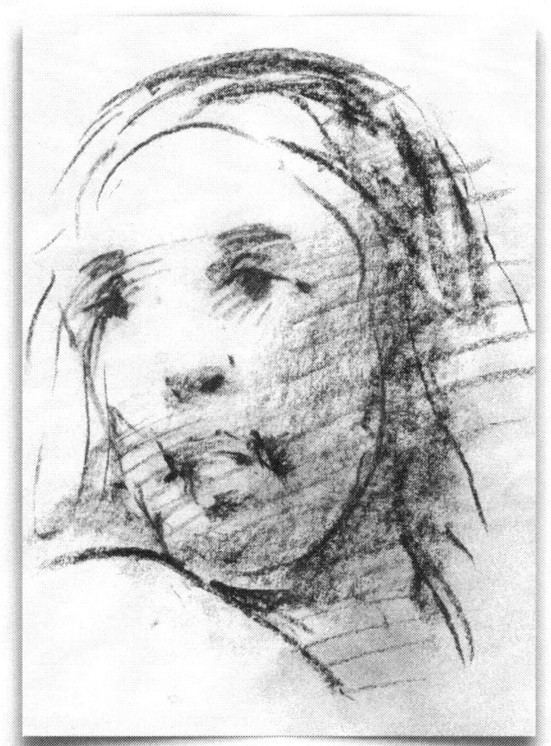

THE HEAD AS AN ENDLESS EXAMPLE OF VARIOUS SHAPES AND SHADOWS

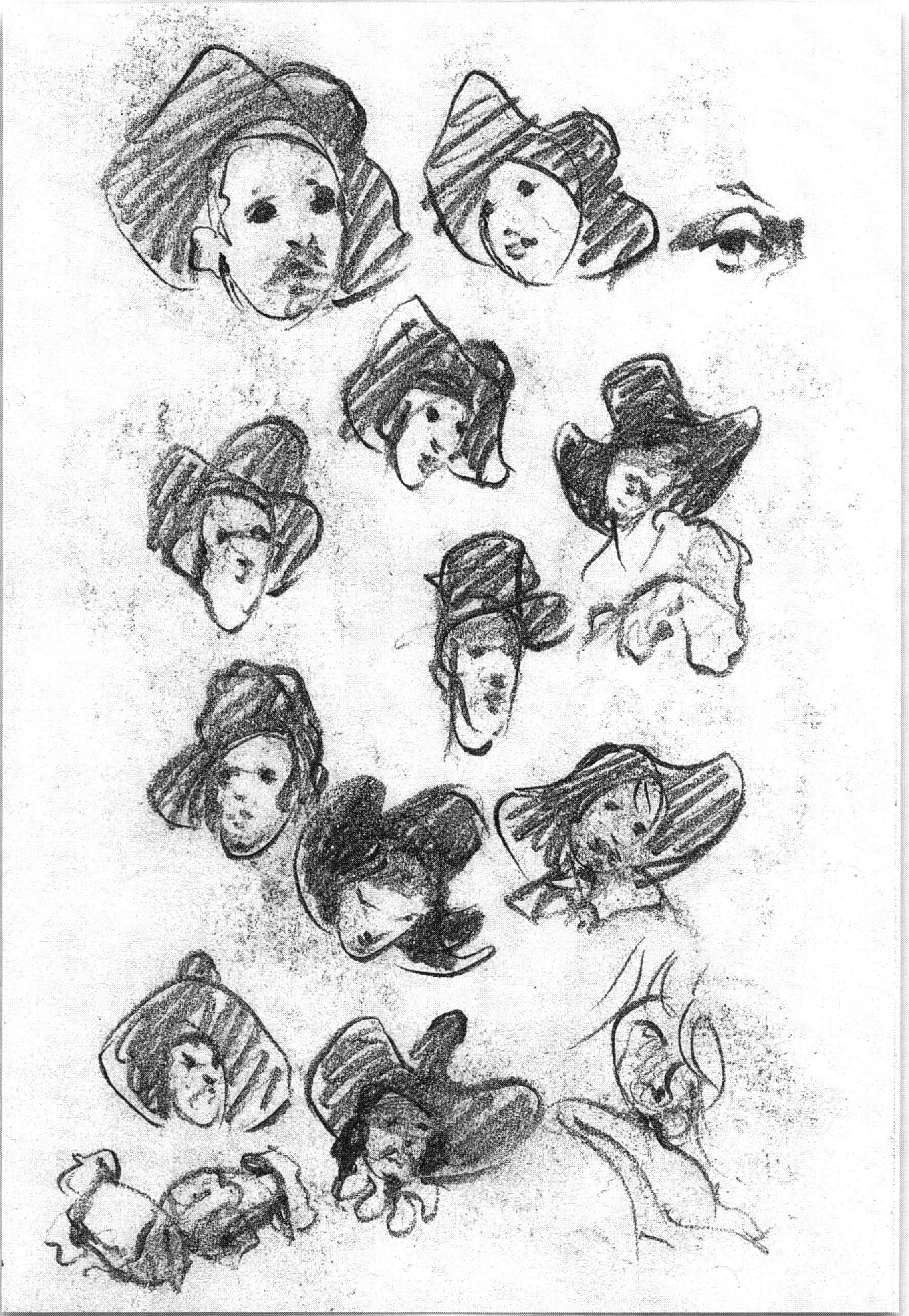

HARMONY OF THE HEAD WITH THE HEADDRESS

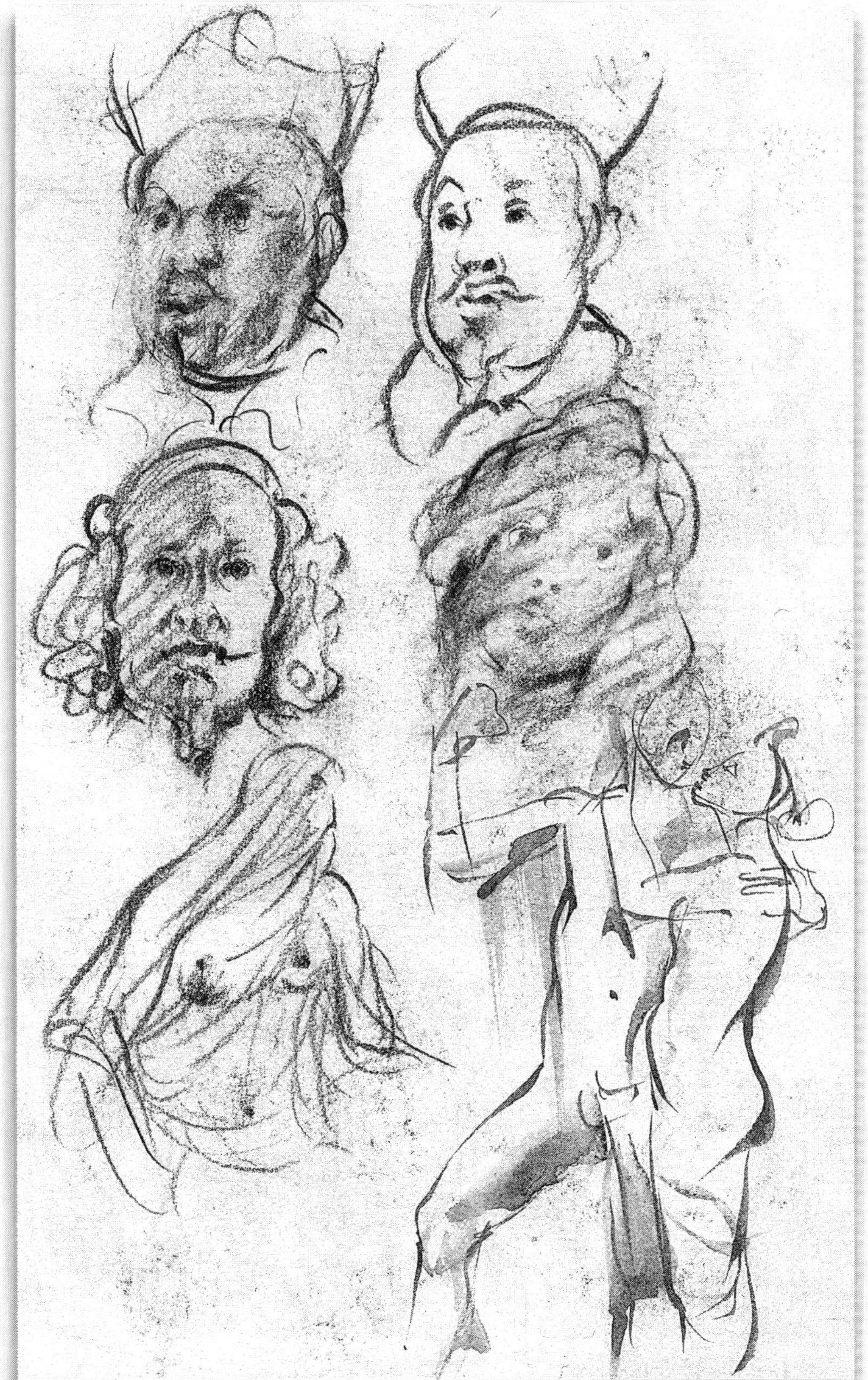

VARIOUS SKETCHES

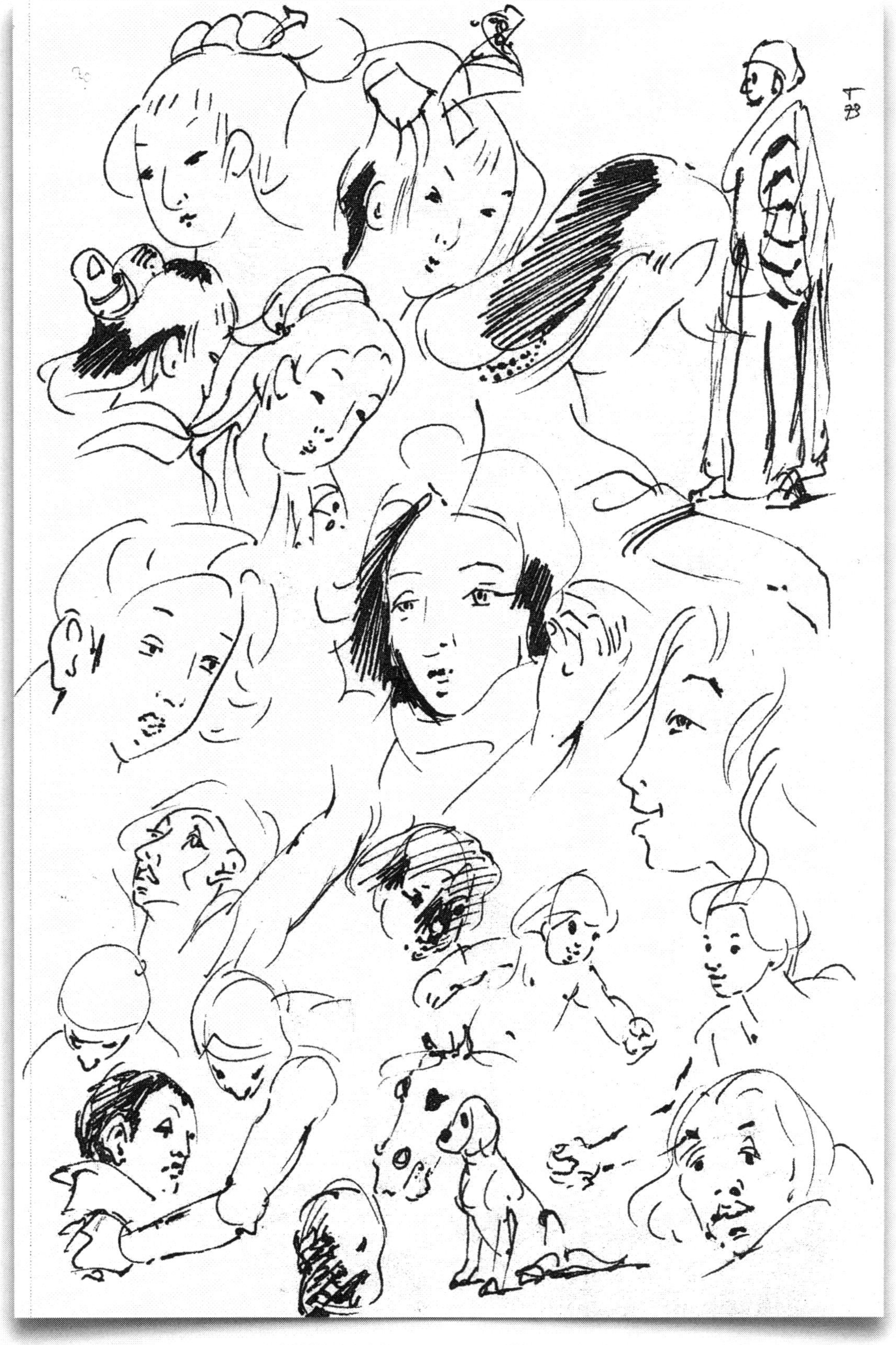

ASIAN APPROACH TO DRAWING

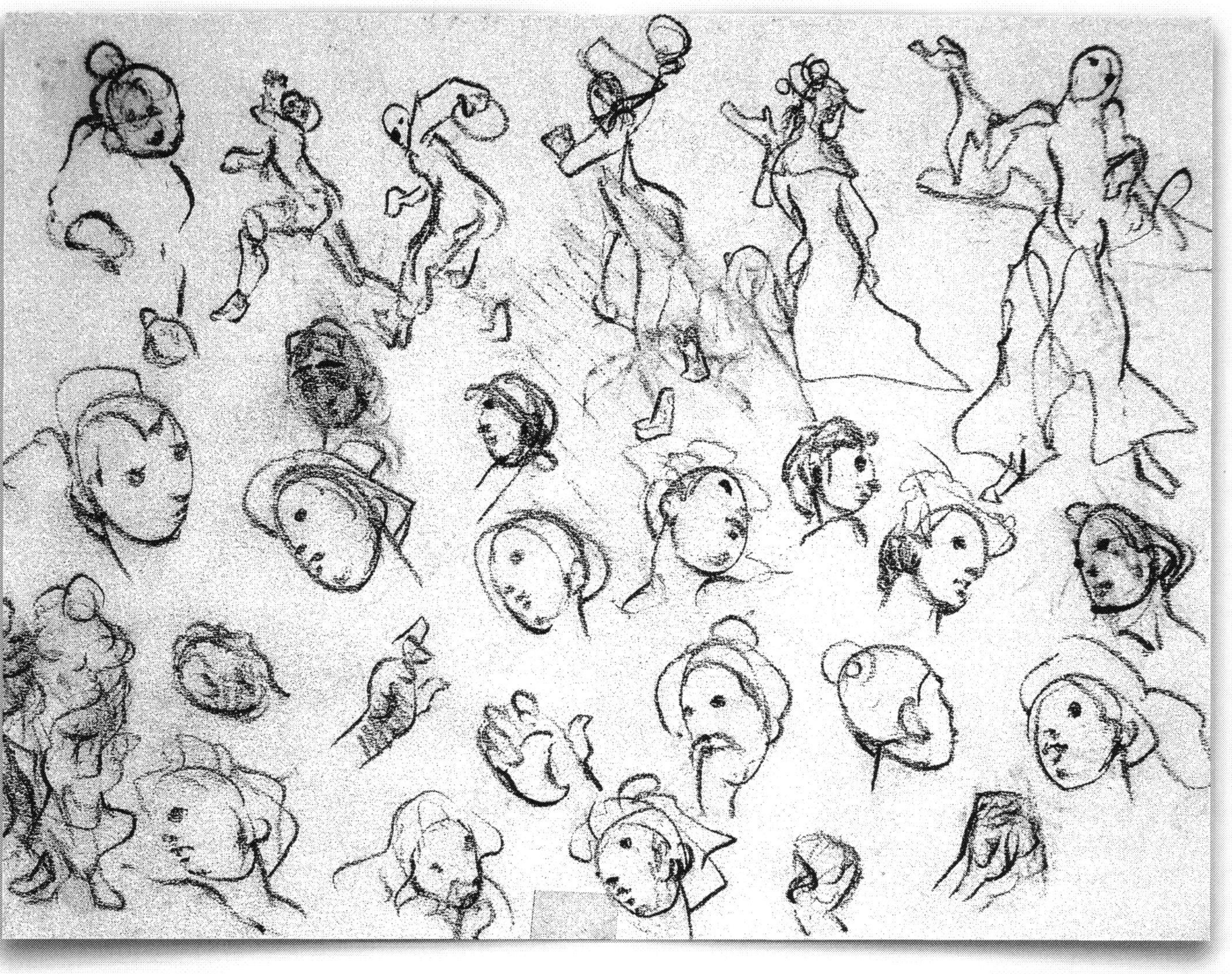

VARIOUS SKETCHES

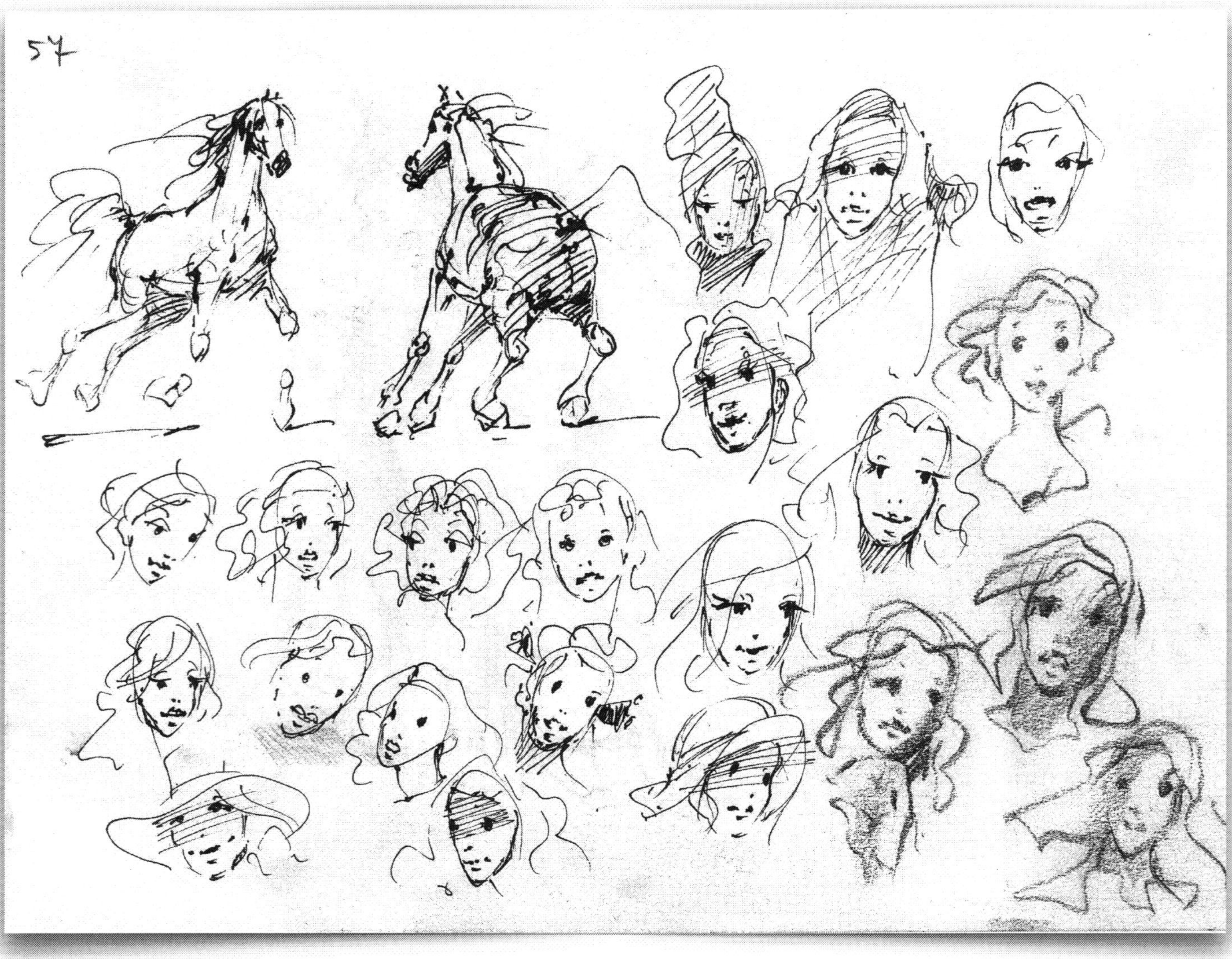

VARIOUS SKETCHES

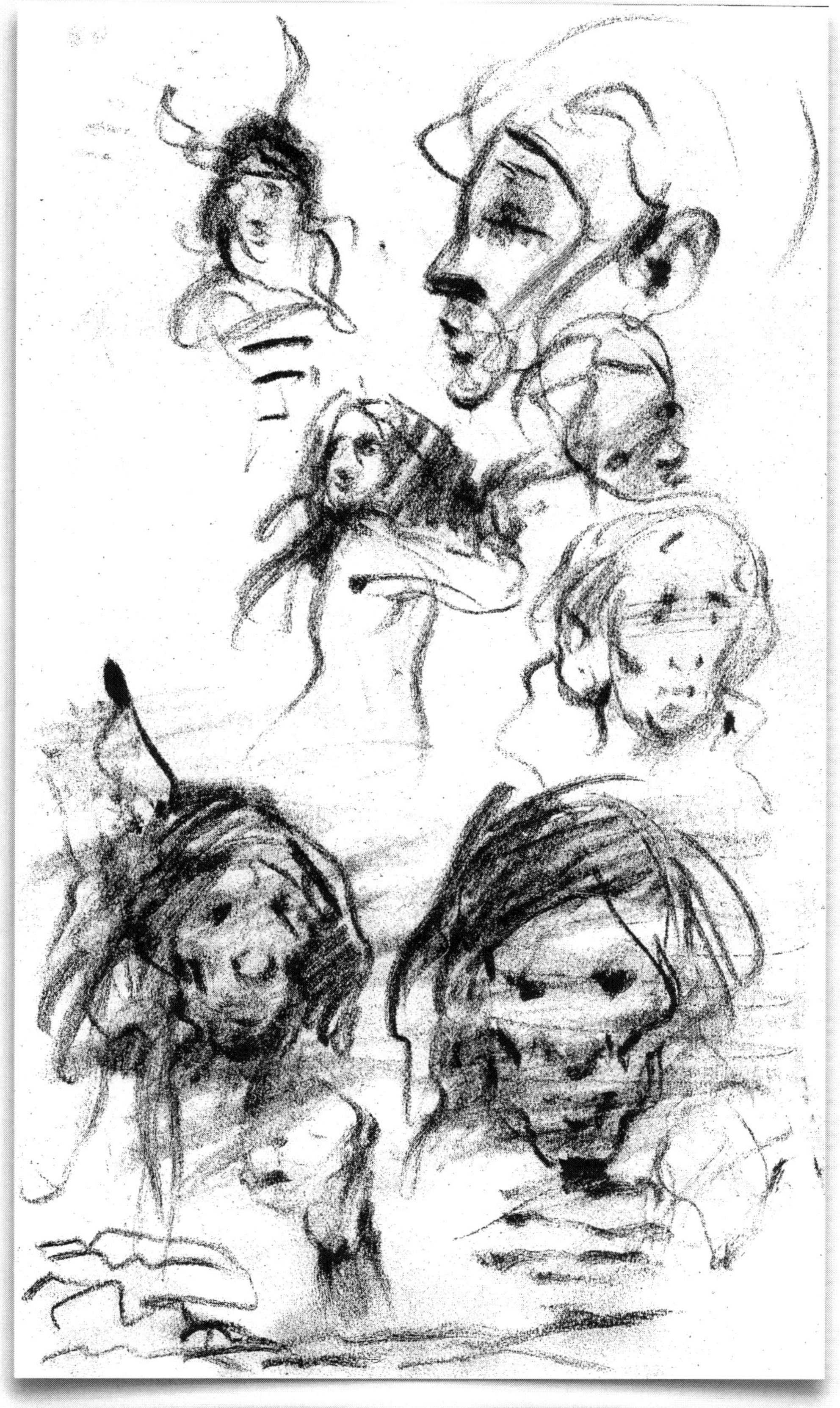

THE CHARACTER OF A RELAXED SKETCH

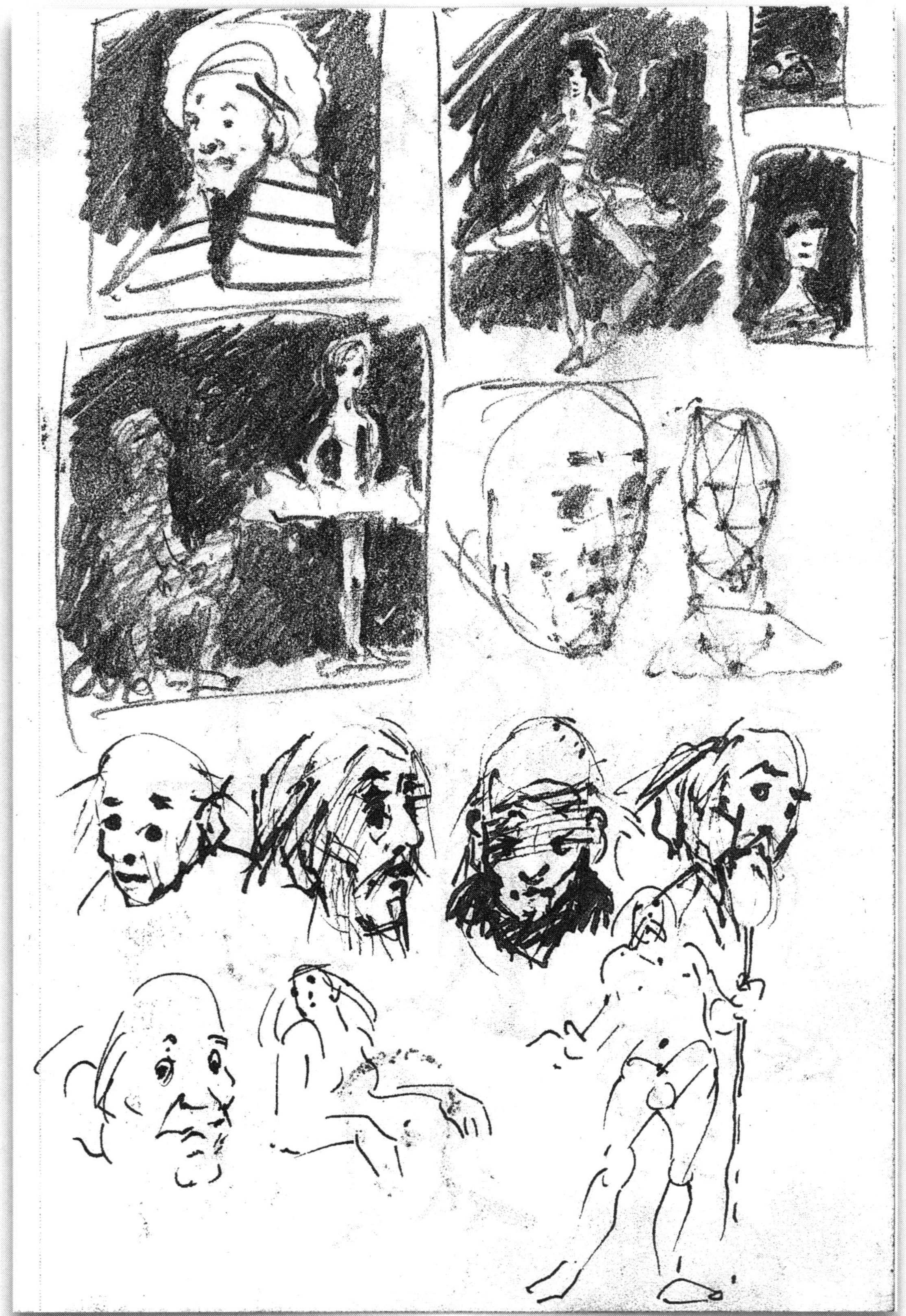

VARIOUS STARTING POINTS FOR PRESENTING
DRAWING CHALLENGES

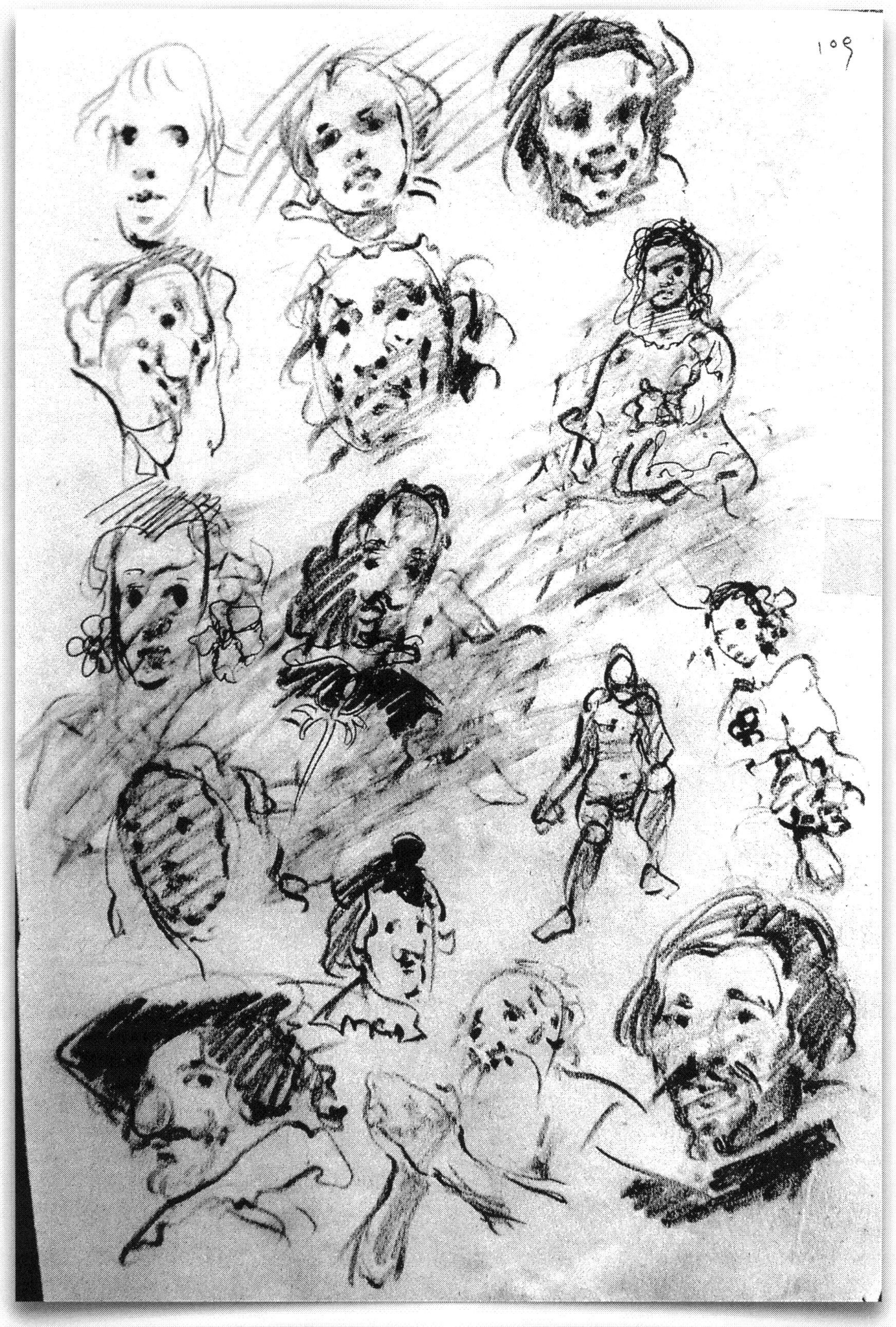

SKETCHES IN THE STYLE OF VELAZQUEZ

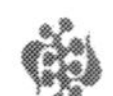

The Full Figure

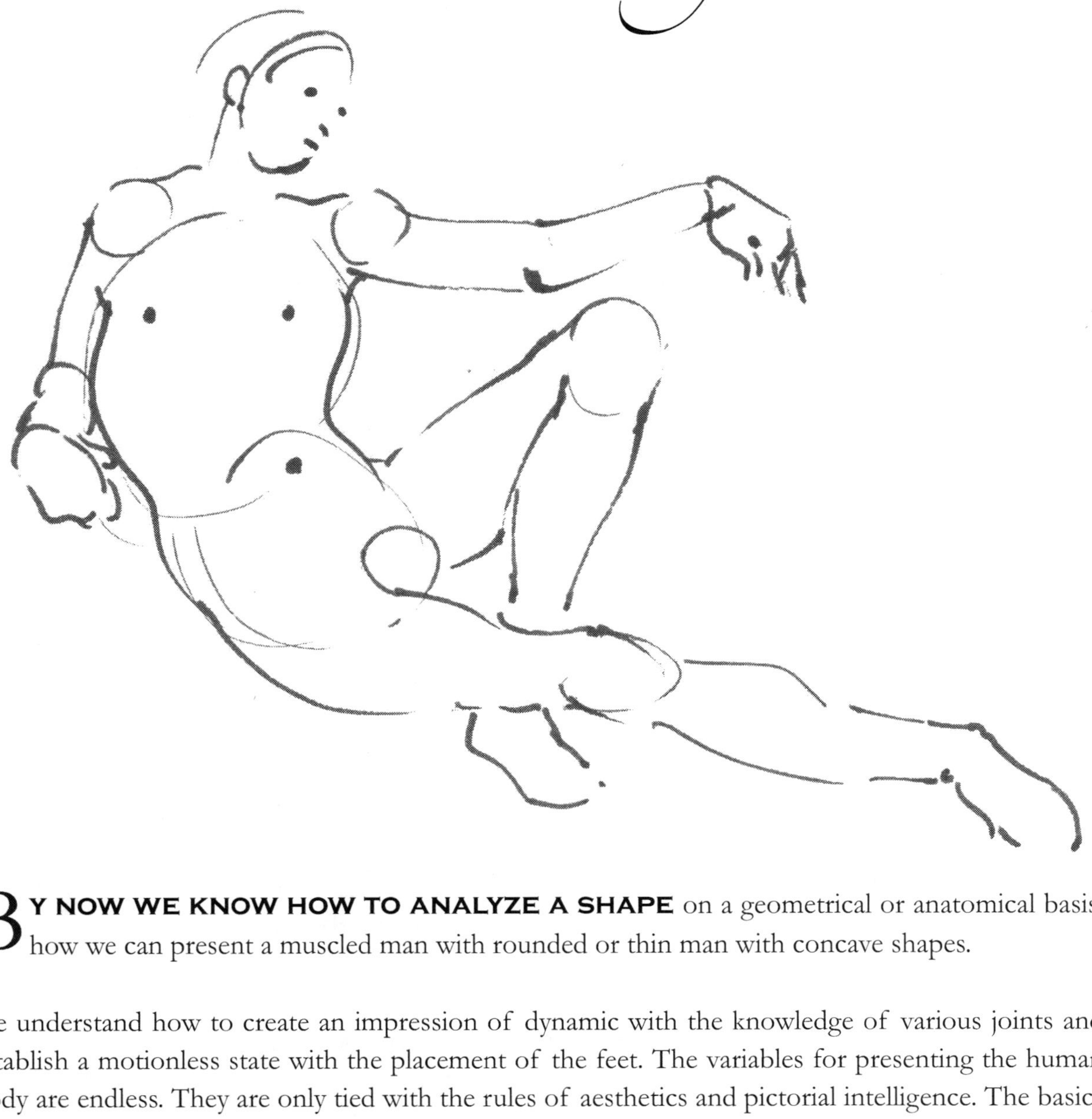

BY NOW WE KNOW HOW TO ANALYZE A SHAPE on a geometrical or anatomical basis, how we can present a muscled man with rounded or thin man with concave shapes.

We understand how to create an impression of dynamic with the knowledge of various joints and establish a motionless state with the placement of the feet. The variables for presenting the human body are endless. They are only tied with the rules of aesthetics and pictorial intelligence. The basics of aesthetics are a man's ability to observe nature. The character of human figure is based on round, elliptic and oval shapes, while the overall view is completed with the principles of architecture.

The ancient cultures of the Mediterranean were moulded on the principles of objective and factual understanding of nature. They left us with magnificent legacies of Egypt, Crete, and Athens. The Greek and Roman classics. In the field of the arts, the human figure represented the highest value.

When drawing the human figure, we follow the same rules of presentation as when drawing separate parts; geometrical analysis based on angular and oval shapes, completed with anatomical character. Likewise the dynamic of the body is observed in its entirety, so that the intention of drawing the figure continues into placement and position. The main sense of the pose is within its harmony with the principles of esthetics.

According to scientific criteria, esthetics is not a science, since it is not based on epistemology - the theory of knowledge. It a matter of individual taste. The rules of esthetics in painting are exact and factual. They are grounded in strong base of human optical perception; human perception of visual nature, gravity, light, symmetry, reflection, pattern, rhythm, calligraphy, passages and contrasts, covering over, translucence, the common characteristics of organisms and their tendency to connect with the environment. Perhaps a few more.The human figure is an example of a most demanding formation and structure. Mastering drawing and painting of human figure form demands the highest level of expertise and technical ability.

TECHNICAL ADVICE AND SUGGESTIONS

THE MOST IMPORTANT PART are the drawings. Each idea is only an expressed opinion, that is not binding. The drawings are a tangible indicator that speaks for itself, without explanation and commentary; the drawings are the essence of every drawing study.

Drawing with reflection is one approach to learn. Drawing and redrawing is the other. Both paths are equal. The number of drawings that you have created one way or another is very important for your progress as a drawing artist. Successful drawings prove the level of practical knowledge, less successful ones can signify a high level of understanding - pictorial intelligence, which is indeed a rarity in today's confusing state of the arts.

The drawings are made with ease and stimulate your creativity, your imagination, more so than any accompanying words. The most important is your regular practice, as it is the only indicator of your deeper understanding of drawing. Who ever questions the level of intelligence when observing Leonardo's paintings? Or the IQ level of Rembrandt? The drawings as examples can serve as a starting point for different interpretations: different technique, size, analysis of the details in various combinations.

Always remember that you are drawing for your inner joy and individual interest. Do not care for praise or disapproval. You are the only judge of your quality now that you tested your abilities. Now you know that depicting the human figure is the most demanding test of artist's abilities and knowledge.

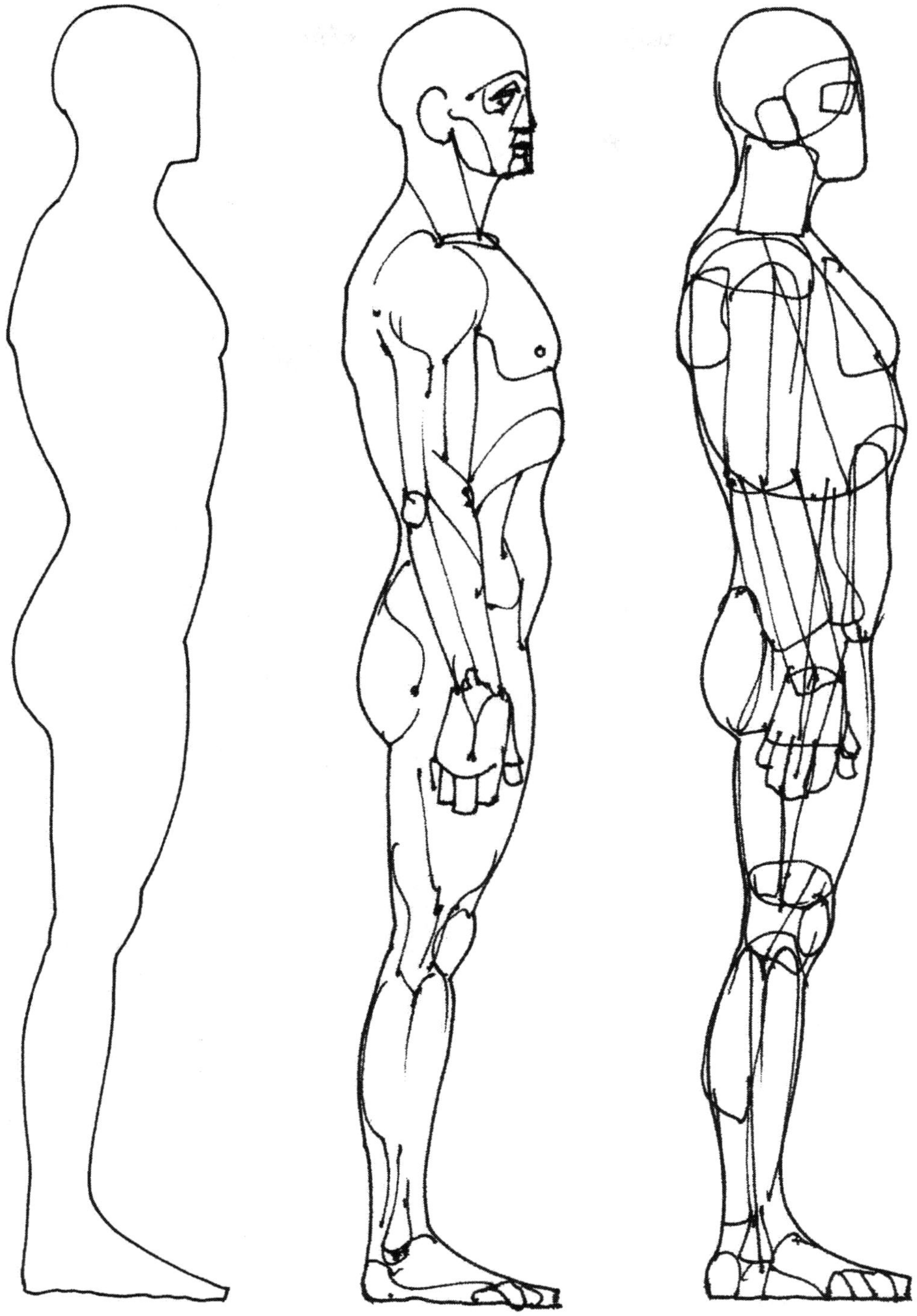

THE DETAILS WITHIN A SILHOUETTE

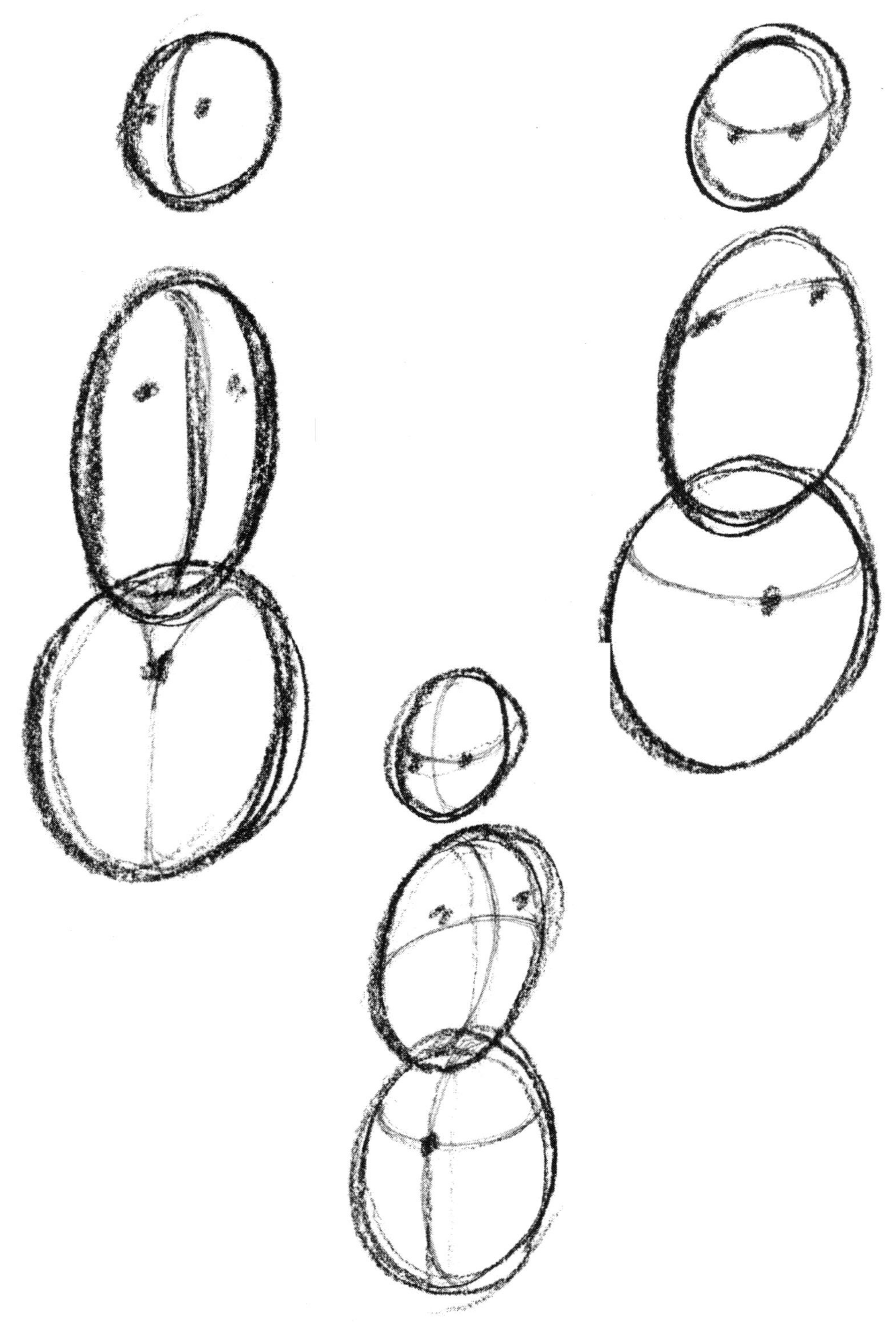

**THE ROTATION AND BENDING OF HUMAN BODY
COVERS THE HEAD, CHEST AND HIPS**

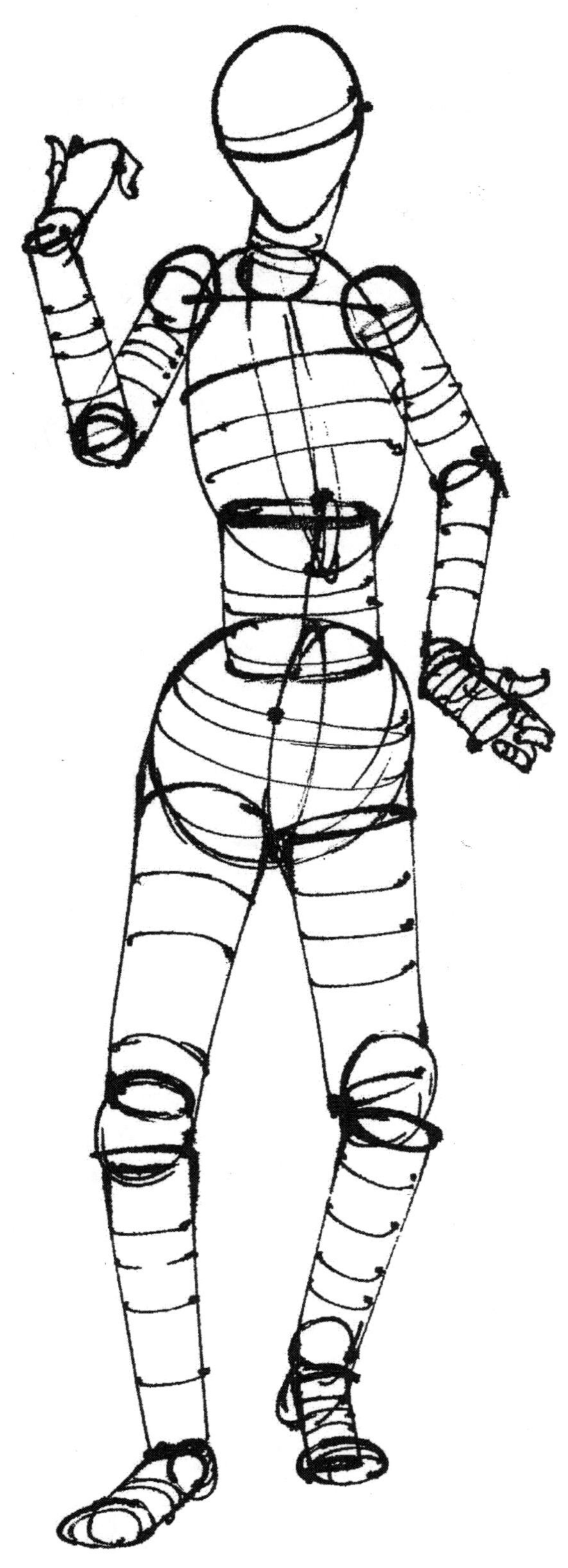

THE LINES DRAWN ON SHAPES INDICATE DIRECTIONS

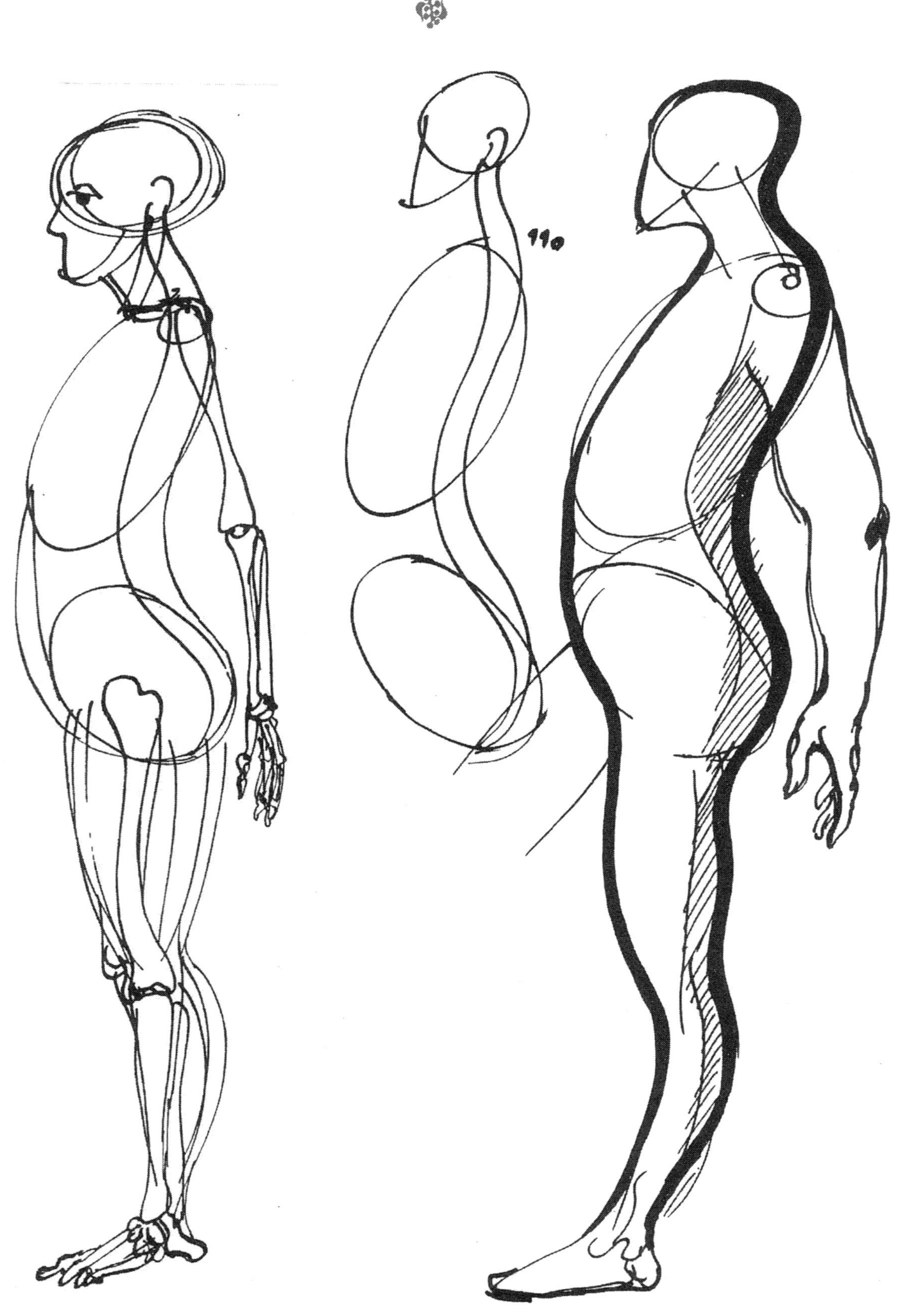

THE BASIC DYNAMICS OF THE FIGURE DEPENDS ON MOBILITY OF THE TORSO IN THE DIRECTION OF BENDING AND ROTATION

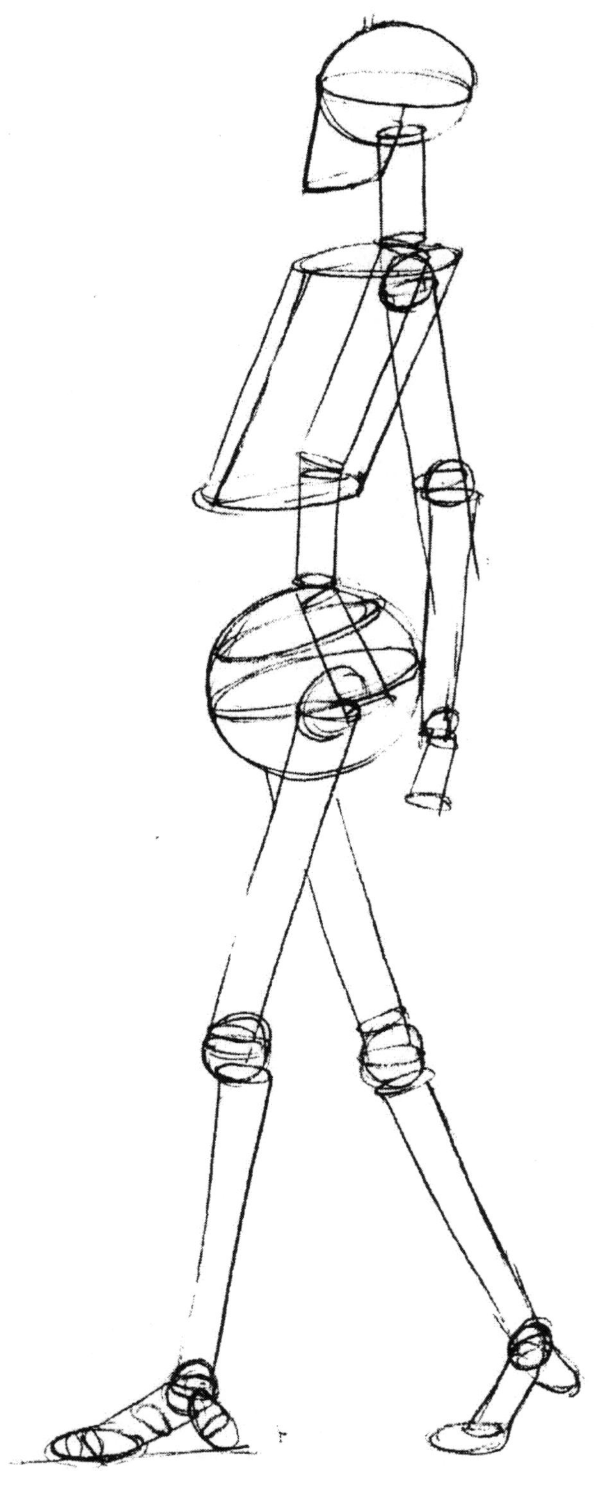

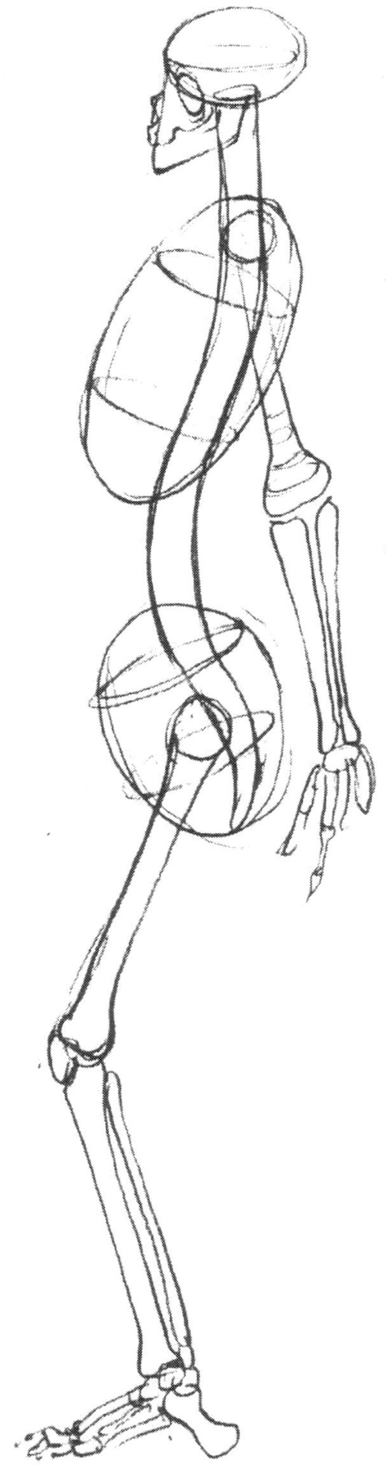

FROM GEOMETRY TO ANATOMY

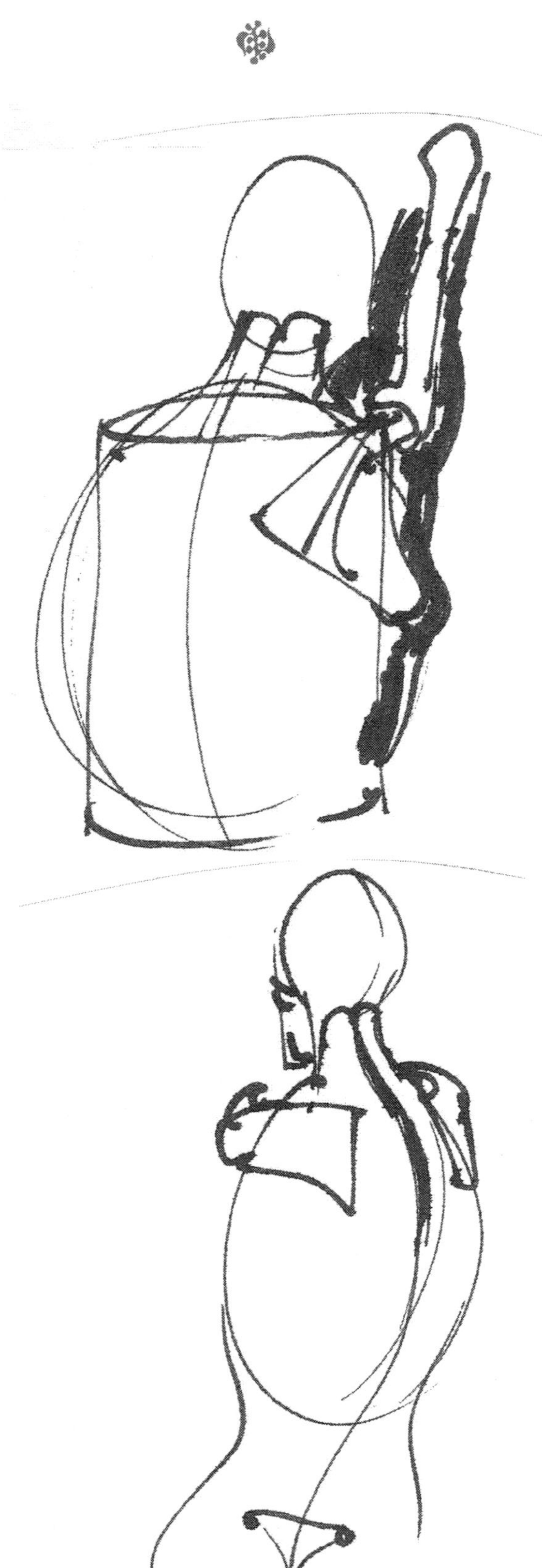

THE ROTATION MOVEMENT OF THE SPINE

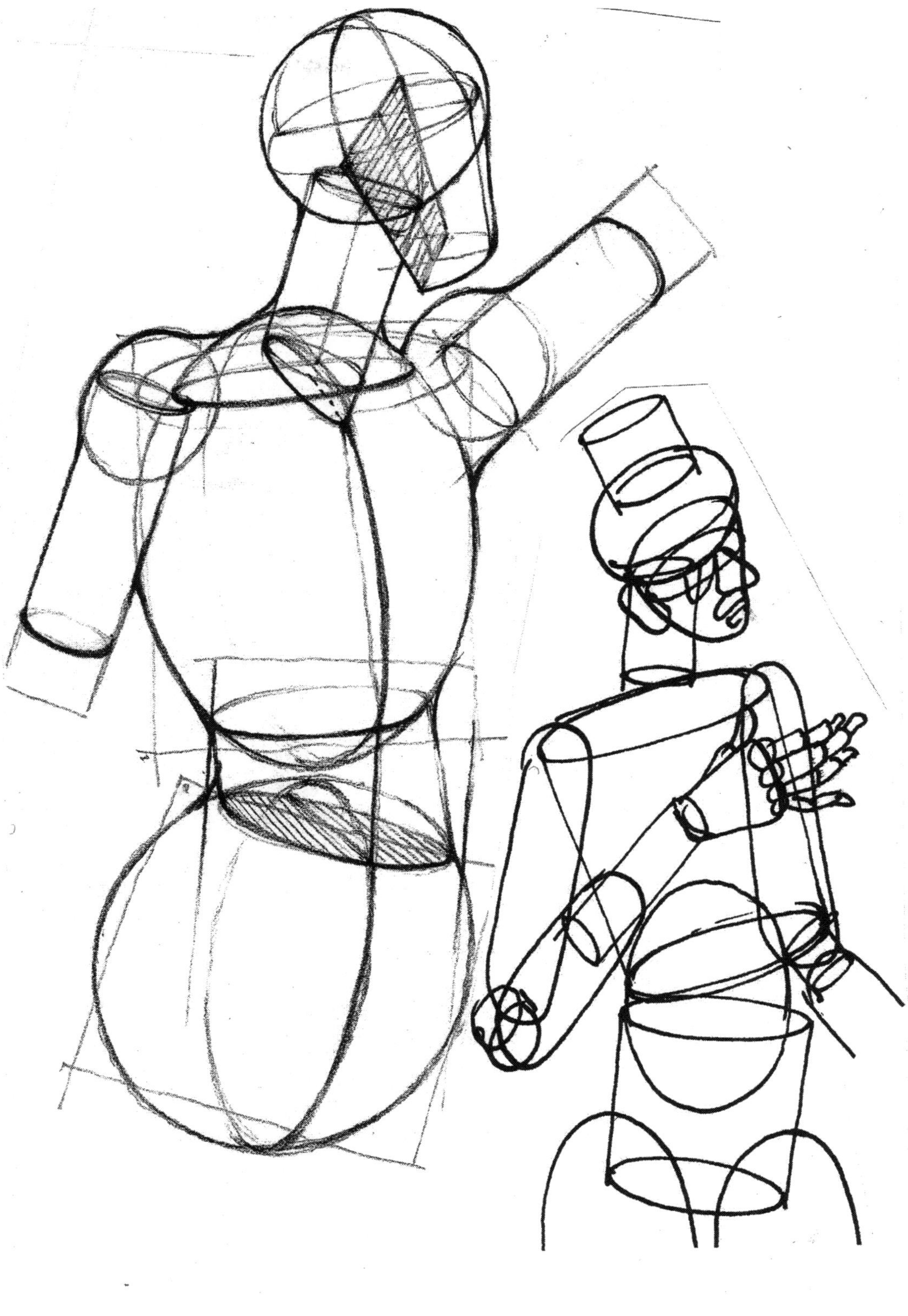

AN EXAMPLE OF SHAPE COMPOSITES

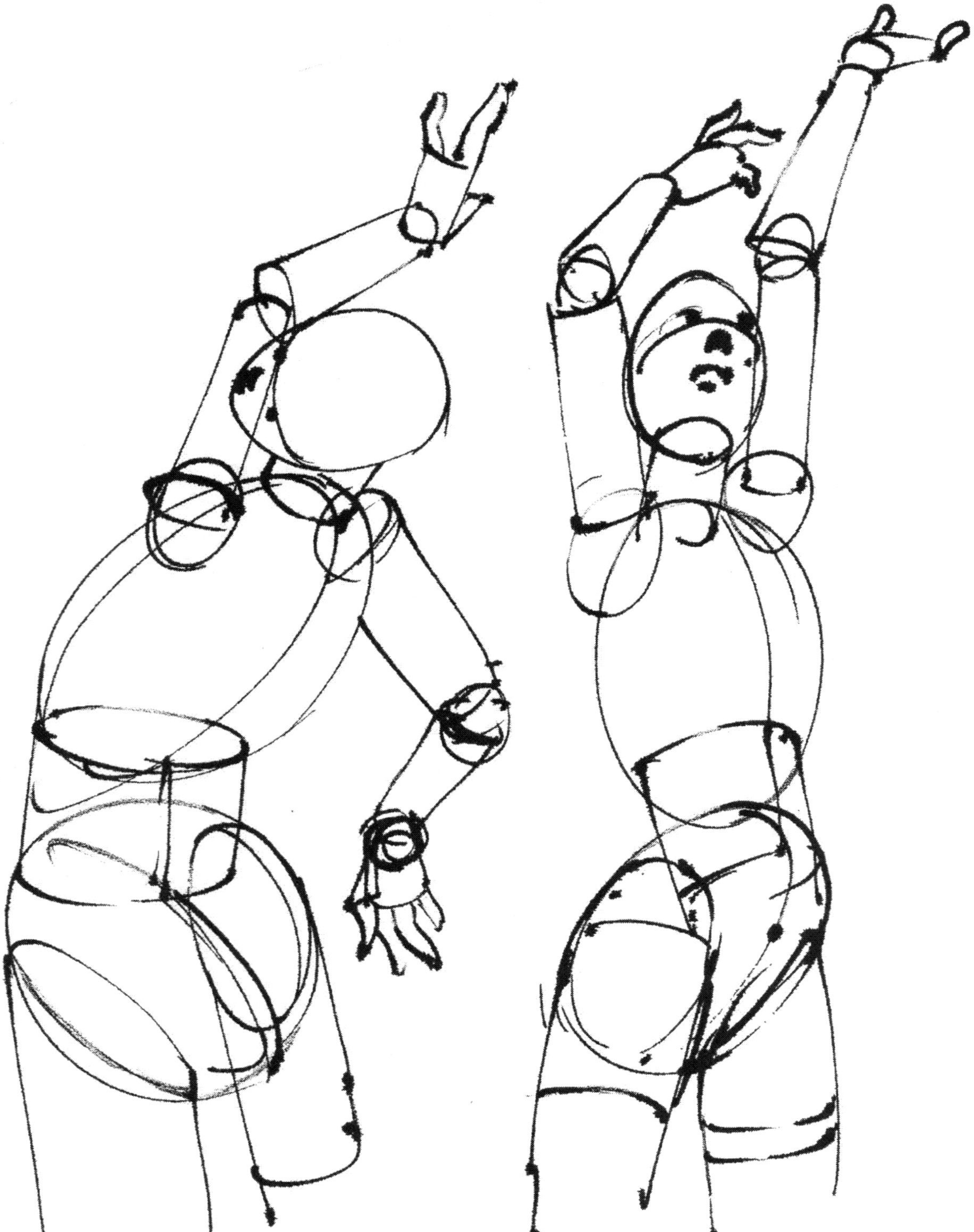

GEOMETRIC ANALYSIS OF MOVEMENT

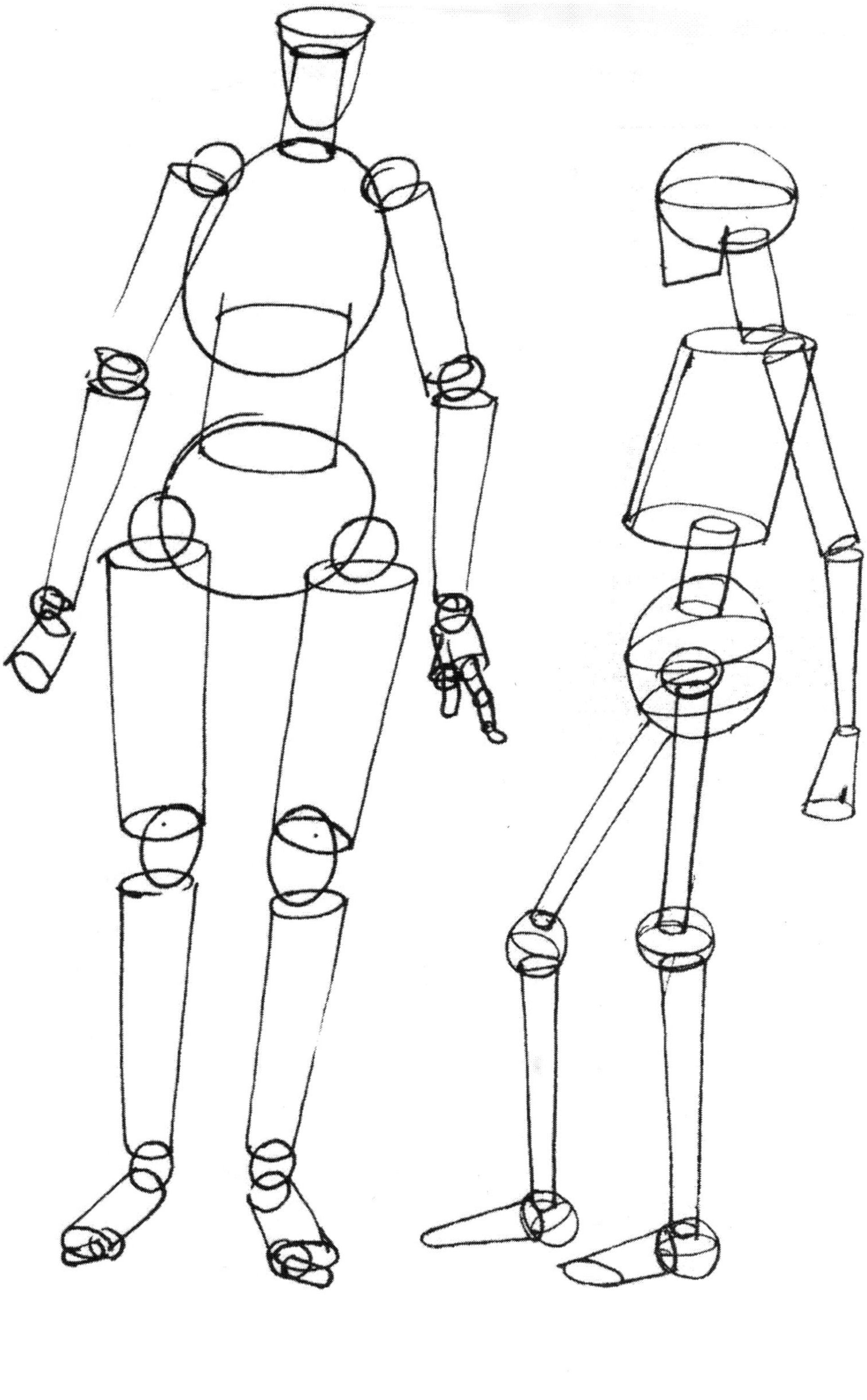

EXAMPLES OF HUMAN GEOMETRY

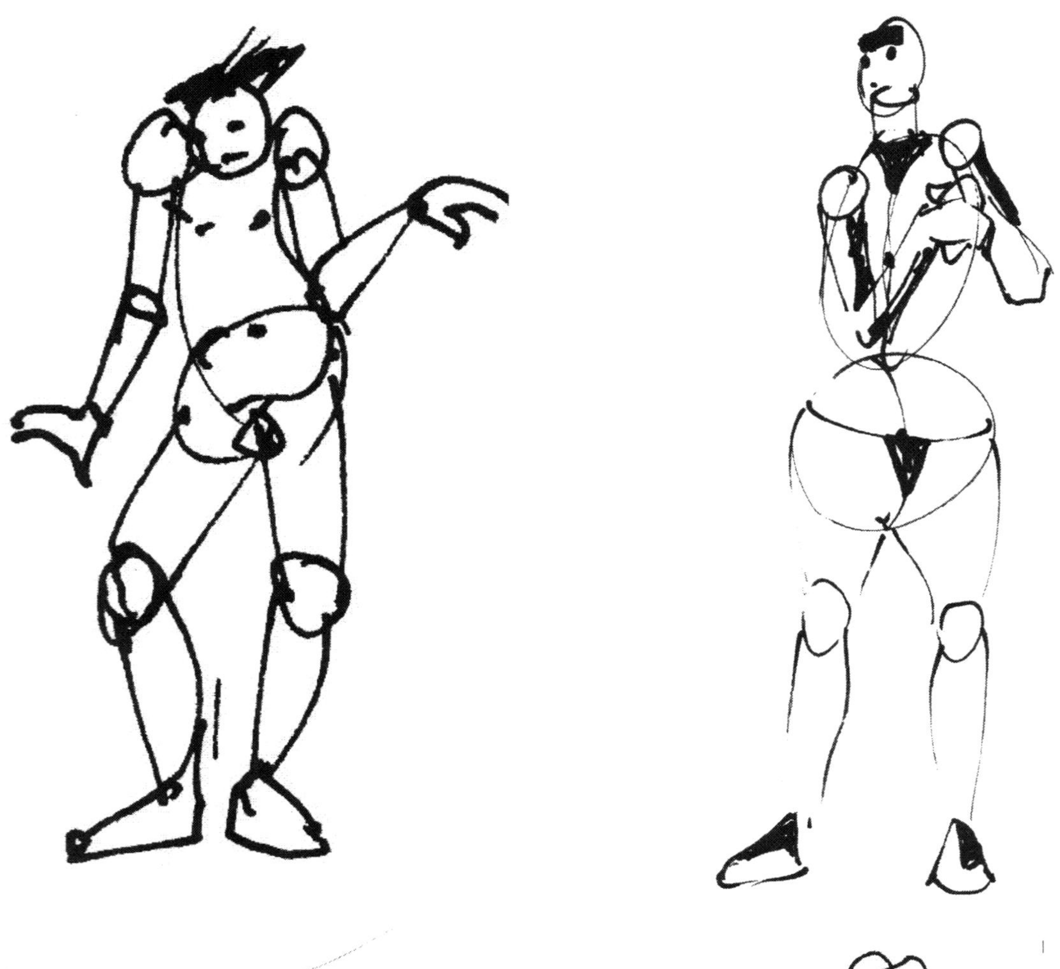

STATIC POSITION AND DYNAMIC MOVEMENT

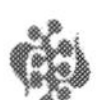

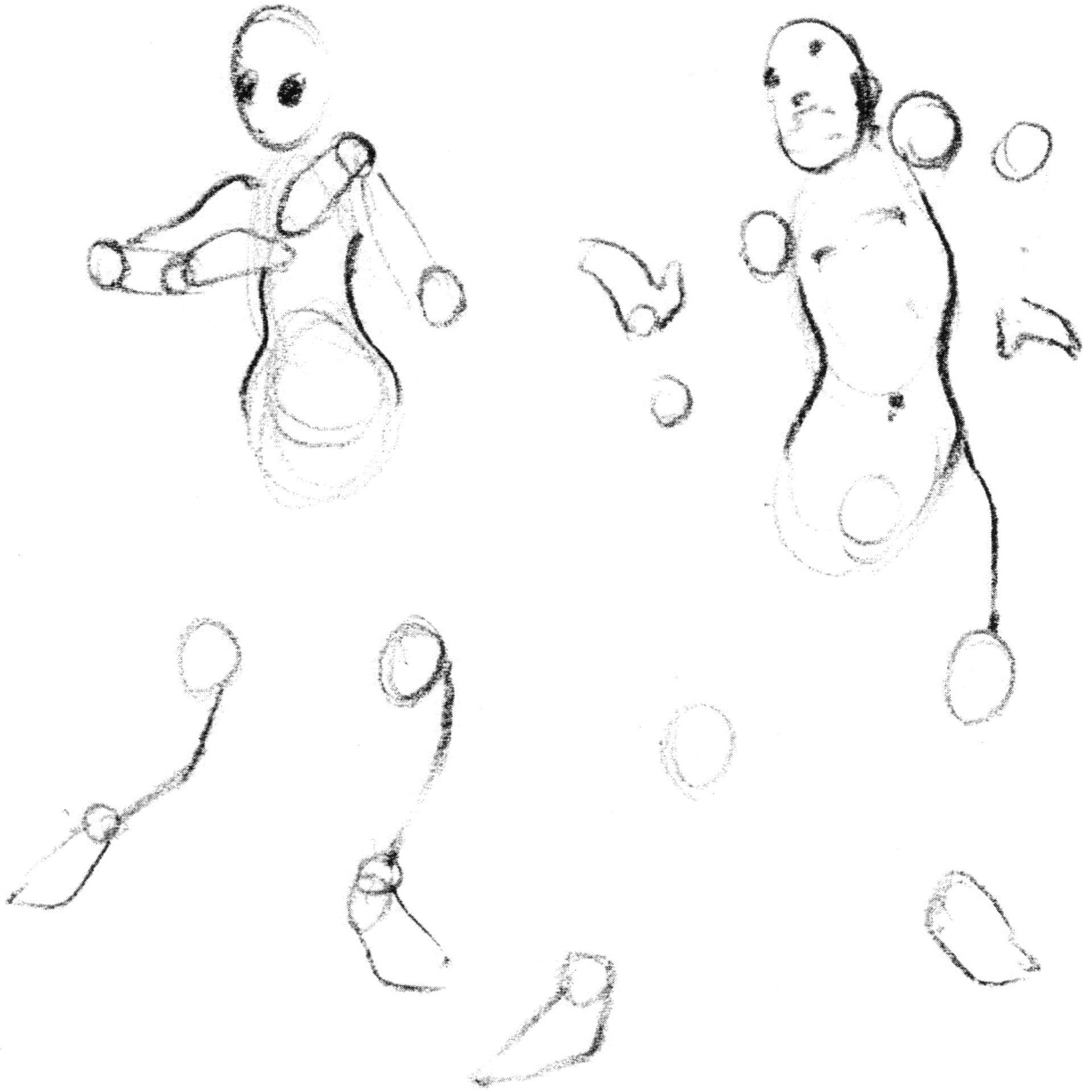

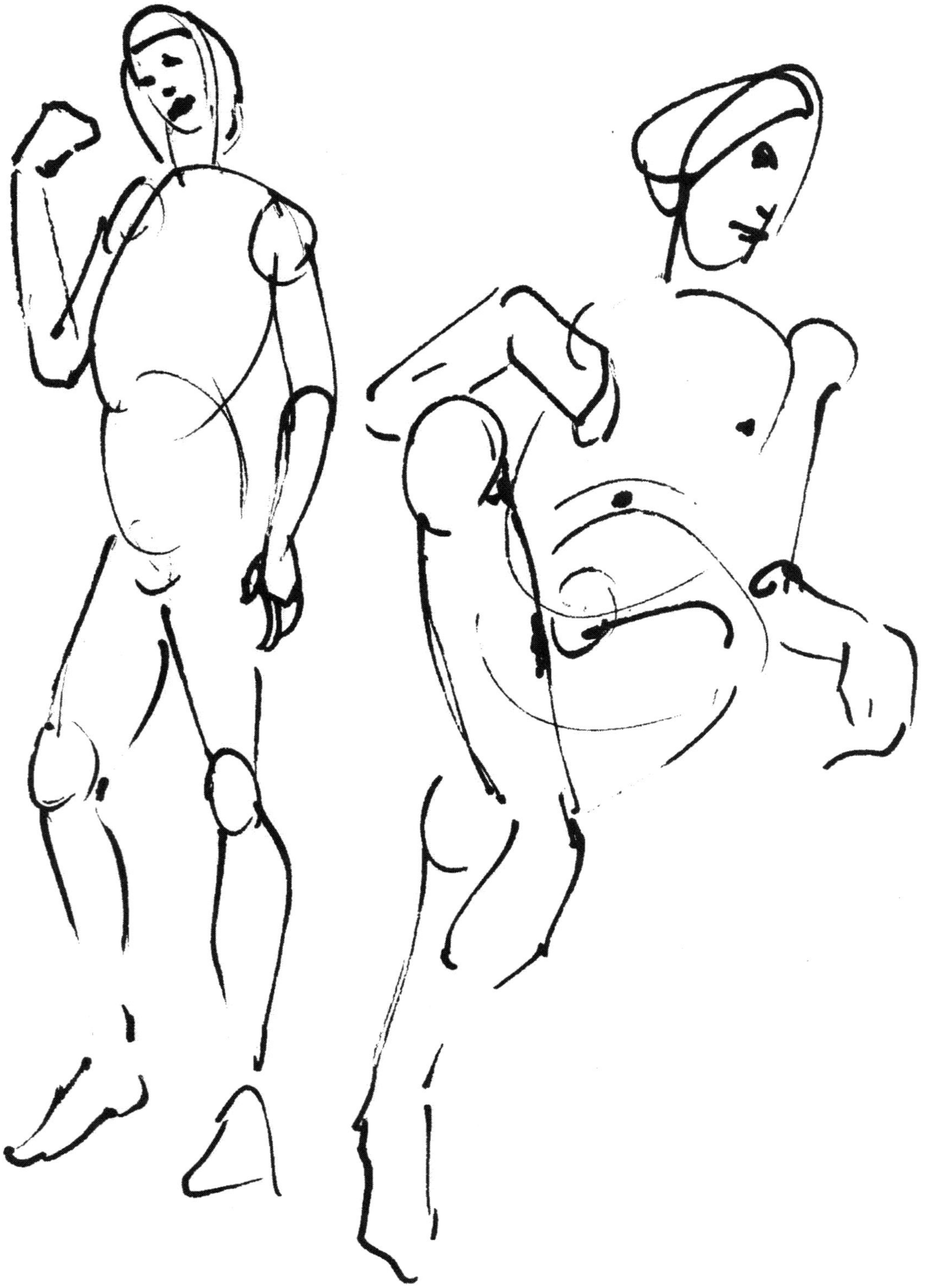

EXAMPLES OF FIGURE DIRECTION

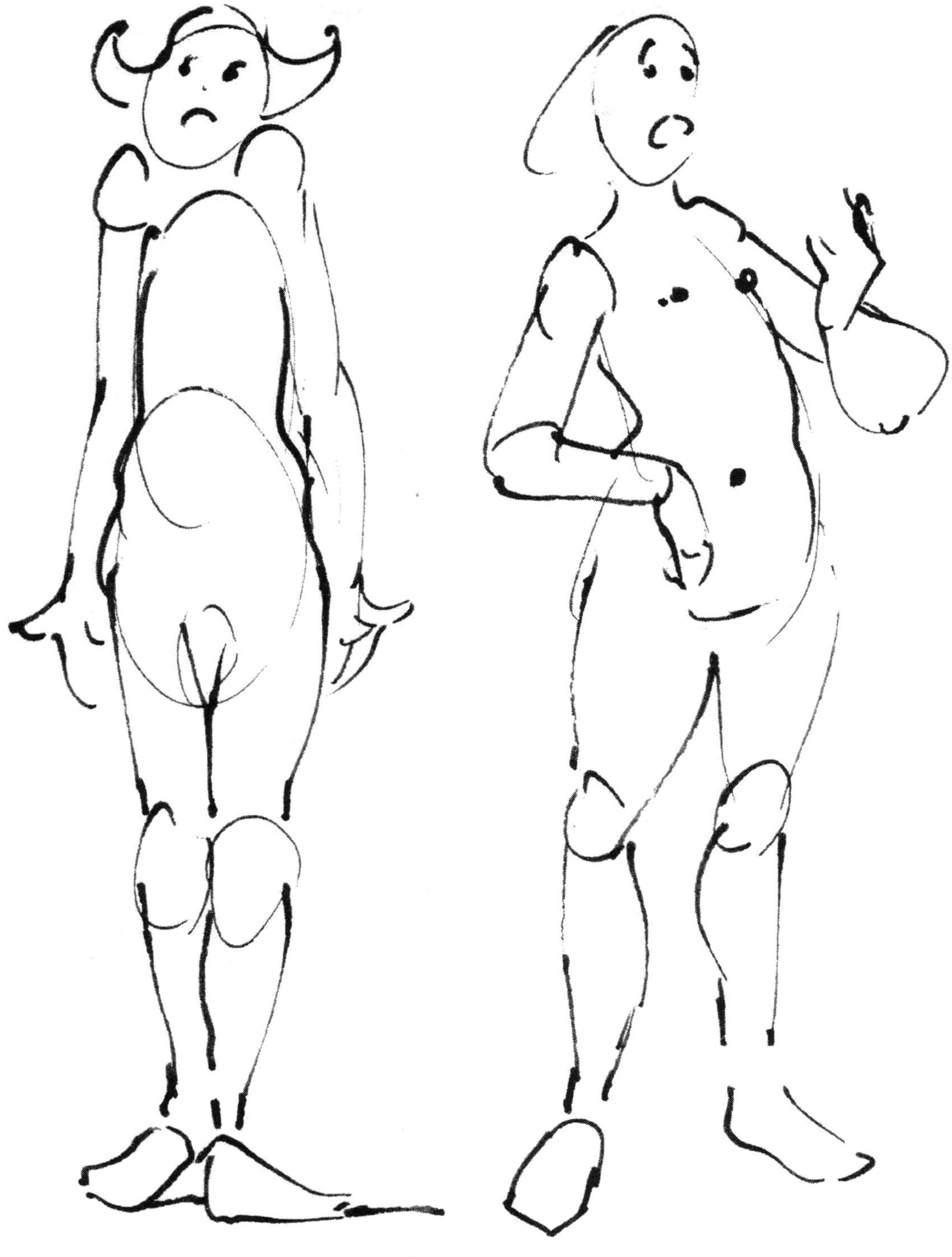

EXAMPLES OF EXPRESSIVE FIGURE POSITION

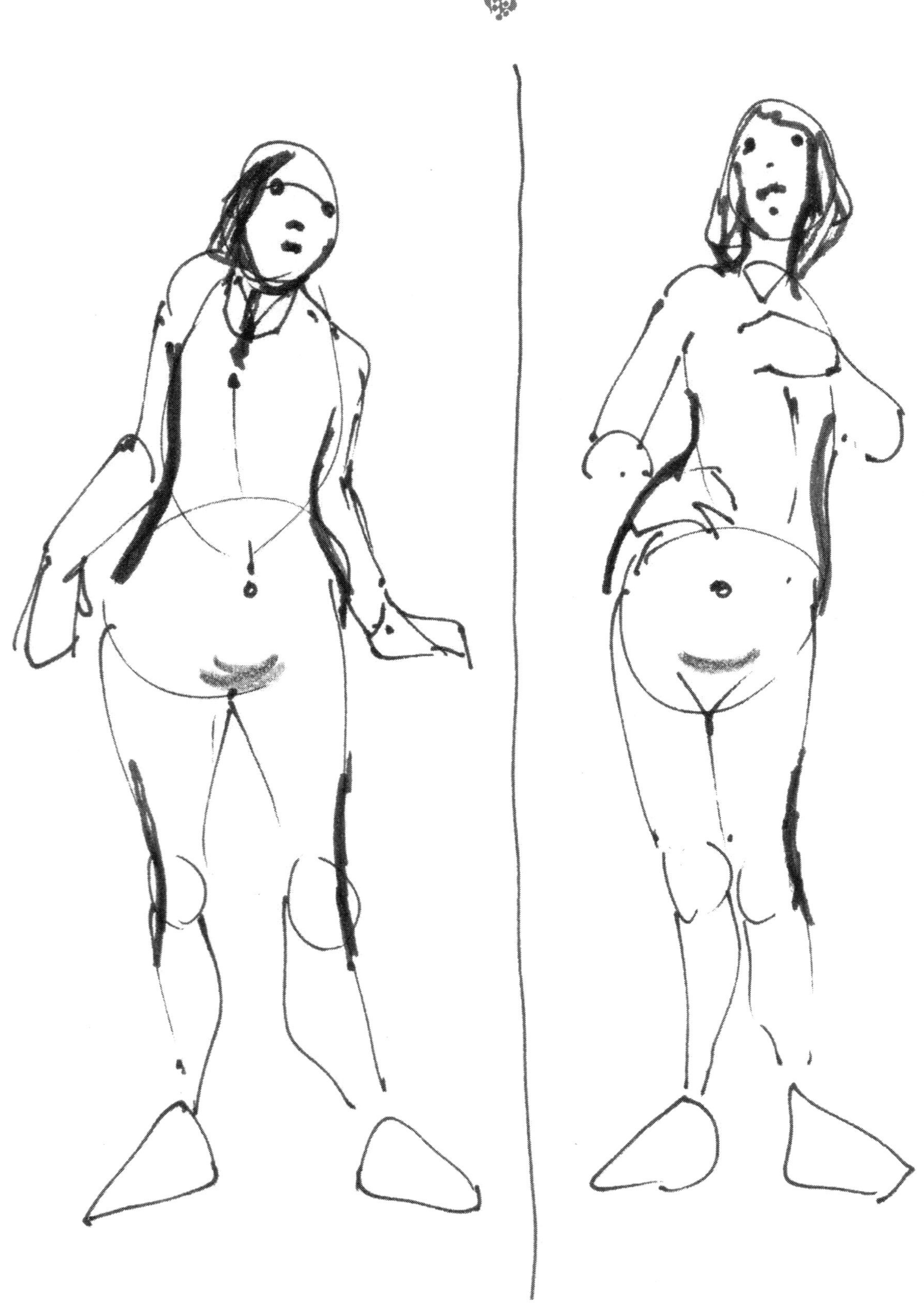

THICK LINES REPRESENT THE MAIN AREAS
OF FIGURAL MOVEMENT

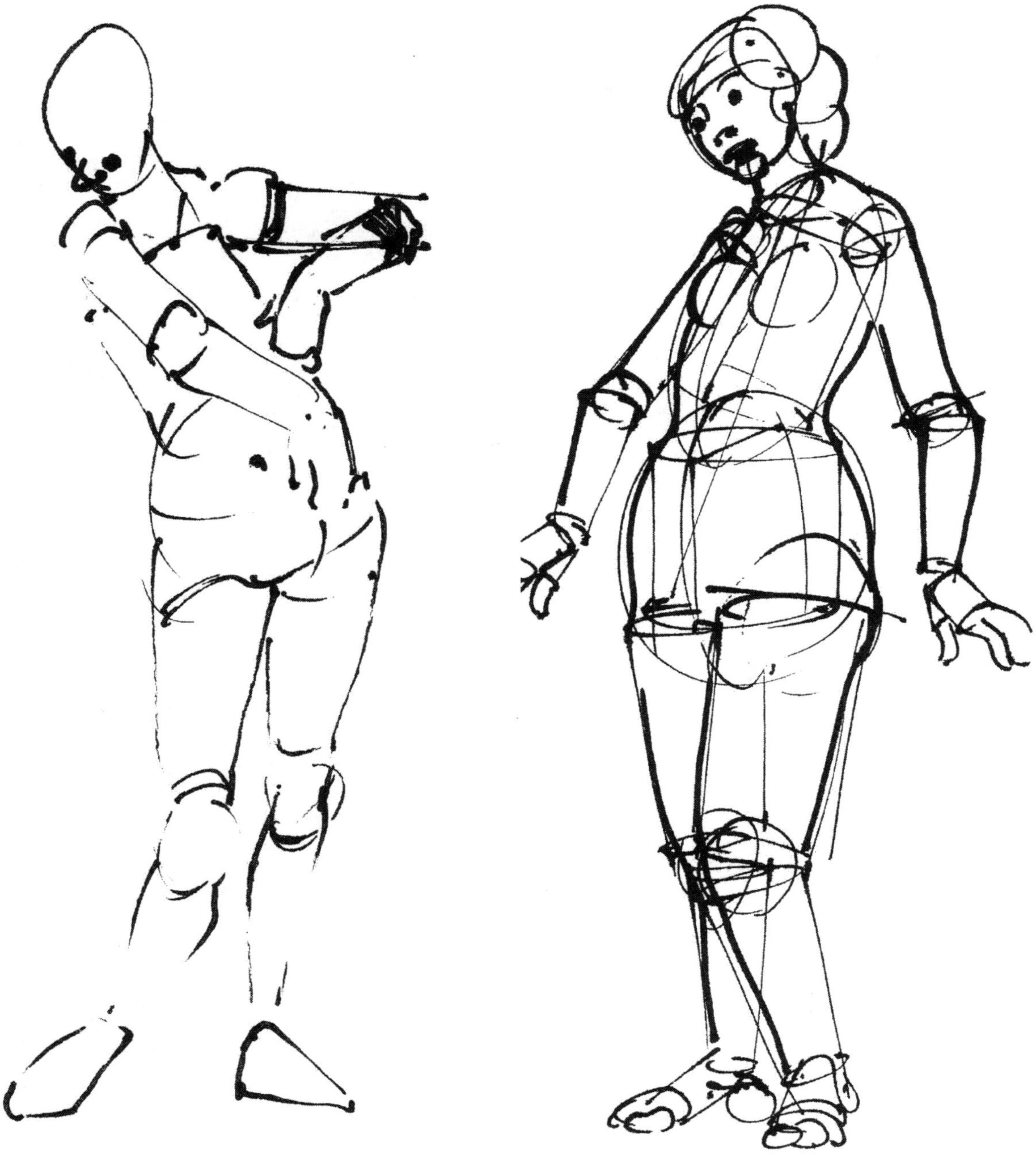

EXAMPLES OF FIGURE IN MOTION

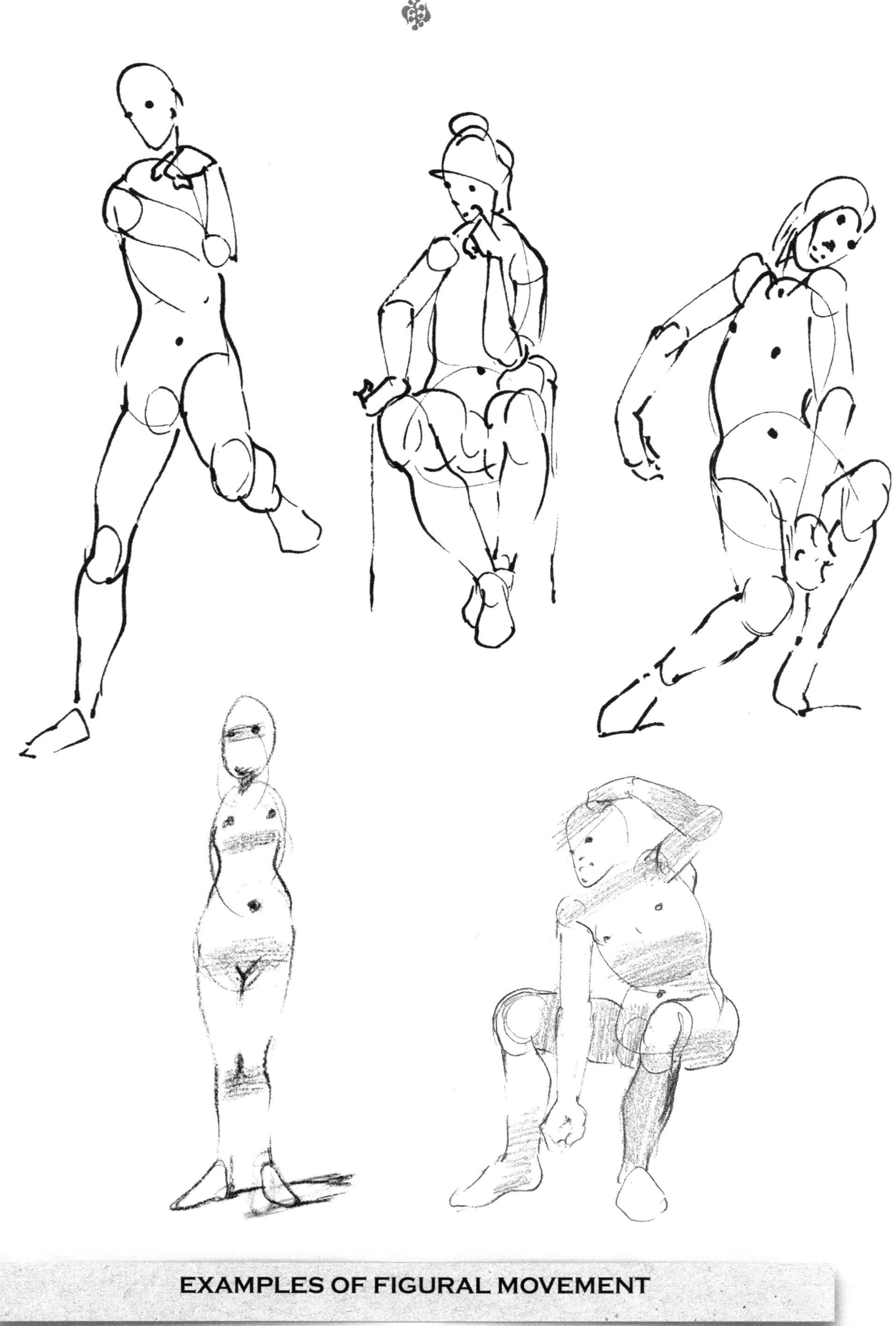

EXAMPLES OF FIGURAL MOVEMENT

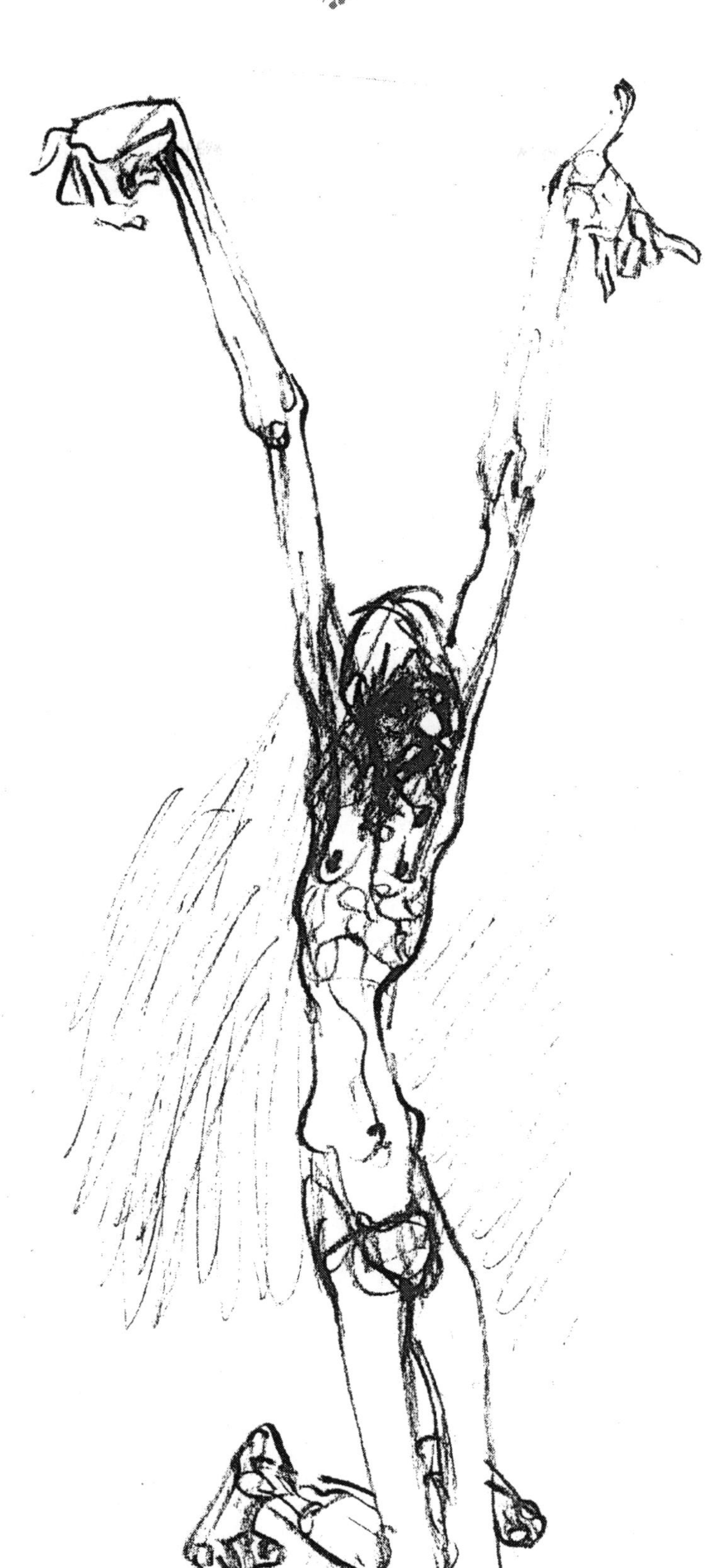

EXAMPLES OF DRAMATIC FIGURE POSITION

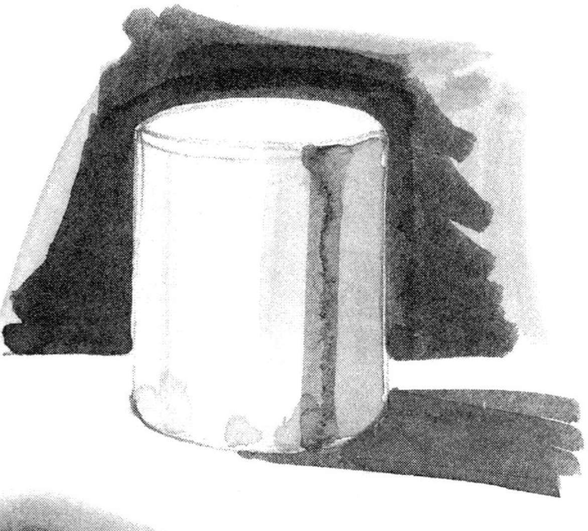

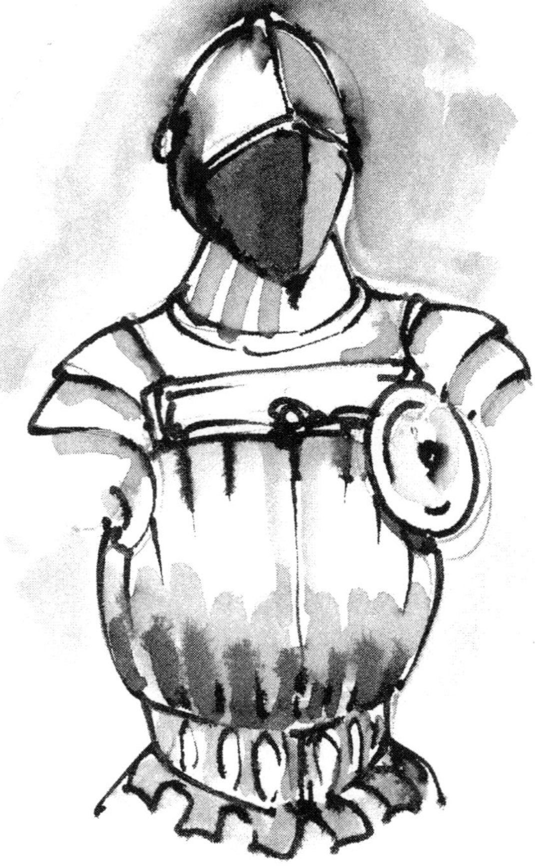

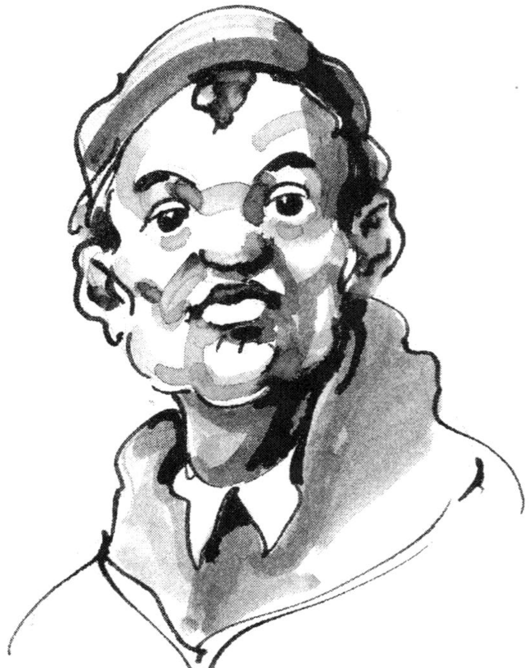

EXAMPLES OF LIGHT AND SHADOW CONTRAST

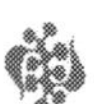

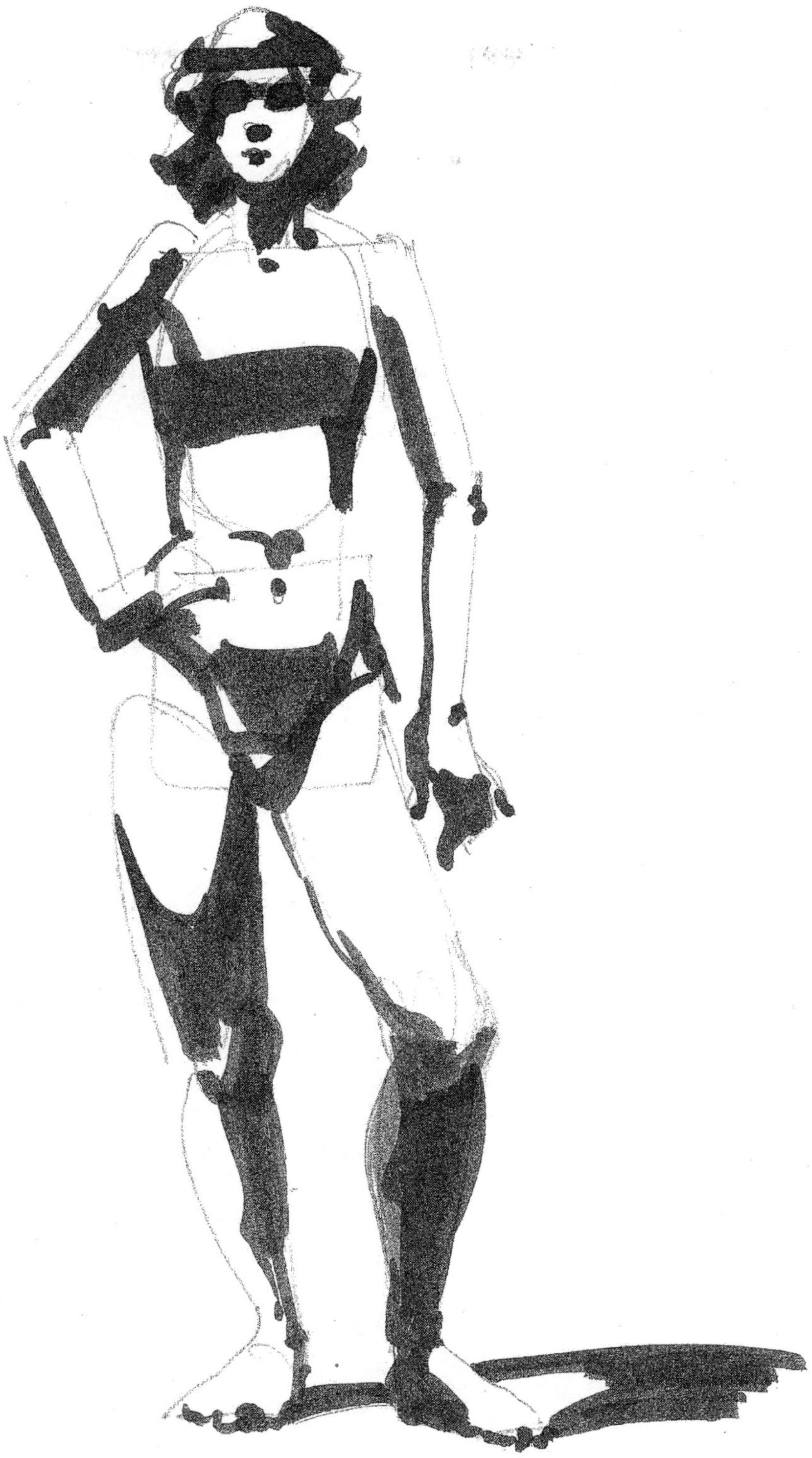

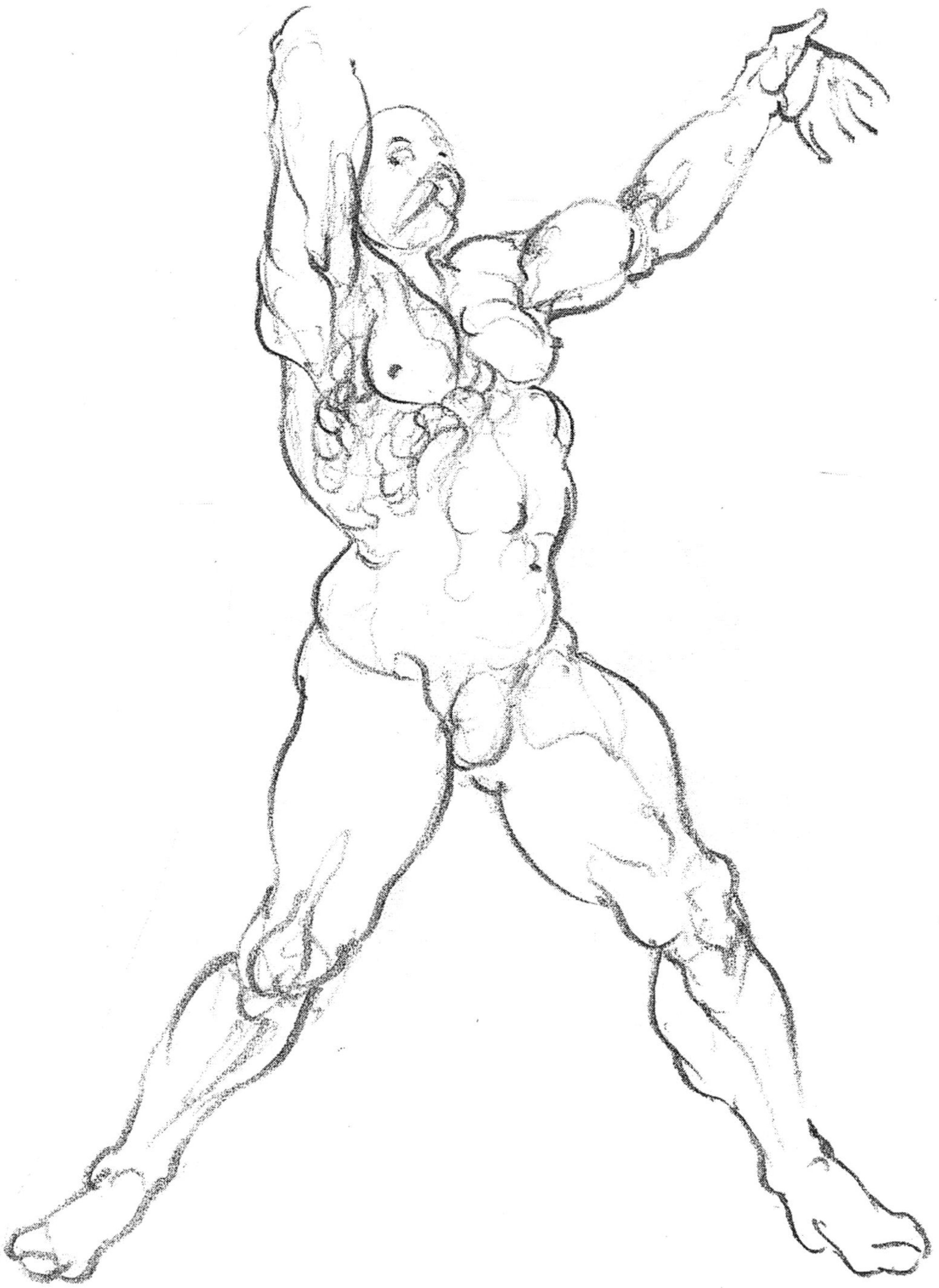

BULGING SHAPES DEFINE MUSCLES

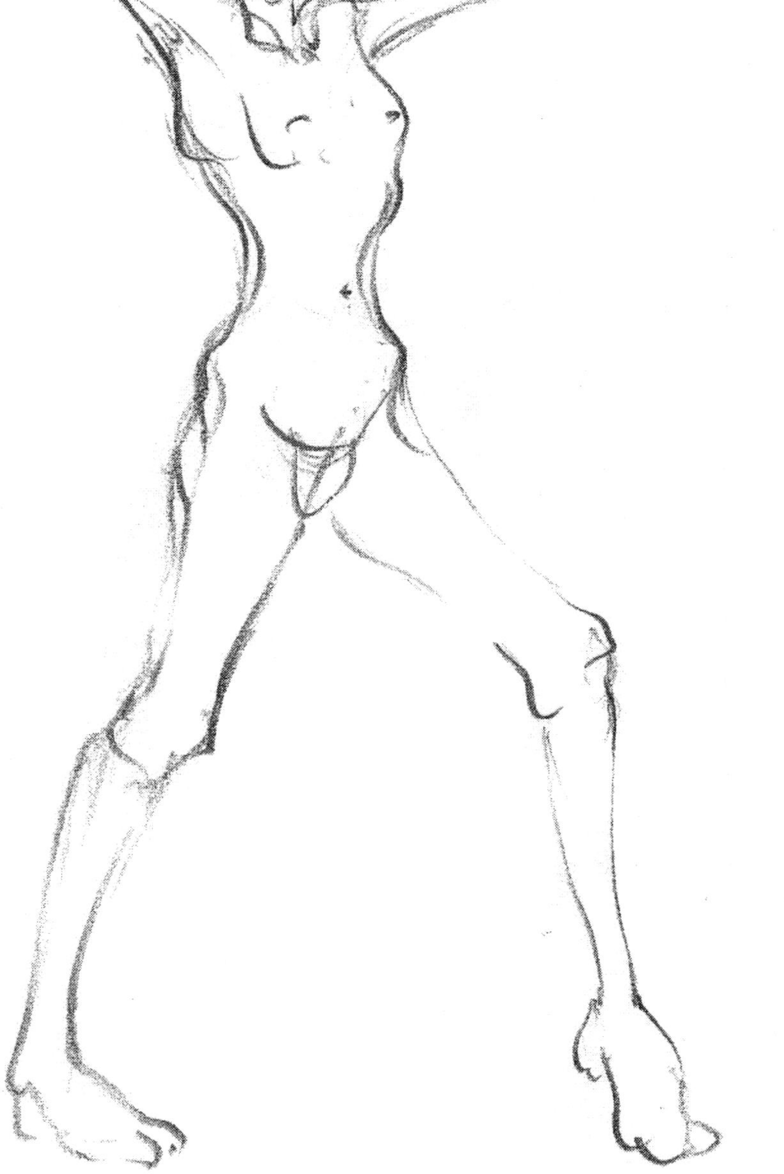

INDENTATIONS ACCENTUATE THE SKELETON

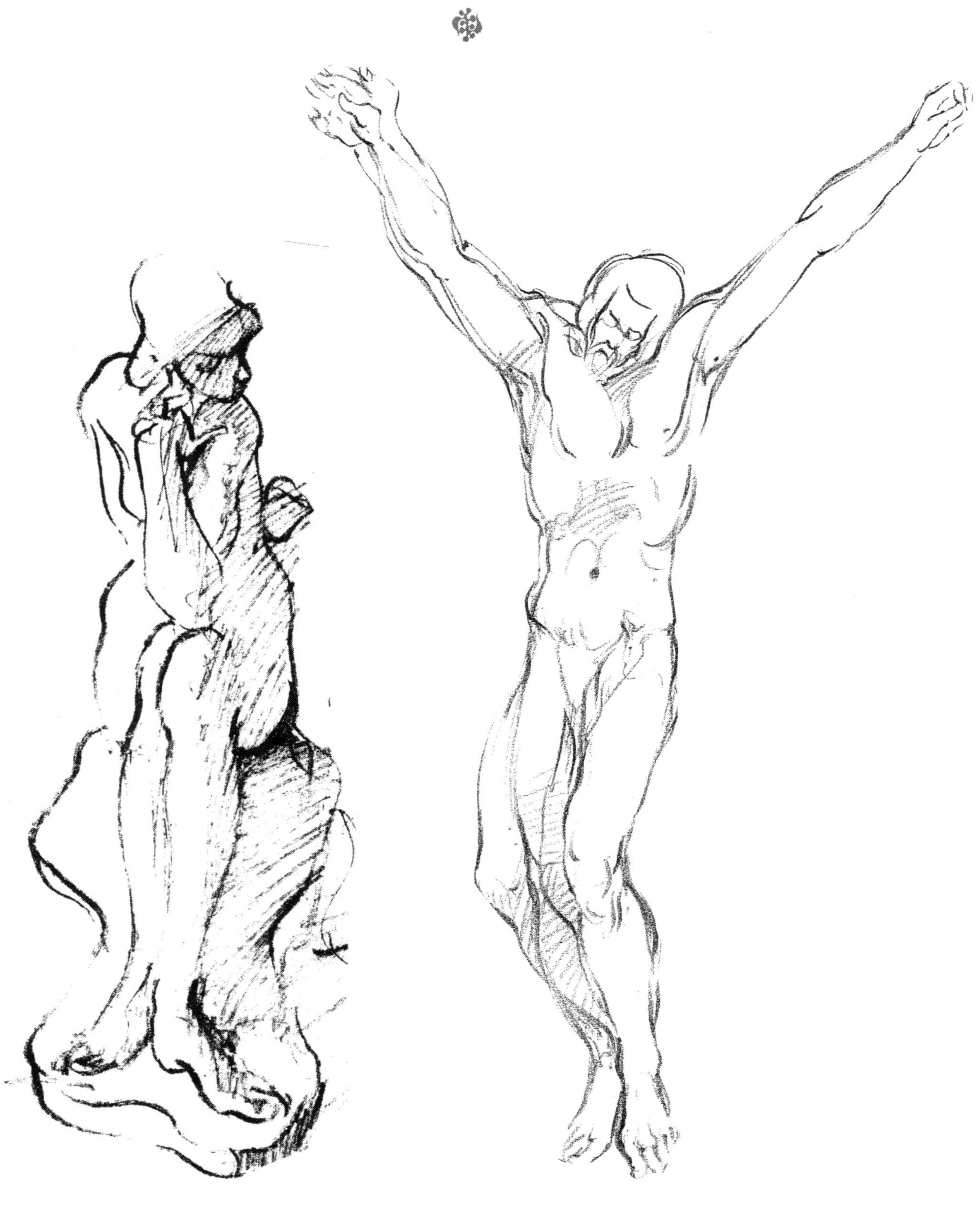

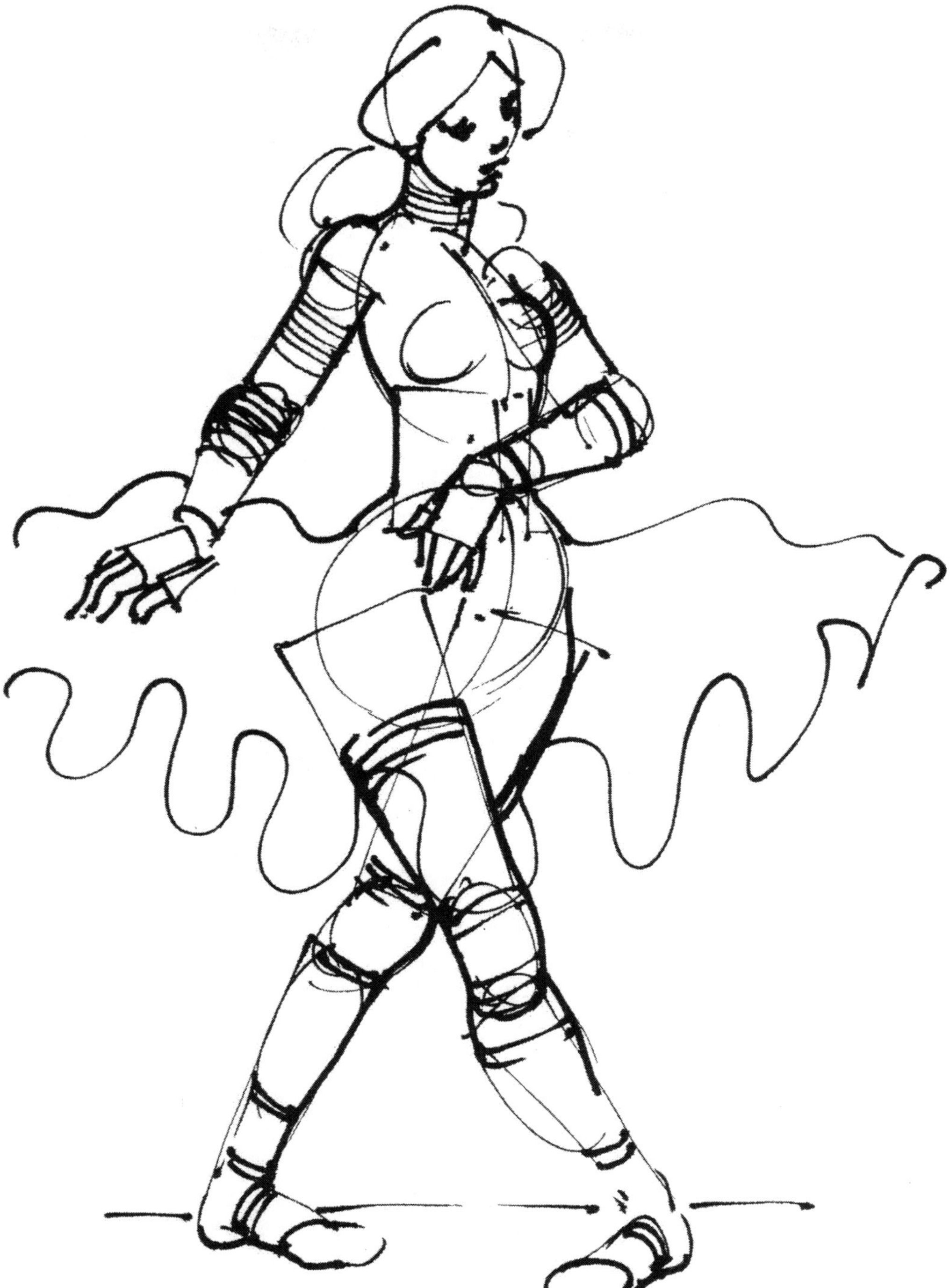

GEOMETRIC ANALYSIS OF SHAPES

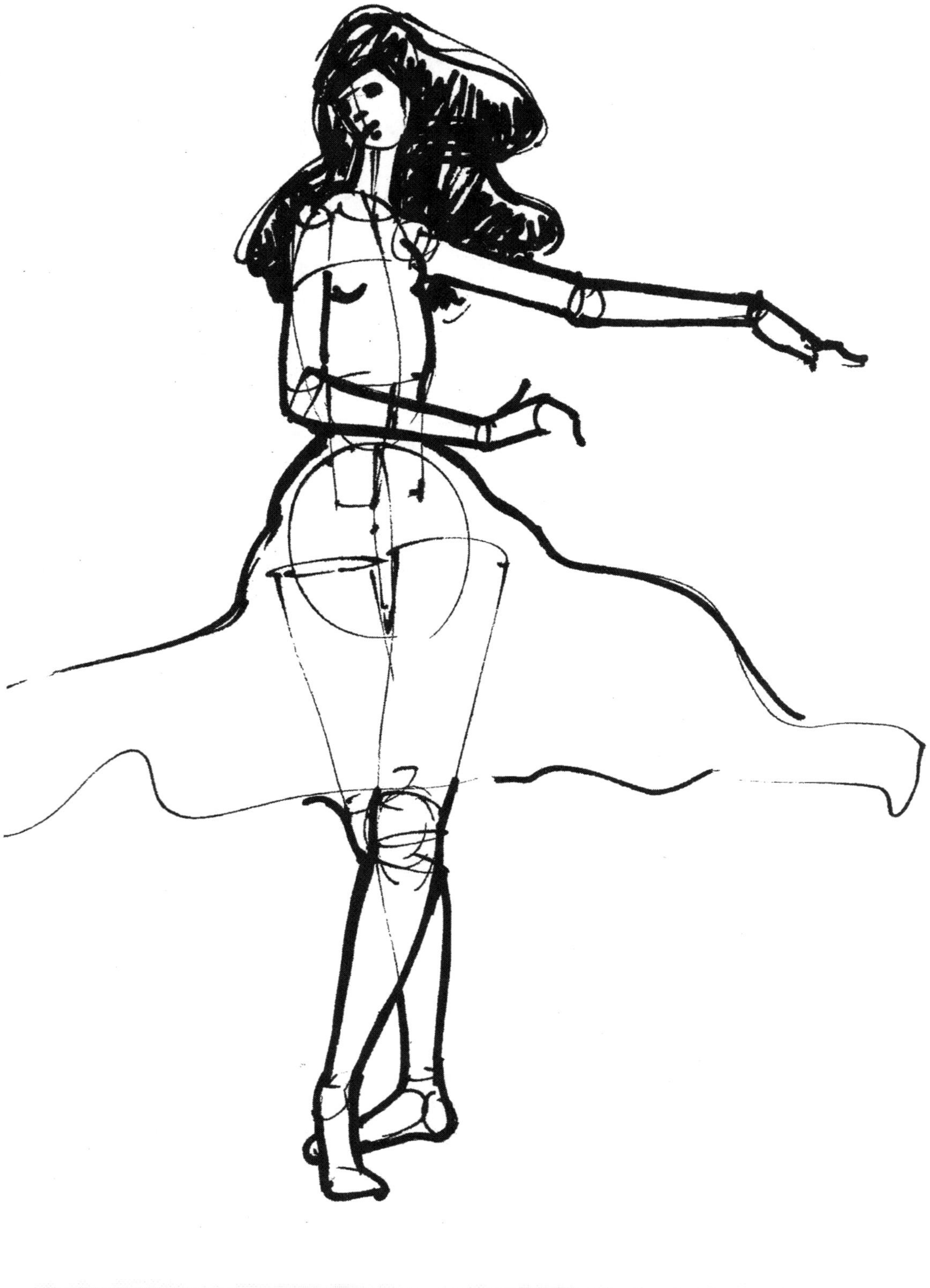

EXAMPLES OF FIGURE ROTATION

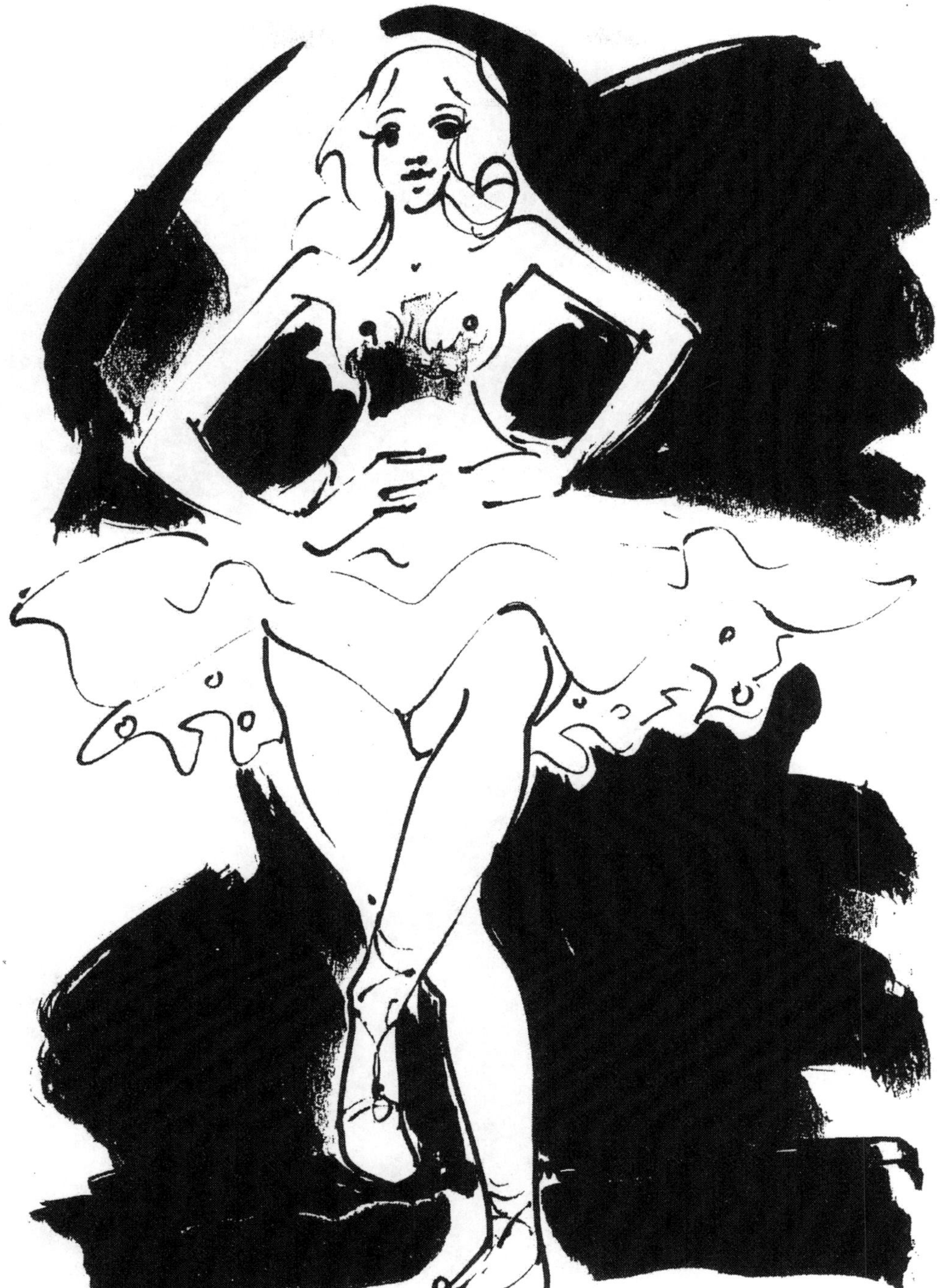

A STUDY OF DANCE MOVEMENT

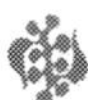

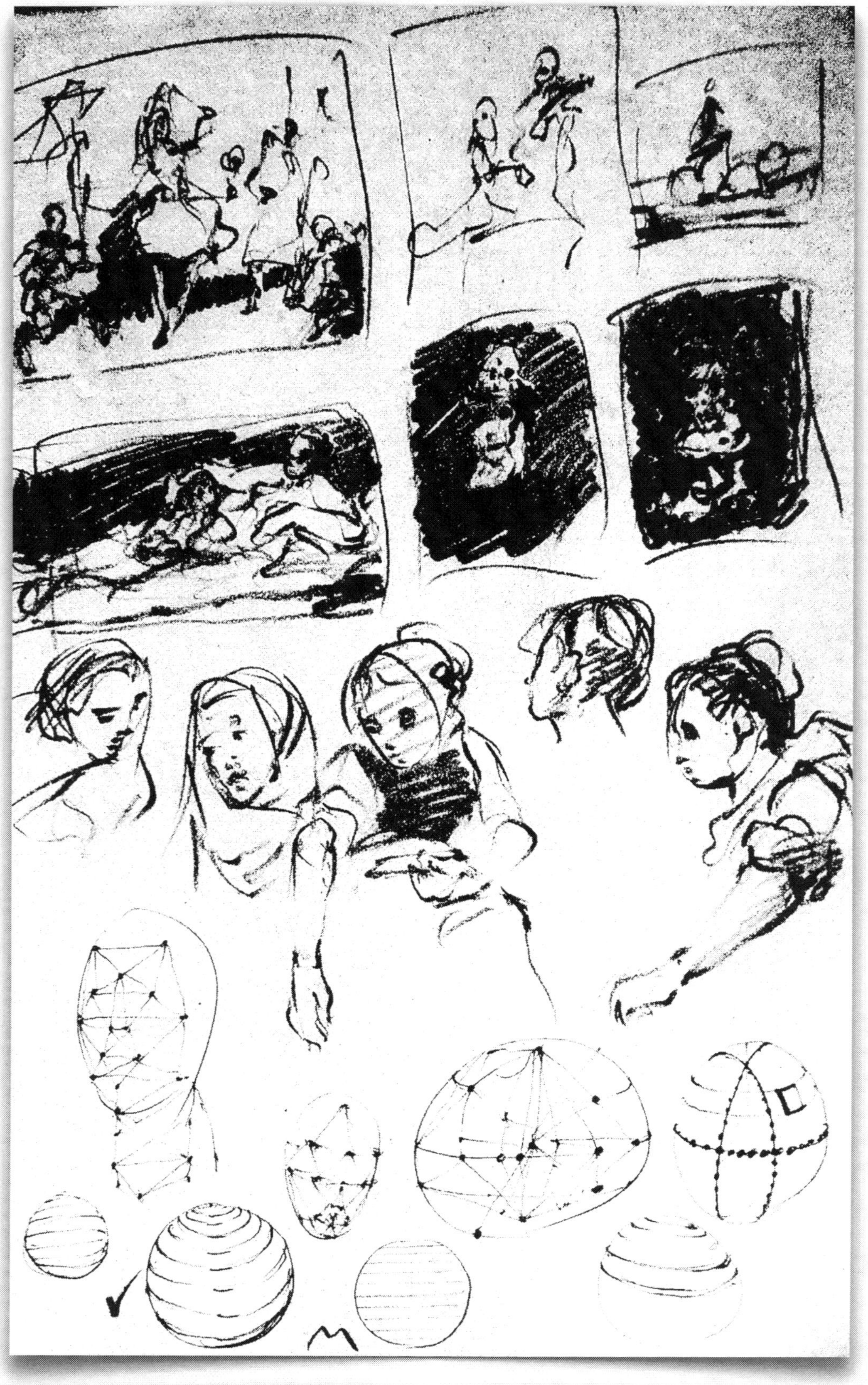

VARIOUS DRAWING STUDIES

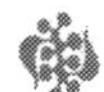

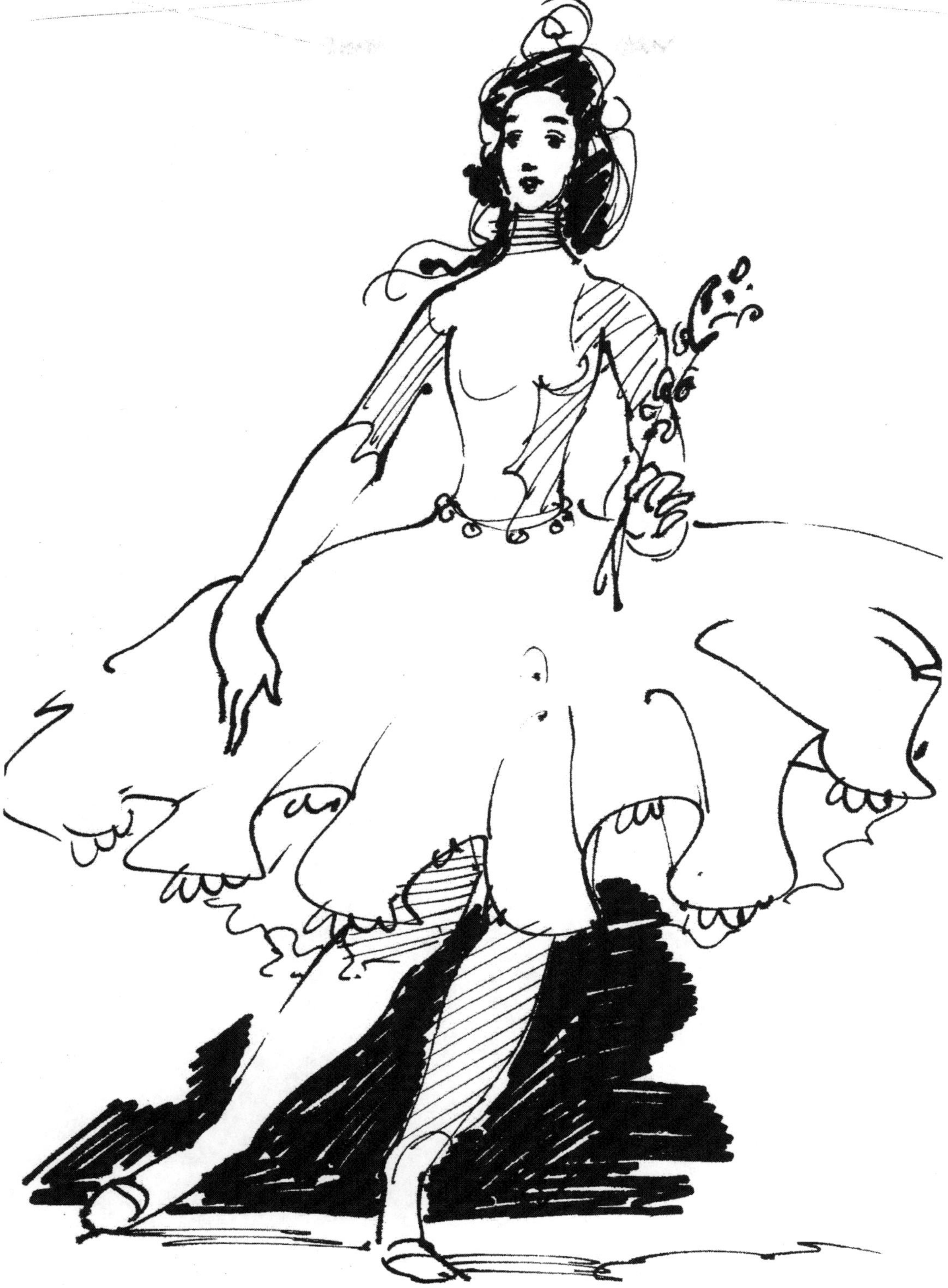

A STUDY OF DANCE MOVEMENT

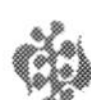

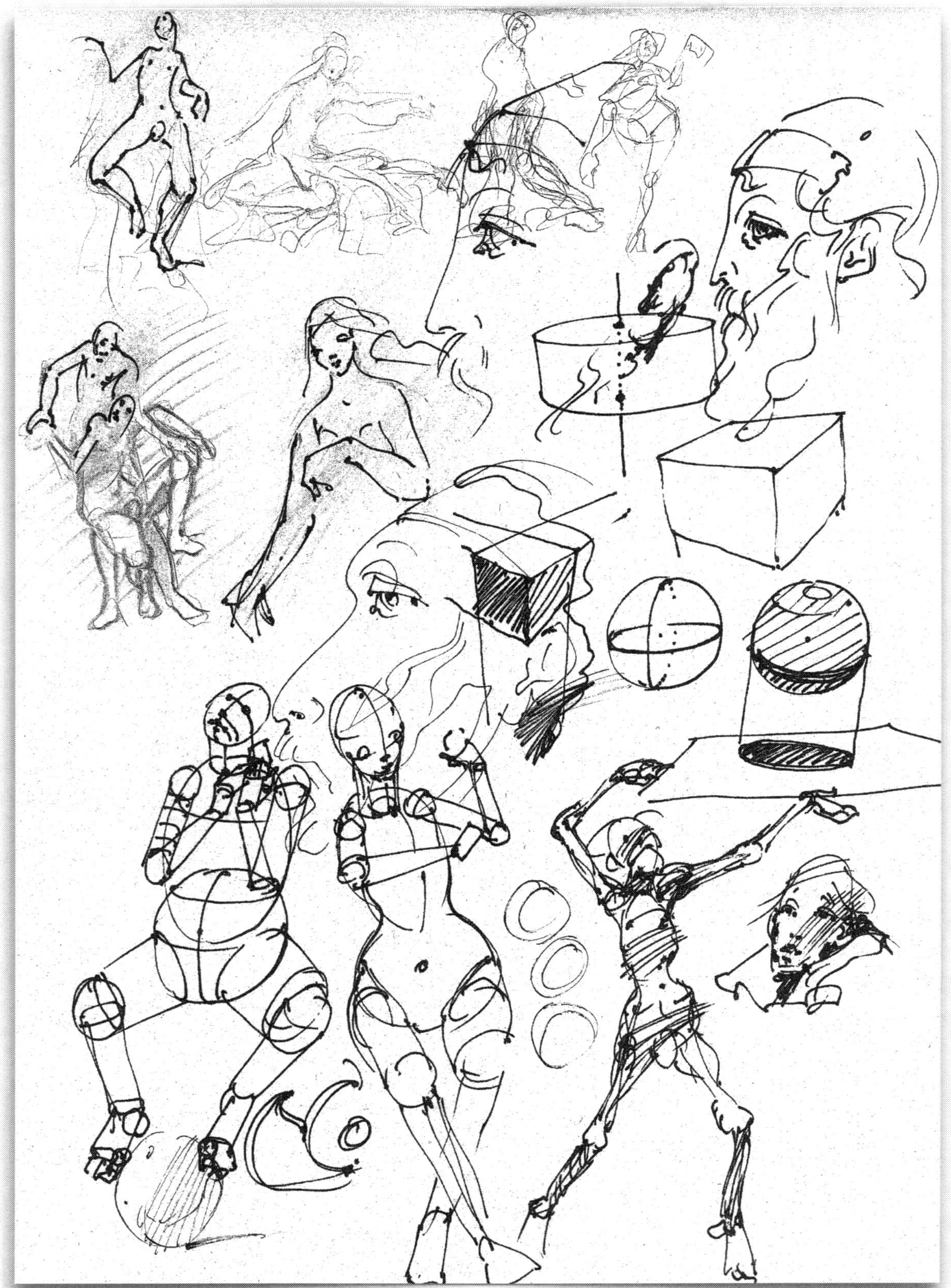

VARIOUS DRAWING STUDIES

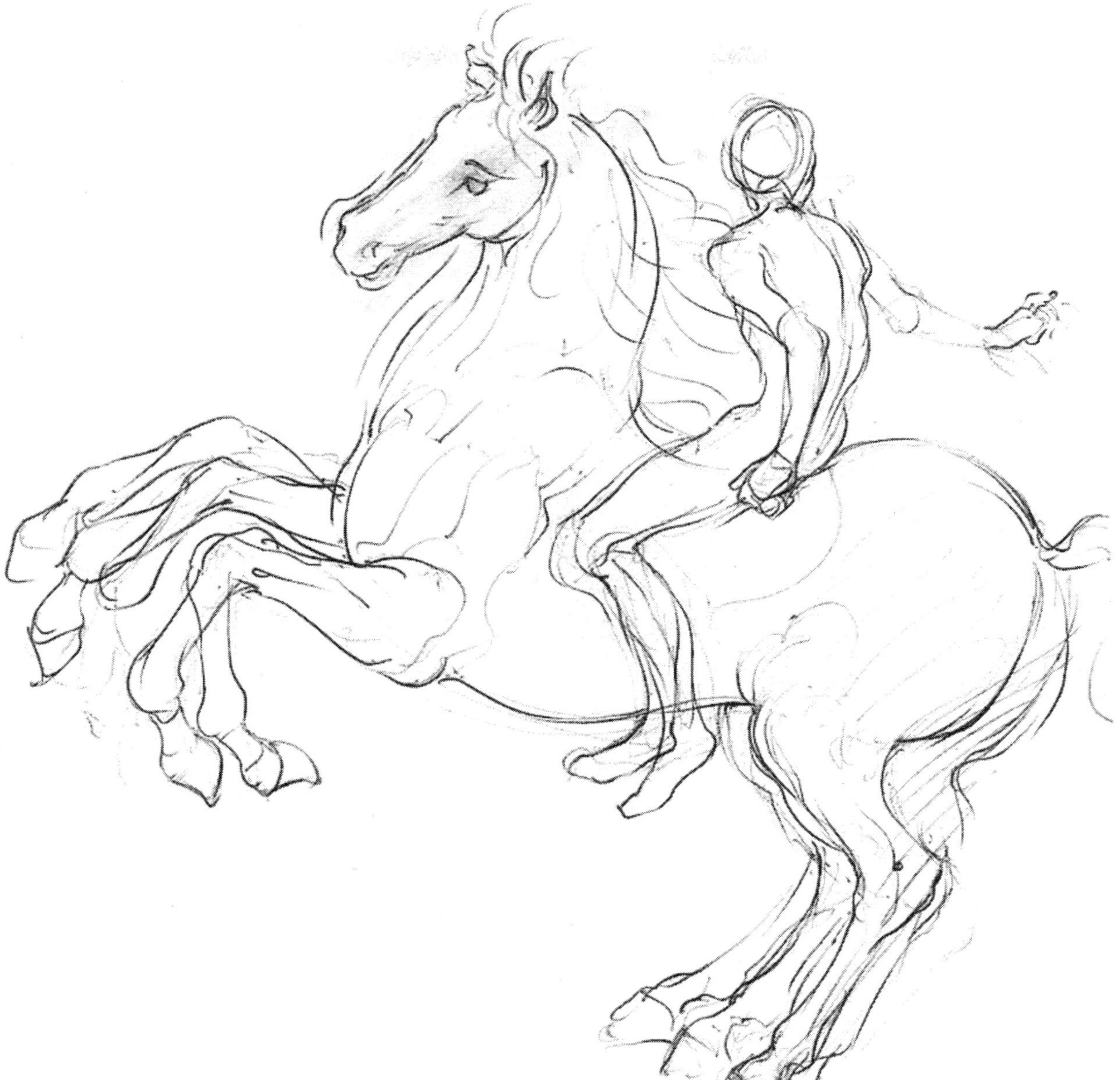

REPEATING THE LINES IN THE DRAWING ACCENTUATES THE DYNAMIC MOVEMENT

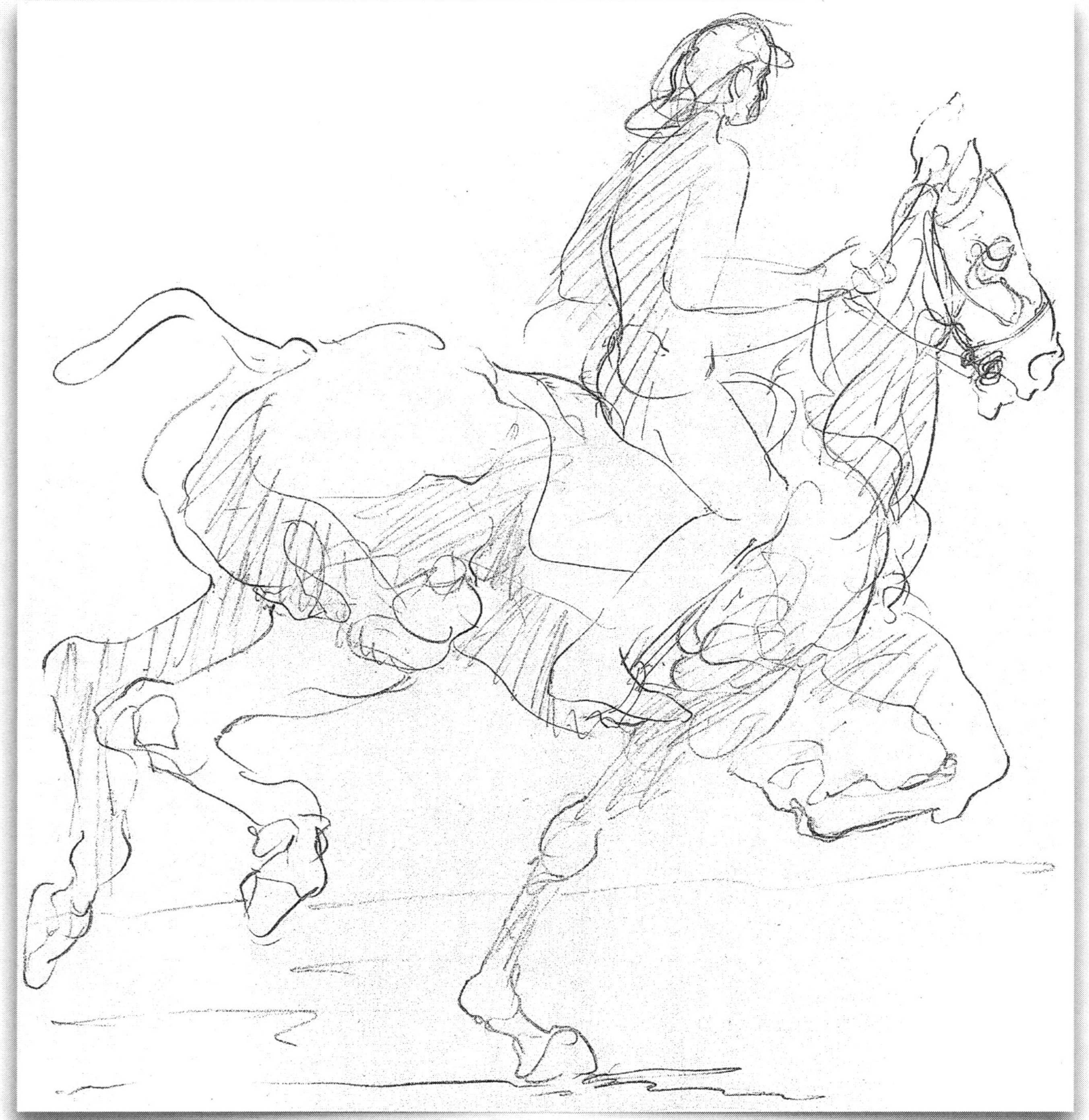

MOVEMENT CAUGHT WITHIN A MOMENT

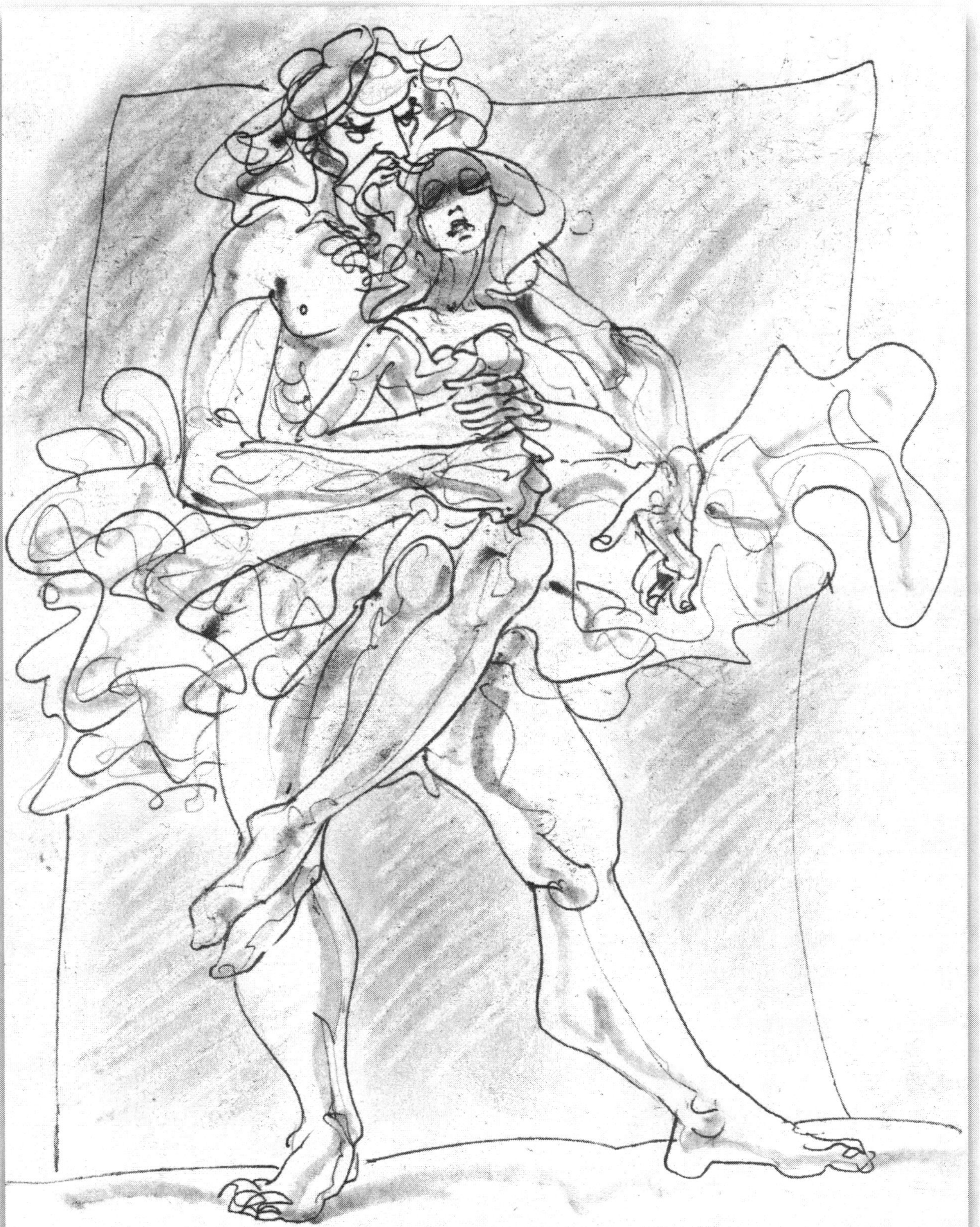

MOVEMENT CAUGHT WITHIN A MOMENT.
SPACE PRESENTED WITH A TONAL BACKGROUND,
THE SCENE OF A HAPPENING

I hope you've enjoyed this fascinating journey through the Drawing Mastery. My final words of advice as mentioned numerous times throughout the book are; practice, practice, practice. So my dear artist, get to work!

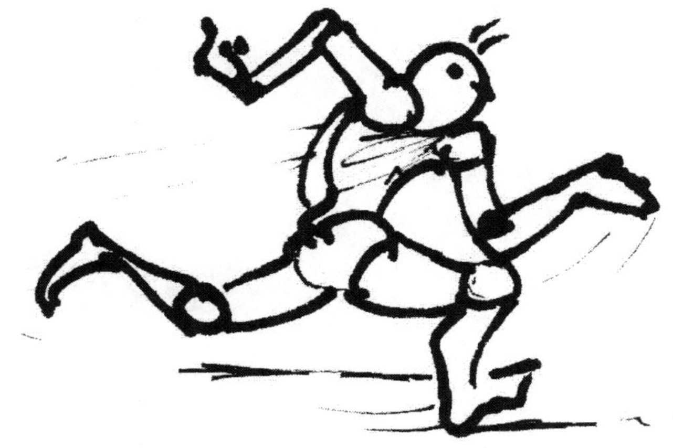

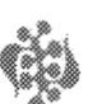

About the Author

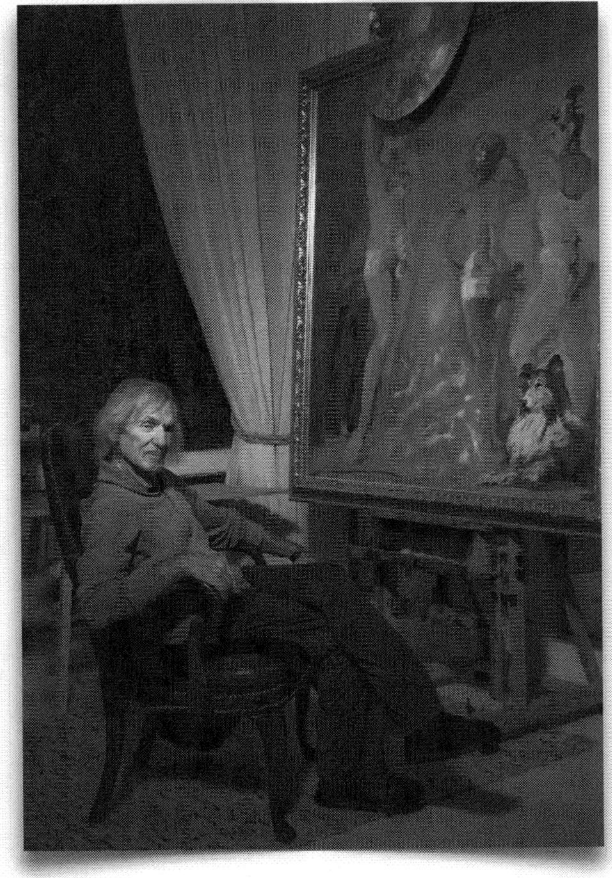

Professor Kiar Mesko is a European American award-winning Artist. He received his diploma from the Art Academy in Slovenia and the Fine Art Hochschule fur Bildende Kunste in West Berlin, Germany. He had the distinction of being the youngest Dean and Professor of Painting and Graphic Print Arts at the National Art Academy in Slovenia. Kiar exhibited throughout Europe, Japan, Egypt and the US, including at the MOMA and has received numerous international awards. He is known for his classical figurative old masters oil paintings, graphic print art as well as marble, bronze and granite sculpture monumental work, displayed in numerous city squares in Europe. Kiar's oils and prints can be found in various Galleries, Museums, private, public and corporate collections worldwide including the permanent collection at the National Gallery of Art in Washington, DC.

VISIT AUTHOR WEBSITE AT

WWW.KIARMESKO.COM

Made in United States
Orlando, FL
04 May 2023

32792667R00137